The Battle for Florida

UNIVERSITY PRESS OF FLORIDA STATE UNIVERSITY SYSTEM

Florida A&M University, Tallahassee
Florida Atlantic University, Boca Raton
Florida Gulf Coast University, Ft. Myers
Florida International University, Miami
Florida State University, Tallahassee
University of Central Florida, Orlando
University of Florida, Gainesville
University of North Florida, Jacksonville
University of South Florida, Tampa
University of West Florida, Pensacola

edited by Lance deHaven-Smith

University Press of Florida

Gainesville · Tallahassee · Tampa · Boca Raton · Pensacola · Orlando · Miami · Jacksonville · Ft. Myers

The Battle for Florida

An Annotated Compendium of Materials
from the 2000 Presidential Election

Copyright 2005 by Lance deHaven-Smith
Printed in the United States of America on recycled, acid-free paper

10 09 08 07 06 05   6 5 4 3 2 1

A record of cataloging-in-publication information is available from
the Library of Congress.

ISBN 0-8130-2819-1

The University Press of Florida is the scholarly publishing agency
for the State University System of Florida, comprising Florida A&M
University, Florida Atlantic University, Florida Gulf Coast University,
Florida International University, Florida State University, University
of Central Florida, University of Florida, University of North Florida,
University of South Florida, and University of West Florida.

University Press of Florida
15 Northwest 15th Street
Gainesville, FL 32611-2079
http://www.upf.com

Contents

List of Illustrations   ix
Preface   xi

1. Studying the 2000 Election   1

Compendium Overview   1
Election Emotions   3
The Election as Drama   4
The Anticlimax of December 12   4
Foolish Certitude   6
The Main Question in 2000   7
Questions Now and for the Future   9
Some Preliminary Answers   11

Appendix to Chapter 1
Frequently Asked Questions   12
Election Timeline   15

2. Who Really Won?   25

Enduring Confusion   26
Sources of Error in Casting and Tabulating Votes   27

Florida's Election Law Reforms of 1989   28
Reforms in 1999   29
Ballot Spoilage and Voter Error in 2000   30
Partisan Differences in Error Rates   31
The Butterfly Ballot   32
Valid Votes among the Discarded Ballots   34
Valid Overvotes   35
What Counts as a Legally Valid Vote?   37
The Election Outcome: When All Votes Are Counted   38
Why the Public Remained Uninformed   39

Appendix to Chapter 2

Federal, Florida, and Texas Election Law in 2000   43
Frequently Asked Questions about the National Opinion Research
    Center's "Florida Ballot Project"   55
NORC Media "Read_me" File: Supplemental Tables and Analytical
    Assumptions   58
Examples of Gadsden County Ballots   87
Official Election Certification   88

3. **Law, Politics, and Administration   89**

Overview of Judicial Decision Making in 2000   90
The Candidates' Positions in a Nutshell   91
The Opening Salvo   91
Initial Issues Resolved by the State Courts   93
Side Issues   94
Legislative Saber Rattling   95
First Ruling of the U.S. Supreme Court   96
Points Scored by Gore in the Election Contest   98
Why Gore Lost the Contest Phase   100
The U.S. Supreme Court Steps in Again   103
Constitutional Origins of the Judicial Breakdown   106
Legal Ambiguity and the Partisan Conspiracy of Florida Legislators
    106
Déjà Vu in 2000: The Disputed Election of 1876   107

Appendix to Chapter 3

Principal Judicial Decisions in the 2000 Election   109

Excerpts from Florida Supreme Court Decision Changing Recount
    Deadline 112
Excerpts from Bush's First Motion on Equal Treatment Issues 133
U.S. Supreme Court Writ Stopping All Recounting 138
U.S. Supreme Court Decision of December 12 141
Florida Attorney General Advisory Opinion of November 14 187
Remarks by Florida Senate President 192
Transmittal Letter for Legislative Report on Special Session 193
Excerpt from Ruling by Florida Supreme Court Mandating
    Statewide Manual Recount 193

4. The Electoral and Partisan Context 195

Why Voting Patterns Were Ignored 196
An Unnoticed Surprise 197
Republican Fears in 2000 198
The Modern Ascendance of Republican Power 199
Florida's Three-Party System 200
What Republicans Learned from the Old He Coon 203
Lessons from Jeb's Victory in 1998 204
Courting the Blue Dogs in 2000 205
Voting Patterns in 2000 206
Republican Strategies for Expanding the Party's Electoral Base 206
Republican Embattlements 207
Misfeasance and Malfeasance Related to the 2000 Election 209
The End or the Beginning? 212

Appendix to Chapter 4

1999 Law on Felon Disenfranchisement 214
Transcript of Remarks by Florida Speaker of the House, Tom Feeney,
    November 22, 2000 216
Special Session Proclamation 230
Duke University Study of Partisanship in the Military 231

5. The Failure of Post-Election Reform 243

Parting Words 244
Sore/Loserman 245
Running Out the Clock 246
Partisan Perspectives on American Politics, Society, and History 247

Ideology and Politics in the Post-Election Response   251
Troubling Questions about Possible Conspiracies   254
The Task Force of Governor Jeb Bush   257
2001 Revisions to Florida's Election Laws   259
Official Evidence of Criminal Acts   264

Appendix to Chapter 5

Al Gore's Concession Speech   269
George W. Bush's Victory Speech   272
George W. Bush's Inaugural Address   276
Jeb Bush's Executive Order Establishing a Task Force   280
Oath of Office from the Florida Constitution   282

Epilogue   283

Critical Categories in Western Political Thought   284
Institutional Failures   287
Failures of Leadership   291
Failures of Citizenship   294
Implications for Speech and Action   295

Bibliography   301
Index   315

Illustrations

Figures

2.1. Graph of Reform Party registration by Buchanan votes
in Florida counties   33
2.2. Precinct undervotes, overvotes, and percent voting Gore   36
2.3. Gadsden County ballot   87
2.4. Sample ballot, Gadsden County   87
2.5. Certification of Florida vote   88
3.1. Memo to Judge Lewis with handwritten notes   194
4.1. Proclamation for Special Session of Florida legislature   230

Tables

2.1. Florida voting systems by number of counties and number
of uncertified ballots examined by NORC   36
2.2. NORC tabulations   39
3.1. Principal judicial decisions in the 2000 election   110
4.1. Voter registrations and deletions, 1995–2000   218

4.2. Voter turnout percentages   219

4.3. Official results, federal overseas absentees   220

4.4. 2000 election, official results by county, with absentees separated out   224

4.5. Campaign finance information for George W. Bush and Al Gore, 2000 presidential election   228

4.6. Percentage of registered voters registered as Democrats, Republicans, and Independents, 1950–2002   229

4.7. Breakdown of ballots received before and after November 7   229

4.8. Breakdown of flawed ballots accepted and rejected, by county   229

Preface

This book originated in my concerns about American government and politics after the disputed 2000 presidential election. I had watched the controversy closely and in person, because much of it took place in Tallahassee, where I live. As an expert on Florida government and politics, I had been able to see through the distortions and misinformation put out by the contending parties, and I had been aware throughout the controversy that Florida's election laws were being undermined and subverted by the very people who were responsible for assuring their proper execution.

However, this recognition was not what caused the concerns behind this book. While I was disappointed by the behavior of many officials during the controversy, I was not afraid for our democracy, because I knew that it had survived far worse. Election fraud and manipulation have been part of American politics from the earliest days of the republic, and yet they have typically led not to lasting breaches in popular control of government but to important reforms. The election dispute of 1800 was followed by the 12th Amendment to the Constitution, and the dispute of 1876 spawned Title III of the federal code. Hence I expected the dispute in 2000 to stimulate similar improvements in electoral processes. In particular, I thought that citizens would push for reforms to remove partisanship from election administration, for the obvious problem in 2000 had been that Florida's election system was in the hands of partisan election officials, many of whom had direct, personal stakes in the outcome of the election.

What alarmed me was not the malfeasance and misfeasance of high officials but rather the inability of both the public and the media to see what was happening and, worse, their widespread reluctance, later, to conduct a postmortem of the election fiasco, determine who was responsible for the electoral breakdown, hold officials accountable for any crimes they may have committed, and enact constitutional and statutory reforms as necessary to root out corruption and to correct flaws in the system. To my amazement and dismay, immediately after George W. Bush was inaugurated the nation suddenly turned from *arguing* about the election to trying to *forget* it. In literally no more than a week or two, and without any warning or explanation, the 2000 presidential election became conversationally taboo. How, I wondered, could an issue that had been the focus of worldwide interest—an election outcome that would have implications long into the future and about which many questions remained unanswered—have been removed so quickly and so thoroughly from public discourse?

Of course, I could understand why a few elements of the electorate might prefer to purge their memories of the brouhaha. Undoubtedly those citizens who toil for a living and who are minimally engaged in political life were tired of the rancor and confusion, not to mention the frequent interruptions to scheduled television. Likewise many Republicans wanted to avoid further consideration of the matter, because they were defensive about how their candidate had ascended to the presidency. Clearly I had no reason to be surprised when these and similarly situated groups wanted to forget the whole matter.

However, at least two other groups—the national news media and the National Democratic Party—had much to gain from keeping the issue alive, and their silence after the inauguration was beyond comprehension. The media had made big investments in learning about the election system as they reported on the controversy, and several of the top newspaper companies had joined together to pay an independent research organization to count all the votes in the months ahead. Nonetheless, immediately after the inauguration, the media dropped the issue like a stinky diaper. A few big stories appeared later in the year—the *Washington Post* did a wrap-up series in the spring, and the *New York Times* did a series in the summer—but these stories were presented in isolation, and the findings were treated, in the articles themselves and in the TV stories about them, as subject to dispute because of objections from one or both of the political parties. Consequently, even though the articles contained circumstantial evidence of malfeasance and felonious crimes by Florida officials at the highest levels and of election fraud involving the military and perhaps members of Congress, they never generated much attention. In a world where all perspectives are treated as equals, the truth becomes merely one more conjecture.

Just as shocking as the media response was the sudden silence of the National Democratic Party, which only weeks before the inauguration had warned that Bush was stealing the election by preventing a full and accurate count of the votes. Democrats had everything to gain by continuing to raise doubts about the election, and yet they said almost nothing, even after they took control of the Senate and had the ability to initiate congressional investigations. Hearings were held on the election-night coverage by the national television media, and a congressional study was conducted on the nature and extent of vote-tabulation error nationally, but, with one exception, no effort was made to assign responsibility for the election problems themselves or to investigate alleged crimes.

The exception did not involve the Democrats. It was a report prepared by the U.S. Civil Rights Commission, which conducted hearings in Florida in January and February 2001. The Commission turned up evidence of a possible conspiracy by Florida's Republican Secretary of State and other high-ranking Republican officials, perhaps including Florida Governor Jeb Bush (George W. Bush's brother), to illegally remove predominantly Democratic voters from the registration rolls under the guise of removing felons, who, by Florida law, are ineligible to vote unless they have their civil rights restored by the governor and cabinet. Incredibly the Commission's hearings received no live television coverage, and media stories about them always included Republican accusations that the Commission was biased because a majority of its members were Democrats or Democratic appointees. A few months later, when the Commission issued its draft report, the findings were written off as a hatchet job engineered by the chair, a black female who had come into conflict with Jeb Bush a year earlier. Apparently fearful of being depicted similarly, congressional Democrats took no action on the report. Thus, after this brief interruption by the Civil Rights Commission, the post-inaugural silence resumed.

To my further amazement, the hush among America's opinion leaders over the 2000 election went largely unnoticed among the general population. Indeed, the citizenry was as intent on avoiding the topic as were public officials, organized interests, and the media. In everyday conversations between coworkers and friends, some mysterious force seemed to place the election controversy off-limits. People acted as if it were entirely natural to move on to other matters—the flagging economy, the warm winter weather, the basketball season. In fact, the desire to continue to discuss the election was widely diagnosed as a sign of immaturity and inflexibility. Those who persisted were swatted with hostile phrases normally used only by insensitive teenagers. "Get over it!" "Let it go!" "Move on!"

I am sure that I, too, would have become infected with this avoidance reaction were it not for my education, which had inoculated me against this particular instance of mass denial. I have spent my adult life pursuing an uncommon line of study combining research on the details of American politics and government with knowledge of classical political philosophy and the political history of Western civilization. Although our political institutions are new, their design originated in the ancient world, and the history of this institutional framework has much to teach us about the political challenges facing us today. It has been filled with more turmoil than stability, more violence than peace, and more oppression than freedom. Our present liberties and our limited control over America's political institutions, police forces, intelligence apparatus, and military troops are fragile and historically rare. During the past 2,500 years, Western civilization has been able to maintain self-government for only brief periods. With no exceptions aside from perhaps the English-speaking nations of the modern era, our republican governments have always come under the sway of one or another of the small but intense factions that seem always to war within us: the poor, the rich, the military, and organized religion.

The system of checks and balances in modern representative democracies was devised in ancient Athens and Rome to pit these factions against one another in a struggle for control. Historically, so long as the balance between factions has been kept in a healthy tension, the system has produced large, vibrant, competitive nations that have led the world in military valor, artistic creativity, and intellectual insight. However, when any one of the major factions has gained unrivaled power, it has always instituted a tyranny in its own image.

The freedom and self-government achieved in ancient Athens and Rome did not endure much longer than the United States has lasted already, and the decline of these political systems into tyranny was marked by characteristics eerily similar to those of the 2000 election. In both the Athens of Socrates and the Rome of Cicero, the end of popular sovereignty originated in political rivalries between families not unlike the Bushes and Gores; the first step of degeneration was a subversion of law in the name of higher values, such as stability and national security; and the decline into tyranny went unchecked by institutionalized oversight bodies, which we now refer to as the courts, because these bodies themselves became involved in the rivalry fueling the downward spiral. For those with the background to see it, the sequence of events in the disputed 2000 presidential election looked like a movie of ancient political decline shown in fast-forward, with each step down the slope mirroring the historic pattern but taking only days rather than decades.

Also comparable in content but more rapid in development in the 2000 election was the peculiar communication pathology that took hold of the citizenry. In the fallen republics of the past, leaders and citizens alike gradually lost their ability to communicate meaningfully about politics and government as they became increasingly polarized along lines of wealth and status. They continued to use the same words—such as equality, justice, truth, democracy, and law—but each side started to define the common words of political discourse differently. The working classes would say they wanted more *isomorphia* ("equality" or "equal treatment"), and the upper classes would agree, but, for the former, *isomorphia* entailed a redistribution of wealth, whereas for the latter it implied that the working and upper classes would have comparable rights to control their own property. As the classes talked past each other in this and other ways, their frustration mounted. Rather than try to sort out the dispute by clarifying the terms of disagreement, each side became increasingly angry at the other side's seemingly self-serving refusal to follow reason and recognize the obvious.

Eventually, according to the reports of Plato and Aristotle, most people became emotionally unbalanced, in the sense that the intensity of their feelings became inversely proportional to the depth of their understanding. Those who knew least, cared most. Hence the populous in general, which is always poorly informed, began to seethe with anger and cynicism, and ultimately it embraced tyranny. In this state of collective madness— this condition of being unable to reason—the Athenians convicted and executed Socrates, the wisest and most just man of their day. Similarly the conflicted citizenry of Rome chose Caesar over Cicero and became absorbed in the bloodlust of the Coliseum.

The hostility and confusion of Americans during the 2000 election took this same form. Arguments developed by the leaders on each side were constantly repeated by elites and masses alike, regardless of the objections and evidence against them. My impression from listening to these citizen debates was that most people were aware of the criticisms against both sides, but none knew enough about the facts at issue to judge the validity of any of the arguments. Frankly this was also true of almost all the pundits, public officials, and commentators on national TV. Consequently public discourse at all levels became a pointless, albeit intense, exchange between formulaic attacks and counterattacks. Even the wording used by different people on each side remained consistent. Whether the debate was between pundits on TV or citizens on the bus, observers would hear phrases such as "count every vote," "changing the rules in the middle of the game," "rent-a-riot," "Carnac," "running out the clock," and so on.

This book is my effort to replicate, in a form appropriately modified for modern audiences, the therapeutic practice devised in classical political philosophy to work on the dysfunctional communication patterns in de-clining republics. This therapy is political philosophy itself, which was originated by men who had lived through the political degeneration of Athens. They concluded that self-government falls apart when citizens lose their ability to talk meaningfully about the issues. Because of intense divisions between social and economic classes, the people begin not simply to disagree but to attribute diametrically opposed meanings to words that are central to their government and its politics.

Clearly the dysfunctional communication pattern described in Athens during its political decline by the first political philosophers was evident with respect to many of the terms that kept coming up in the 2000 election controversy. A good example is how the contending parties used the word *vote*. The Gore side pushed for counting all the "votes," while the Bush side claimed that all the "votes" had already been tallied. Obviously Republicans were defining a vote as a ballot that could be read by a vote-tabulating machine, whereas, for Democrats, votes were any discernable indication of the voters' intention, regardless of its machine readability.

We can see from our experience in the election dispute that pseudo-debates like this generate bad feelings, whether citizens are watching them on TV or mouthing the positions themselves. One reason why they are upsetting is because, when people who are using words incommensurably are unaware of the confusion in their discussion, they cannot understand why those with whom they are speaking do not recognize the obvious. One person says that the votes have obviously been counted, and the other says that obviously they have not been. They both believe they are right, and in a sense they are.

These kinds of word confusions are also upsetting even when they are fully recognized by all the people in the conversation. The problem is that the underlying disagreement, while being raised by the word play, is not addressed and resolved. The emotional effects are similar to the feelings caused by sarcasm, backhanded compliments, and other verbal slights that convey ridicule between the lines.

Socrates sought to reverse the political degeneration of Athens by provoking arguments about the meaning of important terms. Xenophon, one of Socrates' young friends or students, tells us that Socrates was always asking, What is justice? What is love? What is knowledge?

We see the same method in Plato's dialogues. They have all the components of plays—settings, characters, plots, and scenes—but they focus on the meaning of words. Plato used this dramatic form to reveal the different ways in which the same words are understood by different people, depending on their social class, audience, character, and motives.

The disputed 2000 presidential election taught thoughtful Americans that the words used in everyday politics can have diverse and contested meanings, not only words like *justice* and *fairness*, which have a complexity everyone recognizes, but also words that we treat as merely descriptive of known objects or actions, words like *vote* and *count*. Unfortunately, however, many people are concluding from this that the truth about political matters can never be known, including the truth about close elections. This is the same cynicism that came to characterize ancient Rome. When Jesus told Pontius Pilate that he, Jesus, was a witness to the truth, Pilate responded with a rhetorical question: What is truth?

As an emergent trait in America's political culture, such cynicism signals danger. Public cynicism is alarming not merely because it was widespread in the democracies of antiquity as they slid into tyranny. Cynicism implicitly challenges the very possibility of self-government. If the truth cannot be known, then neither can a lie. In the midst of such a culture, political parties will inevitably fall into an arms race of manipulation, dirty tricks, and abuse of office.

This book is offered as a phylactery in the Socratic tradition.

Chapter 1

Studying the 2000 Election

Questions are keys that unlock the doors of reform. In the long run, how we as a nation respond to the disputed 2000 presidential election will depend on the questions we ask and the implications we consider. If, as has generally been the case thus far, Americans continue to focus on issues related to voting technologies and vote-counting procedures, we may discover ways to increase the accuracy of voting and vote tabulation, but we will learn little about enhancing the capacity of our political institutions to produce open elections or to handle future election disputes without bias and intrigue.

Compendium Overview

This book combines an analysis of the 2000 election with an extensive compilation of laws, legal documents, statistical data, and other materials pertinent to the controversy. The book's purpose is twofold. One is to summarize and document what is known about the election. The other is to help citizens learn how to reason productively about matters political.

These aims are related, because they both flow from my assessment of why most voters have never really understood what happened in the 2000 election. In part, the citizenry has remained befuddled because much of the information presented by the mass media has been slanted, incomplete, and contradictory. The nation's confusion is also a consequence of voters' limited skills in judging political arguments. If the voters could see clearly for themselves, the blindness of the mass media would not lead them astray, but when those who are being led by the blind are blind themselves, they all fall in a ditch.

To document the election I have assembled a diverse array of resource materials, many of which were not easily obtained, and some of which cannot be found elsewhere. Among them are statutes, legal documents, official letters, photos, voting data, court transcripts, government records, academic studies, and other items bearing on the election and its implications. Of course, the materials are not exhaustive; far more documents and data exist than could be held in a single book, and, in any event, the corpus continues to grow as new research is conducted, new accounts of events are written by the participants, and more consequences of the election become visible. Materials in this compendium are augmented by others on-line at www.dehaven-smith.com. The special value of the materials selected for inclusion here is their direct relevance to the issues in dispute during the election controversy and to current questions about the election's meaning for democratic governance in the United States.

In the analysis accompanying the resource materials I often point to specific documents and data to support my own conclusions about the disputed election and its implications. This approach is designed to help readers gain some appreciation both for the import of particular documents and for the role of evidence in political inquiry and debate generally.

The book has five chapters, and each chapter contains an appendix in which its resource materials have been placed and organized. The text of each chapter is an essay describing the appendix contents, highlighting key facts, and explaining the meaning and importance of particular items. Additional documents and other resources are referenced in the chapter essays and notes.

The present chapter introduces readers to the controversy surrounding the election, and discusses the nature and scope of the issues addressed in the rest of the book. Unlike other chapters, this one does not review any official documents or reports. It is in part a summary of my conclusions, and also an effort to recall and convey how the election controversy was experienced at the time. The emotional character of the election is important for understanding why many crimes that apparently occurred in relation to the election were never prosecuted, why obvious misfeasance in office was subsequently ignored, and why, for at least the first few years following the election, citizens were reluctant to revisit the controversy even though it had revealed serious weaknesses in the nation's political institutions and civic culture.

Election Emotions

For those in future generations, who will not have personally witnessed the disputed 2000 presidential election, it may be difficult to appreciate how dramatic the controversy became as it unfolded. Even today, people who had followed the controversy closely as it occurred have probably forgotten the intensity of feeling and magnitude of spectacle surrounding it.

Before 2000 the present generation had already seen many disturbing events of historic significance: in the 1960s, the assassinations of John Kennedy, Robert Kennedy, Martin Luther King, and Malcolm X; state attacks on peaceful civil rights demonstrators in the South, and on antiwar protestors at the Democratic National Convention and Kent State University; urban riots in Watts, Oakland, Chicago, and more than 200 other cities; in the 1970s and 1980s, the Watergate and Iran-Contra scandals; the disclosures of American involvement in foreign assassinations and coups; the corruption, collapse, and subsequent bailout of the savings and loan industry; the resignation of Richard Nixon, and the near assassination of Ronald Reagan; and, in the 1990s, the Whitewater investigation and the impeachment of Bill Clinton.

These events were shocking, and they contributed to large increases in citizen cynicism and steep declines in voter turnout. However, they occurred at some remove from the citizenry itself. Citizens mourned the deaths of leaders, watched the political struggles of others, and observed turmoil that seemed sporadic and isolated from mainstream society.

The disputed 2000 presidential election was different. In contrast to earlier tumults and tragedies, in which the bulk of the citizenry had played no active role, the 2000 election and subsequent controversy engaged the citizenry directly. Most Americans had cast votes in the election, and everyone, regardless of whether they had voted, had good reasons to think that their opinions would affect how the dispute would be handled, because their judgments mattered to the candidates as well as to the election officials in Florida, all of whom would eventually face voters in future elections.

The Election as Drama

For these and other reasons, the disputed 2000 presidential election was an event of Shakespearean proportions. As if scripted by the bard himself, the drama revolved around an intense conflict between two men, each of whom was the favorite son of a dynastic family in American politics. Both were fighting as much for glory as for policy. One sought to restore the immanence of his family by vindicating the reputation of his father, who had been defeated in political battle eight years earlier by a talented but sometimes unscrupulous commoner. The other was this same commoner's second, who, despite his noble birth, had long been in the commoner's shadow and now desperately yearned for recognition in his own right.

The conflict between these two heroes took place in only a handful of days, but they were days with many shifts of fortune that taught timeless lessons, for strange fate had placed the protagonists on a battlefield with few ramparts and no exits. Like kings on a chessboard, the heroes encamped on opposite sides at some distance from the front, leaving their troops to be commanded in combat by old and famous generals and young, ambitious lieutenants. Enacted on the virtual stage of live television, the play was organized around a series of battles, each for control of a different piece of political ground.

Suspense mounted from one scene to the next as the action moved back and forth between several locations. From the hilltops by the battlefield the generals announced their battle plans. Political infantrymen positioned themselves along the main roadways, waving battle signs and taunting their enemies. In the center of the field small troops of attorneys collided in hand-to-hand combat, hurling accusations and stabbing fine points of law into the hearts of their opponents' cases. Watching from their encampments, the two kings plotted and fretted. Back at the front, the generals soliloquized to an audience of cameras.

The Anticlimax of December 12

Only one aspect of the drama lacked Shakespearean grandeur: the ending. The combat lasted much longer than expected, and suspense had mounted as first one side and then the other had gained momentary advantage. But just as the final, decisive confrontation was getting under way, the highest tribunal in the land called a halt to the contest, giving victory not necessarily to the side that would have prevailed had the contest been allowed to play out but instead to the contender who happened to have the upper hand at that moment.

When it issued its final decision on December 12, 2000, the U.S. Supreme Court endorsed manual recounts, but it said that Florida's statewide recount could not continue to completion because time had run out for submitting new results to Congress. This awkward conclusion to the dispute was both anticlimactic and incomplete. It was anticlimactic, because it meant that George W. Bush had won the election on a technicality. It was incomplete, because it called for recounting the ballots with clear standards but then prevented the recount from occurring.

Questions were immediately raised about the Supreme Court's objectivity and the reasoning of its decision. Gore supporters claimed that all the justices in the majority had been appointed by Republican presidents. The Court was criticized for contradicting its own policy of states rights, and rumors circulated that some of the conservative justices wanted a Republican in the White House so they could retire and be replaced by another conservative. The Court's ruling was ridiculed for being unsigned; for setting an impractical precedent that seemed to require uniform voting procedures across the states; and for being inconsistent with the U.S. Constitution, which leaves election disputes to be decided by Congress. Nonetheless the Court's ruling was final, and the election, if not the controversy surrounding it, was over.

The dispute had lasted thirty-six days. For the nation, it had been an exhausting episode even though it had offered an exciting display of legal tactics and political strategy. Its sudden and troubling conclusion left many Americans shaking their heads.

At the time, however, it appeared to be as good an outcome as could be expected in the circumstances, because no one knew the full circumstances. At least two facts of critical importance had not yet been discovered. One was that a thorough recount of all the ballots would have been able to determine a clear winner. During the controversy it appeared that any recount would inevitably be arbitrary in its procedures and outcome. Hence the Court's action was seen as bringing a valid end to an arbitrary recount, not bringing an arbitrary end to a valid recount.

The other fact that was not yet known was the extent to which Florida's system of election administration had been corrupted by partisan influences. This did not come out until months later and only in bits and pieces. By then Americans had put the election behind them, and the principal direction of election reform had already been set.

Partisan intrigue and manipulation during the election dispute are documented in the timeline contained in the appendix at the end of this chapter. The timeline differentiates between events and actions that took place, so to speak, on stage, and those that occurred behind the scenes. The former, of which the public was aware at the time, are listed in regular type, and the latter, which were revealed subsequently by investigative journalism, voting studies, and other methods, are in bold. During the dispute, partisan influences were evident at both the highest level, where election policies are formulated and interpreted, and at the base of the system, where the laws are supposed to be faithfully implemented.

Foolish Certitude

Divisions and distortions in public discourse mirrored and reinforced the partisan corruption of Florida's system of election administration. During the controversy, political leaders and the media (and hence almost all citizens paying attention to the dispute as well) focused on the behavior of the candidates and their advocates, and on the issues as the combatants defined them, which centered on questions about the equipment used to cast and count votes. As the candidates and their advocates selected and interpreted the facts to support their own prospects, the mass public became polarized along partisan lines, and people on each side adopted, almost word for word, the opinions of those who spoke for the particular candidate with whom they were aligned.

Most voters had never in their lives looked carefully at a punch-card ballot, and even fewer knew anything about Florida election law or Florida history, but their overwhelming ignorance caused no run on the nation's libraries nor did it produce any hesitancy of opinion. Quite the opposite, for while most voters saw no need for any background knowledge beyond the superficial information dribbling from their televisions, they nevertheless became very intense in their views and believed that they understood the controversy sufficiently to render emphatic judgments. Moreover, although public opinion was divided sharply along partisan lines, most people seemed to think that their judgments paralleled their partisan interests only by coincidence. Such widespread certitude combined with such overwhelming ignorance and self-satisfied confidence was a phenomenon to behold. Apparently ignorance is not bliss; it is angry stupidity.

Of course, many people stood back from the controversy with cynical disdain and mocked those who took the dispute seriously. Admittedly some of the jokes were hilarious. Some targeted Florida or, as people began to say, "Flori-*duh*." Others belittled the key players. Secretary of State Katherine Harris, ridiculed for wearing heavy makeup, was compared to Cruella, an evil woman in a popular Disney movie. Sketches on *Saturday Night Live* sometimes rivaled the parodies of Aristophanes. Certainly their popularity was understandable; in an age of heat, the cool are king, or at least they receive high ratings.

However, when it came to the health of the republic, the comics who joked about the 2000 election were naive. For, unlike Aristophanes, who recognized the dangers of his times, those in 2000 presupposed that the controversy was much ado about nothing, when, for all they really knew, they could have been laughing at the rise of an American Nero. When a nation may be falling, all irony is ironic.

Equally odd for the circumstances was how quickly the election controversy ended after December 12. The same people who for a month had been rabid in their opinions and furious that the candidate they opposed was trying to steal the election suddenly became as silent as citizens ever are. Media commentators attributed the hush to America's political culture, which in their view produced uncritical acceptance of the Supreme Court's decision because the culture calls for adherence to the rules of the game.

But the media could see the silence in only this way; their professional ethos and market circumstances prevent them from reporting on non-events. They can interject opinions into disputes about which they are reporting; editorializing is encouraged. But they have no way to comprehend and comment on a dispute that should have occurred but did not. Man bites dog is news; man bites no one, is not.

The Main Question in 2000

This book seeks both to answer questions raised during the disputed 2000 presidential election, and to pose and address additional issues that have been neglected, overlooked, or suppressed. The question asked most often during the election controversy was "Who really won?" The data and other materials necessary to make this determination have been available since the autumn of 2001, but, until now, they have not been assembled and analyzed in a single work. This is because most books on the election were written before the votes in Florida had been reviewed by the National Opinion Research Center (NORC) at the University of Chicago. In a year-long study paid for by the nation's most important newspapers, NORC carefully examined and evaluated all the 175,010 ballots that had remained uncounted at the end of the dispute. However, NORC did not prepare a written study of the results. Moreover, newspaper and television reports on the study were sketchy and confusing, and they contained many conflicting claims from commentators about the study's meaning and implications.

In chapter 2 of this Compendium the laws that governed voting in Florida at the time of the election are presented and explained, and NORC's data are tabulated on the basis of what counted as a legally valid vote. The chapter shows that the presidential candidate who received the largest number of legally valid votes in Florida's 2000 election was Al Gore. This conclusion is unambiguous and unavoidable.

Today most Americans are under the mistaken impression that the true winner of the 2000 presidential election could not be definitively determined. Many recognize that more Floridians intended to vote for Gore than for Bush, but they think that Bush probably received more legally valid votes and, in any event, that efforts to salvage improperly marked ballots yield unreliable results.

Americans hold this erroneous opinion because they were misled and confused by journalists, political consultants, academics, and others who, during and immediately after the controversy, analyzed the election data in many different ways. Some investigated the issue by trying to discern for whom most Floridians *intended* to vote. Others sought to gauge the results after adjusting for voter errors caused by poor ballot designs in Palm Beach County and poor ballot instructions in Duval and Gadsden counties. Still other analysts asked what the outcome would have been had the partial recount requested by Gore been completed.

However, these and similar analyses were conducted before the NORC data became available. The analyses seemed reasonable at the time, because the central question appeared to be how ballots with ambiguous marks on them should be counted. This issue naturally led analysts to examine how the tally of votes would be affected by different vote-counting criteria.

It turns out, however, that these ambiguously marked ballots were not important to the outcome of the election. Yes, these were the ballots that election officials agonized over in Palm Beach, Broward, and Miami-Dade counties; they were the kinds of ballots that were the focus of the trial in Tallahassee; and they were the central issue on which the U.S. Supreme Court intervened to stop the recount. But they were just a red herring. When voter intent could be discerned, these ballots tended to be split fairly evenly between Bush and Gore.

The uncounted ballots that actually turned out to be decisive for the outcome had been entirely overlooked by most observers throughout the controversy. These were ballots that had been spit out by vote-tabulating machines because they included both a mark for one of the listed presidential candidates and a name written into the space for write-in candidates. Many of these ballots contained clear, legally valid votes, and they heavily favored Gore. Once they are added to the previous vote totals, Gore has the most votes. Although questions may remain about why a full recount did not occur and who was responsible, the issue of who received the most legally valid votes has been settled.

Questions Now and for the Future

The questions addressed by the Compendium that have heretofore gone unasked and unanswered fall into three broad categories. One set is comprised of issues that follow from the observation that America's political institutions produced a flawed outcome in the 2000 presidential election. Many of the questions in this category deal with responsibility and accountability. For example, who, if anyone, was responsible for the breakdown of Florida's system of election administration? Was the election fiasco in any way planned by public officials or precipitated by their actions? Why did the judicial system fail to assure that the true winner of the election was actually determined? Although not all these issues are raised explicitly in the chapters ahead, the materials and their discussion are intended to open this line of inquiry and assemble much of the relevant evidence.

The second category of questions that guided my selection of items for inclusion and discussion have to do with America's political culture, broadly defined. The Compendium contains materials that can be used by readers to probe the nation's apparently limited capacity for sifting through political claims and counterclaims to arrive at reasonable conclusions. For example, chapter 5 examines some of the studies and investigations conducted after the election controversy had ended. It shows that the research and analysis were often poorly framed and that many crucial but sensitive issues were sidestepped.

The third category of issues covered in the Compendium is related to political reform. Within this subject matter, public officials and the media have focused on changes to state and federal election laws. These legislative initiatives are important, and in chapter 5 I have reviewed them and have offered an assessment of whether they are likely to be able to prevent election fiascos in the future.

My main criticism is that the reforms focused on voting equipment and technology rather than on election administration. The problem actually revealed by the 2000 election was not technology but rather partisan corruption in election administration. Currently many Florida counties and many governments in other parts of the nation are expending large amounts of energy and money to replace punch-card voting machines with systems that are totally electronic and often produce no paper records of votes. A study of the new voting machines was recently conducted by The Johns Hopkins University, which found them to be vulnerable to hacking and other forms of manipulation. Deploying this equipment in an administrative context that continues to be highly partisan is like installing a video monitoring system for the fox that is guarding the henhouse.

Moreover, many other questions need to be raised about American government and politics in light of the problems in 2000, not just questions about election reform. For example, a determination needs to be made about what part of the election breakdown in 2000 was a consequence of unlawful or unprofessional behavior by election officials, and what part reflected systemic problems in our institutions. We need to ask whether the constitutional framework of checks and balances in our system of representative democracy is functioning properly. We also need to consider whether the current system of election administration is consistent with the role assigned to elections in American government and politics. These and similar questions are touched on throughout the Compendium.

Some Preliminary Answers

When the election controversy was unfolding, many rumors and accusations circulated about official wrongdoing, but their validity could not be determined then because events were moving too fast and not much hard evidence was available. Now, however, much more is known about what happened. The appendix to this chapter contains a table on "Frequently Asked Questions." It lists typical questions about the election, along with my best judgment on the answers based on the materials contained in the chapters ahead.

Of immediate significance is evidence that crimes were committed by men and women who currently hold high public offices. Under the statute of limitations, these crimes may no longer be punishable, but for the nation's sake they still need to be investigated so that reforms can be devised to prevent their occurrence in the future. Evidence of wrongdoing is discussed in several chapters but is covered in most detail in chapter 5.

Appendix to Chapter 1

Frequently Asked Questions

Who actually received the most votes in Florida's 2000 presidential election?
Al Gore. State election officials ultimately declared Bush the winner by a margin of 537 votes, but during and after the election dispute, questions remained about the uncounted ballots of 175,010 voters, ballots that had been rejected by error-prone tabulating machines employed in many Florida counties. Confusion and conflict, much of it generated by partisan intrigue, prevented these ballots from being counted during the election controversy. However, in 2001 every uncounted ballot was carefully examined in a scientific study by the University of Chicago, which found that, when all the votes were counted, more votes had been cast for Gore than for Bush.

Why did some earlier post-election studies say just the opposite, that is, that Bush had actually won after all?
They did not really say this. They reported, instead, that Bush might have

kept his lead if the manual recounts of machine-rejected ballots had been completed along the lines either requested by Gore or initially mandated by the Florida Supreme Court. In these recount scenarios, not all the machine-rejected ballots would have been included. However, just before the U.S. Supreme Court intervened, the judge overseeing the final state-wide recount was preparing to announce that the recount would cover all the previously uncounted ballots.

Are manual recounts inherently biased or subjective?

No. In any election, many discarded ballots contain votes that are completely unambiguous. Of particular importance in the 2000 election were the ballots on which a selection had been made from the list of candidates and then a name had also been printed in the space for write-ins. Although these "write-in overvotes" were automatically excluded by tabulating machines, they contained unambiguous and legally valid votes whenever the write-in candidate matched the candidate chosen from the list preceding it. In its comprehensive study of all the uncounted ballots, the University of Chicago found that these write-in overvotes heavily favored Gore.

Why were more errors like this made by Democrats than by Republicans?

Because of the characteristics and voting experience of Florida Democrats. The two groups making the most errors were African Americans and seniors, who are core constituencies of the Florida Democratic Party. Seniors probably made errors because of weak eyesight and other physical limitations caused by aging. In contrast, African Americans often made the mistake of casting "write-in overvotes"; they would select Gore on the list of presidential candidates and then write Gore's name on the line available for write-in candidates. Presumably African Americans were more likely than other voters to do this, because they wanted to avoid any ambiguity as to whom they were supporting. Since the Era of Reconstruction when they were first granted the right to vote, African Americans have regularly faced efforts to prevent them from voting and to reject as unreadable or improperly marked those ballots that they have succeeded in casting. African Americans may have made other errors because of the anxiety they are likely to feel at the polls, where in the not so distant past they would have routinely faced threats, violence, police harassment, and worse.

Why should ballots with mistakes on them have been counted at all?
The law required all discernable votes to be counted. Rejecting ballots only because they contain technical errors would have been a violation of Florida election law (Section 101.5614[5]), which stated that no vote "shall be declared invalid or void if there is a clear indication of the intent of the voter." This legal restriction had been enacted years ago, because previously election officials in Florida had used technicalities to throw out many of the votes of African Americans.

Did Florida officials faithfully execute the election laws of the state?
No. The *New York Times* and the *Washington Post* discovered evidence that Florida's governor, secretary of state, and Speaker of the House, all Republicans with close ties to George W. Bush, used their offices to manipulate the election controversy and secure Bush's victory. During the controversy they collaborated either directly or through intermediaries with the legal and political advisers of George W. Bush to (1) put pressure on the state's top law firms not to work for Gore; (2) bend the rules on absentee ballots to allow improperly marked absentee ballots to be counted; (3) block, stall, or discredit manual recounts; and (4) create fears of a constitutional crisis so that the U.S. Supreme Court would intervene.

Will changes to Florida's election laws that were enacted in 2001 prevent the same problems from reoccurring?
No. In fact, the badly named Florida Election Reform Act is in many respects a step backward. It was enacted before the *Times* and the *Post* reported that Florida's public officials at the highest levels had collaborated with George W. Bush's advisers to block fair and proper execution of Florida's election laws. Consequently the legislation focused on modernizing Florida's vote-casting and vote-tabulating equipment but failed to deal with the much more serious problem of partisan corruption in the state's system of election administration.

What can be done to assure that Florida's election system is administered properly to minimize voter confusion, count all valid votes, and reduce bias associated with race and age?
Amend the Florida Constitution. Florida elections are unlikely to be fair and accurate until their administration is constitutionally removed from the hands of partisan officials and prohibited from being biased against senior

citizens, African Americans, and other categories of individuals who face special challenges when voting.

Election Timeline

Note: The following table differentiates between facts that were known at the time of the election controversy and those that became public later. The latter are in bold print.

November 7: Election Day. Before 8:00 p.m. Eastern Standard Time the television networks call Florida for Gore on the basis of exit polls conducted and analyzed by the Voter News Service (VNS). At 9:38 p.m. Voter News Service reports that it erred in calling Duvall County for Gore. At 9:50 p.m. the networks air a videotape of Bush saying, "The people actually counting the votes have come to a different perspective." At 10:00 p.m., CBS, ABC, and CNN all move Florida into the undecided category. At 10:13 p.m., VNS says that it is retracting its call for the entire state of Florida.

Phone records show that a call was made from the cell phone of Florida secretary of state Katherine Harris, a Republican and co-chair of the Bush presidential campaign in Florida, to the Texas governor's mansion.

November 8: The first statewide vote totals reported to Florida's secretary of state are 2,909,135 for Bush to 2,907,351, a margin 1,784. A recount required by state law reduces the margin.

In the morning hours, on instructions from his brother, George W., Florida governor Jeb Bush, who was co-chair of the Bush presidential campaign in Florida, leaves Texas and returns to Florida by private jet.

At 3:30 a.m. Frank Jimenez, general counsel for the governor of Florida, begins gathering information for the Bush campaign by making the first of what will be eight phone calls to the Florida Division of Elections over the course of the next forty-eight hours.

At 4:00 a.m. Ed Kast from the Florida Division of Elections was being interviewed by CNN when Jimenez has him pulled off the air for fear he might hurt the Bush cause. Jimenez then goes to the office of the Division of Elections to find Clay Roberts, the division's director, whom the media describe as a "Bush loyalist."

At 6:15 a.m. state employees in the Florida governor's legal office begin phoning Florida's top law firms to discourage them from working for Al Gore during the recount.

At 2:07 p.m. Don Rubottom, a lawyer for the Florida House of Representatives, sends an e-mail authorized by Florida House Speaker Tom Feeney (a Republican and Jeb Bush's running mate in the Florida gubernatorial election of 1994) through an intermediary to Jeb Bush suggesting that the Florida legislature intervene and select Florida's Electoral College electors for George W. Bush. Rubottom also sends similar e-mails to Secretary Harris and her general counsel.

Legal staff in Governor Jeb Bush's office, including the governor's general counsel, Frank Jimenez, look for ways to prevent a recount.

Florida attorney general Bob Butterworth, a Democrat and co-chair of the Gore campaign in Florida, urges the Gore camp to hang tough and fight. Butterworth appears on television to present the manual recounts in a favorable light. From this time forward Butterworth keeps in close contact with the Gore campaign and legal team.

Governor Jeb Bush calls Austin to discuss whether he should recuse himself. He subsequently recuses himself from participation on the Florida Elections Commission, which must eventually certify the election results.

Division of Elections staff prepare a press release for Secretary of State Harris that says overseas ballots must be "postmarked or signed and dated" by Election Day. It was never released.

November 9: Manual recounts are requested by the Gore campaign in Palm Beach, Broward, Miami-Dade, and Volusia counties.

Jimenez, the general counsel for Governor Jeb Bush, continues placing calls to the Florida Division of Elections to gather information for the team of George W. Bush.

Florida governor Jeb Bush meets with the Bush legal and political team at the headquarters of the Republican Party in Florida and advises against seeking or supporting any manual recounts.

An unnamed Bush campaign official contacts Mac Stipanovich, a well-known Republican campaign strategist, and convinces him to join Harris's staff as an adviser during the controversy.

November 10: The Palm Beach County Canvassing Board begins an initial manual recount of 1 percent of the ballots to determine if the overall machine count may be in error. The canvassing board agrees in advance to count a partially punched chad as a vote if light passes through the ballot at the proper place. This was referred to as the "sunshine rule." Democrats ask instead for a more generous rule that would also count as votes any chads that were merely indented.

The canvassing board breaks for lunch and the chair, Circuit Judge Charles Burton, an appointee of Jeb Bush, meets privately with an attorney from the office of Secretary of State Harris. When the canvassing board reassembles, Burton changes the rule to require two of a chad's four corners to be detached for it to count as a vote.

November 11: The Bush campaign commences a federal lawsuit in U.S. District Court to halt manual recounts, asserting that the recounts violate the equal protection clause of the 14th Amendment to the U.S. Constitution. Private individuals initiate a lawsuit in the circuit court in Palm Beach County to require a revote because of the confusion surrounding the county's butterfly ballot. At about 2 a.m. the Palm Beach County Canvassing Board concludes its initial manual recount of 1 percent of the ballots and, over the objections of Burton, decides to proceed with a full manual recount.

At 6:00 p.m. Jimenez, general counsel to Jeb Bush, calls Clay Roberts, the director of the Division of Elections, to see if the secretary of state could legally issue an advisory opinion saying that the full manual recount in Palm Beach County was unlawful because the difference between the machine count and the manual recount had not been the result of a mechanical failure. Clay told Jimenez that the opinion would have to be requested by a political party. Jimenez contacts Al Cardenas, chairman of the Republican Party, to ask him to make the request, and Cardenas faxes one to Roberts.

November 12: Palm Beach County begins the manual recount. In the evening an opinion is faxed from the Florida Division of Elections to the Palm Beach County Canvassing Board saying that the manual recount was not justified.

Foreseeing the possibility that the Division of Elections might try to stop the recount in Palm Beach County, staff in the Florida attorney general's office contact an intermediary with the Palm

Beach County Canvassing Board and suggest that the latter seek a legal opinion from the attorney general on whether the recount is lawful.

November 13: Counting partly pushed chads only if at least two corners have been severed, the Broward County Canvassing Board conducts a manual recount of 1 percent of the ballots and votes against a full recount after finding only a 4 vote gain for Gore, which, if projected to 100 percent, would yield only a 400 vote gain for Gore, not enough (at the time) to change the election outcome.

The Palm Beach County Canvassing Board finds the fax from the Division of Elections in its fax machine. Later that day the board receives a fax from the Florida attorney general contradicting the opinion from the Division of Elections.

The U.S. District Court rejects Bush's request to stop recounts. Volusia County sues in the Florida Circuit Court to be allowed complete manual recounts past the November 14 deadline in Florida election law. Gore and the Palm Beach County Canvassing Board are allowed to join the Volusia suit.

In her first statement on the issue, Ms. Harris says that overseas ballots have to be "executed" on or before Election Day. They are not required "to be postmarked on or prior to" Election Day. Democrats complain that she was blurring the rules.

November 14: Florida Circuit Court rules that the Florida secretary of state can enforce the November 14 deadline for accepting returns but cannot be arbitrary in doing so. Canvassing boards are told in the ruling that they may submit amended returns at a later date, and Harris can decide whether to accept them. Broward and Palm Beach County canvassing boards return to manual recounting. Harris faxes a letter to the counties instructing them to state their reasons, in writing, by 2 p.m., November 15, for wanting to submit vote totals later than November 14.

After the circuit court rules that late submissions are legal, the Miami-Dade Canvassing Board finally meets to respond to Gore's request on November 9 for a manual recount. The board conducts a 1 percent recount, from which Gore receives a net gain of 6 votes. The board votes 2 to 1 against a complete manual recount on the grounds that Gore would not gain enough votes for the election outcome to be altered.

November 15: Volusia Canvassing Board appeals the circuit court ruling to Florida's First District Court of Appeals.

After receiving letters from four counties by the 2 p.m. deadline, Florida's secretary of state says that she rejects the reasons given by counties for late filings, says she will not consider any subsequent returns, and announces that the election returns received on or before November 14 will be certified on November 18, the day after the deadline for receiving overseas absentee ballots.

In the evening Al Gore appears on national television and proposes that a manual recount be conducted statewide and that he and Bush meet. Bush appears on television soon thereafter to reject both the meeting and the statewide recount.

Mark Herron, a Democratic consultant, writes a legal guide for Democratic lawyers to challenge flawed ballots, including those cast by members of the military.

November 16: Gore files suit in the Florida Circuit Court seeking to compel Secretary Harris to accept amended returns.

November 17: Deadline for receiving overseas absentee ballots.

The Florida Circuit Court refuses Gore's request to compel Harris to consider late returns. Gore appeals the circuit court ruling to Florida's First District Court of Appeals.

The Florida Supreme Court, on its own initiative, uses its "pass through jurisdiction" to take up both the Volusia and the Gore appeals. In its order taking jurisdiction, the court says that the manual recounting can continue and prohibits the secretary of state from certifying the election returns on November 18 as planned.

The U.S. Court of Appeals for the 11th Circuit refuses to grant Bush's appeal to stop manual recounts in Broward and Palm Beach counties.

Despite their gains, Republicans are incensed by Democratic challenges to military ballots and begin attacking the Democrats as unpatriotic.

Amid intense lobbying by both campaigns, canvassing boards across Florida meet to weigh the legality of the overseas ballots and count those that are accepted. Mr. Bush has a net gain of 630 votes.

November 19: After the Florida Supreme Court allows the recounts in the other counties to continue, one of the Miami-Dade County Canvassing Board members, Circuit Judge Myriam Lehr, changes her vote, and Miami-Dade begins a manual recount.

Senator Joseph Lieberman appears on national television, saying that members of the military should get the "benefit of the doubt."

In Broward County Gore has gained only 79 votes over Bush from the manual recount after more than 40 percent of the precincts have been counted. On advice from Andrew Meyers, an assistant county attorney, the Broward Canvassing Board decides to change its recount standard to consider slightly indented or "dimpled" chads as indications of voter intent, and to go back through the ballots already reviewed.

Meyers, the assistant attorney for Broward County, is not assigned to advise the canvassing board but shows up unsolicited and suggests that the canvassing board should change its standard to conform to a Texas statute, which accepts "dimpled" chads in manual recounts. Meyers's wife was assisting the Gore legal team.

November 20: Oral arguments are made to the Florida Supreme Court over the secretary of state's decision to stop the recounts and certify the election returns.

In response to the suit on the butterfly ballot, the circuit court in Palm Beach County rules that a revote cannot be granted. This decision is appealed.

Speaker of the Florida House of Representatives advocates a special legislative session, claiming that the State Legislature can name the electors itself.

Attorney General Robert A. Butterworth, a Democrat, urges canvassing boards to revisit the issue of military ballots.

In the morning Michael Carvin, a lawyer for George W. Bush, was told by Joseph Klock, an attorney selected by Florida secretary of state Katherine Harris to represent her office during the dispute, that the Florida Supreme Court justices had already decided the case and had drafted an opinion allowing five more days for manual recounts.

November 21: Florida Supreme Court rules that manual recounts can continue. The court sets a new deadline for submitting the amended returns. The deadline is Sunday, November 26, at 5:00 p.m. if the secretary of state's office is open, or November 27 at 9:00 a.m. if the office is closed on the 26th. James Baker publicly criticizes the decision and suggests that the Florida legislature should step in. Gore praises the decision, again proposes a meeting with Bush, and says that he will not support any efforts by Democrats to convince Bush electors to the Electoral College to switch their votes.

From this point on, the Bush legal team, Jeb Bush, and Florida Republican chairman Al Cardenas begin planning, with Florida House Speaker Feeney and Florida Senate president John McKay, the timing of the legislature's intervention.

November 22: Bush appeals the Florida Supreme Court ruling to the U.S. Supreme Court.

In response to a suit from Gore, the circuit court in Palm Beach County rules that the Palm Beach County Canvassing Board cannot automatically reject ballots with dimpled chads but must seek to discern the voters' intent per Florida election law.

The Miami-Dade Canvassing Board meets at 8 a.m. because of concerns that its recount cannot be completed by November 26. The board decides to limit the recount to undervotes only, but after a loud demonstration outside the room used for the recount, the board breaks at 10:30 a.m., reconvenes at 1:30 p.m., and votes unanimously to end the recount.

The Bush campaign sues fourteen canvassing boards to try to get them to reconsider rejected military ballots.

Gore personally calls Alex Penelas, the mayor of Miami-Dade County. Gore thinks that Penelas agrees to issue a statement calling for the recount to resume and providing all necessary resources to meet the deadline, but Penelas does not issue a statement.

November 23: Miami-Dade County stops its manual recount. Gore asks the Florida Supreme Court to require Miami-Dade to complete the manual recount, but the court rejects the request.

November 24: U.S. Supreme Court agrees to hear Bush's appeal of the Florida Supreme Court decision allowing the recounts to proceed. The issue it agrees to consider is not whether the recounts violated equal treatment requirements in the U.S. Constitution but whether the Florida

Supreme Court, in setting a new deadline for submitting amended returns, had changed Florida election law after the election, in violation of Title III of the U.S. Code.

November 24–26: In what Democrats called the "Thanksgiving stuffing," canvassing boards reconvene and accept previously rejected ballots, giving Mr. Bush a net gain of 109 votes.

November 26: At 12:34 p.m. the Palm Beach County Canvassing Board faxes a letter to Florida secretary of state Harris asking to be allowed to submit amended returns on Monday, November 27, which the Florida Supreme Court's order authorized if the secretary's office were closed on November 26. Secretary Harris immediately denies the request.

Florida secretary of state certifies the election returns, with 2,912,790 votes for Bush and 2,912,253 votes for Gore, giving Bush a victory by 537 votes. At 8:41 p.m. Governor Jeb Bush signs the certificate designating Florida's electors to his brother, George W.

At 7:06 p.m. the Palm Beach County Canvassing Board faxes its amended return to the secretary of state; it adds 215 votes to Gore's total.

To prevent Gore's legal team from being able to have an injunction served to block the certification from being transmitted to Congress before the election was contested in the circuit court per the Florida election law, Florida governor Jeb Bush gives the document to an obscure staff member to take home with her and mail the next morning.

November 27: Gore files an action in Florida Circuit Court to contest the election returns in Palm Beach, Miami-Dade, and Nassau counties.

November 28: Circuit court judge orders disputed ballots in Palm Beach and Miami-Dade counties to be brought to the court in Tallahassee.

November 29: Gore asks the Florida Supreme Court to immediately begin the recounts in order to complete the recounting in Palm Beach and Miami-Dade counties.

November 30: A committee of the Florida House recommends a special session.

December 1: Oral arguments are heard in the U.S. Supreme Court on Bush's appeal of the Florida Supreme Court decision to allow the recounts to continue until November 25–26.

The Florida Supreme Court upholds the circuit court decision on the butterfly ballot in Palm Beach County.

December 2–3: Circuit trial on Gore's action to contest the election.

December 4: Gore's election challenge is rejected by the circuit court judge. The U.S. Supreme Court vacates the decision of the Florida Supreme Court to extend the deadline for manual recounts and returns the decision to the Florida court for clarification.

December 6: Separate trials begin in Martin and Seminole counties over alleged illegalities involving absentee ballots.

Republican leaders of the Florida legislature announce plans to call a special session to consider having the legislature pick the electors itself.

December 7: Florida Speaker of the House and president of the Senate formally call a special legislative session to commence on December 8.

The intent of the special session was to overrule the Florida Supreme Court after December 12 if this became necessary. The session was announced and held prior to the 12th to put pressure on the Florida Supreme Court and create a sense of impending constitutional crisis, which would help draw in the U.S. Supreme Court.

December 8: The Florida Supreme Court rules in favor of Gore's appeal of the circuit court decision, orders a statewide manual recount of all undervotes, and adds 383 votes to Gore's total, bringing Bush's margin to 154 votes. In an effort to prevent the recount, Bush appeals to the Florida Supreme Court, the U.S. Court of Appeals, and the U.S. Supreme Court.

Circuit courts rule in the Seminole and Martin County absentee ballot cases that irregularities and illegalities occurred but that the absentee ballots cannot be thrown out. These decisions are appealed to the Florida Supreme Court.

Florida Supreme Court denies Bush's appeal to stop the recount.

U.S. Court of Appeals also rejects Bush's appeal but reinstates Bush's 537-vote lead as certified.

Almost immediately after this decision is announced, the U.S. Supreme Court orders the recounting to stop and agrees to hear Bush's appeal.

The Florida Supreme Court decision includes a dissent by Justice Wells that expresses intense concern that the U.S. Supreme Court has already shown (in its earlier remand of the Florida court's first decision) that the high court will overrule the Florida court. Wells's dissent also reveals his concerns about provoking the Florida legislature.

December 11: The U.S. Supreme Court hears oral arguments.

Committees in the Florida House and Senate pass a resolution for consideration by their full bodies to appoint the electors pledged to Bush.

December 12: The Florida Supreme Court upholds circuit court decisions not to throw out absentee ballots in Martin and Seminole counties.

At 10:00 p.m. U.S. Supreme Court issues a ruling that the Florida Supreme Court must set standards for manual recounting, but the court concludes that the time has run out to do this.

December 13: Gore concedes.

Chapter 2

Who Really Won?

To determine who actually won the disputed 2000 presidential election, two questions need to be answered: What is the standard for a legally valid vote, and how many legally valid votes did Bush and Gore receive? With the information available today, these questions are not especially difficult to answer. They could have been answered during the election controversy if the laws of Florida had been interpreted reasonably and administered in good faith. The Bush campaign staff and legal team knew this, and they feared that a recount in any form might give sufficient additional votes to Gore for him to be declared the winner. Hence they immediately began to sew doubts about Florida's election laws and the reliability of manual recounts.

In America's highly competitive political arena, such tactics are legal and even normal, notwithstanding their disservice to the electorate. But controversy and confusion were fomented not merely by the Bush legal and political team but also by public officials at the highest levels of Florida government, some of whom were tied directly to the Bush campaign. As a result, the recount process mandated by Florida law was delayed, disrupted, and ultimately blocked.

Enduring Confusion

So successful were the Republicans' tactics that much of the confusion they caused in 2000 persists to this day. Through a combination of public announcements, legal suits, administrative decisions, memorable metaphors, and orchestrated demonstrations, Republican strategists propagated subtle but significant misconceptions that prejudiced the public's perception of the controversy. Among these manufactured impressions were two that continued to distort popular perceptions months and years later, even as new facts emerged revealing the Republicans' conspiracy to undermine Florida's election laws both in advance of the 2000 election and during the election dispute. The same mistaken beliefs that had skewed citizens' perceptions of the election controversy prevented them from seeing later that they had been bamboozled.

One prejudicial misconception was the idea that Florida's election laws were poorly written and did not anticipate and therefore provide for the incredibly close results of 2000. As this chapter will demonstrate, nothing could have been further from the truth. In the decades leading up to the 2000 presidential contest, two statewide elections in Florida had been decided by very close margins, exposing the imprecision of high-speed, punch-card readers and demonstrating the need for manual recounts when election outcomes fall within the machines' margin of error. In response, Florida election laws had been revised to specify the conditions under which ballots would be recounted, and the procedures that would be used.

Florida's experience in this regard was well known to the state's election officials when they were preparing for the 2000 election and when they saw the indecisive outcome on Election Day. One of the two close elections discussed above involved George W. Bush's brother, Jeb. His loss to Lawton Chiles in the 1994 governor's race had been, at the time, the second closest outcome in a statewide election in modern Florida history. Despite whatever they may have said in public, Republicans knew from firsthand experience that Florida's election laws were well designed to deal with close races.

The other misconception that continued to distort popular perceptions long after the election controversy had passed was the notion that manually counting votes is less accurate than counting them with high speed, ballot-reading machines. This view turns the truth upside down. Two articles written long before the 2000 election about the inaccuracy of ballot-reading machines are posted on-line at www.dehaven-smith.com. Mechanical vote tabulations are notoriously inaccurate. Manual recounts were not the problem; they were the solution.

Nor was Florida alone in recognizing the need to count ballots by hand when election outcomes are close. The appendix contains the manual recount provisions in the election laws in Texas, and the recount provisions of other states are available on-line. They are a routine practice. That manual recounting became suspect to most Americans during the election controversy of 2000 testifies to the power of disinformation.

Sources of Error in Casting and Tabulating Votes

The 2000 election revealed that counting votes with machines can and often does yield results that are significantly in error. This is true regardless of the type of vote-casting and vote-tabulating equipment currently in use in Florida, although error rates do vary from one type to another. Errors in machine counts are caused by a variety of factors, including inadequately maintaining the vote-casting or vote-tabulating machines, problems in the manufacture of the equipment, improperly feeding ballots into the tabulation machines, incorrectly programming the tabulation machines, and voter errors in completing the ballots.

Other, non-mechanical factors can also cause election outcomes to differ from voters' intentions. These include confusing ballot designs, faulty practice ballots, and incorrect or incomplete instructions at the polling place or on the ballot itself. In the 2000 election a notorious example of poor ballot design was the so-called butterfly ballot in Palm Beach County. This ballot is discussed in detail later in this chapter. An example of poor ballot instructions occurred in Gadsden County. A sample ballot from Gadsden is shown in the appendix.

During the 2000 election the imprecision of machine tabulations had been evident the very first day after the election, but so much happened immediately after this that the fact dropped from view. At the end of election night the vote count reported by Florida's county elections supervisors to the secretary of state had George W. Bush ahead by 1,784 votes. The next day the votes were recounted, and, of course, in the twenty-five counties using the punch-card system, the recounting was by machines. Across the state roughly 185,000 ballots had been discarded as unreadable for one reason or another. In the recount Bush's lead dropped by half, to a little over 900 votes.

Most of the increase for Gore occurred because reading punch cards through the vote-tabulating machines causes partially punched chads to break free, with the results that votes previously obscured become visible. Chads are small, numbered, square perforations associated with the names of candidates on the cardboard sheets used as ballots in the punch-card system. Photographs of punch-card ballots are contained in the chapter appendix. I took these pictures in Miami-Dade County when I was re-counting ballots as part of a national news show filmed shortly after the election.

The vote-tabulation machine reads the votes by shining a light on the cards and registering votes when the light shines through the hole that is made when the chad is punched out. If chads are only partially broken free, they can become like swinging doors that may open or close when they are run through the counter. Often a valid vote can be missed during the first count if the chad is left hanging, because a door-like, swinging chad can be folded closed as the ballot goes through the machine. However, when the ballot is run through the machine again, this same vote will be recognized because the chad breaks free. This phenomenon is well known to election officials and is why many states, including Florida, have procedures for ballots to be recounted by hand when elections are very close.

Florida's Election Law Reforms of 1989

The election laws as they stood in Florida for the 2000 election are repro-duced in the appendix. They contained well-thought-out provisions for dealing with the issues that hit in 2000, because the state's election laws had been revised in both 1989 and 1999 to address problems of election error and fraud in earlier elections.

The reforms of 1989 were in response to the very close election between Buddy MacKay and Connie Mack for the U.S. Senate. This was a highly publicized election in which Mack attacked MacKay by concluding his ads with the sentence, "Hey Buddy, you're a liberal." At the tail end of the Reagan administration and long before Newt Gingrich emerged to give conservatism a somewhat negative connotation, the liberal label was anathema in Florida. After losing by the narrowest margin in Florida his-tory up to that time, MacKay asked for manual recounts in several coun-ties, but the county canvassing boards refused. MacKay took the issue to court, but he was told that Florida election law gave him no authority to demand a review. Knowing what we know now after the disputed 2000 presidential election, it is reasonable to think that MacKay might well have won if the ballots had been carefully examined.

In 1988, however, Florida law did not provide for automatic mechanical recounts or any procedures for requesting manual recounts. Hence one of the reforms made to Florida's election laws in 1989 was to add an automatic recount provision, which set the stage for the recount in the disputed 2000 presidential election. The package of 1989 reforms specified the circumstances and procedures for recounts. Any election in which the margin of victory was one-half of a percent or less of the total number of votes cast automatically triggered a recount by whatever the procedure the local canvassing board chose to use. If, after the recount, the margin remained one-half of a percent or less of the total vote, any of the candidates could ask for a manual recount. Local canvassing boards had the option of accepting or rejecting the candidates' requests. If the canvassing board agreed to the recount, the board was required to draw a sample of 1 percent of the ballots and count them manually. Then, if the difference between the initial count and the manual recount was sufficiently large to suggest that a full manual recount might alter the election outcome, the canvassing board was required to manually recount all ballots.

Reforms in 1999

The election reforms of 1999 were added in response to a 1998 election for the mayor of the City of Miami. In this election the outcome was subsequently overturned because of fraud. The main problem occurred with absentee ballots, which were submitted for dead voters, unregistered voters, and others unqualified to participate. The 1999 reforms placed requirements on how absentee ballots were to be requested, the time by which they had to be mailed, and the conditions when absentee voting was authorized.

In addition, the secretary of state was assigned the responsibility of culling the election rolls to remove duplicate listings, deceased voters, and persons convicted of felonies in Florida or elsewhere. With respect to the latter, convicted felons had always been prohibited from voting in Florida unless their civil rights had been restored by the governor and cabinet, but the legislative mandate for a special project to inspect and clean the registered-voter roles was something new.

In chapter 5 evidence is discussed that the secretary of state or staff under her direct supervision intentionally rigged the project to help Republicans in 2000 and create havoc at polling places serving black and low-income communities. Also examined in chapter 5 is the documented failure of both Secretary of State Harris and Governor Jeb Bush to make any special preparations for the high voter turnout that was widely expected. These acts of malfeasance and misfeasance should be kept in mind when considering the problems experienced by Florida's voters in properly completing their ballots. The actions of Florida's top elected officials assured that many polling places, especially those serving traditional Democratic constituencies, would be overcrowded and chaotic.

Ballot Spoilage and Voter Error in 2000

Within a day or two after the ballots had been cast in the 2000 presidential election, most of the people who were observing the ensuing controversy recognized that the official vote count in Florida failed to accurately reflect the intent of the Florida electorate. George W. Bush held a slight advantage in the tabulation, and he would eventually be declared to have won. But it was clear that a majority of Floridians who cast ballots in the 2000 election intended to vote—and thought they had voted—for Al Gore.

Many votes cast for Gore simply ended up not counting or counting for another candidate. The same thing sometimes happened to Bush votes but much less often. Three types of voter error were common, two of which caused ballots to be tossed out or misread by the vote-tabulation equipment. One of the errors that caused ballots to be rejected is referred to as an *undervote*. It occurred when voters marked their ballots in such a way that the vote-tabulation equipment could not recognize any vote at all for a presidential candidate. Sometimes this happened because the small, perforated square, or "chad," next to the candidate selected by the voter in a county with a punch-card voting system was not pressed with sufficient force to be dislodged. In counties with paper ballots read by optical scanners, undervotes could happen when voters circled their choice or marked it with an "X" rather than filling in the bubble next to the candidate's name. The second type of voter error that caused ballots to be rejected by vote-tabulation machines is the so-called *overvote*, which occurred when more than one presidential candidate was selected on the same ballot or when the same candidate was selected twice—once by selecting the candidate in the list of candidates and second by writing the candidate's name in the space provided for write-ins. The third type of error—the kind that did not cause the ballot to be rejected or misread but that nevertheless represented a failure of the system to correctly reflect the voters' intentions—occurred when voters became confused by the ballot design and marked one candidate's name while intending to vote for another.

Partisan Differences in Error Rates

It should be stressed that the mere existence of voter error was not the problem in Florida's 2000 presidential election. What caused the vote tabulation to depart from the electorate's intent was that Gore supporters made errors more often than Bush supporters did. If voter error had been distributed evenly across the electorate then it would have had no effect on the outcome, because errors by each candidate's supporters would have been canceled out by the errors of the supporters of other candidates. Thus the real problem in the disputed 2000 presidential election was not voter error in general but the fact that Florida's election system resulted in more voter spoilage for Democrats than for Republicans.

Mistakes in the polling booth were more common among Democrats than among Republicans for at least three reasons. First, the two social groups making the most errors were African Americans and seniors, and they are the core constituencies of Florida's Democratic Party. Significantly the higher error rate among these groups was true regardless of the type of voting equipment in use. At the time of the election forty counties used an optical scan system, twenty-five used the punch-card system, one used paper ballots, and one used a lever machine. When counties with optical scan systems and punch-card systems are examined separately, counties with higher proportions of seniors and blacks have higher error rates than other counties using the same type of equipment. The county with the highest error rate (12 percent of all votes cast) was Gadsden, the only majority-black county in Florida. Gadsden uses the optical scan system, which, other things being equal, would be expected to have produced a low rate of mistakes.

Second, the Democratic vote in Florida was understated relative to voters' intentions because counties providing the biggest source of Democratic votes used the punch-card system, which is the system with the highest error rate. The proportion of votes miscast in the counties with the punch-card system was roughly three times the proportion of miscast votes in counties using optical scanners. Of the 51 precincts in which more than 20 percent of ballots were rejected, 45 (88 percent) used punch cards. Of the 336 precincts in which more than 10 percent were tossed, 277 (78 percent) used punch cards. Two counties—Broward and Palm Beach—consistently provide Democrats with a large proportion of the party's totals in statewide elections. In the 2000 election Gore came away from these two counties alone with over 300,000 more votes than Bush. At the time of the election, both counties used the punch-card system. This meant that Democrats faced a handicap in what is by far their most important territory.

A third factor that caused vote totals in Florida to understate voters' support for Gore was confusion caused by election materials in a few counties. The best known of these problems was the butterfly ballot in Palm Beach County.

The Butterfly Ballot

Normally ballots in a punch-card system like Palm Beach County's are laid out with the candidates in a list and a series of holes along the left side of the candidates' names. Voters look down the list and then push a stylus into the hole next to their choice, thus (it is hoped) punching out the appropriate chad on the machine-readable card they have inserted into the lectern-like ballot holder. However, the elections supervisor in Palm Beach County was concerned that the list of presidential election candidates was so long that it would run across two pages, which would require voters to turn the page to see all the candidates. The list, which included ten separate tickets, was longer in 2000 than in any other presidential election in Florida history, because a 1998 revision to the Florida Constitution made it easy for independent and minor-party candidates to get their names on the ballot. Wanting voters to be able to see all the presidential candidates at once, the Palm Beach County elections supervisor designed the ballot to open like a book or butterfly, with presidential candidates listed on both the left page or wing and the right, and with the punch-holes running down the middle between them. This design was approved prior to the election by county officials from both the Democratic and Republican parties, all of whom failed to anticipate the voter errors it would cause. Voters, and especially Palm Beach County seniors who are overwhelmingly Democrats, became confused about which punch-holes belonged to which presidential candidates, and many, thinking they were voting for Gore, voted instead for Patrick Buchanan.

Setting aside for the moment the inaccuracy of machine tabulations, the butterfly ballot alone cost Gore the election. The graph shown in Figure

2.1 plots the counties of Florida along two axes: the number of voters registered in the Reform Party in the county and the number of votes received by Buchanan in the 2000 presidential election. With one exception, the counties are arrayed along a line indicative of a close relationship between numbers of Reform Party members and Buchanan votes. The exception is the outlying county in the upper-right quadrant of the graph: Palm Beach County. The large number of votes for Buchanan in this county (about 3,500) relative to the number of voters registered with the Reform Party (about 330) indicates that more than two thousand Gore supporters mistakenly cast their votes for Buchanan.

A more detailed statistical analysis by six political scientists from Harvard University, Cornell University, Northwestern University, and the University of California-Berkeley concluded that the numbers were probably even higher than this. The study found that Palm Beach County's butterfly ballot probably cost Gore at least 3,400 votes because of double punches and up to another 2,400 votes that were mistakenly cast for Buchanan. Had these votes been properly cast, Gore would have won

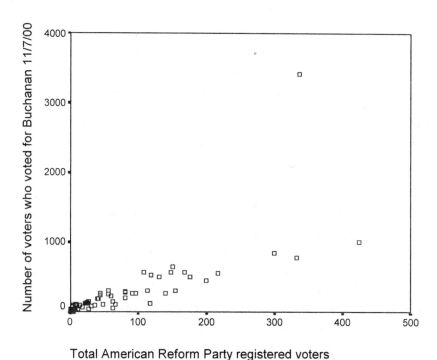

Total American Reform Party registered voters

Figure 2.1. Graph of Buchanan vote by Reform Party voter registration

Florida by about 1,500 votes despite the many other errors Gore supporters made elsewhere in the state.

After the votes had been cast on election day, nothing short of a revote in Palm Beach County could have been done to correct the problem caused by the butterfly ballot. As discussed in the next chapter, a revote was indeed sought through legal action on behalf of Palm Beach County voters but no authority for a revote existed in Florida election law, and the request was denied.

Valid Votes among the Discarded Ballots

Still, even without the ability to undo the voter error caused by the butterfly ballot, Florida's election system, if it had been properly administered, was capable of showing that Gore had actually won. Although the system placed Gore at a disadvantage because his supporters were more likely than other voters to cast overvotes and to be voting on machines with high ballot-spoilage rates, manual recounts of all the undervotes and overvotes at the time of the election controversy would definitely have found that Gore received more votes than Bush.

Manual recounts and other analyses were conducted after the election controversy had ended, when the ballots had become available for public inspection. They showed that many votes unreadable by machines were easily decipherable by human beings and that Gore would have ended up with a majority had those votes been taken into account.

Of course, during the election controversy, the Bush legal team, Republican leaders in the Florida legislature, Florida's Republican secretary of state, the governor of Florida who is George W. Bush's brother, and George W. Bush himself argued that machines alone are capable of reading ballots objectively. Claiming that those votes unreadable by machines were ambiguous when examined by human eyes, Bush partisans denigrated the manual recounts in southeast Florida by saying that the canvassing boards "were not counting votes, they were casting them." However, this argument was simply incorrect. It may have contained an element of validity with respect to punch cards with chads that were only slightly indented or "dimpled," but as a statement about all votes unrecognized or rejected by tabulation machines, it was absolutely false.

There were certain types of both undervotes and overvotes that mechanical devices kicked out but that could be read easily by human beings, and without any uncertainty at all. One type of unambiguous vote unreadable by machines and rejected as undervotes was any vote cast on a punch card by marking the appropriate chad with a pencil or pen. While machines recorded nothing when they scanned such ballots, the intent of the voter was obvious to a person, because a person can see the pencil mark whereas the machine cannot. The same is true for votes cast on an optical scan system when the wrong type of marker was used on the ballot. Such votes were fairly common for both punch-card and optical-scan systems.

A second type of undervote requiring no interpretation was what might be called a "false undervote." These occur with the punch-card system when the ballot is left with a hanging chad, and the chad folds closed when going through the card reader but swings open or falls off entirely on the way out. In such cases the machine fails to register a vote, but a manual inspection of the ballot shows the vote quite clearly.

Valid Overvotes

Turning now to overvotes, the unambiguous votes they contained were those where a candidate's name had been punched or marked in the list of candidates and then the same name had been printed in the space available for write-ins. Vote-tabulating machines for both the optical-scan and the punch-card systems rejected ballots with this type of error, but a manual inspection of such ballots reveals with complete certainty the voters' intent.

Write-in overvotes were the most common form of voter error in the election and were also more likely to have been cast by Gore supporters. The National Opinion Research Center at the University of Chicago provided a summary table on the types and frequency of different errors in the ballots left uncounted at the end of the 2000 election (Table 2.1). Overvotes accounted for about two-thirds of the errors, and undervotes accounted for about one-third.

That overvotes were more often the ballots of Gore supporters than Bush supporters can be seen by comparing the precinct characteristics associated with each type of error. Figure 2.2 is a chart I compiled by merging NORC's dataset of the 175,010 uncounted ballots with a dataset from the Florida Redistricting Economic and Demographic System (FREDS). The latter provides detailed profiles of the characteristics of each election precinct in Florida. By linking each ballot in NORC's data to each precinct in the FREDS data, it was possible to determine the characteristics of the precincts in which different types of errors occurred. As shown in Figure

Table 2.1. Florida Voting Systems by Number of Counties and Number of Uncertified Ballots Examined by NORC

Voting System	Number of Counties	Undervotes	Overvotes	Total No. of Ballots
Votomatic[a]	15	53,215	84,822	138,037
Datavote[b]	9	771	4,427	5,198
Optical scan[c]	41	7,204	24,571	31,775
Lever[d]	1	[f]		
Paper[e]	1	[g]		
Total	67	61,190	113,820	175,010

a. Voters use a hand-held stylus to punch out the chad for the selected candidate.
b. Voters use a mechanical punching mechanism to select candidates.
c. Voters fill in ovals or connect arrows that correspond to the selected candidates. An optical scanning machine reads the forms. In some counties, a prescribed writing implement must be used because regular black pens and lead pencils cannot be read by the scanners.
d. Coders working in the lever county used the Datavote coding materials.
e. Coders working in the paper county used the optical-scan coding materials.
f. Vote totals for the lever county are summed into the vote totals for the Datavote counties.
g. Vote totals for the paper county are summed into the vote totals for the optical-scan counties.

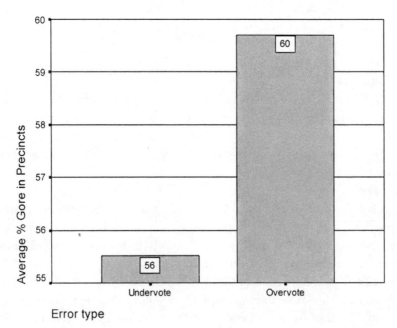

Figure 2.2. Precinct undervotes, overvotes, and percent voting Gore

2.2, the election outcome in precincts in which overvotes occurred averaged 60 percent in favor of Gore, while the precincts of undervotes supported Gore by an average of only 56 percent.

What Counts as a Legally Valid Vote?

One might argue that none of the ballots with undervotes and overvotes should count, because they involve failures on the part of voters to follow directions. But rejecting such ballots would be a violation of Florida election law (Section 101.5614[5]), which states that no vote "shall be declared invalid or void if there is a clear indication of the intent of the voter." It would also run counter to Florida judicial decisions going back almost a century. In *Boardman v. Esteva* (1975), for example, the Florida Supreme Court stated that, in an election dispute,

> the real parties in interest here, not in the legal sense but in realistic terms, are the voters. They are possessed of the ultimate interest and it is they whom we must give primary consideration. The contestants have direct interests certainly, but the office they seek is one of high public service and of utmost importance to the people, thus subordinating their interest to that of the people. Ours is a government of, by and for the people. Our federal and state constitutions guarantee the right of the people to take an active part in the process of that government, which for most of our citizens means participation via the election process. The right to vote is the right to participate; it is also the right to speak, but more importantly the right to be heard. We must tread carefully on that right or we risk the unnecessary and unjustified muting of the public voice. By refusing to recognize an otherwise valid exercise of the right of a citizen to vote for the sake of sacred, unyielding adherence to statutory scripture, we would in effect nullify that right.

Other, similar precedents by the Florida Supreme Court include *State ex rel. Chappell v. Martinez* (Fla. 1988), holding that voter disenfranchisement is improper where the intent of voter can be ascertained, and *Beckstrom v. Volusia County Canvassing Board* (1998), ruling that courts should not frustrate the will of voters if that will can be determined. In Florida, so long as intent can be discerned, all votes are to be counted regardless of whether errors are made by the voters themselves, elections officials, or anyone else.

The Election Outcome: When All Votes Are Counted

If all the legally valid votes in the Florida 2000 presidential election had been counted, Al Gore would have been the winner. This would have been true as a result of the recount in Palm Beach County alone if the canvassing board had had time to review all the undervotes, but, to save time, the board decided not to review any ballots on which Democratic and Republican observers, who reviewed the ballots before they went to the canvassing board, had disagreed about the voters' intention. The *Palm Beach Post* examined the 4,513 ballots discarded for this reason, and the *Post* concluded that 2,500 of the ballots had votes that were unambiguously for Gore and 1,818 votes for Bush, leaving Gore with a net gain of 682 votes. This would have given Gore the election even without the additional 174 votes the canvassing board found for Gore but that were not accepted by the secretary of state because they were turned in ninety minutes after the 5:00 p.m. deadline on November 25.

By the same token, Gore would have also won if a manual recount had simply been made of ballots with overvotes involving write-ins. Thousands more Gore votes than Bush votes were lost because of these "write-in overvotes," a fact revealed by studies undertaken in the aftermath of the controversy. The *Washington Post* conducted a computerized analysis of 2.7 million votes from Florida's eight largest counties to see which candidates' names had been punched on ballots with overvotes. The tabulation machines could not see that the candidate selected from the list and the candidate written-in were often the same, because the machines, while capable of telling when a name had been printed in the space for write-ins, could not actually read the name itself. In its analysis of overvotes, the *Washington Post* found that Gore's name was punched on 46,000 of the overvote ballots it examined, whereas Bush's name was marked on only 17,000. Although the analysis could not determine how many of these overvotes were "write-in overvotes," other reviews of the Florida ballots reveal that this was indeed a very common type of overvote. For example, an *Orlando Sentinel* analysis of overvotes in Escambia County, a Republican stronghold, found 118 legally valid write-in overvotes for Gore and 49 for Bush. None of these votes had been counted in the official election totals, but, if they had been, they would have meant a net gain of 69 votes for Gore in just this one small Republican county.

Of course, the definitive study of the uncounted ballots was conducted by NORC. It found that the undervotes split roughly evenly between the two candidates. There was some variation in the division, depending on the criteria used to decide when and how to count partially punched chads, but the variation did not matter in the final vote total when the overvotes were included. Shown in Table 2.2 are the results for each of the different criteria that would have met Florida's legal standard for recounts.

Regardless of which criteria are used for counting undervotes, Gore has the most votes when all votes are counted. This is true if a single standard is applied statewide or if each county applied its own standards independently. Gore's margin of victory ranges between 9 and 158 votes.

Why the Public Remained Uninformed

The national and state electorates have continued to misunderstand that Gore received more votes than Bush, in part because the NORC findings were not clearly communicated either by NORC or by the study's media sponsors. Incredibly NORC did not issue a final report on the research. Instead, it released a number of data files along with text files describing the dataset layouts and variables, and explaining the decisions that went into the data coding. The most informative of these explanatory text files is contained in this chapter's appendix (see "NORC Media 'Read_Me' File"). Although it is clearly written, only someone with extensive techni-

Table 2.2. NORC Tabulations

	Bush	Gore	Winner	Margin
Prevailing statewide standard[a]	2,916,261	2,916,270	Gore	9
County standards[b]	2,924,452	2,924,508	Gore	56
Two-corner detached, statewide[c]	2,916,377	2,916,523	Gore	146
Most restrictive[d]	2,915,044	2,915,202	Gore	158
Most inclusive[e]	2,924,641	2,924,789	Gore	148

a. For punch cards, accepts a single-corner detached chad as an indicator of voter intent. For optical scan, accepts all affirmative marks as indicators of voter intent. Volusia County's certified result is accepted.

b. Accepts the certified results from Broward and Volusia counties and applies county-by-county standards to both undervotes and overvotes in the sixty-five remaining counties.

c. Accepts punch-card ballots with at least two corners of a chad detached as an adequate indication of voter intent.

d. Accepts only so-called perfect ballots that machines somehow missed and did not count, or ballots with unambiguous expressions of voter intent. Also accepts punch-card ballots where voters made choices with pencil markings.

e. Applies a uniform standard of "dimple or better" on punch marks and "all affirmative marks" on optical ballots to overvotes and undervotes statewide.

cal skills could understand it, much less use it to analyze the data files and determine what they meant for the election outcome. Moreover, in releasing the data as it did—without a final report or even a definitive press statement—NORC implied that there were so many possible criteria for judging dimpled chads, hanging chads, and so on, that many outcomes could be reached, some favoring Bush and others favoring Gore. Yet NORC did not even provide a summary table listing the vote tabulations under different scenarios, instead leaving even this most basic information to be derived by others.

NORC's actions were undoubtedly approved by the sponsors of the study. One can only speculate about why these media companies, which had spent millions of dollars to fund the project, later decided, in effect, to bury the findings, but their decision did not go unnoticed. For example, articles appeared in the *New Yorker* magazine and in a major newspaper in London, the *Guardian*, pointing out that NORC and its media sponsors appeared to have suffered a loss of nerve. One clue about why was the timing of NORC's release of the data files. The research had been completed shortly before September 11, 2001, but after the terrorist attacks on the World Trade Towers and the Pentagon, NORC announced that the scheduled release of its research findings was going to be pushed back several weeks. Presumably this was to avoid embarrassing the nation's president during a national crisis. Of course, there would have been no embarrassment if the data supported President Bush's claim to the White House, so it appears that NORC and its media sponsors decided to bury the findings because circumstances had changed.

Another reason why the national and state electorates have continued to misunderstand that Gore received more votes than Bush was because they were misled by two post-election studies that had come out earlier and appeared to reach the opposite conclusion, namely, that when the machine-rejected ballots were recounted by hand, a majority of Florida voters had actually cast their ballots for Bush after all. No doubt the authors of these two reports never intended for them to be misleading, but the way that the research was framed and the findings were stated did indeed create a misunderstanding. (For a response to reader criticism, see Tom Fiedler, "Votes Aren't Sacred," *Miami Herald*, April 8, 2001.) One study was a recount by the *Miami Herald* of the undervotes in Miami-Dade County. During the election controversy Gore's legal team, as well as many media commentators, believed that a complete manual recount of the Miami-

Dade undervotes would have delivered a net gain for Gore sufficient to give him the election. The other study was funded by several media companies and conducted by an independent accounting firm to see if Gore would have won if the recount ordered by the Florida Supreme Court had not been halted by the U.S. Supreme Court. The studies concluded that Gore probably would not have come up with more votes than Bush even if one or both of these recounts had been allowed. (For summaries of both studies, see Martin Merzer, "Overvotes Leaned to Gore," *Miami Herald*, May 11, 2001.) Since these two types of recounts were the only ones on the judicial table when the controversy ended, the implication seemed to be that Bush had actually been the winner.

But this conclusion was based on an erroneous assumption, namely, that the types of recounts being litigated were those that would truly have yielded a reasonably accurate determination of the voters' intentions. In fact, the post-controversy recounts revealed not that Bush had actually won but rather that, if a manual recount had been limited to *under*votes, it would have produced an inaccurate picture of the electorate's position. As we now realize, additional net votes for Gore were contained in the *over*votes, because many Gore voters made the mistake of selecting Gore in the list of presidential candidates and also printing Gore's name in the space for write-ins. Both the optical-scan and the punch-card systems rejected ballots with this type of error, but a manual inspection of such ballots reveals with complete certainty the voters' intent. The *Herald* study found that 3,146 overvotes contained clear and therefore legally valid votes not counted in any of the manual recounts during the dispute. Most were write-in overvotes. Of the total, 1,871 were for Gore and 1,189 were for Bush, a gain of 682 votes—more than enough to offset Bush's certified lead. (The other 86 legible overvotes went to other candidates.) The bottom line is that Gore did indeed receive more votes than Bush in Florida, but because time was running out during the recounts, not all the ballots rejected in mechanical tabulations were counted.

To be sure, one could argue that time constraints existed because of the U.S. Constitution and Title III of the U.S. Code, which specify the dates by which electors must be selected and the Electoral College must cast its votes. This is indeed true. But rather than putting an end to concerns about who was responsible for the election breakdown, it magnifies the importance of the actions of Florida's highest public officials in their handling of the dispute. Partisan maneuverings, primarily by Republican elected officials heading the state's executive and legislative branches, most of whom had close personal ties to George W. Bush, repeatedly caused disruption and delay clearly intended to prevent a manual recount from being conducted.

Without these delays and disruptions there would have been plenty of time to address procedural issues and conduct a full manual count of all machine-rejected ballots. When the statewide recount began after being mandated by the Florida Supreme Court on December 8 and before being preempted by the U.S. Supreme Court, teams in Tallahassee under the circuit court's supervision were counting 300 votes per hour. No county had more than a combined total of 65,000 undervotes and overvotes, a number that could have been counted in 216 hours, or nine 24-hour days. The presidency went to the wrong man, in large part because some of the very people in Florida responsible for assuring fair and accurate elections disrupted and delayed the process to keep a thorough recount from happening.

Appendix to Chapter 2

Federal, Florida, and Texas Election Law in 2000

Constitution of the United States

Article II

Section 1, Clause 2. Presidential Electors

Each State shall appoint, in such Manner as the Legislature thereof may direct, a Number of Electors, equal to the whole Number of Senators and Representatives to which the State may be entitled in the Congress: but no Senator or Representative, or Person holding an Office of Trust or Profit under the United States, shall be appointed an Elector.

United States Code

3 U.S.C. § 1. Time of Appointing Electors

The electors of President and Vice President shall be appointed, in each State, on the Tuesday next after the first Monday in November, in every fourth year succeeding every election of a President and Vice President.

3 U.S.C. § 2. Failure to Make Choice on Prescribed Day
Whenever any State has held an election for the purpose of choosing electors, and has failed to make a choice on the day prescribed by law, the electors may be appointed on a subsequent day in such a manner as the legislature of such State may direct.

3. U.S.C. § 5. Determination of Controversy as to Appointment of Electors
If any State shall have provided, by laws enacted prior to the day fixed for the appointment of the electors, for its final determination of any controversy or contest concerning the appointment of all or any of the electors of such State, by judicial or other methods or procedures, and such determination shall have been made at least six days before the time fixed for the meeting of the electors, such determination made pursuant to such law so existing on said day, and made at least six days prior to said time of meeting of the electors, shall be conclusive, and shall govern in the counting of the electoral votes as provided in the Constitution, and as hereinafter regulated, so far as the ascertainment of the electors appointed by such State is concerned.

3 U.S.C. § 15. Counting electoral votes in Congress
Congress shall be in session on the sixth day of January succeeding every meeting of the electors. The Senate and House of Representatives shall meet in the Hall of the House of Representatives at the hour of 1 o'clock in the afternoon on that day, and the President of the Senate shall be their presiding officer. Two tellers shall be previously appointed on the part of the Senate and two on the part of the House of Representatives, to whom shall be handed, as they are opened by the President of the Senate, all the certificates and papers purporting to be certificates of the electoral votes, which certificates and papers shall be opened, presented, and acted upon in the alphabetical order of the States, beginning with the letter A; and said tellers, having then read the same in the presence and hearing of the two Houses, shall make a list of the votes as they shall appear from the said certificates; and the votes having been ascertained and counted according to the rules in this subchapter provided, the result of the same shall be delivered to the President of the Senate, who shall thereupon announce the state of the vote, which announcement shall be deemed a sufficient declaration of the persons, if any, elected President and Vice President of the United States, and, together with a list of the votes, be entered on the

Journals of the two Houses. Upon such reading of any such certificate or paper, the President of the Senate shall call for objections, if any. Every objection shall be made in writing, and shall state clearly and concisely, and without argument, the ground thereof, and shall be signed by at least one Senator and one Member of the House of Representatives before the same shall be received. When all objections so made to any vote or paper from a State shall have been received and read, the Senate shall thereupon withdraw, and such objections shall be submitted to the Senate for its decision; and the Speaker of the House of Representatives shall, in like manner, submit such objections to the House of Representatives for its decision; and no electoral vote or votes from any State which shall have been regularly given by electors whose appointment has been lawfully certified to according to section 6 of this title from which but one return has been received shall be rejected, but the two Houses concurrently may reject the vote or votes when they agree that such vote or votes have not been so regularly given by electors whose appointment has been so certified. If more than one return or paper purporting to be a return from a State shall have been received by the President of the Senate, those votes, and those only, shall be counted which shall have been regularly given by the electors who are shown by the determination mentioned in section 5 of this title to have been appointed, if the determination in said section provided for shall have been made, or by such successors or substitutes, in case of a vacancy in the board of electors so ascertained, as have been appointed to fill such vacancy in the mode provided by the laws of the State; but in case there shall arise the question which of two or more of such State authorities determining what electors have been appointed, as mentioned in section 5 of this title, is the lawful tribunal of such State, the votes regularly given of those electors, and those only, of such State shall be counted whose title as electors the two Houses, acting separately, shall concurrently decide is supported by the decision of such State so authorized by its law; and in such case of more than one return or paper purporting to be a return from a State, if there shall have been no such determination of the question in the State aforesaid, then those votes, and those only, shall be counted which the two Houses shall concurrently decide were cast by lawful electors appointed in accordance with the laws of the State, unless the two Houses, acting separately, shall concurrently decide such votes not to be the lawful votes of the legally appointed electors of such State. But if the two Houses shall disagree in respect of the counting of such votes, then, and in that case, the votes of the electors whose appointment shall have been certified by the executive of the State, under the seal thereof, shall be counted. When the two Houses have voted, they shall immediately again meet, and the presiding officer shall then announce the decision of the questions submitted. No votes or papers from any other State shall be acted upon until the objections previously made to the votes or papers from any State shall have been finally disposed of.

Florida Constitutional Provisions

Florida Constitution—Article III, Legislature
§ 1. Composition
The legislative power of the state shall be vested in a legislature of the State of Florida, consisting of a senate composed of one senator elected from each senatorial district and a house of representatives composed of one member elected from each representative district.

Article V
Judiciary
§ 3. Supreme court
(a) Organization.—The supreme court shall consist of seven justices. Of the seven justices, each appellate district shall have at least one justice elected or appointed from the district to the supreme court who is a resident of the district at the time of the original appointment or election. Five justices shall constitute a quorum. The concurrence of four justices shall be necessary to a decision. When recusals for cause would prohibit the court from convening because of the requirements of this section, judges assigned to temporary duty may be substituted for justices.
(b) Jurisdiction.—The supreme court:
(1) Shall hear appeals from final judgments of trial courts imposing the death penalty and from decisions of district courts of appeal declaring invalid a state statute or a provision of the state constitution.
(2) When provided by general law, shall hear appeals from final judgments entered in proceedings for the validation of bonds or certificates of indebtedness and shall review action of statewide agencies relating to rates or service of utilities providing electric, gas, or telephone service.
(3) May review any decision of a district court of appeal that expressly declares valid a state statute, or that expressly construes a provision of the

state or federal constitution, or that expressly affects a class of constitutional or state officers, or that expressly and directly conflicts with a decision of another district court of appeal or of the supreme court on the same question of law.

(4) May review any decision of a district court of appeal that passes upon a question certified by it to be of great public importance, or that is certified by it to be in direct conflict with a decision of another district court of appeal.

(5) May review any order or judgment of a trial court certified by the district court of appeal in which an appeal is pending to be of great public importance, or to have a great effect on the proper administration of justice throughout the state, and certified to require immediate resolution by the supreme court.

(6) May review a question of law certified by the Supreme Court of the United States or a United States Court of Appeals which is determinative of the cause and for which there is no controlling precedent of the supreme court of Florida.

(7) May issue writs of prohibition to courts and all writs necessary to the complete exercise of its jurisdiction.

(8) May issue writs of mandamus and quo warranto to state officers and state agencies.

(9) May, or any justice may, issue writs of habeas corpus returnable before the supreme court or any justice, a district court of appeal or any judge thereof, or any circuit judge.

(10) Shall, when requested by the attorney general pursuant to the provisions of Section 10 of Article IV, render an advisory opinion of the justices, addressing issues as provided by general law.

(c) Clerk and marshal.—The supreme court shall appoint a clerk and a marshal who shall hold office during the pleasure of the court and perform such duties as the court directs. Their compensation shall be fixed by general law. The marshal shall have the power to execute the process of the court throughout the state, and in any county may deputize the sheriff or a deputy sheriff for such purpose.

Article XI
Amendments
§ 1. Proposal by legislature
Amendment of a section or revision of one or more articles, or the whole,

of this constitution may be proposed by joint resolution agreed to by three-fifths of the membership of each house of the legislature. The full text of the joint resolution and the vote of each member voting shall be entered on the journal of each house.

Florida Statutes

Fla. Stat. Ann § 101.5614. Canvass of returns

(1)(a) In precincts in which an electronic or electromechanical voting system is used, as soon as the polls are closed, the election board shall secure the voting devices against further voting. The election board shall thereafter open the ballot box in the presence of members of the public desiring to witness the proceedings and count the number of voted ballots, unused ballots, and spoiled ballots to ascertain whether such number corresponds with the number of ballots issued by the supervisor. If there is a difference, this fact shall be reported in writing to the county canvassing board with the reasons therefor if known. The total number of voted ballots shall be entered on the forms provided. The proceedings of the election board at the precinct after the polls have closed shall be open to the public; however, no person except a member of the election board shall touch any ballot or ballot container or interfere with or obstruct the orderly count of the ballots.

(b) In lieu of opening the ballot box at the precinct, the supervisor may direct the election board to keep the ballot box sealed and deliver it to a central or regional counting location. In this case, the election board shall count the stubs removed from the ballots to determine the number of voted ballots.

(2)(a) If the ballots are to be tallied at a central location or at no more than three regional locations, the election board shall place all ballots that have been cast and the unused, void, and defective ballots in the container or containers provided for this purpose, which shall be sealed and delivered forthwith to the central or regional counting location or other designated location by two inspectors who shall not, whenever possible, be of the same political party. The election board shall certify that the ballots were placed in such container or containers and each container was sealed in its presence and under its supervision, and it shall further certify to the number of ballots of each type placed in the container or containers.

(b) If ballots are to be counted at the precincts, such ballots shall be counted pursuant to rules adopted by the Department of State, which rules shall provide safeguards which conform as nearly as practicable to the safe-guards provided in the procedures for the counting of votes at a central location.

(3)(a) All proceedings at the central or regional counting location or other designated location shall be under the direction of the county canvassing board and shall be open to the public, but no person except a person employed and authorized for the purpose shall touch any ballot or ballot container, any item of automatic tabulating equipment, or any return prior to its release. If the ballots are tabulated at regional locations, one member of the canvassing board or a person designated by the board to represent it shall be present at each location during the testing of the counting equipment and the tabulation of the ballots.

(b) If ballots are tabulated at regional locations, the results of such election may be transmitted via dedicated teleprocessing lines to the main computer system for the purpose of compilation of complete returns. The security guidelines for transmission of returns by dedicated teleprocessing lines shall conform to rules adopted by the Department of State pursuant to § 101.015.

(4) If ballot cards are used, and separate write-in ballots or envelopes for casting write-in votes are used, write-in ballots or the envelopes on which write-in ballots have been cast shall be serially numbered, starting with the number one, and the same number shall be placed on the ballot card of the voter. This process may be completed at either the precinct by the election board or at the central counting location. For each ballot or ballot and ballot envelope on which write-in votes have been cast, the canvassing board shall compare the write-in votes with the votes cast on the ballot card; if the total number of votes for any office exceeds the number allowed by law, a notation to that effect, specifying the office involved, shall be entered on the back of the ballot card or in a margin if voting areas are printed on both sides of the ballot card. Such votes shall not be counted. All valid votes shall be tallied by the canvassing board.

(5) If any ballot card of the type for which the offices and measures are not printed directly on the card is damaged or defective so that it cannot properly be counted by the automatic tabulating equipment, a true duplicate copy shall be made of the damaged ballot card in the presence of witnesses and substituted for the damaged ballot. Likewise, a duplicate ballot card shall be made of a defective ballot which shall not include the invalid votes. All duplicate ballot cards shall be clearly labeled "duplicate," bear a serial

number which shall be recorded on the damaged or defective ballot card, and be counted in lieu of the damaged or defective ballot. If any ballot card of the type for which offices and measures are printed directly on the card is damaged or defective so that it cannot properly be counted by the automatic tabulating equipment, a true duplicate copy may be made of the damaged ballot card in the presence of witnesses and in the manner set forth above, or the valid votes on the damaged ballot card may be manually counted at the counting center by the canvassing board, whichever procedure is best suited to the system used. If any paper ballot is damaged or defective so that it cannot be counted properly by the automatic tabulating equipment, the ballot shall be counted manually at the counting center by the canvassing board. The totals for all such ballots or ballot cards counted manually shall be added to the totals for the several precincts or election districts. No vote shall be declared invalid or void if there is a clear indication of the intent of the voter as determined by the canvassing board. After duplicating a ballot, the defective ballot shall be placed in an envelope provided for that purpose, and the duplicate ballot shall be tallied with the other ballots for that precinct.

(6) If an elector marks more names than there are persons to be elected to an office or if it is impossible to determine the elector's choice, the elector's ballot shall not be counted for that office, but the ballot shall not be invalidated as to those names which are properly marked.

(7) Absentee ballots may be counted by automatic tabulating equipment if they have been punched or marked in a manner which will enable them to be properly counted by such equipment.

(8) The return printed by the automatic tabulating equipment, to which has been added the return of write-in, absentee, and manually counted votes, shall constitute the official return of the election. Upon completion of the count, the returns shall be open to the public. A copy of the returns may be posted at the central counting place or at the office of the supervisor of elections in lieu of the posting of returns at individual precincts.

Fla. Stat. Ann. § 102.166. Protest of Election Returns; Procedure
(1) Any candidate for nomination or election, or any elector qualified to vote in the election related to such candidacy, shall have the right to protest the returns of the election as being erroneous by filing with the appropriate canvassing board a sworn, written protest.

(2) Such protest shall be filed with the canvassing board prior to the time

the canvassing board certifies the results for the office being protested or within 5 days after midnight of the date the election is held, whichever occurs later.

(3) Before canvassing the returns of the election, the canvassing board shall:

(a) When paper ballots are used, examine the tabulation of the paper ballots cast.

(b) When voting machines are used, examine the counters on the machines of nonprinter machines or the printer-pac on printer machines. If there is a discrepancy between the returns and the counters of the machines or the printer-pac, the counters of such machines or the printer-pac shall be presumed correct.

(c) When electronic or electromechanical equipment is used, the canvassing board shall examine precinct records and election returns. If there is a clerical error, such error shall be corrected by the county canvassing board. If there is a discrepancy which could affect the outcome of an election, the canvassing board may recount the ballots on the automatic tabulating equipment.

(4) (a) Any candidate whose name appeared on the ballot, any political committee that supports or opposes an issue which appeared on the ballot, or any political party whose candidates' names appeared on the ballot may file a written request with the county canvassing board for a manual recount. The written request shall contain a statement of the reason the manual recount is being requested.

(b) Such request must be filed with the canvassing board prior to the time the canvassing board certifies the results for the office being protested or within 72 hours after midnight of the date the election was held, whichever occurs later.

(c) The county canvassing board may authorize a manual recount. If a manual recount is authorized, the county canvassing board shall make a reasonable effort to notify each candidate whose race is being recounted of the time and place of such recount.

(d) The manual recount must include at least three precincts and at least 1 percent of the total votes cast for such candidate or issue. In the event there are less than three precincts involved in the election, all precincts shall be counted. The person who requested the recount shall choose three precincts to be recounted, and, if other precincts are recounted, the county canvassing board shall select the additional precincts.

(5) If the manual recount indicates an error in the vote tabulation which could affect the outcome of the election, the county canvassing board shall:
(a) Correct the error and recount the remaining precincts with the vote tabulation system;
(b) Request the Department of State to verify the tabulation software; or
(c) Manually recount all ballots.
(6) Any manual recount shall be open to the public.
(7) Procedures for a manual recount are as follows:
(a) The county canvassing board shall appoint as many counting teams of at least two electors as is necessary to manually recount the ballots. A counting team must have, when possible, members of at least two political parties. A candidate involved in the race shall not be a member of the counting team.
(b) If a counting team is unable to determine a voter's intent in casting a ballot, the ballot shall be presented to the county canvassing board for it to determine the voter's intent.
(8) If the county canvassing board determines the need to verify the tabulation software, the county canvassing board shall request in writing that the Department of State verify the software.
(9) When the Department of State verifies such software, the department shall:
(a) Compare the software used to tabulate the votes with the software filed with the Department of State pursuant to § 101.5607; and
(b) Check the election parameters.
(10) The Department of State shall respond to the county canvassing board within 3 working days.

Fla. Stat. Ann § 102.168. Contest of election
(1) Except as provided in § 102.171, the certification of election or nomination of any person to office, or of the result on any question submitted by referendum, may be contested in the circuit court by any unsuccessful candidate for such office or nomination thereto or by any elector qualified to vote in the election related to such candidacy, or by any taxpayer, respectively.
(2) Such contestant shall file a complaint, together with the fees prescribed in chapter 28, with the clerk of the circuit court within 10 days after midnight of the date the last county canvassing board empowered to canvass the returns certifies the results of the election being contested or within 5

days after midnight of the date the last county canvassing board empowered to canvass the returns certifies the results of that particular election following a protest pursuant to § 102.166(1), whichever occurs later.

(3) The complaint shall set forth the grounds on which the contestant intends to establish his or her right to such office or set aside the result of the election on a submitted referendum.

The grounds for contesting an election under this section are:

(a) Misconduct, fraud, or corruption on the part of any election official or any member of the canvassing board sufficient to change or place in doubt the result of the election.

(b) Ineligibility of the successful candidate for the nomination or office in dispute.

(c) Receipt of a number of illegal votes or rejection of a number of legal votes sufficient to change or place in doubt the result of the election.

(d) Proof that any elector, election official, or canvassing board member was given or offered a bribe or reward in money, property, or any other thing of value for the purpose of procuring the successful candidate's nomination or election or determining the result on any question submitted by referendum.

(e) Any other cause or allegation which, if sustained, would show that a person other than the successful candidate was the person duly nominated or elected to the office in question or that the outcome of the election on a question submitted by referendum was contrary to the result declared by the canvassing board or election board.

(4) The canvassing board or election board shall be the proper party defendant, and the successful candidate shall be an indispensable party to any action brought to contest the election or nomination of a candidate.

(5) A statement of the grounds of contest may not be rejected, nor the proceedings dismissed, by the court for any want of form if the grounds of contest provided in the statement are sufficient to clearly inform the defendant of the particular proceeding or cause for which the nomination or election is contested.

(6) A copy of the complaint shall be served upon the defendant and any other person named therein in the same manner as in other civil cases under the laws of this state. Within 10 days after the complaint has been served, the defendant must file an answer admitting or denying the allegations on which the contestant relies or stating that the defendant has no knowledge or information concerning the allegations, which shall be

deemed a denial of the allegations, and must state any other defenses, in law or fact, on which the defendant relies. If an answer is not filed within the time prescribed, the defendant may not be granted a hearing in court to assert any claim or objection that is required by this subsection to be stated in an answer.

(7) Any candidate, qualified elector, or taxpayer presenting such a contest to a circuit judge is entitled to an immediate hearing. However, the court in its discretion may limit the time to be consumed in taking testimony, with a view therein to the circumstances of the matter and to the proximity of any succeeding primary or other election.

(8) The circuit judge to whom the contest is presented may fashion such orders as he or she deems necessary to ensure that each allegation in the complaint is investigated, examined, or checked, to prevent or correct any alleged wrong, and to provide any relief appropriate under such circumstances.

Texas Statutes and Codes

Election Code
Title 8. Voting Systems
Chapter 127. Processing Electronic Voting System Results
Subchapter E. Processing Results at Central Counting Station
§ 127.130. Manual Counting

(a) Electronic system ballots that are not to be counted automatically and the write-in votes not counted at the polling places shall be counted manually at the central counting station.

(b) If the automatic counting of electronic system ballots becomes impracticable for any reason, the manager may direct that the ballots be counted manually at the central counting station.

(c) The procedure for manual counting is the same as that for regular paper ballots to the extent practicable. The manager is responsible for the manual counting of ballots at the central counting station.

(d) Subject to Subsection (e), in any manual count conducted under this code, a vote on a ballot on which a voter indicates a vote by punching a hole in the ballot may not be counted unless:

(1) at least two corners of the chad are detached;

(2) light is visible through the hole;

(3) an indentation on the chad from the stylus or other object is present and indicates a clearly ascertainable intent of the voter to vote; or

(4) the chad reflects by other means a clearly ascertainable intent of the voter to vote.

(e) Subsection (d) does not supersede any clearly ascertainable intent of the voter.

Frequently Asked Questions about the National Opinion Research Center's "Florida Ballot Project"

NORC, a national organization for research at the University of Chicago, is an independent social science research center. NORC has completed examination of the uncertified ballots in the Florida presidential race. This effort was conceived and sponsored by a group of the nation's largest media organizations.

What did NORC hope to accomplish?

Our goal was to gather data on the appearance of the ballots that were not certified in the November 2000 election in Florida and to create an archive of the markings. This archive will be available to the public on the day the media organizations publish and air their stories. NORC will also use this data to examine the reliability of the various voting systems used in Florida.

Which news organizations are involved?

This project was conceived and sponsored by the *New York Times*, the *Wall Street Journal*, the *Washington Post*, Tribune Publishing (which includes the *Chicago Tribune*, the *Los Angeles Times*, and a number of other newspapers), CNN, the Associated Press, the *St. Petersburg Times*, and the *Palm Beach Post*. The news organizations were responsible for securing county cooperation, for paying all associated county fees, and for ensuring proper presentation of the uncertified ballots. The news organizations will conduct individual analyses of the data and prepare reports for publication and broadcast.

How many uncertified ballots were there?

NORC examined 175,010 uncertified ballots, including 113,820 overvotes (the voter selected more than one candidate for president) and 61,190 undervotes (the voter did not select a candidate for president or, for some reason, the vote counting mechanism did not register a vote for president).

When did the examination begin?

NORC staff went to Florida in late January 2001 and began an extensive training effort. Ballot examination began Monday, February 5, 2000, and continued through May.

How did NORC examine the ballots?

In each of the counties local election officials assigned county workers to display the ballots. NORC coding teams (one or three coders per team) reviewed each ballot and recorded the markings they observed. The team of coders sat side by side, but members worked independently of one another and made individual determinations regarding the appearance of the ballots. They did not talk among themselves or consult one another in any way.

What specifically did NORC coders look for?

Coders recorded the condition of each ballot examined. Thus, for Votomatic (and to some extent Datavote) ballots, coders noted whether chads were dimpled and, if so, whether light was shining through the dimple. (Each coder worked with a small light table that helped coders to examine for light.) Coders also noted whether chads were completely punched or hanging by one, two, or three corners. For optical scan ballots and any Votomatic or Datavote absentee ballots completed outside the voting booth, coders noted whether the ovals or arrows were fully filled or otherwise marked (with a check, slash, X, etc.). Coders noted whether there were stray marks on the ballot that would confuse a scanning machine and whether ballots were uncertified because the wrong color ink was used. Finally, coders recorded verbatim any written notations on the ballots.

Was every ballot reviewed by three coders?

No. All undervotes and the overvotes from three test counties (Polk, Pasco, Nassau) were reviewed by three coders. In the three test counties (one Votomatic, one Datavote, and one optical scan) NORC coders reviewed each overvote to determine whether three coders were necessary. High agreement among the three coders indicated that overvotes were easier to code than undervotes, and so the decision was made to code the remaining overvotes with one coder. Indeed, overvotes were easier to code because it requires more than one fully punched chad or more than one fully completed oval or arrow (markings more easily identified than dimples) to produce an overvote.

What was done to ensure accuracy in the field?

Because this data set is intended to be the authoritative description of the uncertified ballots, a number of steps were taken to ensure high quality. First, only qualified individuals were hired to review the ballots. Because of the nature of the task, all coders were administered a near-point vision test before being staffed on this project. Project coders were trained and tested on coding procedures before being allowed to code. Team leaders—who were long-term NORC employees—conducted the training and worked closely with the coders to ensure consistently high performance. Every evening, prior to shipping the coding forms to Chicago, the team leaders reviewed the forms for completeness and legibility of coding. NORC also attempted to verify the accuracy of the coding by randomly selecting ballots from every county to recode. This recoding was later matched with the original coding and reviewed for consistency of coding.

What happened next with the data?

Information on the ballot markings was recorded on coding forms that were sent daily to the NORC offices in Chicago. In Chicago, a trained team of data entry specialists entered the information into electronic files.

What was done to ensure accuracy of the data entry?

Each data form was entered twice (by two different data entry clerks). The results of both data entry tasks were compared, and data entry supervisors conducted an adjudication process. Differences between the two data entries were reviewed and appropriate corrections made. Supervisors consulted coding forms as necessary. Typos, out-of-range codes, and other anomalies were reconciled during this process.

Were there other steps as well?

In the final step of data review, NORC assigned an independent team of statisticians to examine the data. These statisticians reviewed the information and approved it for release to the media group and to the public.

What is the final product?

NORC compiled 17.5 million pieces of information into two primary data sets. One is a ballot-level database (the raw database) that contains information on every chad or candidate space on every ballot across the sixty-seven counties. This file does not attempt to align candidate information across ballots; it simply reflects the reality of the disparate ballot designs used throughout the state of Florida. The second is an aligned database that does reconcile every coder's information for every ballot for each presidential and U.S. Senate candidate. This file contains the first processing step necessary to facilitate comparison of the coding for each candidate regardless of his or her various ballot positions across the state. The raw database is the definitive historical archive of every mark on the uncertified ballots. The aligned file is an analyst's tool, presenting only the markings related to the various candidate positions on each county's ballot.

Secondary data sets include the ballot notations copied verbatim by NORC coders, the demographic characteristics of the coders, the re-coding data collected while coding, and a number of files produced by the media group. The media group files contain qualitative and quantitative county- and precinct-level information used by the media in their analyses.

All data files will be released on the day that the media group members publish their stories. Scholars, journalists, and anyone else interested in examining these data may go to the website for access to our files.

NORC Media "Read_me" File: Supplemental Tables and Analytical Assumptions

Table of Contents
I. Data Analysis Working Group
II. Analytical Assumptions and Terminology
    A. Evaluating levels of coder agreement
    B. Re-ordering NORC codes into a hierarchy (optional)
    C. Defining standards
    D. Rules
III. Exceptional Counties
    A. Volusia County
    B. Broward County
    C. Orange County
    D. Other counties with official hand-count results
IV. Coder-comment override table

V. Coder issues

VI. Scenarios

    A. Concepts

    B. Definitions

    1. Prevailing statewide standard scenario

    2. Supreme Court "simple" scenario

    3. Supreme Court "complex" scenario

    4. 67-county custom standards scenario

    5. Two-corners-detached statewide scenario

    6. "Most inclusive" statewide scenario

    7. "Most restrictive" statewide scenario

    8. The Gore 4-county recount strategy scenario

    9. "Dimples when other dimples present" scenario

VII. Relating NORC-coded ballot data to state-certified vote totals

    A. Adjusted certified totals

    B. Court-based scenarios

    C. Precision of ballot segregation

VIII. Tabulator

IX. County data

    A. The Florida Newspaper Survey (voting standards)

    B. The DAWG Survey (election administrative procedures)

X. Precinct data

    A. Nov. 7, 2000 presidential election, certified Florida voting results

    B. Precinct demographic data

    C. Flagged Miami-Dade County precincts

XI. Consortium Steering Committee Representatives

XII. Appendices

    A. Coder-comment override assumptions

    B. Listing of supplemental table names

I. Data Analysis Working Group

A group of national and Florida news organizations commissioned the National Opinion Research Center (NORC) to view and characterize the ballots that did not register a vote for president in the November 2000 Florida election. NORC's ballot-data archive does not classify ballots as votes or non-votes, and contains no analysis of the ballots. However, the consortium steering committee in April 2001 established a Data Analysis Working Group (DAWG) made up of database specialists from participating news organizations. This working group met over several months to develop, in advance, common logic and assumptions for analyzing the NORC aligned dataset (the table organizing ballot-level data according to candidate names, see NORC documentation). These rules and assumptions are the consortium's best judgments about how to interpret and apply the complex laws and practices of vote recounts to an unprecedented social survey, and, in general, they were applied by all the members of the consortium in their separate analyses. This README file, and the procedures and tables described herein, are the work product of the DAWG, made up of the following individuals:

Sharon Crenson (Associated Press)
Ford Fessenden, co-leader (*New York Times*)
Ed Foldessy (*Wall Street Journal*)
Keating Holland (Cable News Network)
Sean Holton (*Orlando Sentinel*)
Connie Humburg (*St. Petersburg Times*)
Elliot Jaspin (Cox Newspapers)
Dan Keating, co-leader (*Washington Post*)
Richard O'Reilly (*Los Angeles Times*)
Archie Tse (*New York Times*)

Consultants
Database: Diana Jergovic (National Opinion Research Center)
Steering-committee: Jane Caplan (Cable News Network)
Voting standards and technology: Bob Drogin (*Los Angeles Times*)

II. Analytical Assumptions and Terminology

A. Evaluating Levels of Coder Agreement

NORC ballot coders did not "award" votes to candidates. They reported what they saw at the Presidential and Senate positions on the ballot through the use of descriptive codes that were later entered into a database. In the case of "undervote" ballots three coders reviewed each ballot and reported their observations independently of one another. In the case of most "overvote" ballots, one coder reviewed each ballot. (See NORC documentation for definitions and details). The DAWG analyzed and tabulated that data, not the ballots themselves. Analysis involves examining NORC coding for a ballot and deciding if it contained evidence of voter intent. For ballots viewed by more than one NORC coder, the

DAWG defined a method to measure whether the coders agreed on what they saw. The DAWG measured agreement in two ways. For "general" agreement, each ballot-viewing was evaluated to determine whether it met the standard being applied to award a vote. For "precise" agreement, the exact marks recorded in the presidential areas were compared.

Four levels of agreement were characterized in assessing voter intent:

1. Two-coder general agreement: At least two coders report marks that meet the standard being applied. (If there was only one coder, as in most overvote ballots, the single coder's result is also included in this category.)

2. Unanimous general agreement: All coders who viewed a ballot reported marks that meet the standard being applied.

3. Two-coder precise agreement: At least two coders report precisely the same markings on each of the 10 presidential positions, the same number of markings in chads not assigned to candidates and the same write-in code (WIPCODE) field. (Also includes all ballots with only one coder.)

4. Unanimous precise agreement: All coders who viewed a ballot report precisely the same markings on each of the 10 presidential positions, the same number of markings in chads not assigned to candidates and the same write-in code (WIPCODE) field.

B. Re-ordering NORC Codes into a Hierarchy (Optional)

Some researchers may choose to re-order the NORC codes into a hierarchy for the sake of unified analysis across voting technologies (HIERARCHY codes). The suggested hierarchy is as follows:

For punch-card ballots (Votomatic and Datavote):

NORC 0 = HIERARCHY 0 (blank, no mark seen)

NORC 8 = HIERARCHY 1 (dimple on border of chad area, with or without sunlight)

NORC 7 = HIERARCHY 2 (dimple within chad area, off chad, with or without sunlight)

NORC 5 = HIERARCHY 3 (dimpled chad, no sunlight)

NORC 6 = HIERARCHY 4 (dimpled chad, with sunlight)

NORC 1 = HIERARCHY 5 (1–corner of chad detached)

NORC 2 = HIERARCHY 6 (2–corners of chad detached)

NORC 3 = HIERARCHY 7 (3–corners of chad detached)

NORC 4 = HIERARCHY 8 (4–corners of chad detached, clean
   punch)
NORC 9 = HIERARCHY 9 (chad marked with pencil or pen)
(Note: Any Votomatic ballots with NORC codes 7 and 8 were considered
ambiguous, and weren't tabulated as expressing voter intent under any
scenario. Datavote precinct ballots are punched with a lever machine,
which always punches ballots cleanly, so analysts have no issues of dangling
chads to contend with. Datavote absentee ballots are similar to Votomatic
precinct ballots.)
   For optical-scan ballots:
   NORC 00 = HIERARCHY 0 (blank, no mark seen)
   NORC 99 = HIERARCHY 0 (negated mark)
   NORC 88 = HIERARCHY 0 (marked and erased or partially erased)
   NORC 11 = HIERARCHY 3 (circled party name)
   NORC 12 = HIERARCHY 3 (other mark on or near party name)
   NORC 21 = HIERARCHY 3 (circled candidate name)
   NORC 22 = HIERARCHY 3 (other mark on or near candidate
      name)
   NORC 31 = HIERARCHY 3 (arrow/oval mark other than fill: circle,
      x, /, check, scribble)
   NORC 32 = HIERARCHY 3 (other mark near oval/arrow)
   NORC 44 = HIERARCHY 8 (arrow/oval filled)
(Note: The only practical way for DAWG to assign optical-scan ballots
into a hierarchy was to create an "all affirmative marks" standard for most
scenarios, and an "arrow-oval filled" standard for use in only the most
restrictive scenarios.)

C. Defining Standards

Coders did not apply standards to ballots or make judgments about which
marks might constitute a "vote." They only reported markings on ballots
in categories designed to reflect the issues that canvassing boards have
deemed important in determining voter intent. The DAWG developed
assumptions for applying accepted definitions of various standards to the
data. Here are four examples of how the DAWG established standards for
assessing voter intent:
   1. Dimple or better standard
      Ballots were considered to have evidence of voter intent under this
      standard if NORC coded them as follows:

On punch-card ballots, NORC codes 1, 2, 3, 4, 5, 6, 9 (HIERAR-CHY code 3 or higher)

On optical-scan ballots, NORC codes 11, 12, 21, 22, 31, 32, 44 (HIERARCHY code 3 or higher).

2. One-corner detached standard

Ballots were considered to have evidence of voter intent under this standard if NORC coded them as follows:

On punch-card ballots, NORC codes 1, 2, 3, 4, 9 (HIERARCHY code 5 or higher).

On optical-scan ballots, NORC codes 11, 12, 21, 22, 31, 32, 44 (HIERARCHY code 3 or higher).

3. Two-corners detached standard

Ballots were considered to have evidence of voter intent under this standard if NORC coded them as follows:

On punch-card ballots, NORC codes 2, 3, 4, 9 (HIERARCHY code 6 or higher)

On optical-scan ballots, NORC codes 11, 12, 21, 22, 31, 32, 44 (HIERARCHY code 3 or higher).

4. Dimple (if rest of ballot is dimpled) standard

Ballots were considered to have evidence of voter intent under this standard if NORC coded them as follows:

On punch-card ballots, ballots meeting the two-corners detached standard outlined above AND ALSO NORC codes 5,6 and 1 IF the Senate race chad indicates a 5, 6 or 1 code OR IF "othdimpc" value is affirmative (code 1).

On optical-scan ballots, NORC codes 11, 12, 21, 22, 31, 32, 44 (HIERARCHY code 3 or higher).

Note: These standards are distinct from the "scenarios" described in section VI. In general, the term "scenario" refers to the application of one or more standards to a specified set of ballots.

D. Rules

1. Rules on write-ins

Coders recorded the first four letters of the surname of a candidate entered in the write-in area of the ballot. Those write-ins were evaluated for voter intent using Florida law and practice as guidance. For optical and datavote ballots, under the "any affirmative mark" definitions, DAWG interpreted the following as indicating intent to vote:

a. a so-called "write-in overvote," in which the voter has marked for a candidate, and made another mark in the write-in oval or arrow area , but entered the same candidate's name, no write-in name, a competing candidate's vice-presidential running mate or an unqualified write-in, e.g., Mickey Mouse. This rule is based on Florida laws outlined in Chapter 1S-2.0031(7) of Florida's administrative code governing elections.

b. an undervote (no affirmative marks in presidential area or write-in oval/arrow) if a valid candidate's name is written in the text portion of the write-in area (WIPCODE field = 1–12) and the write-in oval or arrow is not coded with a negation mark or erasure.

2. Special rule for ballots with multiple markings

When any coder reports marks for multiple candidates on a ballot, the coding is considered a "multi-marked" ballot with no clear voter intent. No information from that coder is used in assessing voter intent. Any other mark in the presidential area of the ballot is considered a "competing mark" for these purposes (NORC codes, 1, 2, 3, 4, 5, 6, 7, 8, 9, 11, 12, 21, 22, 31, 32, 44, and -6 "invalid data" code).

3. Missing data assumptions

A -3 code means data from a coder are missing, and is treated as a blank for the purposes of determining agreement among coders.

A -6 means an invalid NORC code was entered by the coder. The presumption is that the coder saw something, so the marking must be treated as a "competing mark," which generally causes the ballot to be classified as an overvote. However, if there is a single -6, an acceptable write-in for that same candidate and there are no other competing marks, the -6 is ignored.

4. Negation marks

In optical scan counties, the code for erasures and partial erasures (88) and the code for a negated mark (99) are generally treated as blanks, not as competing marks. They are viewed as competing marks only in certain scenarios in selected counties where officials said they would not always accept a negation or erasure as a clear indicator of voter intent on an overvoted ballot. Those cases are flagged by fields in the County table (DAWG DATASETS.XLS). In punch-card counties, negations were sometimes indicated by voter marks on ballots and dealt with in the Coder Comment Override Table explained in Section IV.

5. Pencil marks on punch-card ballots

Pencil marks on a chad, unless explained as negations in the coder-comments field, are treated as affirmative marks equivalent to a clean punch. These appear as a code "9" in the data file or once coder-comment overrides are applied.

III. Exceptional Counties

A few counties are notable for the way they handled ballots during the Election recount period or in isolating uncounted "overvote" and "under-vote" ballots for review by NORC coders:

A. Volusia County

Volusia County completed a hand count that ultimately produced its final certified presidential election results. However, the 346 ballots that remained as non-votes after the completion of that hand count were not maintained separately from the certified votes. Instead, county elections officials later co-mingled those ballots with the rest of the ballots during an attempt to sort out all overvotes and undervotes for a news media review that preceded the NORC review. The result was a segregation of ballots that bore no relation either to totals from the certified hand count or totals from the initial vote tally reported by machines on Election Day, when the county reported 447 undervotes and 155 overvotes. NORC coders were shown 339 undervotes and 171 overvotes by Volusia officials, and the codings are included in the archive. However, because of the poor quality of the segregation and the inclusion of the hand recount in the certified results, DAWG chose to exclude those codings from its analysis and recommends other researchers do so as well. Volusia County's certified results are used in all scenarios.

B. Broward County

Broward County officials maintained the segregation of undervoted and overvoted ballots that remained after the completion of its certified hand count, and those ballots were viewed and coded by NORC. However, NORC did not view contested ballots that were awarded to candidates in the hand count and included in the county's certified results. Thus the ballots with a PRECVERS value of "C" indicate only those contested ballots that ultimately were not awarded to any candidate—not the complete universe of contested ballots in Broward. The Broward certified vote is treated as a valid result for all county-specific scenarios and as a valid baseline for adding NORC-coded ballots in any other scenario. This approach prevented the double-counting of contested ballots that were ultimately certified in official totals. (Note: The PRECVERS variable is also used to identify some, but not all, of the contested ballots from Palm Beach County hand counts)

C. Orange County

The 966 undervotes and 1,383 overvotes reported by Orange County in the Election Day tally that ultimately produced its certified totals could not be segregated completely by county officials for viewing by NORC coders. The coders were shown only 640 undervotes and 1,197 overvotes. More than 400 of the ballots rejected by machines on Election Day simply could not be distinguished from ballots that were accepted and counted —they appeared to be properly completed. Explanations for why optical-scanning machines did not detect votes on these ballots range from low carbon content in the ink pens used to mark them, to humidity and dust, to misalignment of the ballot as it is fed into the tabulator. However, the county segregation of ballots for the media was accomplished via a manual review and classification of all the approximately 282,000 ballots cast. As part of this process, county officials agreed not only to sort out the undervotes and overvotes, but assign other ballots to candidate piles and ultimately provide new unofficial "tallies" for Bush and Gore. In this fashion, officials identified 134,701 ballots clearly for Bush and 140,469 clearly for Gore (bringing their county totals to 134,715 and 140,485, respectively, when federal overseas absentee votes certified by Orange on Nov. 17 are included). That represented gains over each candidate's certified vote totals amounting to 184 for Bush and 249 for Gore. The process accounted for 433 of the uncounted ballots from Election Day that could not be isolated in the segregation, and that adjustment is dealt with in the DAWG precinct table as explained below, in the section of this file entitled "Relating NORC-coded ballot data to state-certified totals."

(NOTE: Orange County officials ultimately fed its properly completed ballots into machines in a final effort to find those that were not counted. In this process, many of the machine-rejected ballots were identified and coded by NORC, but not enough to justify substituting that data for the tallies from the full manual segregation. So those data are not part of the main dataset. However, NORC is providing data from those codings in two separate tables (ORNG-RAW and ORNG-ALIGN, see NORC documentation). They may be of interest to researchers studying types of ballots rejected by optical-scanner machines.)

D. Other counties with official hand-count results

During the post-election contest, officials in Palm Beach County completed a recount of ballots and officials in Miami-Dade County completed a recount of 139 precincts. In addition, a handful of counties completed recounts on Dec. 9 before the U.S. Supreme Court intervened and halted counting. Totals from these counts are used in some scenarios, and can be found in the COUNTY table fields BUSHDEC9 and GOREDEC9.

IV. Coder-comment Override Table

A number of ballots contained written notations or markings made by voters, or other unusual characteristics that could not be assigned numeric codes. NORC coders used a "comments" area on their coding sheets to record this information. In all, 5,407 ballot records in the data archive contain such coder comments. The DAWG reviewed the comments and concluded that, in the vast majority of cases, they did not affect the assessment of voter intent. However, the DAWG did find cases where comments provided evidence of intent. For example, on one Bay County undervote all three coders reported that the voter, who left all ovals blank, wrote: "I forgot my glasses and cannot see this. Please put Bush down for my vote." Other cases were found where coders indicated negations or marks of affirmation in the comments field but not in the coding areas. In all, the DAWG found evidence of intent in the comments on 234 ballots. Those are summarized in a separate table within the Tabulator, as described in Section VIII. All the consortium members used these judgments in tabulating their assessments of voter intent.

V. Coder Issues

Baker County Coder
Of the 153 coders who worked for this project, only one displayed questionable coding. Under recommendation from NORC, the DAWG did not analyze the 79 Baker County undervotes that this coder viewed. In-

stead, the judgments of the other two coders were used for these ballots. No other ballots display questionable coding.

VI. Scenarios

A. Concepts

A "scenario" means applying a standard to a defined set of ballots in the dataset. A mixture of standards can be applied from county to county, or to undervotes only, or to both undervotes and overvotes in all counties. (Volusia County is always excepted, for reasons outlined above.) The DAWG has developed a set of assumptions for nine scenarios. Some apply a single standard uniformly to all counties. Others take only selected counties into consideration and adjust totals in other counties to simulate conditions imposed by various court actions during the election contest period. Still others apply county-specific standards based on answers local election officials gave to survey questions. Each of the scenarios may be implemented at the four evaluation levels for coder agreement as described in section II-A.

B. Definitions

1. Prevailing statewide standard scenario

This standard is based on responses from county elections officials to the Florida Newspaper Survey described in section IX-A. Officials in a majority of punch-card counties said they would accept a single-corner detached chad as an indicator of voter intent, and officials in a majority of optical scan counties said they would accept all affirmative marks as described in NORC codes as indicators of voter intent. These standards are applied to both undervotes and overvotes to the NORC aligned dataset. Volusia County's certified result is accepted. Results are added to adjusted certified totals (BUSHAFTER and GOREAFTER fields in County table, as explained in Section VII). Coder agreement may be evaluated at four levels of two-coder general, unanimous general, two-coder precise and unanimous precise.

2. Supreme Court "simple" scenario

On Dec. 8, the Florida Supreme Court ordered a statewide hand count of undervotes in all counties, with the exception of counties that had already completed hand counts at that point: Volusia, Broward, Palm Beach and Miami-Dade (partial, 139 precincts only). This scenario accepts the results of those hand counts as its baseline and attempts to implement the court order literally on other counties at a range of uniform standards to gauge what the outcome might have been had the U.S. Supreme Court not intervened. It is limited to ballots presented to NORC coders as undervotes (BALTYPE1 = 1) and applies the range of four standards outlined in section II-C(1–4), evaluating each at all four levels of coder agreement. Results are added to adjusted certified totals.

3. Supreme Court "complex" scenario

This scenario starts with the same baseline as Supreme Court Simple (accepting the four sets of hand counts that were accepted in the order) but elsewhere applies various standards to varying sets of ballots, by county, in an attempt to gauge what was really happening that day. Many counties did not follow a literal interpretation of the Dec. 8 Florida Supreme Court order, according to the Florida Newspaper Survey. And each county applied individual standards. Officials in nine counties—most notably Lake County—planned to review and count overvote ballots on Dec. 9. Circuit Judge Terry Lewis, who was overseeing the statewide count, has said in an interview that he probably would have held a hearing sometime that afternoon to consider whether to accept voter intent found on overvotes. Other counties were refusing to count, and NORC data from those counties are excluded in this scenario. Some counties managed to complete their hand counts that day and report new totals before the U.S. Supreme Court intervened, and NORC data are excluded while BUSHDEC9 and GOREDEC9 adjustments for the counties are added to their certified results in this scenario. Results from NORC data everywhere else are applied to adjusted certified totals. DAWG applied the scenario at four levels of coder agreement. (Note: When asked in the survey where they would begin to derive voter intent along the spectrum of NORC codes, officials in Martin, Indian River and Sarasota counties answered "possibly" for all codes, including clean punches. For these counties, DAWG applied the most widely accepted standard of one-corner detached. In all other cases, a county answer of "possibly" to a question in the survey was treated as a "no.")

4. 67-county custom standards scenario

This scenario attempts to apply the answers to the Florida Newspaper

Survey to a broader set of ballots. It accepts the certified results from Broward and Volusia counties as a baseline, and applies county-by-county standards to both undervotes and overvotes in the 65 remaining counties. It is the best guess at what the results of an unrestricted statewide hand recount might have been. Results are applied to adjusted certified totals. DAWG applied the scenario at all four levels of coder agreement. (Note: Treatment of Martin, Indian River and Sarasota county survey answers is the same as in Scenario 3.)

5. Two-Corners-Detached statewide scenario

This statewide scenario is based on arguments made by George W. Bush's attorneys during the 36-day period following Election Day. Although arguments changed as the post-election contest wore on, Bush representatives generally settled on accepting punch-card ballots with at least two corners of a chad detached as adequate indication of voter intent. Therefore, the DAWG tallied this scenario using NORC codes 2, 3, 4, and 9 as acceptable affirmative indications of voter intent. In the case of an optically scanned ballot, all affirmative marks are accepted.

6. "Most inclusive" statewide scenario

This scenario applies a uniform standard of "dimple or better" on punch marks and "all affirmative marks" on optical ballots to overvotes and undervotes statewide. See section II-C(1). It applies results to adjusted certified totals. DAWG applied it all at all four levels of coder agreement.

7. "Most restrictive" statewide scenario

This scenario would accept only so-called "perfect ballots" that machines somehow missed and did not count, or ballots with unambiguous expressions of voter intent. These include fully punched chads (4–corners detached) that may have been obstructed during tabulation and properly marked optical ballots (Code 44) that scanners could not read because of problems with ink color, carbon content, humidity and misalignment. The scenario also accepts punch-card ballots where voters made choices with pencil markings (Code 9). It applies results to adjusted certified totals. DAWG applied it at all four levels of coder agreement.

8. The Gore 4-county recount strategy scenario

Early in the post-election deadlock, the Gore camp requested hand counts in four heavily Democratic counties: Miami-Dade, Broward, Palm Beach and Volusia. In the weeks ahead, hand counts were completed in three of the counties and in 139 precincts in Miami-Dade County. This scenario attempts to measure the potential results of Gore's early, limited strategy by accepting certified results (see Section VII-B) from 65 counties (including in Broward and Volusia), the results of the completed but uncertified Palm Beach hand count and the partial, uncertified hand count results from Miami-Dade. It then applies to the remaining Miami-Dade precincts the standard of one-corner detached (also accepting pencil marks) and evaluates at four levels of coder agreement. IMPORTANT: Because this scenario assumes no manual review would have taken place outside these four counties, results in this instance should be added to UNADJUSTED certified totals for statewide tabulations.

9. "Dimples when other dimples present" scenario

This scenario applies the theory that voter intent can be derived from a ballot, even if the threshold standard is not met, if the voter marked the entire ballot in the same substandard fashion. NORC codings for the Senate race and the "other dimples" field are used to make that determination. In Palm Beach, officials accepted chads with at least two-corners detached but would also accept dimples and other substandard marks if the entire ballot was similarly marked. The "dimples-if-other-dimples" standard is applied to all punch-card counties statewide and accepts all affirmative marks in optical counties. See section II-C(4).

VII. Relating NORC-coded Ballot Data to State-certified Totals

A. Adjusted certified totals

In the County table (in DAWG DATASETS.XLS), the fields BUSH-AFTER and GOREAFTER are used as the common baseline for adding data from NORC codings. In most cases, these values are simple reiterations of the certified vote total for each candidate in a given county. But in four counties, the values reflect adjustments to candidate totals made for reconciliation purposes when county elections officials sorted uncounted ballots for NORC coder review. In this fashion, county officials were able to account for ballots that they otherwise could not find in the sorting process. Though rejected by machines on Election Day, these ballots appear to election officials as properly marked, perfectly valid votes. Detailed breakdowns can be found in the Precinct table. Most adjustments occur in Orange County (182 precincts). In Orange, officials manually segregated all 282,000 ballots cast into piles of overvotes, undervotes and new piles of votes for each candidate. They tallied the ballots in the candidate piles and provided those totals for the study. The differences this process made for each candidate in each precinct can be seen in the Precinct-table fields BUSHADJ, GOREADJ and OTHADJ, which are added to the certified result to produce values in BUSHAFTER, GOREAFTER and OTH-AFTER. Similar adjustments were made in a total of 12 precincts in Baker, Leon and St. Johns counties.

B. Court-based scenarios

In three scenarios based on political strategies or court orders, baseline candidate totals are adjusted with data from official hand counts as well as NORC ballot-coding data. In the County table of DAWG DATA-SETS.XLS, the fields SIMPLEFLAG, COMPLEXFLAG, BUSHDEC9 and GOREDEC9 control these adjustments. (See value descriptions in County table layout for details.) The Precinct table field MIADADE139 is necessary to make the precinct-level adjustment for Miami-Dade County. (1) The Supreme Court Simple scenario uses totals from hand counts in four counties that the Florida Supreme Court accepted as part of its Dec. 8 order: For Broward and Volusia counties, the results of those hand counts are the same as the final certified totals. No NORC data should be added. For Palm Beach County the hand-count adjustments to certified totals are in the BUSHDEC9 and GOREDEC9 fields of the County table in the DAWG dataset, and should be used instead of NORC ballot-coding data for Palm Beach. For Miami-Dade County, the court-accepted hand count covered only 139 precincts before it was interrupted on Nov. 22. The adjustment for those precincts in BUSHDEC9 and GOREDEC9 should be added to certified totals, along with NORC data from the remaining Miami-Dade precincts (where MIADADE139 = 0).
(2) The Supreme Court Complex scenario starts with the same adjustments as Supreme Court Simple and adds adjusted totals for other counties that completed their hand counts Dec. 9 before the U.S. Supreme Court intervened: Escambia, Liberty, Manatee and Madison. NORC data from those counties are excluded, as is NORC data from four counties that refused to count (Gadsden, Hamilton, Lafayette and Union).
(3) The Gore 4-county scenario uses the same adjustment as Supreme Court Simple, but adds the results from those four counties to UNAD-JUSTED certified totals from the rest of the state. This is because no

recounts or sorting adjustments would have altered the certified totals in Orange, Baker, Leon, and St. Johns counties in this scenario.

Adjustments to BUSHAFTER and GOREAFTER in court-based scenarios:

County
    Supct Simple
    Supct Complex
    Gore 4-county
Volusia
    none (use certified)
    none (use certified)
    none (use certified)
Broward
    none (use certified)
    none (use certified)
    none (use certified)
Palm Beach
    add "DEC9" fields
    add "DEC9" fields
    add "DEC9" fields
Miami-dade
    add NORC+"DEC9" fields
    add NORC+"DEC9" fields
    add NORC+"DEC9" fields
Escambia
    add NORC data
    add "DEC9" fields, no NORC
    use certified (unadjusted)
Liberty
    add NORC data
    add "DEC9" fields, no NORC
    use certified (unadjusted)
Manatee
    add NORC data
    add "DEC9" fields, no NORC
    use certified (unadjusted)
Madison
    add NORC data

add "DEC9" fields, no NORC
use certified (unadjusted)
Refusals
add NORC data
add DEC9 "0," no NORC
use certified (unadjusted)
All Others
add NORC data
add NORC data
use certified (unadjusted)
Overvotes
Ignore all
Count where in play
include in NORC count

C. Precision of Ballot Segregation

While the Florida ballot data archive provides the best achievable historical record of Florida's uncounted ballots, it cannot be said to include every
ballot that was not counted, nor can it be said to include only ballots that
were not counted. Any effort to segregate and analyze Florida's rejected
ballots is, from the start, limited by the same flawed county systems that
failed to count, or inconsistently counted, all the ballots on Election Day.
For this project, undervotes and overvotes were sorted both by machine
and by hand, and sometimes by a combination of both. The NORC
archive includes data abstracted from a total of 175,010 ballots statewide.
That amounts to more than 99 percent of the total 176,446 uncounted
ballots expected statewide, based on county precinct reports that produced
the final, state-certified vote totals. In fact, NORC's codings of 61,190
undervotes fell just 9 short of the 61,199 rejected ballots indicated in precinct reports.

At the county level, such apparent precision proved more elusive. In 11
counties, NORC coders were shown the precise number of rejected ballots
as expected. In 38 counties, coders were shown a total of 1,862 ballots
fewer than had been expected and in the remaining 18 counties, coders
were shown a total of 426 ballots more than had been expected. Those
numbers yield an absolute variance of 2,288 ballots, or 1.3 percent from
the number of the total ballots expected. Analytical adjustments in Orange

and Volusia counties described in the Exceptional Counties section of this file bring that county-level variance below 1 percent.

For a number of reasons related to irregularities in precinct-naming conventions, election-night tabulation, subsequent sorting methods, and other county accounting practices, variances are magnified when studied at precinct level or when distinctions between "overvotes" and "undervotes" are drawn. County officials showed NORC coders uncounted ballots from 6,151 precincts. Of those, 3,877 precincts (63 percent) yielded the exact total of uncounted ballots (84,592 ballots) as expected based on county precinct reports. In 5,583 precincts (91 percent of NORC-coded precincts, 141,922 ballots overall), the number of ballots shown in each precinct fell within 5 ballots of what had been expected. Among individual precincts within that 91 percent, coders saw a total of 1,682 fewer ballots than had been expected in some precincts and a total of 1,368 more ballots than expected in other precincts. (In many of the remaining 9 percent of precincts, ballots shown by county elections officials cannot be systematically related to county precinct reports. But discrepancies can often be explained individually. For instance, Escambia County could not assign its countywide total of 4,372 uncounted ballots to precincts, whereas the precinct dataset calculates that breakdown for each precinct using the UN-ACCOUNTED field. In Duval County, NORC coders were shown ballots assigned to numbered "absentee precincts" whereas that distinction was not made in county precinct reports. In Duval, NORC coders were shown only 3 ballots of 96 uncounted ballots expected in precinct "8S." A likely explanation for the apparent shortfall: NORC coders were shown 79 ballots in a precinct indicated as precinct "85," which is not a precinct designation on Duval's election totals. But because such disparities could not be eliminated with certainty, NORC did not adjust the precinct names in its dataset.)

To a great extent, the precision of ballot segregation for the Florida ballot study mimics what was already taking place or was about to take place all over the state had the Dec. 9 hand count not been halted. In that sense, it may provide a useful baseline for statisticians and students of election processes and reforms who wish to gauge the accuracy of such processes under time constraints. (Note: County elections officials are not required to report "certified" numbers of overvotes and undervotes to the state. However, most counties produce election reports containing those numbers, which can be found in the precinct dataset in the OVERVOTES,

UNDERVOTES and OVER-UNDER UNSPECIFIED fields. In Escambia and Lafayette counties only, the UNACCOUNTED field was used as a measure of uncounted ballots because officials could provide no other accounting).

VIII. Tabulator

DAWG member Elliot Jaspin (Cox Newspapers) created a ballot tabulator that is being released to the public (DAWG.MDB). It is a Microsoft Access 2000 interface with an automated front end that allows point-and-click application of all built-in scenarios, creation of new scenarios and reporting of results. It includes as a base table the NORC aligned dataset (renamed FLORIDA) containing extra analytical fields, including a field called CANSELECT, which allows researchers a ballot-level view of how the application of DAWG assumptions in any given scenario affects a given ballot. Detailed instructions are included with the tabulator, along with a built-in version of the Coder-comment override table named DAWG DECISIONS. The results from this tabulator in all scenarios were cross-checked, verified and replicated with four other tabulators created by DAWG members Richard O'Reilly (*Los Angeles Times*), Ford Fessenden (*New York Times*), Dan Keating (*Washington Post*) and Sharon Crenson (Associated Press, in conjunction with software engineer Dave Stonehill). Test data were used initially, and tabulators were verified again after the release of the complete ballot data archive.

IX. County Data (Dawg Datasets.xls)

The county dataset contains basic information from each of Florida's 67 counties pertaining to elections officials and voting technology, ballot design and standards for voter-intent as well as information on how ballots were segregated for NORC coders and other NORC administrative details. It includes county-level certified vote totals for each candidate, as well as adjusted totals as outlined in section VII-A. These numbers may be used as the baseline when adding tabulations from the ballot data archive. Other fields provide the necessary information for running scenarios with county-specific standards (VI-B, 3&4). The county table also reports questions and answers collected in two surveys of county officials.

A. The Florida Newspaper Survey

This survey distills information collected in interviews with 194 local elections officials in 67 counties across the state, including 165 members of county canvassing boards. It reports on procedures and voter-intent standards those officials were prepared to follow and apply in the Dec. 9 hand count. It also draws upon letters that 53 counties wrote outlining established protocols and procedures to Circuit Judge Terry Lewis, who was overseeing the Dec. 9 recount. Where counties had not developed specific standards of voter intent, individual canvassing-board members were questioned at length about standards they had used in previous hand counts and what they personally viewed as a measure of voter intent. The reporting was done by David Damron of the *Orlando Sentinel*, Tom Tobin and Alicia Caldwell of the *St. Petersburg Times*, Fred Schulte of the *Sun-Sentinel* of South Florida, Bill Douthat and Meghan Meyer of the *Palm Beach Post* and Jeff Zeleny of the *Chicago Tribune*. In the table, answers to questions are indicated with codes: 0 = no, 1 = yes, 2 = possibly and -9 = no data.

B. The DAWG Survey

This survey, coordinated by the Associated Press and Cable News Network, collected information on basic elections administration and procedures followed Nov. 7, 2000, throughout the contested election. In the table, answers to questions are indicated with codes, as described in the record layout.

X. Precinct Data (Dawg Datasets.xls)

The precinct data file contains 6,657 records, with variables for certified election results, adjustments made for analytical purposes, demographic data and a field flagging Miami-Dade County precincts that should be excluded from certain scenarios.

A. Nov. 7, 2000, Florida Election Final Certified Results

These results were compiled for the Florida ballot review project by the *Orlando Sentinel* from public records of the state of Florida and its 67 counties. Sources include data-entry from certified total, precinct-level printouts generated by county election supervisors or electronic files imported directly from county websites. In many cases, elections officials were questioned at length in an attempt to account for every ballot cast and resolve other discrepancies. The baseline for reconciliation is the final, Nov. 26 certification of county-by-county vote totals, which is included as a supplemental table and is also available in spreadsheet form at the Florida Secretary of State, Division of Elections website (at http://election.dos.state.fl.us). A separate spreadsheet at that site provides a county breakdown of the late overseas absentee votes (FedAbs) certified on Nov. 17. In the cases of five counties (Lafayette, Marion, Nassau, Suwannee and Washington), the state-certified results spreadsheet contains mistakes in vote totals for some minor candidates due to clerical errors by elections officials. In these cases, the state-published totals remain the baseline and the county figures are adjusted and explained accordingly in this documentation. The state does not certify totals for ballots cast, overvotes, undervotes and unqualified write-ins. In this dataset, those numbers are based on county records.

Each of the dataset's 6,657 records represents a physical precinct, absentee precinct, or pseudo-precinct with certified candidate vote totals along with write-in votes, undervotes and overvotes for that precinct. The record set is complete, so each candidate column reconciles vertically with that candidate's official certified statewide vote total and county-by-county vote total. However, 271 records (4 percent) cannot be reconciled internally (horizontally) because county officials could not provide complete and accurate information about the number of ballots cast, overvotes or undervotes. In those cases, the sum of ballots documented as counted and uncounted either fall short of or exceed the reported number of ballots cast. There is an UNACCOUNTED field in the dataset that reports that number for each precinct. There is also an OVER-UNDER UNSPECIFIED field that reports the combined total of overvotes and undervotes for a precinct when county officials could not provide a breakdown. The WRITE-IN field includes votes for unqualified as well as qualified write-in candidates, a distinction that is explained below.

Unreconciled precincts (271)

The two counties with the most discrepancies are Orange and Escambia.

Orange County: (113 unreconciled precincts) Officials said election workers inconsistently reported total ballots from precinct to precinct. In some instances, votes cast for unqualified write-in candidates were not included in the total ballots. In other cases, the ballots cast totals were not adjusted upward to reflect so called "red-stripe" ballots initially listed as "not counted" by machines in precincts but later canvassed and found to contain votes.

Escambia County: (109 unreconciled precincts) Officials said they simply did not keep track of overvotes and undervotes by precinct, not even a combined figure, and declined to compile such a record. But the "unaccounted" field may be used as a general guide to the combined number of overvotes and undervotes that might be found in a given precinct.

Calhoun: (6 unreconciled precincts). County officials blame inconsistent tabulation of ballots cast.

Collier: (1 unreconciled precinct) County officials said they discovered 25 uncounted absentee ballots in a still-sealed envelope after the rest of the absentees had been counted and recounted; 21 of these ballots contained votes ultimately included in certified totals, but officials cannot report if the remaining 4 were undervotes, overvotes or unqualified write-ins. A pseudo-precinct called "ABFOUND" is created to account for the 25 ballots.

Glades: (10 unreconciled precincts) Officials said they had no machine tabulation of overvotes and undervotes by precinct, but later compiled estimates for media reviews. Those numbers are included in the data, even though they are not official. While these figures are not official and leave several precincts unreconciled, they may be more helpful than no numbers at all.

Holmes: (1 unreconciled precinct) Election officials said they mistakenly tabulated 3 unqualified write-in ballots in Precinct 10 as spoiled ballots. This would explain the shortfall of 3 ballots in that precinct.

Jefferson: (2 unreconciled precincts). Precinct 5 and Absentee precinct figures each fall one ballot short of reconciliation. However, total ballots cast for county matches the county's machine-generated total. County officials could not explain the discrepancy.

Lafayette: (6 unreconciled precincts). County elections supervisor could not specify how many uncounted ballots in each precinct are overvotes, undervotes or unqualified write-ins.

Martin: (1 unreconciled precinct) County officials first reported that all 280 absentee ballots showing no votes were either undervotes or overvotes. However, they were only able to positively identify 177 undervotes and 56 overvotes, leaving 47 ballots unaccounted for.

Nassau: (18 unreconciled precincts) This is another county where no "official" tallies for undervotes or overvotes were produced by machines—but the county was able to produce incomplete tallies based on a manual search in response to media requests. The database includes those unofficial figures. Also, for reasons they can't explain because control of the office has changed hands, county officials combined the overvote-undervote tallies for precincts 7 and 21. That combined total—7 undervotes and 75 overvotes—could not be assigned to either precinct, so it is not in this database. However, including those figures in the county total brings the total number of undervotes and overvotes reported in Nassau (1,491) to within one ballot of the number viewed by NORC project coders (1,492).

Osceola: (1 unreconciled precinct). County and state certification documents report one legal write-in vote for candidate May Chote (one of only two qualified write-in candidates statewide). County precinct results do not assign this vote to a precinct, so a psuedo precinct was created ("Hand" precinct). At the same time, this ballot was not added to the county's "total ballots" figure, because county officials were unwilling to concede that the number should be adjusted.

St. Johns: (3 unreconciled precincts) County officials found four precincts unreconciled after their official machine recount. A subsequent hand count of those four resulted in some adjustments that made it into the certification, and brought one precinct into line but left small, still unexplained discrepancies in the remaining three.

Pseudo-precincts
"FedAbs" (67)
The precinct table reports all federal overseas absentee ballots certified by each county on Nov. 17 in a separate precinct created for that county called "FedAbs." The majority of counties did not include any of these votes in the detailed data they provided, so the Florida Secretary of State was used as the source. In a few cases, however, counties did include the late overseas absentees as part of their overall absentee totals. For the sake of simplicity and consistency across counties, those numbers were adjusted downward to reflect the shift of some of those votes into the new FedAbs precinct.

"ERROR" (4)
Franklin—An apparent computer-tabulation glitch in Franklin County awarded one extra vote to Gore countywide, but that vote cannot be traced

to any individual precinct. Neither county officials nor tabulation system vendors can explain this simple addition error. Since this mistake was certified in the official results, it is accounted for in the database as an ERROR precinct showing one vote (+1) for Gore. Had this mistake not been made, Bush's official statewide margin of victory would have been 538 votes rather than 537.

Lafayette—County officials stand by their precinct-level report itemizing a total of 3 votes countywide for James Harris. However, they certified only two votes for Harris in documents they filed with the secretary of state. To reconcile the difference, an ERROR precinct was created with a value of (-1) in the Harris field.

Marion—The county's official certification documents report 662 votes for Harry Browne, even though they maintain he received only 332 votes and precinct totals show only 332 votes. The apparent clerical error by the county in typing up the certification documents was dealt with by creating an ERROR precinct with 300 (+300) votes for Browne.

Nassau—In this case, an apparent data-entry error by the state recorded the total Nader vote as 253 (his vote in the initial Election Day count). In fact, Nader was certified in the recount as having 255 votes in this county. An ERROR precinct with a (-2) value for Nader was created to bring the number in line with the mistaken state total.

"HAND" (4)

Miami-Dade—HAND precinct reflects six Gore votes found in a manual recount and certified by canvassing board on Nov. 15.

Osceola—HAND precinct created for a single May Chote write-in vote that county cannot trace to a precinct. Total ballots field remains at zero, because county officials insisted total ballots cast figure should not be adjusted.

Pinellas—HAND precinct created to account for three ballots discovered after the election. Two of these ballots were recovered on Nov. 18 in a transfer box, resulting in one more vote each for Gore and Bush. The third ballot (a Bush vote) was found Nov. 22 in a previously unreviewed write-in envelope. County officials could assign none of these votes to precincts.

Volusia—HAND precinct created to account for a Harry Browne write-in vote that was picked up in a canvass of absentee votes. The vote was not assigned to any precinct in the county data.

"FEDWRI" (1)

Miami-Dade—Some overseas voters use generic, write-in ballots available at embassies, Army bases, etc., if they fear they won't get the overseas absentee ballot they requested in time. In Miami-Dade, these write-ins were counted by hand and included 41 Bush votes, 38 Gore votes and 2 Browne votes. The numbers were not included in the county precinct reports, so the database creates a precinct called FEDWRI to reflect those numbers.

"NOV13" (1)

Polk—County officials did an early count and certification of federal overseas absentees ballots on Nov. 13, even though the final certification of those ballots was not due until Nov. 17. The ballots included 11 votes for Bush, 3 votes for Gore and 1 for Nader, and the totals are in an artificial precinct called NOV13.

"ABSRED" (1)

Volusia—Because of the complexity of the county record-keeping involved in the hand recount completed and certified in Volusia County, it was most practical to aggregate all absentee ballots and 110 so-called "Red Envelope" ballots into a single, artificial precinct. Red Envelope ballots are those placed in special bins at polling places if and when the AccuVote tabulating machine breaks down. At the end of the night, workers feed these ballots into a properly functioning AccuVote machine. If a ballot was marked incorrectly and is rejected at that point, it is placed in a red envelope and sent to the canvassing board for review.

"ABFOUND" (1)

Collier—County officials said they discovered 25 uncounted absentee ballots in a still-sealed envelope after the rest of the absentees had been counted and recounted; 21 of these ballots contained votes ultimately included in certified totals, but officials cannot say if the remaining four were undervotes, overvotes or unqualified write-ins. So a precinct called "ABFOUND" was created to account for the 25 ballots.

Other Disparities between County and State Data

Suwannee—County officials mistakenly certified all 16 unqualified write-ins as votes for May Chote, when she in fact received zero votes there. There was no need to adjust the database to account for this mistake, however, since the write-in field makes no distinction between qualified and unqualified write-ins.

Washington—County canvassing board mistakenly certified 3 write-in votes for May Chote, when in fact she received zero votes. There was no need to adjust the database, for the same reasons cited in Suwannee County.

Write-ins: Qualified and Unqualified

Counties are expected to certify to the state votes for qualified write-in candidates, and there were only two such candidates in Florida in the 2000 election: May Chote and Ken McCarthy. However, in precinct-level data reports, counties typically reported write-in votes for qualified and unqualified candidates together simply as "write-in." That number sufficed for the purposes of reconciling precincts in this database. However, it should be noted that many counties classify unqualified write-ins as "undervotes." The logic is that if the names of non-candidates such as Donald Duck, Colin Powell, John McCain or Ziggy are written in, it's actually a non-vote. The following 21 counties report no unqualified write-ins whatsoever, indicating that such ballots very likely are to be found among ballots classified as undervotes.

County	Write-in Total
Broward	0
Collier	0
Dixie	0
Glades	0
Hamilton	0
Highlands	0
Hillsborough	0
Indian River	0
Jefferson	1
Lafayette	0
Liberty	0
Marion	0
Martin	0
Miami-Dade	0
Nassau	0
Osceola	1
Palm Beach	0
Pasco	0

Pinellas	0
Sarasota	0
Union	0

B. Precinct Demographic Data

Variables detailing precinct by precinct statistics for registered voters by race, party and age and registration date come from a dataset built by the staff of the Florida Legislature. This dataset (called FREDS 2000) contains demographic information that is an integral part of the Florida Redistricting System.

Note on precinct shapefiles: Researchers attempting to link the DAWG precinct dataset to Arcview mapping shapefiles from the FREDS dataset must make some adjustments for changes in precinct names. The DAWG files and the NORC datasets use precinct names in use before the FREDS 2000 data were available

C. Flagged Miami-Dade County Precincts

In the precinct dataset, the field MIADADE139 contains flags that identify the 139 Miami-Dade County precincts that had been completed in a partial hand count and accepted by the Supreme Court (1 = was counted by hand, 0 = was not counted). In some scenarios, NORC ballot-coding data from these 139 precincts are excluded and the results from the official hand count of those precincts are substituted.

XI. Consortium Steering Committee Representatives

The Florida ballot project was overseen by a steering committee made up of one representative from each participating organization. This committee made broad policy decisions and guided the DAWG on some individual non-technical matters.

The Associated Press: Kevin Walsh
Cable News Network: Tom Hannon
New York Times: John Broder
Palm Beach Post: Bill Rose
St. Petersburg Times: Chuck Murphy
Tribune Co.: Doyle McManus
Wall Street Journal: Phil Kuntz
Washington Post: Bill Hamilton

XII. Appendices

A. Coder-comment Override Assumptions

1. The DAWG comment override dataset prioritizes ballots on which comment interpretation would change the outcome of an assessment of voter intent from that ballot (i.e., if a comment changes a ballot's tabulation from a "non-vote" to a "vote" or vice versa, or from two-coder agreement to three-coder agreement, or vice versa).

2. Comments from multiple coders about the same ballot were considered in aggregate.

3. When the comments specify that the write-in name is "McCain" the DAWG re-coded the WIPCODE field to indicate "13" and the WIPTXT field to say CAIN. This avoids confusion with the proper WIPTXT value for McCarthy, a state-qualified write-in candidate.

4. If two candidates were marked and one was X-d, no determination was made of whether the X was an affirmation or negation of the mark. If multiple candidates were marked and all but one X-d by the voter, the group of X-d candidates were treated as negations and changed to a blank code of 0. If multiple candidates are marked and one is circled, it is considered an affirmation of the circled candidate, and the other candidate codes are changed to 0.

5. When a comment indicates the first name of a legitimate candidate has been written, and the write-in field has the vice-presidential name of the same candidate, WIPTXT is coded to the correct four-letter sign of the legitimate candidate.

6. A chad taped back into place on a punch-card ballot is considered an attempt by the voter to correct an unintended punch, and is treated as a negation, but is coded "0" rather than "99."

7. When a comment indicates the coder clearly didn't follow coding instructions, fields are changed to reflect correct use of codes. (e.g., if a coder said chad was "completely gone," but didn't properly code that as a "4").

8. When comments indicate the chad is in place, but has been flipped, spun or twisted around backward, the chad is coded as "5." This is done under a rationale that says the coders clearly noted a disruption, but that it should be coded at the lowest level of disruption and captured only in the broadest, most inclusive assessments of voter intent.

9. When comments indicate a candidate name is written in the "margin," the candidate oval is recoded to "31."

B. Listing of Supplemental Table Names

1. DAWG DATASETS.XLS (Contains Precinct and County datasets, with record layouts, Microsoft Excel)
2. DAWG.MDB (Tabulator, Microsoft Access 2000)
3. README.doc (readme file, Microsoft Word)
4. README.txt (readme file, text version)
5. OFFICIAL FLORIDA ELECTION RESULTS.XLS (Florida Secretary of State certified election results, by county).

Examples of Gadsden County Ballots

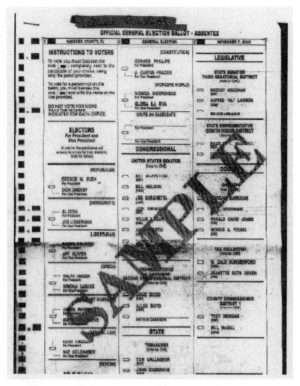

Figure 2.3. Gadsden County ballot

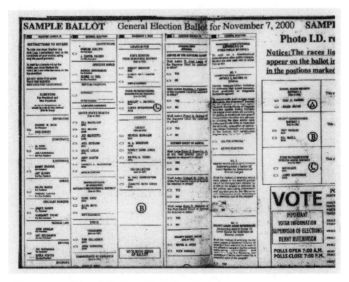

Figure 2.4. Sample ballot, Gadsden County

Official Election Certification

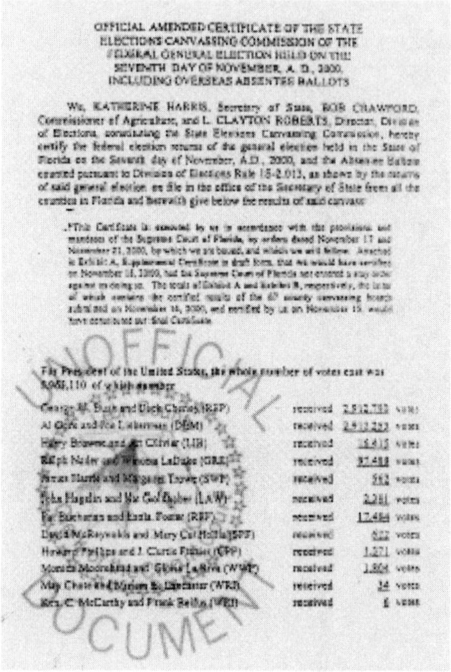

OFFICIAL AMENDED CERTIFICATE OF THE STATE
ELECTIONS CANVASSING COMMISSION OF THE
FEDERAL GENERAL ELECTION HELD ON THE
SEVENTH DAY OF NOVEMBER, A. D., 2000,
INCLUDING OVERSEAS ABSENTEE BALLOTS

We, KATHERINE HARRIS, Secretary of State, BOB CRAWFORD, Commissioner of Agriculture, and L. CLAYTON ROBERTS, Director, Division of Elections, constituting the State Elections Canvassing Commission, hereby certify the federal election returns of the general election held in the State of Florida on the Seventh day of November, A.D., 2000, and the Absentee Ballots counted pursuant to Division of Elections Rule 1S-2.013, as shown by the returns of said general election on file in the office of the Secretary of State from all the counties in Florida and herewith give below the results of said canvass:

*This Certificate is executed by us in accordance with the provisions and mandates of the Supreme Court of Florida, by orders dated November 17 and November 21, 2000, by which we are bound, and which we will follow. Attached is Exhibit A, Supplemental Certificate in draft form, that we would have certified on November 18, 2000, had the Supreme Court of Florida not entered a stay order against us doing so. The totals of Exhibit A and Exhibit B, respectively, the latter of which contains the certified results of the 67 county canvassing boards submitted on November 14, 2000, and certified by us on November 15, would have constituted our final Certificate.

For President of the United States, the whole number of votes cast was 5,963,110 of which number

George W. Bush and Dick Cheney (REP)	received	2,912,790	votes
Al Gore and Joe Lieberman (DEM)	received	2,912,253	votes
Harry Browne and Art Olivier (LIB)	received	16,415	votes
Ralph Nader and Winona LaDuke (GRE)	received	97,488	votes
James Harris and Margaret Trowe (SWP)	received	562	votes
John Hagelin and Nat Goldhaber (LAW)	received	2,281	votes
Pat Buchanan and Ezola Foster (REF)	received	17,484	votes
David McReynolds and Mary Cal Hollis (SPF)	received	622	votes
Howard Phillips and J. Curtis Frazier (CPF)	received	1,371	votes
Monica Moorehead and Gloria La Riva (WWP)	received	1,804	votes
Mary Chote and Miriam B. Lancaster (WRI)	received	34	votes
Eva C. McCarthy and Frank Beltin (WRI)	received	6	votes

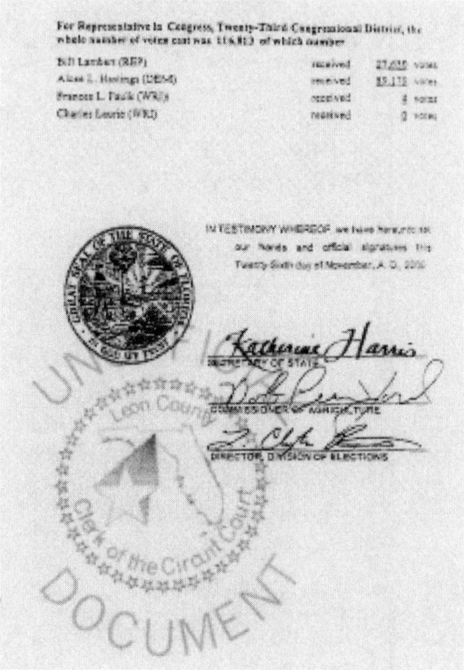

For Representative in Congress, Twenty-Third Congressional District, the whole number of votes cast was 116,813 of which number

Bill Lambert (REP)	received	27,035	votes
Alcee L. Hastings (DEM)	received	89,179	votes
Frances L. Faulk (WRI)	received	4	votes
Charles Laurie (WRI)	received	0	votes

IN TESTIMONY WHEREOF, we have hereunto set our hands and official signatures this Twenty-Sixth day of November, A. D., 2000.

Katherine Harris
SECRETARY OF STATE

COMMISSIONER OF AGRICULTURE

DIRECTOR, DIVISION OF ELECTIONS

Figure 2.5. Certification of Florida vote

Chapter 3

Law, Politics, and Administration

Making sense of the judicial process surrounding the disputed 2000 presidential election requires some understanding of the U.S. Constitution and the violent history of federalism. The litigation triggered by the controversy was fed by contradictions in the Constitution and by the intergovernmental conflict that flows from these contradictions. America's judicial system failed the nation in 2000 because the constitutional framework governing the electoral process and the role of the courts within it is deeply flawed.

The purpose of this chapter is to help readers understand the historical and legal context of judicial decision making in the 2000 election. This purpose directs our attention to particular rulings in the election dispute and also structures our investigation of individual cases. Hence the analysis does not cover every legal issue that came up during the controversy, nor does it examine every aspect of the cases thus considered. It aspires to be incisive rather than exhaustive so that the judicial landscape as a whole can be comprehended.

Overview of Judicial Decision Making in 2000

The 2000 presidential election generated litigation at every level of the state and national court system. Table 3.1 in the appendix to this chapter lists all the issues that had a significant bearing on the outcome of the dispute and indicates who brought each issue forward and with what results. In many instances different courts were deliberating simultaneously on related cases. Normally cases enter the Florida system at the two lowest levels—county courts and circuit courts—and move higher only on appeal, but cases of particular significance can be taken directly to the appellate courts, which include District Courts of Appeal and the Florida Supreme Court. At the *federal* level, cases almost always enter at the circuit court level and move upward to the district court and on to the U.S. Supreme Court. Generally matters are taken up in federal circuit courts either on appeal from state courts, as trials of federal law, or as cases involving state actions alleged to be in violation of the U.S. Constitution.

The overarching legal question in 2000 was which level of the nation's judicial system, state or federal, should have jurisdiction. The answer to this question would largely determine how the disputed Florida ballots would be handled. If the federal courts took up the election dispute, they would be concerned mainly with assuring that ballots would be given the same weight by whatever recounting procedures were used. This requirement follows from the Equal Protection Clause of the 14th Amendment to the U.S. Constitution, and if the U.S. Supreme Court or lower federal courts became involved in the election, their involvement was likely to be on this issue. Ballots would not have to be counted in exactly the same way statewide—variations in equipment across counties precluded such uniformity—but ballots from different counties would have to have similar chances of being included in the statewide totals.

Significantly this emphasis gives little or no consideration to the actual quality of the tabulations. From the federal perspective, it is perfectly lawful for ballots to be discarded or misread so long as they are discarded or misread with equal frequency and under the same conditions for all categories of voters. The priority is equal treatment, not election accuracy.

In contrast, the Florida courts would be primarily interested in assuring that every discernable vote is accurately counted and properly reflected in the electoral tabulations. This requirement was imposed by Florida law and was supported by almost a century of judicial precedents. In relation to the federal courts above it, the difficulty for the Florida Supreme Court was to specify procedures for counting and recounting ballots that would be consistent with Florida law and would also give the ballots in all counties equal consideration. This difficulty arose because Florida election law did not envision statewide recounts; it assumed that disputes over vote tabulations would arise, just as they had in the Mack-MacKay race, on a county-by-county basis, because in Florida each county tabulates its votes independently.

The Candidates' Positions in a Nutshell

The chapter appendix contains many of the legal motions made on behalf of the candidates during the dispute. On the question of jurisdiction, the lawyers representing Bush and Gore stated their respective positions most clearly and directly in their November 23 submissions to the U.S. Supreme Court. At this point in the election controversy the legal dispute had been going on for less than two weeks. Bush was appealing a ruling by the U.S. Court of Appeals for the 11th Circuit, which had denied his request for an injunction to stop the Florida recount. Two weeks later the argument made by Bush's legal team in this appeal would be accepted by the U.S. Supreme Court as the basis for the ruling that ended the election controversy with Bush as the winner; a slim and fractious majority on the Court would agree with Bush that Florida's procedures for counting machine-rejected ballots treated voters unequally and therefore violated the equal protection provisions of the 14th Amendment. This was not what the Court ruled in response to the November 23 filings, but Bush's motion in these filings states what ultimately becomes the winning argument.

Gore's position on the question of jurisdiction is laid out in response to the Bush motion in a brief filed the same day on Gore's behalf by Laurence Tribe. Tribe argued that the State of Florida's statutorily mandated process for manual recounts was "indistinguishable from the laws of other states and reflected procedures that had been applied throughout the nation for centuries." Tribe urged the U.S. Supreme Court to stay out of the election dispute because the Florida Supreme Court's interpretation of Florida law was a routine matter and posed no constitutional issues that called for a decision from the nation's highest court.

The Opening Salvo

The motion addressed by the Bush and Gore lawyers in their November 23 filings had been submitted thirteen days earlier. It was the first election lawsuit involving either of the candidates. Bush initiated it after the Florida Democratic Party requested a manual recount of ballots in four counties where Gore had outpolled Bush by substantial margins. On November 10 the Palm Beach County Canvassing Board began the initial manual recount of 1 percent of the ballots (as required by Florida's recount provisions) to determine if the overall machine count had been in error. On the same day the Bush campaign commenced a federal lawsuit in U.S. District Court to halt all manual recounts. Bush's position from the beginning was that the recounts violated the equal protection clause of the 14th Amendment to the U.S. Constitution.

At the same time that Bush's lawyers were filing their motion in federal court, Republican public officials in charge of Florida's election system were taking steps to block the recounts administratively. In the early morning hours of November 11 the Palm Beach County Canvassing Board had concluded its initial manual recount of 1 percent of the ballots and had decided to proceed with a full manual recount. When the county's manual recount began on November 12 Clay Roberts, a partisan Republican who directed the Division of Elections in the office of Secretary of State Katherine Harris, issued an advisory opinion saying that the manual recount in Palm Beach County was not legally authorized. His reasoning in the opinion was biased and superficial, and had been formulated collaboratively with the chairman of Florida's Republican Party. The opinion claimed that the manual recount provisions in Florida law applied only to situations where machines were miscounting ballots that had been *properly completed by voters*. The situation in Palm Beach County, the opinion claimed, involved ballots that had been rejected by vote-tabulating machines because they had been filled out *incorrectly*. A copy of Roberts's opinion was immediately sent to Palm Beach County election officials.

While Roberts was preparing his opinion, Florida attorney general Bob Butterworth somehow heard about it, and he sent a letter to the Palm Beach County canvassing board contradicting Roberts's opinion. Butterworth's position was well reasoned and accurately stated the meaning and implications of the law. Moreover, unlike Roberts's opinion, Butterworth's analysis cited the history of Florida election law, pertinent judicial precedents, and opinions issued previously *by Roberts's own office*. Butterworth's letter is contained in the appendix.

The next day another step to head off the manual recounts administratively was taken by Secretary of State Harris. She issued a press release saying that state election law required all county tabulations to be certified by the county canvassing boards and submitted to her office no later than one week after the election. The election had taken placed on November 7, so Harris said that the deadline was November 14. The press release was immediately followed by a letter from Clay Roberts to all of Florida's election supervisors reiterating Harris's legal interpretation.

Given the large number of ballots that had to be manually inspected, it would be impossible for the counties to complete their manual recounts by November 14. Although Harris was correct that Florida election law set a one-week timetable for the counties to submit their amended returns, the law also contained provisions for the manual recounts. As head of the election process, she had the authority to develop procedures that would address and resolve these kinds of legislative glitches, and in other cases, such as the state's legislation on felon disenfranchisement, she had demonstrated a willingness to take advantage of the discretionary power of her office. If she truly wanted to implement the statutory provisions for manual recounts but felt bound by the deadline that made the recounts impractical, she could have requested an opinion from the attorney general or the Florida Supreme Court about how to deal with the legislative glitch. Indeed, the attorney general, Democrat Bob Butterworth, had already pointed out that Florida needed to conduct a statewide recount to avoid running afoul of the 14th Amendment, and he had urged Harris and others to use their administrative authority to devise a recount process that would proceed smoothly and with fairness to the voters. However, Harris was clearly more interested in preventing manual recounts altogether than in carrying out her responsibilities in good faith; she stuck to the deadline with a vengeance.

Initial Issues Resolved by the State Courts

Harris's position on the deadline along with the conflicting opinions of Roberts and Butterworth became the first issues in the 2000 election to move all the way through the Florida courts. The canvassing board in Palm Beach County requested a ruling from the Florida Supreme Court on the disagreement between Roberts and Butterworth, and Gore submitted a motion to the Florida Circuit Court requesting the court to stop Harris from enforcing the November 14 deadline. The circuit court issued two rulings on Gore's motion, both supporting Harris, and Gore's lawyers then appealed them to the Florida Supreme Court, which overturned the Circuit Court and imposed a new deadline of November 24 for the amended returns to be submitted by the counties.

The court's reasoning was straightforward: Every practical effort must be made by election officials to discern the intent of the voters, and state election law must be interpreted and applied so as not to penalize voters for the delays or mistakes of public officials.

The court's logic was perhaps best displayed by Justice Periente in her questioning of one of Harris's attorneys during oral argument. While the attorney was making a case for Harris's November 14 deadline, he was interrupted by a question from Periente. She asked what should be done in a hypothetical situation where the election personnel simply took off for a few days and could not complete the recount because they had been derelict in their duties. Should the state penalize the voters for the actions of these officials? The attorney responded that, yes, the voters should be penalized. The answer was less than convincing and seemed to make Periente's point for her.

Side Issues

The decision of the Florida Supreme Court was immediately appealed to the U.S. Supreme Court by Bush's attorneys, but the recounts in Palm Beach and Broward counties continued as the appeal was being filed and considered. At the same time the Miami-Dade Canvassing Board decided to reconsider its earlier decision, following the initial recount of 1 percent of the ballots, not to conduct a full recount because Gore had not gained enough additional votes in the 1 percent test for the board to expect a full recount to change the outcome of the election. The earlier decision of the Miami-Dade board had been made when the recounts in Palm Beach and Broward counties had not been far along and Bush's lead over Gore had been larger. Later, as the Palm Beach and Broward recounts proceeded, Bush's margin shrank, and the number of additional votes that Gore had gained in Miami-Dade's preliminary (1-percent) recount started to appear sufficient to require a full recount.

Another issue that entered the Florida judicial system at this time had to do with the standards being used in Palm Beach County to decide how to interpret dimpled ballots. Palm Beach County had a preexisting policy of counting a dimpled chad as a vote only if there were other dimpled chads on the same ballot. This policy was based on the idea that multiple dimples indicated a problem with the voting machine. Later, during the contest phase of the dispute, which took place in Florida Circuit Court, Gore's lawyers would argue that ballots were likely to be dimpled only for the presidential race because most voters cast a vote for this race, which caused chads to accumulate in the voting machine's repository directly underneath the presidential column of the punch-card ballot, thus preventing voters from fully inserting their stylus when voting for president but not for other offices. However, in the County Court of Palm Beach County, the Gore team argued simply that law and precedent made any single rule for handling dimpled ballots illegal. The issue was heard twice in county court, and in both instances the judge agreed with Gore's argument. However, the court's decision had little if any effect on how the canvassing board actually operated when it reviewed the ballots.

Legislative Saber Rattling

Back in Tallahassee, leaders of the Florida legislature began threatening to intervene. Republicans were in control of both the House and the Senate, and the House Speaker and Senate president, both of whom were Republicans, held positions that were second in power only to the office of governor. Moreover, Tom Feeney, the Speaker, had a close personal relationship with Florida governor Jeb Bush. He had been Jeb's running mate in the 1994 gubernatorial race that Lawton Chiles had won narrowly.

In a series of statements later discovered to have been orchestrated by the Bush legal team, Feeney held press conferences to publicly criticize the decisions of Florida's Supreme Court and to threaten legislative preemption. Public statements by the Speaker of the Florida House of Representatives and the president of the Florida Senate are included in the appendix. Also included are legislative proclamations for a special legislative session and for House and Senate hearings on the election dispute.

As discussed further in chapter 5, this saber rattling was planned and coordinated by the Bush legal team and the Speaker of the Florida House to create the appearance of a constitutional crisis so that the U.S. Supreme Court would be more likely to intervene in the controversy. Republicans assumed that if the federal courts became involved, they would be likely to raise questions about the equal-treatment implications of Florida's vote tabulation procedures. The Speaker of the House asserted, and the Senate president more or less acceded to his assertion, that the Florida legislature could decide the election in Florida regardless of rulings by the Florida Supreme Court, because, in the Speaker's view, the U.S. Constitution and Title III of the U.S. Code vested this power in state legislatures.

In fact, the Florida legislature would have had a role in deciding the election only if Florida had been unable to choose its slate of Electoral College electors before December 12. This was the date on which the deadline fell that is set in Title III for the so-called safe harbor. This provision was enacted after the disputed election of 1876, in which Florida, as in 2000, had played a central role. The outcome of the 1876 presidential election had come into question in large part because of shifting partisan fortunes in Florida. Shortly after the election the state had reported that its Electoral College votes had been won by the Republican candidate, but then, two months later after the Democrats elected in 1876 took office, Florida awarded its electoral vote to the Democrat. When the electoral college votes were submitted to Congress they were contested, and the election outcome could not be determined.

Under the safe harbor clause of Title III, election results submitted to Congress by states prior to the deadline cannot be contested subsequently when the states' Electoral College votes are officially transmitted. In threatening legislative action, Florida's Speaker had knowingly created the false impression that, if the dispute continued to December 12, Florida's electoral slate might be excluded entirely from the Electoral College vote. In truth, however, Florida had submitted its election results as soon as they were certified. This meant that the state's electoral votes had already met the safe harbor requirement. If the dispute were not resolved judicially by December 12, the results originally certified and submitted would stand, and Congress would be obligated to accept them. By implication, any amendments to the results would have to be made by December 12 or they would have no effect. Thus Florida was never in danger of having its electoral votes dismissed.

First Ruling of the U.S. Supreme Court

On November 24 the U.S. Supreme Court agreed to hear Bush's appeal of the Florida Supreme Court decision allowing the recounts to proceed under a new deadline, which was itself November 24. However, the issue that the court decided to consider was not whether the recounts violated the equal-treatment requirements of the U.S. Constitution but whether the Florida court, in setting a new deadline for submitting amended returns, had changed Florida election law after the election, in violation of Title III of the U.S. Code.

Toward the end of the oral argument before the court, a surprising turn occurred in the discussion that would have unexpected significance later. Justice Scalia asked rhetorically on what basis the Florida court had arrived at a new deadline. There was no clear answer in the ruling of the Florida Supreme Court. In the ensuing discussion among Scalia and the other justices, a consensus seemed to emerge that the only acceptable route by which the Florida court could have arrived at the new deadline was via a careful interpretation of the Florida statutes. If, instead, the Florida court had based its reasoning for the new deadline on the Florida Constitution, then the Florida court's ruling would be open to challenge for potentially failing to take into account the implications of the U.S. Constitution and Title III of the U.S. Code. The Constitution gives the authority to choose electors to the state legislatures, which, like Florida, normally exercise this authority by enacting state election laws. Title III of the U.S. Code says that the procedures in place at the time of an election to federal office cannot be changed afterward when the winner is being determined. If the Florida court had based the new deadline on the Florida Constitution, then it had violated the provision in the U.S. Constitution assigning to state legislatures the power to select electors.

In its ruling on the matter, the U.S. Supreme Court sent the case back to the Florida court for a clarification of the state court's opinion. In effect, the U.S. Supreme Court was requiring that the Florida court revise its opinion so that it was clearly reasoned from the letter of the state's election laws. This was easy enough for the Florida court to do, because the Florida election laws clearly said that candidates had a right to request manual recounts and that county canvassing boards had to conduct full manual recounts when they determined by a count of 1 percent of the votes that a manual recount could alter the election outcome. As a practical matter, Florida's urban counties could not complete these mandated recounts within the time frame specified by the law, and yet some sort of deadline had to be set because the law also included a process for candidates to contest the election. Thus the Florida Supreme Court did not need to call on the Florida Constitution to justify its decision establishing a new deadline. Presumably the court had referenced the state constitution just to add to the weight of its ruling. The ruling of the U. S. Supreme Court would therefore have no immediate consequence, but the ruling would have significance later because it meant that the Florida Supreme Court, when addressing subsequent issues in the election dispute, had to reason solely from state statutes and case law. It would not have the flexibility provided by reasoning from the state constitution.

Points Scored by Gore in the Election Contest

By December 4, when the U.S. Supreme Court issued its first ruling, the election controversy had already moved beyond the issue of deadlines for recounting the machine-rejected ballots. On November 26, when the Court was just beginning to consider the case for which this ruling was written, Florida's secretary of state and the other two members of the state Elections Commission certified the election returns, with 2,912,790 votes for Bush and 2,912,253 votes for Gore, giving Bush victory by 537 votes. Governor Jeb Bush immediately signed the certificate designating Florida's electors to his brother, George W. To prevent Gore's legal team from being able to have an injunction served to block the certification from being transmitted to Congress before the election was contested in circuit court per Florida election law, the governor gave the document to an obscure staff member to take home with her and mail the next morning.

On December 2 and 3 a trial was held in Florida Circuit Court on Gore's action to contest the election results thus certified. Presiding over the trial was Judge N. Sander Sauls. The premise on which Sauls eventually decided the case was that, for the election outcome to be overturned, Gore's advocates had to prove that further recounting was likely to make Gore the winner instead of Bush.

David Boise, Gore's lead attorney throughout the election dispute, thought that this would be a very easy standard to reach, because the election was clearly very close and the manual recount had not been completed in Miami-Dade County. The Miami-Dade recount had been halted prematurely after Bush supporters, some of whom were operatives for the national Republican Party and had come to Florida from other states, flooded into the county administration building and boisterously protested the canvassing board's decision to undertake the full recount.

It is unclear whether Boise had realized by the end of the trial that Sauls expected him to actually prove that a full recount in Miami-Dade would be very likely to give the election to Gore, but, in any event, the evidence presented by Boise on this point was inconclusive, and Sauls ruled against him.

Throughout the election dispute Boise demonstrated remarkable legal and political skills, especially in understanding how legal issues played out in public perceptions and vice versa, and if the trial in circuit court had been heard by a jury, he would probably have won easily. He understood that, in the arena of public and pundit opinion, the central question was whether the manual recounts were truly arriving at the will of the voters or, instead, assigning false meanings to ballots that were inherently ambiguous. A joke being circulated was that the people holding up ballots with hanging chads looked like Carnac the Magnificent, a character jokingly played by Johnny Carson on the *Tonight Show* in an occasional skit. Wearing a turban and looking like an Eastern mystic, Carson would hold an envelope in front of his forehead and try to use psychic powers to see its contents. When he announced what he saw, Carnac was always wrong, and the actual message in the envelope would be a hilarious punch line. As long as the manual recounts were vulnerable to being belittled as loony exercises in divination, any claim that further recounting would reveal the true winner of the election would be unconvincing.

Even though they did not meet the legal test that Sauls would apply in his ruling, Boise and the rest of the Gore legal team did succeed in vindicating the manual recounts, first with their own witnesses and then with a masterful cross-examination of one of the witnesses for Bush. The Gore witnesses made two points. The first was that the cause of dimpled chads, hanging chads, and undervoting in general could have been the result of a failure to properly clean the voting equipment. Testimony revealed that machines had been allowed to accumulate chads for many years without being emptied or cleaned a single time. The implication was that "chad buildup" from past elections could eventually prevent voters from being able to push all the way through the punch-card ballots.

Second, the Gore team brought in a statistician to prove that the frequency of undervotes in Palm Beach, Broward, and Miami-Dade counties, all of which used punch cards, was far greater than the frequency of undervotes in counties using paper ballots, lever machines, and optical scanning.

This suggested that undervotes were being caused by the equipment rather than by voter errors or failure to follow directions. The statistician pointed out further that the manual recounts tended to bring the error rate of the punch-card counties into line with the error rates in other counties. The upshot of these points was that a manual recount was necessary to determine the true intent of voters in punch-card counties.

The Bush team brought in one of the inventors and manufacturers of the type of punch-card machine used in southeast Florida. Questioning by the Bush lawyers was intended to refute the theory of chad buildup that had been introduced by earlier witnesses for Gore. However, upon cross-examination, the witness admitted flatly that when elections were very close, punch-card ballots had to be manually inspected to arrive at precise results.

Why Gore Lost the Contest Phase

Although at this point it appeared that Boise had successfully made the case for a full recount in Miami-Dade County and perhaps a new recount in Palm Beach County, he had actually overlooked a crucial point that would cost him the case. A crucial claim in Gore's argument remained to be proven; Judge Sauls expected Gore's advocates to demonstrate that a manual recount would probably give Gore the election. All that the Gore team had shown was that machine tabulations of punch-card ballots will fail to read about 3 percent of the ballots containing valid votes, and that such unread votes can in fact be accurately discerned through human observation. These were important points to make, especially in the larger arena of public opinion, but they would have no bearing on the outcome of the trial unless it could also be shown that the ballots targeted by Gore for recounting would alter the outcome of the election.

The fatal flaw in the case presented by Gore's lawyers was stated in paragraph 4(d) in their initial filing. Earlier in the filing, the Gore team had totaled up the net additional votes that had been found for Gore in the county recounts but that had not been included when the election results had been certified. These additional Gore votes came from the results certified originally by Nassau County but later amended; the recount results submitted late by Palm Beach County; and the recounting that had been completed in Miami-Dade County before its recount had been terminated. However, even with all these additions, Gore did not move into the lead. Consequently the Gore team was forced to make the more speculative claim in paragraph 4(d) that Gore would win if a full recount were conducted in Miami-Dade County and if the ambiguous ballots in Palm Beach County were recounted with a standard more flexible than that employed by the Palm Beach County Canvassing Board in violation of the rulings in county court.

Boise failed to prove the claim in 4(d) not because the evidence was unavailable but because the Gore team made a poor choice when selecting one of its expert witnesses. Boise and company needed to demonstrate that, on the basis of the manual recounting completed thus far in Miami-Dade County, a full recount would provide enough additional votes to Gore for him to win. Boise decided to use an expert with impeccable credentials in the field of statistics but with little experience with elections data and no experience with the system of government in Florida. The Gore statistician had the additional impediment of being from Germany and not being completely fluent in English, especially with respect to the technical jargon used to describe elections data.

The expert made a fundamental error in his methodology for projecting the results of a full recount in Miami-Dade County. He took the number of votes gained by Gore in the partial recount and divided it by the total number of ballots recounted. The resulting number was the "vote fraction" that Gore had gained for each recounted ballot. He then multiplied this fraction by the total number of undervotes in Mimai Dade County to estimate the number of votes Gore would gain if all undervotes were counted.

The problem with this methodology was that it failed to take into account that the votes recounted up to that point in Miami-Dade had come from precincts that were not reflective of precincts countywide. The recount had begun with precincts with higher percentages of African Americans and Democrats than the percentages for the county as a whole. This meant that the vote fraction Gore had gained for each ballot recounted thus far was larger than the vote fraction he would be likely to get in other precincts. In other words, Gore may have gained votes in African American and Democratic precincts, but he would not gain as many votes and probably would lose votes in predominantly white, predominantly Cuban, and predominantly Republican precincts.

After Gore's legal team had presented its case, the Bush lawyers presented witnesses in rebuttal. They also recalled Boise's statistician for further questioning. They asked him point blank if his methodology had been flawed in the way I have just described, and he said yes. He admitted further that his calculations therefore did not show that the election outcome would have been different. He asked that he be allowed to redo his work, but the judge told him that this was not allowable.

On December 4 Judge Sauls issued his ruling against Gore's challenge to the election results. How much it surprised the Gore lawyers is unclear. Certainly those who supported Gore from the sidelines were disappointed and doubtful that any further manual recounts would be allowed, much less that Gore might eventually win. The Republican leadership of the Florida legislature had already brought the legislature into special session. (For the proclamation, see the appendix). Hence it seemed unlikely that the Florida Supreme Court would do anything further, since this would require overturning a trial judge and also staring down the U.S. Supreme Court, which had already drawn a line in the sand.

Boise admitted publicly that the case had been thoroughly rejected by the district court judge, and he expressed both disappointment and shock at the judge's ruling. But he also voiced optimism that Gore would prevail on appeal, which he immediately filed in the Florida District Court of Appeals. The latter sent the case directly to the state's highest court.

On December 8 the Florida Supreme Court surprised the world. It overturned the circuit court decision and ordered a statewide manual re-count. It also added 383 votes to Gore's total on the basis of findings in the circuit court trial, and Bush's margin was reduced to just 154 votes.

The court reached its decision by a vote of 4 to 3. The majority was made up of the court's three newest members plus Justice Ansted, who was the only member who would be standing for merit retention election in 2002. Ansted clearly demonstrated great courage in standing with his more recently appointed colleagues.

Two of the three justices in the minority simply dissented without comment, but the third, Chief Justice Wells, issued an emotional dissent. It revealed the impact that had been made on the court by the hostile posturing of the Florida legislature. Wells based his dissent almost entirely on political practicality rather than on considerations of law and precedent. In essence, he warned that the majority's decision risked precipitating a constitutional crisis.

The decision of the Florida Supreme Court to overturn Judge Sauls's ruling was entirely consistent with precedent and with Florida election laws, and it reflected the position expressed all along by the court that all valid votes had to be counted. Why, then, was the court's ruling so surprising? Because it addressed the fundamental issues of the controversy frontally and showed no fear of either the court above it or the Republican-dominated legislature across the street.

The Florida Supreme Court threw out the trial judge's decision on the grounds that he had set too high a standard for the Gore case. Judge Sauls had built his verdict entirely around the premise that the election results could be overturned only if Gore's legal team could demonstrate that Gore had probably won. Although the judge's decision included many arguments, the verdict had been constructed atop this very thin reed. When the Florida Supreme Court plucked this reed from beneath the judge's reasoning, his position collapsed. Ruling that votes legitimately cast by Florida electors and discernible through manual recounts permitted under Florida law had to be included in the vote tabulation, the court mandated a statewide manual recount of all undervoted ballots that had not yet been examined. The court noted further that Florida law provided no guidelines for interpreting ballots beyond the laws' references to voter intentions.

The statewide recount began immediately. The county courts were to oversee the recounting in their jurisdictions, and circuit court judge Terry Lewis was assigned to provide state direction. In his instructions to the counties he required that the recount cover overvoted ballots as well as undervotes, since they, too, might contain legally valid votes and therefore should have been included in the Supreme Court's ruling (see the Lewis memo in the appendix).

The U.S. Supreme Court Steps in Again

In an effort to stop the statewide recount that had been ordered by the Florida Supreme Court and initiated by the counties, Bush's lawyers appealed to the Florida Supreme Court, the U.S. District Court of Appeals, and the U.S. Supreme Court. The first two courts rejected the motions, but the U.S, Supreme Court agreed to hear the case.

Several members of the national Supreme Court must have already decided that they needed not only to prevent Gore from overturning Florida's certified results but also to make it impossible for him to challenge Florida's Electoral College vote when it was transmitted to Congress. Perhaps these justices shared the feelings of Justice Wells in Florida, who feared a political crisis. Perhaps they thought that a Gore victory arrived at through a recount would forever be rejected by Bush supporters, whereas a Gore defeat at this point would provoke little reaction. It would have been natural for the justices to be worried about the potential for social unrest. After all, they had been watching demonstrations in Florida and Texas for days, and had encountered demonstrators personally in the nation's capital where they lived and worked. They had also heard Jim Baker and George W. Bush reject the legitimacy of the Florida Supreme Court when it had overturned the Florida secretary of state's inflexible deadline for completing the manual recounts.

We are unlikely ever to learn exactly what the justices were thinking, but one thing was evident from their actions: they were very concerned about public perceptions, for they not only decided to hear the Bush appeal but also to prohibit any further recounting until their ruling had been issued.

After consuming all the time remaining for Florida to submit amended election results under the safe harbor provision of Title III of the U.S. Code, the United States Supreme Court issued what can only be described as one of the most tortured and embarrassing decisions in its history. Significantly none of the justices claimed authorship for it, and several justices in the majority issued separate opinions that agreed on little. In the majority were Chief Justice Rehnquist and Justices Kennedy, O'Connor, Scalia, and Thomas. The minority included Justices Breyer, Ginsburg, Souter, and Stevens.

The only point holding the majority together was the view that a more detailed set of criteria for recounting the ballots in Florida would be necessary if the manual recounts were going to treat all Florida voters equally. The majority consensus on this point meant that the Court's first ruling, which had required clarification from the Supreme Court of Florida on the latter's decision to overturn the secretary of state's recount deadline, had placed Florida's top court in an impossible situation. The ruling implicitly warned the Florida Supreme Court against straying from Florida election law, even if the law violated the Florida Constitution. This meant that the Florida court could not establish uniform guidelines for interpreting dimpled chads and other ballot markings, because state election laws made reference only to judgments of voter intent. But then, when the Florida court did not include ballot-reading guidelines in its order for a statewide recount, the U.S. Supreme Court intervened to object. The Court supported the Florida court's decision to conduct a statewide manual recount, but it said that uniform standards would be needed to assure that voters are treated equally. The ruling also pointed out that time had run out for further recounting.

In addition to deciding the election by a technicality, the Supreme Court's decision struck many observers as flawed in its reasoning. In particular, the ruling applied the 14th Amendment's equal protection clause selectively and, in so doing, ran counter to the Amendment's historic intent. The 14th Amendment was enacted shortly after the Civil War to prohibit the former Confederate states from governing African Americans differently from other citizens. There was a great deal of evidence from the Florida election that the votes of African Americans were more likely than the votes of other voters to have been spoiled by ballot errors or machine-tabulation failures and were therefore less likely to be counted in the presidential election. However, in the Court's decision, the equal protection clause had been applied not to alleviate this injustice but to let it stand. At the same time the Court ignored all sorts of other forms of unequal treatment in the election system of Florida and in virtually all other states. The inevitable impression left by the decision was that the justices in the majority had twisted their legal reasoning to reach a predetermined conclusion and give the presidency to Bush.

Some of the justices in the majority also appeared to misunderstand the legal basis for Florida's mandated recount procedures. This became obvious from questions asked by the justices during oral arguments. One asked whether Florida had ever conducted recounts like those being used in 2000. The attorney to whom the question was posed was a lawyer for George W. Bush. Presumably out of ignorance, he answered no. In reality, however, nothing could be further from the truth. In very close elections ballots are almost always recounted manually.

If the U.S. Supreme Court justices had actually read the materials submitted to them, this would have been obvious. After all, one of the recurring issues in the controversy had been whether Broward and Palm Beach counties should follow Palm Beach County's preexisting policy on how to interpret dimpled and hanging chads. Obviously, if Palm Beach County had a policy on chads, manual recounts must be a normal course of action. Why one of the Gore lawyers did not correct the Court's misimpression and the erroneous answer given to the question is unknown.

Constitutional Origins of the Judicial Breakdown

That the state and federal courts approached the disputed election differently is not why the courts became gridlocked in 2000. The judicial system burned up the time needed for a full recount because there was no obvious answer to the question of jurisdiction. The U.S. Constitution is simply unclear about the division of authority between the national and state governments.

The framers of the national constitution wanted to delineate a sphere of autonomy for the states while also placing national authority over issues of national significance, but for various reasons the Constitution ended up with a blurred boundary between national and state powers. The Constitution's confusion on this point is visible in the first words of the document: "We the people of the United States . . ." These words imply that the authority of the Constitution flows from the nation, from the country's entire population considered as a collectivity, from "we the people," but the nation's very name implies otherwise—that the nation is a combination of *states*, a "United States."

The positions of Bush and Gore in the election dispute simply recapitulated the tension in the Constitution between state and national authority. Gore believed that the ballots should be manually recounted because the laws of the State of Florida, as interpreted by the Florida Supreme Court, mandated this type of recount under conditions that Gore met. Bush argued, and the U.S. Supreme Court more or less agreed, that the use of different recounting procedures in different counties would violate the equal treatment clause of the Fourteenth Amendment, which requires that all citizens of the United States, irrespective of where they may happen to reside, be afforded comparable rights, privileges, and protections.

Legal Ambiguity and the Partisan Conspiracy of Florida Legislators

Not only did the Constitution's ambiguities about national and state authority pull the courts into a time-exhausting whirlpool of decision making, but they also created openings for partisan manipulation. During the election controversy, both the Florida Supreme Court and the U.S. Supreme Court were considered suspect because of the political orientations of the elected officials who had appointed their members. All the justices of the Florida Supreme Court had been selected by Democrats, whereas a majority of the justices of the U.S. Supreme Court had been chosen by Republicans, one of whom was George W. Bush's father.

Nonetheless, even if accusations of partisan bias were warranted, they mistook the symptoms for the disease. To the extent that partisanship infected the positions of individual justices or judges, it could do so mainly because the legal principles governing elections and election disputes are confused and confusing.

The same was true with respect to the maneuvers of the Florida legislature during the crisis, maneuvers that were unquestionably partisan and unethical, and perhaps criminal. The groundless threats and warnings of the legislature seemed credible only because the U.S. Constitution is so muddled. As the controversy bounced from issue to issue and was batted back and forth from one level and branch of government to another, it seemed to take on a life of its own, but it actually originated in constitutional ambiguity.

Déjà Vu in 2000: The Disputed Election of 1876

The election dispute of 2000 mirrored in many ways the disputed presidential election of 1876, because they both grew from the same constitutional ground and even from some of the same problems of election administration. Just as the 2000 election hinged on the outcome in Florida, so did the election of 1876. The 1876 election also involved questions both about the state's authority to determine the results of the election and about the accuracy of county-level tabulations of the votes.

In 1876 Florida's statewide population was divided about evenly between blacks and whites, but the balance varied widely from county to county. The counties in the so-called Black Belt, where the plantation system of agriculture was prevalent, were overwhelmingly black. For example, blacks comprised 80 percent of the population in Leon County, where Tallahassee is located. In many other counties there were few African Americans.

The 1876 dispute centered on the vote returns from Florida's predominantly white counties. As remains the case today, election administration was handled by officials elected locally at the county level, which meant that the election system in 1876 was being administered in many parts of Florida by public officials who were extremely hostile to the Republican administration both nationally and in the state. In 1876, when the election results came into Tallahassee from these outlying white areas, the vote totals for the Democratic presidential candidate were so high that the state election officials, who were Republicans, threw them out as fraudulent. Florida's electoral votes were then committed by the state to Republican presidential candidate Rutherford B. Hayes, and this, with the votes of the other states he carried, gave Hayes enough electoral votes to win the office.

However, the returns from Florida were subsequently rescinded when a Democratic governor took office on January 1, 1877. He appointed new election officials and recalculated the vote totals, this time with the allegedly fraudulent county returns included. Florida then resubmitted its slate of electors, replacing Republicans with Democrats. The question of which electors to accept was decided by a Republican Congress, but when it selected the Republican, the southern states threatened another Civil War. The Republicans averted this danger by agreeing to end Reconstruction. However, they left the source of the disagreement intact in the Constitution, where it remains like a ticking time bomb, ready to explode as it did in 2000.

Appendix to Chapter 3

Principal Judicial Decisions in the 2000 Election

Table 3.1. Principal Judicial Decisions in the 2000 Election

Court and Level of Government	Issue
Federal	
U.S. Supreme Court	Do manual recounts violate the equal treatment clause of the 14th Amendment?
	Can the Florida Supreme Court change the counties' deadline for submitting revised returns to the Election Commission?
U.S. District Court	Do manual recounts in Florida violate the equal protection clause of the 14th Amendment?
State	
Florida Supreme Court	Can Florida secy. of state require counties to submit returns in seven days?
Florida District Court	All appeals of circuit court decisions in the election dispute were forwarded by the Florida district courts directly to the Florida Supreme Court.
Florida Circuit Court	Can Florida secy. of state require counties to submit returns in seven days?
	Did Florida secy. of state have sound reasons in holding counties to the seven-day deadline?
	Did the vote totals certified by the state and various counties exclude legally valid votes?
	Did election supervisors in Volusia and Seminole counties break the law by giving special assistance to Republican Party officials?
Florida County Court	Can the election be done over?
	What standard should Palm Beach County use in manual recounts?

From	Ruling	Who Is Helped
Bush on appeal from Federal District Court	Must have a statewide standard.	Bush, because time has run out.
Bush	Depends on basis of FSC's ruling. Must be based on Florida Constitution.	Bush, because it signals the FSC to step carefully.
Federal District Court	No.	Gore
Gore on appeal	No. Court sets new deadline.	Gore
Gore	Yes, but must have sound reasons.	Bush
Gore	Yes.	Bush
Gore, contesting the election	No.	Bush
Citizens of the respective counties	Yes, but there is no remedy.	Bush
Several Palm Beach County voters	No.	Bush
Gore	"Voter intent" per election law.	Gore

Excerpts from Florida Supreme Court Decision Changing Recount Deadline

Nos. SC00-2346, SC00-2348 & SC00-2349

PALM BEACH COUNTY CANVASSING BOARD,

Petitioner,

vs.

KATHERINE HARRIS, etc., et al.,

Respondents.

VOLUSIA COUNTY CANVASSING BOARD, et al.,

Appellants,

vs.

KATHERINE HARRIS, etc., et al.,

Appellees.

FLORIDA DEMOCRATIC PARTY,

Appellant,

vs.

KATHERINE HARRIS, etc., et al.,

Appellees.

[November 21, 2000]

PER CURIAM

We have for review two related trial court orders appealed to the First District Court of Appeal, which certified the orders to be of great public importance requiring immediate resolution by this Court (Case Numbers SC00-2348 and SC00-2349). We have jurisdiction under article V, section 3(b)(5) of the Florida Constitution. For the reasons set forth in this opinion, we reverse the orders of the trial court.[1]

I. Facts

A. The Election

On Tuesday, November 7, 2000, the State of Florida, along with the rest of the United States, conducted a general election for the President of the United States. The Division of Elections ("Division") reported on Wednesday, November 8, that George W. Bush, the Republican candidate, had received 2,909,135 votes, and Albert Gore Jr., the Democratic candidate, had received 2,907,351 votes. Because the overall difference in the total votes cast for each candidate was less than one-half of one percent of the total votes cast for that office (i.e., the difference was 1,784 votes), an automatic recount was conducted pursuant to section 102.141(4), Florida

Statutes.[2] The recount resulted in a substantially reduced figure for the overall difference between the two candidates.

In light of the closeness of the election, the Florida Democratic Executive Committee on Thursday, November 9, requested that manual recounts be conducted in Broward, Palm Beach, and Volusia Counties pursuant to section 102.166, Florida Statutes (2000).[3] Pursuant to section 102.166(4)(d), the county canvassing boards of these counties conducted a sample manual recount of at least one percent of the ballots cast. Initial manual recounts demonstrated the following: In Broward County, a recount of one percent of the ballots indicated a net increase of four votes for Gore; and in Palm Beach County, a recount of four sample precincts yielded a net increase of nineteen votes for Gore. Based on these recounts, several of the county canvassing boards determined that the manual recounts conducted indicated "an error in the vote tabulation which could affect the outcome of the election." Based on this determination, several canvassing boards voted to conduct countywide manual recounts pursuant to section 102.166(5)(c).

B. The Appeal Proceedings

Concerned that the recounts would not be completed prior to the deadline set forth in section 102.111(1), Florida Statutes (2000), requiring that all county returns be certified by 5:00 p.m. on the seventh day after an election, the Palm Beach County Canvassing Board, pursuant to section 106.23, Florida Statutes (2000), sought an advisory opinion from the Division of Elections, requesting an interpretation of the deadline set forth in sections 102.111 and 102.112. The Division of Elections responded by issuing Advisory Opinion DE 00-10, stating that absent unforeseen circumstances, returns from the county must be received by 5:00 p.m. on the seventh day following the election in order to be included in the certification of the statewide results.

Relying upon this advisory opinion, the Florida Secretary of State (the Secretary) issued a statement on Monday, November 13, 2000, that she would ignore returns of the manual recounts received by the Florida Department of State (the Department) after Tuesday, November 14, 2000, at 5:00 p.m. The Volusia County Canvassing Board (the Volusia Board) on Monday, November 13, 2000, filed suit in the Circuit Court of the Second Judicial Circuit in Leon County, Florida, seeking declaratory and injunctive relief, and the candidates and the Palm Beach County Canvassing

Board (the Palm Beach Board), among others, were allowed to intervene. In its suit, the Volusia Board sought a declaratory judgment that it was not bound by the November 14, 2000, deadline and also sought an injunction barring the Secretary from ignoring election returns submitted by the Volusia Board after that date.

The trial court ruled on Tuesday, November 14, 2000, that the deadline was mandatory but that the Volusia Board may amend its returns at a later date and that the Secretary, after "considering all attendant facts and circumstances," may exercise her discretion in determining whether to ignore the amended returns.[4] Later that day, the Volusia Board filed a notice of appeal of this ruling to the First District Court of Appeal, and the Palm Beach Board filed a notice of joinder in the appeal.

Subsequent to the circuit court's order, the Secretary announced that she was in receipt of certified returns (i.e., the returns resulting from the initial recount) from all counties in the State. The Secretary then instructed Florida's Supervisors of Elections (Supervisors) that they must submit to her by 2:00 p.m., Wednesday, November 15, 2000, a written statement of "the facts and circumstances" justifying any belief on their part that they should be allowed to amend the certified returns previously filed. Four counties submitted their statements on time. After considering the reasons in light of specific criteria,[5] the Secretary on Wednesday, November 15, 2000, rejected the reasons and again announced that she would not accept the amended returns but rather would rely on the earlier certified totals for the four counties. The Secretary further stated that after she received the certified returns of the overseas absentee ballots from each county, she would certify the results of the presidential election on Saturday, November 18, 2000.

On Thursday, November 16, 2000, the Florida Democratic Party and Albert Gore filed a motion in Circuit Court of the Second Judicial Circuit in Leon County, Florida, seeking to compel the Secretary to accept amended returns. After conducting a hearing, the court denied relief in a brief order dated Friday, November 17, 2000.[6] That day, both the Democratic Party and Gore appealed to the First District Court of Appeal, which consolidated the appeals with the Volusia Board's appeal already pending there, and certified both of the underlying trial court orders to this Court based on the Court's "pass-through" jurisdiction.[7] By orders dated Friday, November 17, 2000, this Court accepted jurisdiction, set an expedited briefing schedule, and enjoined the Secretary and the Elections Canvassing Commission (Commission) from certifying the results of the presidential election until further order of this Court.[8]

II. Guiding Principles

Twenty-five years ago, this Court commented that the will of the people, not a hyper-technical reliance upon statutory provisions, should be our guiding principle in election cases:

[T]he real parties in interest here, not in the legal sense but in realistic terms, are the voters. They are possessed of the ultimate interest and it is they whom we must give primary consideration. The contestants have direct interests certainly, but the office they seek is one of high public service and of utmost importance to the people, thus subordinating their interest to that of the people. Ours is a government of, by and for the people. Our federal and state constitutions guarantee the right of the people to take an active part in the process of that government, which for most of our citizens means participation via the election process. *The right to vote is the right to participate; it is also the right to speak, but more importantly the right to be heard.* We must tread carefully on that right or we risk the unnecessary and unjustified muting of the public voice. By refusing to recognize an otherwise valid exercise of the right of a citizen to vote for the sake of sacred, unyielding adherence to statutory scripture, we would in effect nullify that right.

Boardman v. Esteva, 323 So. 2d 259, 263 (Fla. 1975) (emphasis added)

We consistently have adhered to the principle that the will of the people is the paramount consideration.[9] Our goal today remains the same as it was a quarter of a century ago, i.e., to reach the result that reflects the will of the voters, whatever that might be. This fundamental principle, and our traditional rules of statutory construction, guide our decision today.

III. Issues

The questions before this Court include the following: Under what circumstances may a Board authorize a countywide manual recount pursuant to section 102.166(5); must the Secretary and Commission accept such recounts when the returns are certified and submitted by the Board after the seven-day deadline set forth in sections 102.111 and 102.112?[10]

IV. Legal Opinion of the Division of Elections

The first issue this Court must resolve is whether a County Board may conduct a countywide manual recount where it determines there is an error in vote tabulation that could affect the outcome of the election. Here, the Division issued opinion DE 00-13, which construed the language "er-

ror in vote tabulation" to exclude the situation where a discrepancy between the original machine return and sample manual recount is due to the
manner in which a ballot has been marked or punched.

Florida courts generally will defer to an agency's interpretation of statutes and rules the agency is charged with implementing and enforcing.[11]
Florida courts, however, will not defer to an agency's opinion that is contrary to law.[12] We conclude that the Division's advisory opinion regarding
vote tabulation is contrary to law because it contravenes the plain meaning
of section 102.166(5).

Pursuant to section 102.166(4)(a), a candidate who appears on a ballot, a political committee that supports or opposes an issue that appears
on a ballot, or a political party whose candidate's name appears on the
ballot may file a written request with the County Board for a manual
recount. This request must be filed with the Board before the Board
certifies the election results or within seventy-two hours after the election, whichever occurs later.[13] Upon filing the written request for a manual
recount, the canvassing board may authorize a manual recount.[14] The
decision whether to conduct a manual recount is vested in the sound discretion of the Board.[15] If the canvassing board decides to authorize the
manual recount, the recount must include at least three precincts and at
least one percent of the total votes cast for each candidate or issue, with
the person who requested the recount choosing the precincts to be recounted.[16] If the manual recount indicates an "error in the vote tabulation
which could affect the outcome of the election," the county canvassing
board "shall":
(a) Correct the error and recount the remaining precincts with the vote
tabulation system;
(b) Request the Department of State to verify the tabulation software; *or*
(c) Manually recount all ballots. § 102.166(5)(a)–(c), Fla. Stat. (2000) (emphasis added)

The issue in dispute here is the meaning of the phrase "error in the vote
tabulation" found in section 102.166(5). The Division opines that an "error in the vote tabulation" only means a counting error resulting from
incorrect election parameters or an error in the vote tabulating software.
We disagree.

The plain language of section 102.166(5) refers to an error in the vote
tabulation rather than the vote tabulation system. On its face, the statute
does not include any words of limitation; rather, it provides a remedy for

any type of mistake made in tabulating ballots. The Legislature has utilized the phrase "vote tabulation system" and "automatic tabulating equipment" in section 102.166 when it intended to refer to the voting system rather than the vote count. Equating "vote tabulation" with "vote tabulation system" obliterates the distinction created in section 102.166 by the Legislature.

Sections 101.5614(5) and (6) also support the proposition that the "error in vote tabulation" encompasses more than a mere determination of whether the vote tabulation system is functioning. Section 101.5614(5) provides that "[n]o vote shall be declared invalid or void if there is a clear indication of the intent of the voter as determined by the canvassing board." Conversely, section 101.5614(6) provides that any vote in which the Board cannot discern the intent of the voter must be discarded. Taken together, these sections suggest that "error in the vote tabulation" includes errors in the failure of the voting machinery to read a ballot and not simply errors resulting from the voting machinery.

Moreover, section 102.141(4), which outlines the Board's responsibility in the event of a recount, states that the Board "shall examine the counters on the machines *or the tabulation of the ballots cast in each precinct* in which the office or issue appeared on the ballot and determine whether the returns correctly reflect the votes cast" § 102.141, Fla. Stat. (2000) (emphasis added). Therefore, an "error in the vote tabulation" includes a discrepancy between the number of votes determined by a voter tabulation system and the number of voters determined by a manual count of a sampling of precincts pursuant to section 102.166(4).

Although error cannot be completely eliminated in any tabulation of the ballots, our society has not yet gone so far as to place blind faith in machines. In almost all endeavors, including elections, humans routinely correct the errors of machines. For this very reason Florida law provides a human check on both the malfunction of tabulation equipment and error in failing to accurately count the ballots. Thus, we find that the Division's opinion DE 00-13 regarding the ability of county canvassing boards to authorize a manual recount is contrary to the plain language of the statute.

Having concluded that the county canvassing boards have the authority to order countywide manual recounts, we must now determine whether the Commission[17] must accept a return after the seven-day deadline set forth in sections 102.111 and 102.112 under the circumstances presented.

V. The Applicable Law

The abiding principle governing all election law in Florida is set forth in article I, section 1, Florida Constitution:

SECTION 1. Political power. All political power is inherent in the people. The enunciation herein of certain rights shall not be construed to deny or impair others retained by the people. Art. I, § 1, Fla. Const.

The constitution further provides that elections shall be regulated by law:

SECTION 1. Regulation of elections. All elections by the people shall be by direct and secret vote. General elections shall be determined by a plurality of votes cast. *Registration and elections shall, and political party functions may, be regulated by law*; however, the requirements for a candidate with no party affiliation or for a candidate of a minor party for placement of the candidate's name on the ballot shall be no greater than the requirements for a candidate of the party having the largest number of registered voters. Art. VI, § 1, Fla. Const. (emphasis added)

The Florida Election Code ("Code"), contained in chapters 97–106, Florida Statutes (2000), sets forth specific criteria regulating elections. The Florida Secretary of State is the chief election officer of the state and is charged with general oversight of the election system.[18] The Supervisor of Elections ("Supervisor") in each county is an elected official[19] and is charged with appointing two Election Boards for each precinct within the county prior to an election.[20] Each Election Board is composed of inspectors and clerks,[21] all of whom must be residents of the county,[22] and is charged with conducting the voting in the election, counting the votes,[23] and certifying the results to the Supervisor[24] by noon of the day following the election.[25] The County Canvassing Board ("Canvassing Board" or "Board"), which is composed of the Supervisor, a county court judge, and the chair of the board of county commissioners,[26] then canvasses the returns countywide,[27] reviews the certificates,[28] and transmits the returns for state and federal officers to the Florida Department of State ("Department") by 5:00 p.m. of the seventh day following the election.[29] No deadline is set for filing corrected, amended, or supplemental returns.

The Elections Canvassing Commission ("Canvassing Commission" or "Commission"), which is composed of the Governor, the Secretary of State, and the Director of the Division of Elections, canvasses the returns statewide, determines and declares who has been elected for each office, and issues a certificate of election for each office as soon as the results are compiled.[30] If any returns appear to be irregular or false and the Commission is unable to determine the true vote for a particular office, the Commission certifies that fact and does not include those returns in its canvass.[31] In determining the true vote, the Commission has no authority to look beyond the county's returns.[32] A candidate or elector can "protest" the returns of an election as being erroneous by filing a protest with the appropriate County Canvassing Board.[33] And finally, a candidate, elector, or taxpayer can "contest" the certification of election results by filing a post-certification action in circuit court within certain time limits[34] and setting forth specific grounds.[35]

VI. Statutory Ambiguity

The provisions of the Code are ambiguous in two significant areas. First, the time frame for conducting a manual recount under section 102.166(4) is in conflict with the time frame for submitting county returns under sections 102.111 and 102.112. Second, the mandatory language in section 102.111 conflicts with the permissive language in 102.112.

A. *The Recount Conflict*

Section 102.166(1) states that "any candidate for nomination or election, or any elector qualified to vote in the election related to such candidacy shall have the right to protest the returns of the election as being erroneous by filing with the appropriate canvassing board a sworn written protest." The time period for filing a protest is "prior to the time the canvassing board certifies the results for the office being protested or within 5 days after midnight of the date the election is held, whichever is later.

Section 102.166(4)(a), the operative subsection in this case, further provides that, in addition to any protest, "any candidate whose name appeared on the ballot . . . or any political party whose candidates' names appeared on the ballot may file a written request with the county canvassing board for a manual recount" accompanied by the "reason that the manual recount is being requested." Section 102.166(4)(b) further provides that the written request may be made prior to the time the Board certifies the returns or within seventy-two hours after the election, whichever occurs later:[36]

(4)(a) Any candidate whose name appeared on the ballot, any political committee that supports or opposes an issue which appeared on the ballot, or any political party whose candidates' names appeared on the ballot may file a written request with the county canvassing board for a manual recount. The written request shall contain a statement of the reason the manual recount is being requested.

(b) *Such a request must be filed with the canvassing board prior to the time the canvassing board certifies the results for the office being protested or within 72 hours after midnight of the date the election was held, whichever occurs later.*

§ 102.166, Fla. Stat. (2000) (emphasis added)

A Board "may" authorize a manual recount[37] and such a recount must include at least three precincts and at least one percent of the total votes cast for the candidate.[38] The following procedure then applies:

(5) If the manual recount indicates an error in the vote tabulation which could affect the outcome of the election, the county canvassing board shall:

(a) Correct the error and recount the remaining precincts with the vote tabulation system;

(b) Request the Department of State to verify the tabulation software; or

(c) Manually recount all ballots.

(6) Any manual recount shall be open to the public.

(7) Procedures for a manual recount are as follows:

(a) The county canvassing board shall appoint as many counting teams of at least two electors as is necessary to manually recount the ballots. A counting team must have, when possible, members of at least two political parties. A candidate involved in the race shall not be a member of the counting team.

(b) If a counting team is unable to determine a voter's intent in casting a ballot, the ballot shall be presented to the county canvassing board for it to determine the voter's intent.

§ 102.166, Fla. Stat. (2000)

Under this scheme, a candidate can request a manual recount at any point prior to certification by the Board and such action can lead to a full recount of all the votes in the county. Although the Code sets no specific deadline by which a manual recount must be completed, logic dictates that the period of time required to complete a full manual recount may be substantial, particularly in a populous county, and may require several days. The protest provision thus conflicts with sections 102.111 and 102.112, which state that the Boards "must" submit their returns to the Elections Canvassing Commission by 5:00 p.m. of the seventh day following the election or face penalties. For instance, if a party files a precertification protest on the sixth day following the election and requests a manual recount and the initial manual recount indicates that a full countywide recount is necessary, the recount procedure in most cases could not be completed by the deadline in sections 102.111 and 102.112, i.e., by 5:00 p.m. of the seventh day following the election.

B. *The "Shall" and "May" Conflict*

In addition to the conflict in the above statutes, sections 102.111 and 102.112 contain a dichotomy. Section 102.111, which sets forth general criteria governing the State Canvassing Commission, was enacted in 1951 as part of the Code and provides as follows:

102.111 Elections Canvassing Commission.

(1) Immediately after certification of any election by the county canvassing board, the results shall be forwarded to the Department of State concerning the election of any federal or state officer. The Governor, the Secretary of State, and the Director of the Division of Elections shall be the Elections Canvassing Commission. The Elections Canvassing Commission shall, as soon as the official results are compiled from all counties, certify the returns of the election and determine and declare who has been elected for each office. In the event that any member of the Elections Canvassing Commission is unavailable to certify the returns of any election, such member shall be replaced by a substitute member of the Cabinet as determined by the Director of the Division of Elections. *If the county returns are not received by the Department of State by 5 p.m. of the seventh day following an election, all missing counties shall be ignored,* and the results shown by the returns on file shall be certified.

§ 102.111, Fla. Stat. (2000) (emphasis added)

The Legislature in 1989 revised chapter 102 to include section 102.112, which provides that returns not received after a certain date "may" be ignored and that members of the County Board "shall" be fined:

102.112 Deadline for submission of county returns to the Department of State; penalties.

(1) The county canvassing board or a majority thereof shall file the county returns for the election of a federal or state officer with the Department of State immediately after the certification of the election results. Returns must be filed by 5 p.m. on the 7th day following the first primary and general election and by 3:00 p.m. on the 3rd day following the second primary. *If the returns are not received by the department by the time specified, such returns may be ignored* and the results on file at that time may be certified by the department.

(2) The department shall fine each board member $200 for each day such returns are late, the fine to be paid only from the board member's personal

funds. Such fines shall be deposited into the Election Campaign Financing Trust fund, created by § 106.32.

(3) Members of the county canvassing board may appeal such fines to the Florida Elections Commission, which shall adopt rules for such appeals.

§ 102.112, Fla. Stat. (2000) (emphasis added)

The above statutes conflict. Whereas section 102.111 is mandatory, section 102.112 is permissive. While it is clear that the Boards must submit returns by 5:00 p.m. of the seventh day following the election or face penalties, the circumstances under which penalties may be assessed are unclear.

VII. Legislative Intent

Legislative intent—as always—is the polestar that guides a court's inquiry into the provisions of the Florida Election Code.[39] Where the language of the Code is clear and amenable to a reasonable and logical interpretation, courts are without power to diverge from the intent of the Legislature as expressed in the plain language of the Code.[40] As noted above, however, chapter 102 is unclear concerning both the time limits for submitting the results of a manual recount and the penalties that may be assessed by the Secretary. In light of this ambiguity, the Court must resort to traditional rules of statutory construction in an effort to determine legislative intent.[41]

First, it is well settled that where two statutory provisions are in conflict, the specific statute controls the general statute.[42] In the present case, whereas section 102.111 in its title and text addresses the general makeup and duties of the Elections Canvassing Commission, the statute only tangentially addresses the penalty for returns filed after the statutory date, noting that such returns "shall" be ignored by the Department. Section 102.112, on the other hand, directly addresses in its title and text both the "deadline" for submitting returns and the "penalties" for submitting returns after a certain date; the statute expressly states that such returns "may" be ignored and that dilatory Board members "shall" be fined. Based on the precision of the title and text, section 102.112 constitutes a specific penalty statute that defines both the deadline for filing returns and the penalties for filing returns thereafter, and section 102.111 constitutes a non-specific statute in this regard. The specific statute controls the non-specific statute.

Second, it also is well settled that when two statutes are in conflict, the more recently enacted statute controls the older statute.[43] In the present case, the provision in section 102.111 stating that the Department "shall" ignore returns was enacted in 1951 as part of the Code. On the other hand, the penalty provision in section 102.112 stating that the Department "may" ignore returns was enacted in 1989 as a revision to chapter 102. The more recently enacted provision may be viewed as the clearest and most recent expression of legislative intent.

Third, a statutory provision will not be construed in such a way that it renders meaningless or absurd any other statutory provision.[44] In the present case, section 102.112 contains a detailed provision authorizing the assessment of fines against members of a dilatory County Canvassing Board. The fines are personal and substantial, i.e., $200 for each day the returns are not received. If, as the Secretary asserts, the Department were required to ignore all returns received after the statutory date, the fine provision would be meaningless. For example, if a Board simply completed its count late and if the returns were going to be ignored in any event, what would be the point in submitting the returns? The Board would simply file no returns and avoid the fines. But, on the other hand, if the returns submitted after the statutory date would not be ignored, the Board would have good reason to submit the returns and accept the fines. The fines thus serve as an alternative penalty and are applicable only if the Department may count the returns.

Fourth, related statutory provisions must be read as a cohesive whole.[45] As stated in *Forsythe v. Longboat Key Beach Erosion Control Dist.*, 604 So. 2d 452, 455 (Fla. 1992), "all parts of a statute must be read together in order to achieve a consistent whole. Where possible, courts must give effect to all statutory provisions and construe related statutory provisions in harmony with another." In this regard we consider the provisions of section 102.166 and 102.168.

Section 102.166 states that a candidate, political committee, or political party may request a manual recount any time before the County Canvassing Board certifies the results to the Department and, if the initial manual recount indicates a significant error, the Board "shall" conduct a countywide manual recount in certain cases. Thus, if a protest is filed on the sixth day following an election and a full manual recount is required, the Board, through no fault of its own, will be unable to submit its returns to the Department by 5:00 p.m. on the seventh day following the election. In such a case, if the mandatory provision in section 102.111 were given effect, the votes of the county would be ignored for the simple reason that the Board was following the dictates of a different section of the Code. The

Legislature could not have intended to penalize County Canvassing Boards for following the dictates of the Code.

And finally, when the Legislature enacted the Code in 1951, it envisioned that all votes cast during a particular election, including absentee ballots, would be submitted to the Department at one time and would be treated in a uniform fashion. Section 97.012(1) states that it is the Secretary's responsibility to "[o]btain and maintain uniformity in the application, operation, and interpretation of the election laws." Chapter 101 provides that all votes, including absentee ballots, must be received by the Supervisor no later than 7:00 p.m. on the day of the election. Section 101.68(2)(d) expressly states that "[t]he votes on absentee ballots shall be included in the total vote of the county." Chapter 102 requires that the Board submit the returns by 5:00 p.m. on the seventh day following the election.

The Legislature thus envisioned that when returns are submitted to the Department, the returns "shall" embrace all the votes in the county, including absentee ballots. This, of course, is not possible because our state statutory scheme has been superseded by federal law governing overseas voters;[46] overseas ballots must be counted if received no later than ten days following the election (i.e., the ballots do *not* have to be received by 7:00 p.m. of the day of the election, as provided by state law).[47] In light of the fact that overseas ballots cannot be counted until after the seven-day deadline has expired, the mandatory language in section 102.111 has been supplanted by the permissive language of section 102.112.

Further, although county returns must be received by 5:00 p.m. on the seventh day following an election, the "official results" that are to be compiled in order to certify the returns and declare who has been elected must be construed in pari materia with section 101.5614(8), which specifies that "write-in, absentee *and manually counted results* shall constitute the official return of the election." (Emphasis added.)

Under this statutory scheme, the County Canvassing Boards are required to submit their returns to the Department by 5:00 p.m. of the seventh day following the election. The statutes make no provision for exceptions following a manual recount. If a Board fails to meet the deadline, the Secretary is not required to ignore the county's returns but rather is permitted to ignore the returns within the parameters of this statutory scheme. To determine the circumstances under which the Secretary may lawfully ignore returns filed pursuant to the provisions of section 102.166

for a manual recount, it is necessary to examine the interplay between our statutory and constitutional law at both the state and federal levels.

[SECTION VIII. NOT INCLUDED in this extract]

IX. The Present Case

The trial court below properly concluded that the County Canvassing Boards are required to submit their returns to the Department by 5:00 p.m. of the seventh day following the election and that the Department is not required to ignore the amended returns but rather may count them. The court, however, erred in holding that the Secretary acted within her discretion in prematurely rejecting any amended returns that would be the result of ongoing manual recounts. The Secretary's rationale for rejecting the Board's returns was as follows:

The Board has not alleged any facts or circumstances that suggest the existence of voter fraud. The Board has not alleged any facts or circumstances that suggest that there has been substantial noncompliance with the state's statutory election procedures, coupled with reasonable doubt as to whether the certified results expressed the will of the voters. The Board has not alleged any facts or circumstances that suggest that Palm Beach County has been unable to comply with its election duties due to an act of God, or other extenuating circumstances that are beyond its control. The Board has alleged the *possibility* that the results of the manual recount *could* affect the outcome of the election if certain results obtain. However, absent an assertion that there has been substantial noncompliance with the law, I do not believe that the *possibility* of affecting the outcome of the election is enough to justify ignoring the statutory deadline. Furthermore, I find that the facts and circumstances alleged, standing alone, do not rise to the level of extenuating circumstances that justify a decision on my part to ignore the statutory deadline imposed by the Florida Legislature.

Letter from Katherine Harris to Palm Beach Canvassing Board (Nov. 15, 2000)(emphasis added)

We conclude that, consistent with the Florida election scheme, the Secretary may reject a Board's amended returns only if the returns are submitted so late that their inclusion will preclude a candidate from contesting the certification or preclude Florida's voters from participating fully in the federal electoral process. The Secretary in the present case has made no claim that either of these conditions apply at this point in time.

The above analysis is consistent with *State ex rel. Chappell v. Martinez*,

536 So. 2d 1007 (Fla. 1988), wherein the Court addressed a comparable recount issue. There, the total votes cast for each of two candidates for a seat in the United State House of Representatives were separated by less than one-half of one percent; the county conducted a mandatory recount; the Board's certification of results was not received by the Department until two days after the deadline, although the Board had telephoned the results to the Department prior to the deadline; and the unsuccessful candidate sued to prevent the Department from counting the late votes. The Court concluded that the will of the electors supersedes any technical statutory requirements:

[T]he electorate's effecting its will through its balloting, not the hypertechnical compliance with statutes, is the object of holding an election. "There is no magic in the statutory requirements. If they are complied with to the extent that the duly responsible election officials can ascertain that the electors whose votes are being canvassed are qualified and registered to vote, and that they do so in a proper manner, then who can be heard to complain the statute has not been literally and absolutely complied with?"

Chappell, 536 So. 2d at 1008–09 (quoting *Boardman v. Esteva,* 323 So. 2d 259, 267 (Fla. 1975)

X. Conclusion

According to the legislative intent evinced in the Florida Election Code, the permissive language of section 102.112 supersedes the mandatory language of section 102.111. The statutory fines set forth in section 102.112 offer strong incentive to County Canvassing Boards to submit their returns in a timely fashion. However, when a Board certifies its returns after the seven-day period because the Board is acting in conformity with other provisions of the Code or with administrative rules or for other good cause, the Secretary may impose no fines. It is unlikely that the Legislature would have intended to punish a Board for complying with the dictates of the Code or some other law.

Because the right to vote is the preeminent right in the Declaration of Rights of the Florida Constitution, the circumstances under which the Secretary may exercise her authority to ignore a county's returns filed after the initial statutory date are limited. The Secretary may ignore such returns only if their inclusion will compromise the integrity of the electoral process in either of two ways: (1) by precluding a candidate, elector, or taxpayer from contesting the certification of election pursuant to section

102.168; or (2) by precluding Florida voters from participating fully in the federal electoral process. In either such case, this drastic penalty must be both reasonable and necessary. But to allow the Secretary to summarily disenfranchise innocent electors in an effort to punish dilatory Board members, as she proposes in the present case, misses the constitutional mark. The constitution eschews punishment by proxy.

As explained above, the Florida Election Code must be construed as a whole. Section 102.166 governs manual recounts and appears to conflict with sections 102.111 and 102.112, which set a seven-day deadline by which County Boards must submit their returns. Further, section 102.111, which provides that the Secretary "shall" ignore late returns, conflicts with section 102.112, which provides that the Secretary "may" ignore late returns. In the present case, we have used traditional rules of statutory construction to resolve these ambiguities to the extent necessary to address the issues presented here. We decline to rule more expansively, for to do so would result in this Court substantially rewriting the Code. We leave that matter to the sound discretion of the body best equipped to address it—the Legislature.

Because of the unique circumstances and extraordinary importance of the present case, wherein the Florida Attorney General and the Florida Secretary of State have issued conflicting advisory opinions concerning the propriety of conducting manual recounts, and because of our reluctance to rewrite the Florida Election Code, we conclude that we must invoke the equitable powers of this Court to fashion a remedy that will allow a fair and expeditious resolution of the questions presented here.[56]

Accordingly, in order to allow maximum time for contests pursuant to section 102.168, amended certifications must be filed with the Elections Canvassing Commission by 5:00 p.m. on Sunday, November 26, 2000, and the Secretary of State and the Elections Canvassing Commission shall accept any such amended certifications received by 5:00 p.m. on Sunday, November 26, 2000, provided that the office of the Secretary of State, Division of Elections, is open in order to allow receipt thereof. If the office is not open for this special purpose on Sunday, November 26, 2000, then any amended certifications shall be accepted until 9:00 a.m. on Monday, November 27, 2000. The stay order entered on November 17, 2000, by this Court shall remain in effect until the expiration of the time for accepting amended certifications set forth in this opinion. The certificates made and signed by the Elections Canvassing Commission pursuant to section

102.121 shall include the amended returns accepted through the dates set forth in this opinion.

It is so ordered. No motion for rehearing will be allowed.

WELLS, C. J., and SHAW, HARDING, ANSTEAD, PARIENTE, LEWIS and QUINCE, J. J., concur.

Notes

1. The Palm Beach County Canvassing Board has filed in this Court an "Emergency Petition for Extraordinary Writ" against Secretary of State Katherine Harris and others (Case Number SC00-2346). We have examined our jurisdiction under article V, section 3(b)(8) of the Florida Constitution. However, because the issue raised by that separate petition can be disposed of in our pending case and because we have previously stated in our order of November 16, 2000, that there was "no legal impediment" to the manual recounts continuing, we deem it unnecessary to determine if we have a separate basis of jurisdiction for entertaining the writ. Accordingly, by separate order we dismiss the petition.

2. Section 102.141(4), Florida Statutes (2000), provides in pertinent part:
(4) If the returns for any office reflect that a candidate was defeated or eliminated by one-half of a percent or less of the votes cast for such office . . . the board responsible for certifying the results of the vote on such race or measure shall order a recount of the votes cast with respect to such office or measure.

3. We have not discussed the events in Miami-Dade County because Miami-Dade is not a party nor has it sought to intervene in this case.

4. The trial court's order reads in part:
The County Canvassing Boards are, indeed, mandated to certify and file their returns with the Secretary of State by 5:00 p.m. today, November 14, 2000. There is nothing, however, to prevent the County Canvassing Boards from filing with the Secretary of State further returns after completing a manual recount. It is then up to the Secretary of state, as the Chief Election Officer, to determine whether any such corrective or supplemental returns filed after 5:00 p.m. today are to be ignored. Just as the County Canvassing Boards have the authority to exercise discretion in determining whether a manual recount should be done, the Secretary of State has the authority to exercise her discretion in reviewing that decision, considering all attendant facts and circumstances, and decide whether to include or to ignore the late filed returns in certifying the election results and declaring the winner.

Just as the Secretary cannot decide ahead of time what late returns should or should not be ignored, it would not be proper for me to do so by injunction. I can lawfully direct the Secretary to properly exercise her discretion in making a decision on the returns, but I cannot enjoin the Secretary to make a particular decision, nor can I rewrite the Statute which, by its plain meaning, mandates the filing of returns by the Canvassing Boards by 5:00 p.m. on November 14, 2000. *McDermott v. Harris*, No. 00-2700, unpublished order at 7 (Fla. 2d Cir. Ct. Nov. 14, 2000)

5. The criteria considered by the Secretary are as follows:

Facts & Circumstances Warranting Waiver of Statutory Deadline

1. Where there is proof of voter fraud that affects the outcome of the election. *In re Protest of Election Returns*, 707 So. 2d 1170, 1172 (Fla. 3d DCA 1998); *Broward County Canvassing Bd. v. Hogan*, 607 So. 2d 508, 509 (Fla. 4th DCA 1992).

2. Where there has been a substantial noncompliance with statutory election procedures, and reasonable doubt exists as to whether the certified results expressed the will of the voters. *Beckstrom v. Volusia County Canvassing Bd.*, 707 So. 2d 720 (Fla. 1998).

3. Where election officials have made a good faith effort to comply with the statutory deadline and are prevented from timely complying with their duties as a result of an act of God, or extenuating circumstances beyond their control, by way of example, an electrical power outage, a malfunction of the transmitting equipment, or a mechanical malfunction of the voting tabulation system. *McDermott v. Harris*, No. 00-2700 (Fla. 2d Cir. Ct. Nov. 14, 2000).

Facts & Circumstances Not Warranting Waiver of Statutory Deadline

1. Where there has been substantial compliance with statutory election procedures and the contested results relate to voter error, and there exists a reasonable expectation that the certified results expressed the will of the voters. *Beckstrom. Volusia County Canvassing Bd.*, 707 So. 2d 720 (Fla. 1998).

2. Where there exists a ballot that may be confusing because of the alignment and location of the candidates' names, but is otherwise in substantial compliance with the election laws. *Nelson v. Robinson*, 301 So. 2d 508, 511 (Fla. 2d DCA 1974) ("[M]ere confusion does not amount to an impediment to the voters' free choice if reasonable time and study will sort it out").

3. Where there is nothing "more than a mere possibility that the outcome of the election would have been affected." *Broward County Canvassing Bd. v. Hogan*, 607 So. 2d 508, 510 (Fla. 4th DCA 1992). Letter from Katherine Harris to Palm Beach County Canvassing Board (Nov. 15, 2000).

6. The court's order reads in part:

On the limited evidence presented, it appears that the Secretary has exercised her reasoned judgment to determine what relevant factors and criteria should be considered, applied them to the facts and circumstances pertinent to the individual counties involved, and made her decision. My order requires nothing more. *McDermott v. Harris*, No. 00-2700, unpublished order at 2 (Fla. 2d Cir. Ct. Nov. 17, 2000).

7. *See* Art. V, § 3(b)(5), Fla. Const. ("[The Court may] review any order or judgment of a trial court certified by the district court of appeal in which an appeal

is pending to be of great public importance . . . and certified to require immediate resolution by the supreme court").

8. Subsequently, the Volusia Board moved to voluntarily dismiss its appeal in this Court. The Court granted the motion, but indicated that the case style would remain the same and that Gore and the Palm Beach Board "would continue as intervenors/appellants in this action."

9. *See State ex rel. Chappell v. Martinez*, 536 So. 2d 1007, 1009 (Fla. 1988) (holding that disenfranchisement of voters is not proper where there has been substantial compliance with the election statute and the intent of voter can be ascertained); *Beckstrom v. Volusia County Canvassing Bd.*, 707 So. 2d 720, 726 (Fla. 1998) (holding that courts should not frustrate will of voters if that will can be determined).

10. Neither party has raised as an issue on appeal the constitutionality of Florida's election laws.

11. *See Donato v. American Tel. & Tel. Co.*, 767 So. 2d 1146, 1153 (Fla. 2000); *Smith v. Crawford*, 645 So. 2d 513, 521 (Fla. 1st DCA 1994).

12. *See Donato*, 767 So. 2d at 1153; *Nikolits v. Nicosia*, 682 So. 2d 663, 666 (Fla. 4th DCA 1996).

13. § 102.166(4)(b), Fla. Stat. (2000).

14. § 102.166(4)(c), Fla. Stat. (2000).

15. *See Broward County Canvassing Bd. v. Hogan*, 607 So. 2d 508, 510 (Fla. 4th DCA 1992).

16. *See* § 102.166(4)(d), Fla. Stat. (2000).

17. The Commission is composed of the Secretary of State, the Director of the Division of Elections, and the Governor. *See* § 102.111, Fla. Stat. In this instance, Florida Governor Jeb Bush has removed himself from the Commission because his brother, Texas Governor George W. Bush, is the Republican candidate for President of the United States. Robert Crawford, Florida Commissioner of Agriculture, has been appointed to replace Florida Governor Jeb Bush. *See* § 102.111, Fla. Stat.

18. § 97.012, Fla. Stat. (2000).

19. § 98.015, Fla. Stat. (2000).

20. § 102.012(1), Fla. Stat. (2000).

21. § 102.012(1), Fla. Stat. (2000).

22. § 102.012(2), Fla. Stat. (2000).

23. § 102.012(4), Fla. Stat. (2000).

24. § 102.071, Fla. Stat. (2000).

25. § 102.141(3), Fla. Stat. (2000).

26. § 102.141(1), Fla. Stat. (2000).

27. § 102.141(2), Fla. Stat. (2000).

28. § 102.141 (3), Fla. Stat. (2000).

29. §§ 102.111–.112, Fla. Stat. (2000).

30. §§ 102.111, .121, Fla. Stat. (2000).

31. § 102.131, Fla. Stat. (2000) ("If any returns shall appear to be irregular or false so that the Elections Canvassing Commission is unable to determine the true vote for any office . . . the commission shall so certify and shall not include the returns in its determination, canvass, and declaration").

32. § 102.131, Fla. Stat. (2000) ("The Elections Canvassing Commission in determining the true vote shall not have authority to look beyond the county returns").

33. § 102.166, Fla. Stat. (2000).

34. *See* § 102.168(2), Fla. Stat. (2000) (explaining that the action must be filed within ten days after the last Board certifies its returns or within five days after the last Board certifies its returns following a protest).

35. The grounds for contesting an election are set forth in section 102.168(3), Florida Statutes (2000):

(a) Misconduct, fraud, or corruption . . . sufficient to change or place in doubt the result of the election.

(b) Ineligibility of the successful candidate. . . .

(c) Receipt of a number of illegal votes or rejection of a number of legal votes sufficient to change or place in doubt the result of the election.

(d) Proof that any elector, election official or canvassing board member was given or offered a bribe. . . .

(e) Any other cause or allegation which, if sustained, would show that a person other than the successful candidate was the person duly nominated or elected to the office in question.

36. As discussed in *Siegel v. Lepore*, 2000 WL 1687185 *6 (S.D. Fla. 2000):

On its face, the manual recount provision does not limit candidates access to the ballot or interfere with voters' right to associate or vote. Instead the manual recount provision is intended to safeguard the integrity and reliability of the electoral process by providing a structural means of detecting and correcting clerical or electronic tabulating errors in the counting of election ballots. While discretionary in its application, the provision is not wholly standardless. Rather, the central purpose of the scheme, as evidenced by its plain language, is to remedy "an error in the vote tabulation which could affect the outcome of the election." Fla. Stat. §102.166(5). In this pursuit, the provision strives to strengthen rather than dilute the right to vote by securing, as nearly as humanly possible, an accurate and true reflection of the will of the electorate. Notably, the four county canvassing boards [that were] challenged in this suit have reported various anomalies in the initial automated count and recount. The state manual recount provision therefore serves important governmental interests.

37. The statute does not set forth any criteria for determining when a manual recount is appropriate. *See* § 102.166(4)(c), Fla. Stat. (2000) ("The county canvassing board may authorize a manual recount").

38. § 102.166(4)(d), Fla. Stat. (2000).

39. *See, e.g., Florida Birth-Related Neurological Injury Compensation Ass'n v. Florida Div. of Admin. Hearings,* 686 So. 2d 1349 (Fla. 1997).

40. *See, e.g., Starr Tyme, Inc. v. Cohen,* 659 So. 2d 1064 (Fla. 1995).

41. *See, e.g., Capers v. State,* 678 So. 2d 330 (Fla. 1996).

42. *See, e.g., State ex rel. Johnson v. Vizzini,* 227 So. 2d 205 (Fla. 1969).

43. *See, e.g., McKendry v. State,* 641 So. 2d 45 (Fla. 1994).

44. *See, e.g., Amente v. Newman,* 653 So. 2d 1030 (Fla. 1995).

45. *See, e.g., Sun Ins. Office, Ltd. v. Clay,* 133 So. 2d 735 (Fla. 1961).

46. According to the Secretary, this matter is governed by consent decree with the federal government.

47. *See* Fla. Admin. Code R.1S-2.013 (1998), which provides in relevant part: (7) With respect to the presidential preference primary and the general election, any absentee ballot cast for a federal office by an overseas elector which is postmarked or signed and dated no later than the date of the Federal election shall be counted if received no later than 10 days from the date of the Federal election so long as such absentee ballot is otherwise proper. Overseas electors shall be informed by the supervisors of elections of the provisions of this rule, i.e., the ten-day extension provision for the presidential preference primary and the general election, and the provision for voting for the second primary.

56. At oral argument, we inquired as to whether the presidential candidates were interested in our consideration of a reopening of the opportunity to request recounts in any additional counties. Neither candidate requested such an opportunity.

Excerpts from Bush's First Motion on Equal Treatment Issues

Following are excerpts from two filings in the United States Supreme Court. The first asks for quick action on an appeal of a ruling by the United States Court of Appeals for the 11th Circuit. The second excerpt is the appeal itself.

Motion to Expedite Consideration

This is a case of the utmost national importance, involving the Constitution's most fundamental rights as exercised in the nation's most important election. The outcome of the election for the presidency of the United States may hang in the balance.

Petitioners Bush and Cheney received the most votes in the state of Florida in the presidential election held Nov. 7, 2000. That result was confirmed by a statewide recount and confirmed again after a tabulation of overseas absentee ballots. Yet the Supreme Court of Florida has prevented state officials from certifying the appointment of electors in accordance with the popular vote. Instead, state officials have been compelled to postpone any final decision pending the completion of a selective, capricious and standardless manual count of ballots cast in only a handful of unrepresentative Florida counties. As explained in greater detail in the accompanying petition for certiorari, the manual recount currently being conducted is riddled with severe and pervasive irregularities, including the physical manipulation and degradation of ballots, manifest inconsistencies in counting methods, and a politically charged, partisan atmosphere, all of which have combined to spawn a process that now borders on anarchy.

Petitioners seek a writ of certiorari to review the constitutionality of these arbitrary and ad hoc recount procedures, which are being employed in an apparent effort to influence after the fact the will of the citizens of Florida and possibly to change the outcome of the presidential election. Review by this Court is warranted to ensure the legality, fairness and legitimacy of the election.

This Court's expedited consideration of the petition is warranted to halt the ongoing rampant violations of petitioners' constitutional rights, to address events that are turning the presidential election in Florida into a circus, and to restore stability by bringing the 2000 presidential election to orderly finality in accordance with constitutional law.

Time is plainly of the essence: Florida must certify its representatives to the Electoral College before Dec. 18, 2000, the date on which the College meets to select the next President and Vice President of the United States. If this matter is not resolved prior to that time, not only petitioners but the nation as a whole may suffer injury from the resulting confusion. Indeed, the intense national and worldwide attention on the recount efforts to date only foreshadows the disruption that may well follow if the uncertainty and unfairness that have shrouded this election are allowed to persist. Simply put, the importance of a prompt resolution of the federal constitutional questions presented by this case cannot be overstated.

Should this Court grant the petition for certiorari, an expedited briefing schedule is necessary for the same reasons. Particularly given the importance of the issues presented, it is in the best interests of the parties, as well as the nation, that this Court have as much time as possible to consider the relative merits of the parties' positions and to issue its decision sufficiently in advance of the Electoral College's selection of the next president and vice president on Dec. 18, 2000.

This Court has previously granted expedited treatment of cases involving substantial questions of national importance. The importance of this case is at least equal to, if not greater than, those landmark decisions. The presidency itself is at stake.

Accordingly, petitioners respectfully submit that respondents should be directed to file their response(s) to the petition by 9:00 a.m. on Friday, Nov. 24, 2000; that petitioners submit their reply brief in support of certiorari by 9:00 a.m. on Saturday, Nov. 25; and that the Court issue its ruling on the petition as soon as practicable thereafter.

If certiorari is granted, petitioners submit that opening briefs for petitioners and respondents, together with any amicus curiae briefs, should be filed and served by 7:00 p.m. on Wednesday, Nov. 29, 2000; that reply briefs for petitioners and respondents should be filed and served by 7:00 p.m. on Friday, Dec. 1, 2000; and that oral arguments should be held on the afternoon of Tuesday, Dec. 5, 2000.

Petition for Writ of Certiorari

The selective manual recount process has unquestionably damaged ballot integrity. Representatives of the county respondents have admitted that the more the ballots are handled, the more chads will fall off, making it more likely that the ballot recount (and any future recount under constitutional standards) will produce different numbers from this cause alone. Observers of the manual recounts have consistently reported that ballots have been bent, prodded, poked and aggressively handled. Ballots have been twisted, crumpled, creased, and dropped; some have been stained with ink with pens, and crushed. In some instances, the ballots were even used as fans.

Unsurprisingly, this aggressive mishandling of ballots, especially after two or more machine counts of the ballots, dislodged large numbers of chads, which littered the floors of the recount rooms. When observers attempted to memorialize the presence of dislodged chads, Democratic officials and county employees attempted to sweep away the chads rather than have the physical degradation documented.

Thus, ballots that survive the repeated mechanical and manual recounts to which they have been subjected may not resemble the ballots Floridians actually cast on Nov. 7, and the tabulations that result from this process cannot be said to be an accurate, fair or consistent tabulation of the votes cast by Floridians in that election.

The manual recount process is chaotic, hanging and uncertain. Differing and sometimes self-contradictory guidelines were issued and then retracted.

Other rules were not communicated to the ballot counters. The inevitable result was a complete lack of uniformity across the four counties and within the counties.

For example, a representative of the Palm Beach Board admitted that during the initial manual recount the board had applied inconsistent tests and procedures for determining which ballots to count and had changed its approach to that crucial issue midstream. According to another Palm Beach Board official, the standard for determining which ballots to count manually "is very vague in the law," and "the canvassing board . . . make[s] the rules . . . They can do what they want as far as once they decide amongst themselves."

In Miami-Dade County, the supervisor of elections asked the canvassing board to define the criteria that would be employed in conducting the remaining partial manual recount. In response, the chairman of the board stated that he could not know whether to count a ballot "until I reasonably see it." As he elaborated, "I don't think we should limit ourselves in the parameters by which we would consider. . . . I believe that we will know when we see, so to speak, what we are looking at . . ." The board thus declined to set any standards, leaving the question of which ballots were to be counted to ad hoc, case-by-case discretion applied by officials acting with full knowledge of the election results elsewhere.

As Respondent Florida Democratic Party conceded in its Answer Brief in the Florida Supreme Court, "Different canvassing boards are using different standards. In fact, the Florida Democratic Party (F.D.P.) has sued to insure this divergence occurs.

These widely varying policies (or lack of policies), and the confusing legal challenges to them, have translated into severe problems in the vote tabulating process itself. In Broward County for example, the two-corner rule has apparently not been well communicated to the counters and is, in any event, under legal attack. Other internal counting rules, such as double-counting final stacks of ballots, have been announced, temporarily applied, and then rescinded. In general, confusion, disarray and mistakes are commonplace in the vote-counting process.

The lack of intelligible, uniform standards fatally undermines any claim that manual recounting actually captures the intent of the voters.

The atmosphere has become politically charged with pressure being exerted on the county boards and their lawyers by prominent political figures such as former Secretary of State and current Gore campaign spokesperson Warren Christopher and Florida Attorney General Robert Butterworth. Indeed, observers also noted that the elections officers exhibited partisan bias and even hostility. (guidance to ballot counters expressed hostility to Republican attorney observers and implied that a Republican president would endanger the economy and increase the chances of war). Such external political pressure obviously increases the likelihood that conscious or unconscious bias will further taint the recount.

Other signs of politically driven decision making proliferate. For example, the Broward County Canvassing Boards originally decided not to authorize a countywide manual recount, but then reversed that decision in a 2–1 vote after extensive political lobbying. Media reports have widely recounted the erratic nature of the various canvassing boards and their decisions whether to proceed with manual recounts. The on-again, off-again process further illustrates the unchecked nature of the County Respondents' discretion, and demonstrates that the recounts do not provide a stable, fair, deliberate and objective counting of ballots. . . .

This case is extraordinary. It raises issues of imperative public importance seen only once in a generation. Indeed, not since *United States v. Nixon* (1974) have questions of similar magnitude been brought before this court. . . . This Court's direct and immediate review of the lower courts' refusal to halt the selective manual recount is warranted because this case "is of such imperative public importance" that the Court should deviate from normal appellate practice. As discussed in greater detail below, this case presents important questions regarding the First and Fourteenth Amendments' protections for the fundamental right to vote. Moreover, these questions are presented in the context of one of the closest elections for president in our nation's history.

There is a profound national interest in ensuring the fairness and finality of elections, particularly in an election for the highest office in the land. The constitutionality of the arbitrary recount process currently being implemented by the county respondents in this crucial election presents precisely the type of question that the nation justifiably expects should be decided by this Court. Indeed, absent a decision by this Court, the election results from Florida may lack finality and legitimacy. The consequences may well include the ascension of a President of questionable legitimacy, or a constitutional crisis.

Cite as: 531 U.S. ____ (2000) 1

SCALIA, J., concurring

SUPREME COURT OF THE UNITED STATES

No. 00-949 (00A504)

GEORGE W. BUSH ET AL. v. ALBERT GORE, JR. ET AL.

ON APPLICATION FOR STAY

[December 9, 2000]

The application for stay presented to JUSTICE KENNEDY and by him referred to the Court is granted, and it is ordered that the mandate of the Florida Supreme Court, case No. SC00-2431, is hereby stayed pending further order of the Court. In addition, the application for stay is treated as a petition for a writ of certiorari, and the petition for a writ of certiorari is granted. The briefs of the parties, not to exceed 50 pages, are to be filed with the Clerk and served upon opposing counsel on or before 4:00 p.m. Sunday, December 10, 2000. Rule 29.2 is suspended in this case. Briefs may be filed in compliance with Rule 33.2 to be replaced as soon as possible with briefs prepared in compliance with Rule 33.1. The case is set for oral argument on Monday, December 11, 2000, at 11:00 a.m., and a total of one and one-half hours is allotted for oral argument.

JUSTICE SCALIA, concurring. Though it is not customary for the Court to issue an opinion in connection with its grant of a stay, I believe a brief response is necessary to JUSTICE STEVENS' dissent. I will not address the merits of the case, since they will shortly be before us in the petition for certiorari that we have granted. It suffices to say that the issuance of the stay suggests that a majority of the Court, while not deciding the issues presented, believe that the petitioner has a substantial probability of success. On the question of irreparable harm, however, a few words are appropriate. The issue is not, as the dissent puts it, whether "[c]ounting every legally cast vote [can] constitute irreparable harm." One of the principal issues in the appeal we have accepted is precisely whether the votes that have been ordered to be counted are, under a reasonable interpretation of Florida law, "legally cast vote[s]." The counting of votes that are of questionable legality does in my view threaten irreparable harm to petitioner, and to the country, by casting a cloud upon what he claims to be the legitimacy of his election. Count first, and rule upon legality afterwards, is not a recipe for producing election results that have the public acceptance democratic stability requires. Another issue in the case, moreover, is the propriety, indeed the constitutionality, of letting the standard for determination of voters' intent—dimpled chads, hanging chads, etc.—vary from county to county, as the Florida Supreme Court opinion, as interpreted by the Circuit Court, permits. If petitioner is correct that counting in this fashion is unlawful, permitting the count to proceed on that erroneous basis will prevent an accurate recount from being conducted on a proper basis later, since it is generally agreed that each manual recount produces a degradation of the ballots, which renders a subsequent recount inaccurate.

For these reasons I have joined the Court's issuance of stay, with a highly accelerated timetable for resolving this case on the merits.

Cite as: 531 U.S. ____ (2000) 1
STEVENS, J., dissenting
SUPREME COURT OF THE UNITED STATES
No. 00-949 (00A504)
GEORGE W. BUSH ET AL. v. ALBERT GORE, JR. ET AL.
ON APPLICATION FOR STAY
[December 9, 2000]

JUSTICE STEVENS, with whom JUSTICE SOUTER, JUSTICE GINSBURG, and JUSTICE BREYER join, dissenting.

To stop the counting of legal votes, the majority today departs from three venerable rules of judicial restraint that have guided the Court throughout its history. On questions of state law, we have consistently respected the opinions of the highest courts of the States. On questions whose resolution is committed at least in large measure to another branch of the Federal Government, we have construed our own jurisdiction narrowly and exercised it cautiously. On federal constitutional questions that were not fairly presented to the court whose judgment is being reviewed, we have prudently declined to express an opinion. The majority has acted unwisely. Time does not permit a full discussion of the merits. It is clear, however, that a stay should not be granted unless an applicant makes a substantial showing of a likelihood of irreparable harm. In this case, applicants have failed to carry that heavy burden. Counting every legally cast vote cannot constitute irreparable harm. On the other hand, there is a danger that a stay may cause irreparable harm to the respondents—and, more importantly, the public at large—because of the risk that "the entry of the stay would be tantamount to a decision on the merits in favor of the applicants." *National Socialist Party of America v. Skokie*, 434 U.S. 1327, 1328 (1977) (STEVENS, J., in chambers). Preventing the recount from being completed will inevitably cast a cloud on the legitimacy of the election. It is certainly not clear that the Florida decision violated federal law. The Florida Code provides elaborate procedures for ensuring that every eligible voter has a full and fair opportunity to cast a ballot and that every ballot so cast is counted. See, e.g., Fla. Stat. §§ 101.5614(5), 102.166 (2000). In fact, the statutory provision relating to damaged and defective ballots states that "[n]o vote shall be declared invalid or void if there is a clear indication of the intent of the voter as determined by the canvassing board." Fla. Stat. § 101.5614(5) (2000). In its opinion, the Florida Supreme Court gave weight to that legislative command. Its ruling was consistent with earlier Florida cases that have repeatedly described the interest in correctly ascertaining the will of the voters as paramount. See *State ex rel. Chappell v. Martinez*, 536 So. 2d 1007 (1998); *Boardman v. Esteva*, 323 So. 2d 259 (1976); *McAlpin v. State ex rel. Avriett*, 19 So. 2d 420 (1944); *State ex rel. Peacock v. Latham*, 169 So. 597, 598 (1936); *State ex rel. Carpenter v. Barber*, 198 So. 49 (1940). Its ruling also appears to be consistent with the prevailing view in other States. See, e.g., *Pullen v. Milligan*, __ Ill.2d __, 561 N. E. 2d 585, 611 (Ill. 1990). As a more fundamental matter, the Florida court's ruling reflects the basic principle, inherent in our Constitution and our democracy, that every legal vote should be counted. See *Reynolds v. Sims*, 377 U.S. 533, 544–555 (1964); cf. *Hartke v. Roudebush*, 321 F. Supp. 1370, 1378–1379. (SD Ind. 1970) (STEVENS, J., dissenting); accord *Roudebush v. Hartke*, 405 U.S. 15 (1972). Accordingly, I respectfully dissent.

(Slip Opinion) Cite as: 531 U.S. ____ (2000)
Per Curiam

NOTICE: This opinion is subject to formal revision before publication in the preliminary print of the United States Reports. Readers are requested to notify the Reporter of Decisions, Supreme Court of the United States, Washington, D.C. 20543, of any typographical or other formal errors, in order that corrections may be made before the preliminary print goes to press.

SUPREME COURT OF THE UNITED STATES

No. 00-949

GEORGE W. BUSH, ET AL., PETITIONERS *v.*
ALBERT GORE, JR., ET AL. ON WRIT OF CERTIORARI
TO THE FLORIDA SUPREME COURT

[December 12, 2000]

PER CURIAM.

I

On December 8, 2000, the Supreme Court of Florida ordered that the Circuit Court of Leon County tabulate by hand 9,000 ballots in Miami-Dade County. It also ordered the inclusion in the certified vote totals of 215 votes identified in Palm Beach County and 168 votes identified in Miami-Dade County for Vice President Albert Gore, Jr., and Senator Joseph Lieberman, Democratic Candidates for President and Vice President. The Supreme Court noted that petitioner, Governor George W. Bush asserted that the net gain for Vice President Gore in Palm Beach County was 176 votes, and directed the Circuit Court to resolve that dispute on remand. ___ So. 2d, at ___ (slip op., at 4, n. 6). The court further held that relief would require manual recounts in all Florida counties where so-called "undervotes" had not been subject to manual tabulation. The court ordered all manual recounts to begin at once. Governor Bush and Richard Cheney, Republican Candidates for the Presidency and Vice Presidency, filed an emergency application for a stay of this mandate. On December 9, we granted the application, treated the application as a petition for a writ of certiorari, and granted certiorari. *Post*, p. ___.

The proceedings leading to the present controversy are discussed in some detail in our opinion in *Bush* v. *Palm Beach County Canvassing Bd.*, *ante*, p. ____ *(per curiam) (Bush I)*. On November 8, 2000, the day following the Presidential election, the Florida Division of Elections reported that petitioner, Governor Bush, had received 2,909,135 votes, and respondent, Vice President Gore, had received 2,907,351 votes, a margin of 1,784 for Governor Bush. Because Governor Bush's margin of victory was less than "one-half of a percent . . . of the votes cast," an automatic machine recount was conducted under §102.141(4) of the Florida Election Code, the results of which showed Governor Bush still winning the race but by a diminished margin. Vice President Gore then sought manual recounts in Volusia, Palm Beach, Broward, and Miami-Dade Counties, pursuant to Florida's election protest provisions. Fla. Stat. §102.166 (2000). A dispute arose concerning the deadline for local county canvassing boards to submit their returns to the Secretary of State (Secretary). The Secretary declined to waive the November 14 deadline imposed by statute. §§102.111, 102.112. The Florida Supreme Court, however, set the deadline at November 26. We granted certiorari and vacated the Florida Supreme Court's decision, finding considerable uncertainty as to the grounds on which it was based. *Bush I, ante,* at ___–___ (slip op., at 6–7). On December 11, the Florida Supreme Court issued a decision on remand reinstating that date. ___ So. 2d ___, ___ (slip op. at 30–31).

On November 26, the Florida Elections Canvassing Commission certified the results of the election and declared Governor Bush the winner of Florida's 25 electoral votes. On November 27, Vice President Gore, pursuant to Florida's contest provisions, filed a complaint in Leon County Circuit Court contesting the certification. Fla. Stat. §102.168 (2000). He sought relief pursuant to §102.168(3)(c), which provides that "[r]eceipt of a number of illegal votes or rejection of a number of legal votes sufficient to change or place in doubt the result of the election" shall be grounds for a contest. The Circuit Court denied relief, stating that Vice President Gore failed to meet his burden of proof. He appealed to the First District Court of Appeal, which certified the matter to the Florida Supreme Court.

Accepting jurisdiction, the Florida Supreme Court affirmed in part and reversed in part. *Gore v. Harris,* ___ So. 2d. ____ (2000). The court held that the Circuit Court had been correct to reject Vice President Gore's challenge to the results certified in Nassau County and his challenge to the Palm Beach County Canvassing Board's determination that 3,300 ballots cast in that county were not, in the statutory phrase, "legal votes."

The Supreme Court held that Vice President Gore had satisfied his burden of proof under §102.168(3)(c) with respect to his challenge to

Miami-Dade County's failure to tabulate, by manual count, 9,000 ballots on which the machines had failed to detect a vote for President ("under-votes"). ___ So. 2d., at ___ (slip op., at 22–23). Noting the closeness of the election, the Court explained that "[o]n this record, there can be no question that there are legal votes within the 9,000 uncounted votes sufficient to place the results of this election in doubt." *Id.*, at ___ (slip op., at 35). A "legal vote," as determined by the Supreme Court, is "one in which there is a 'clear indication of the intent of the voter.'" *Id.*, at ___ (slip op., at 25). The court therefore ordered a hand recount of the 9,000 ballots in Miami-Dade County. Observing that the contest provisions vest broad discretion in the circuit judge to "provide any relief appropriate under such circumstances," Fla. Stat. §102.168(8) (2000), the Supreme Court further held that the Circuit Court could order "the Supervisor of Elections and the Canvassing Boards, as well as the necessary public officials, in all counties that have not conducted a manual recount or tabulation of the undervotes . . . to do so forthwith, said tabulation to take place in the individual counties where the ballots are located." ___ So. 2d, at ___ (slip op., at 38).

The Supreme Court also determined that Palm Beach County and Miami-Dade County, in their earlier manual recounts, had identified a net gain of 215 and 168 legal votes, respectively, for Vice President Gore. *Id.*, at ___ (slip op., at 33–34). Rejecting the Circuit Court's conclusion that Palm Beach County lacked the authority to include the 215 net votes submitted past the November 26 deadline, the Supreme Court explained that the deadline was not intended to exclude votes identified after that date through ongoing manual recounts. As to Miami-Dade County, the Court concluded that although the 168 votes identified were the result of a partial recount, they were "legal votes [that] could change the outcome of the election." *Id.*, at (slip op., at 34). The Supreme Court therefore directed the Circuit Court to include those totals in the certified results, subject to resolution of the actual vote total from the Miami-Dade partial recount.

The petition presents the following questions: whether the Florida Supreme Court established new standards for resolving Presidential election contests, thereby violating Art. II, §1, cl. 2, of the United States Constitution and failing to comply with 3 U.S.C. §5, and whether the use of standardless manual recounts violates the Equal Protection and Due Process Clauses. With respect to the equal protection question, we find a violation of the Equal Protection Clause.

II

A

The closeness of this election, and the multitude of legal challenges which have followed in its wake, have brought into sharp focus a common, if heretofore unnoticed, phenomenon. Nationwide statistics reveal that an estimated 2% of ballots cast do not register a vote for President for whatever reason, including deliberately choosing no candidate at all or some voter error, such as voting for two candidates or insufficiently marking a ballot. See Ho, More Than 2M Ballots Uncounted, AP Online (Nov. 28, 2000); Kelley, Balloting Problems Not Rare But Only in a Very Close Election Do Mistakes and Mismarking Make a Difference, Omaha World-Herald (Nov. 15, 2000). In certifying election results, the votes eligible for inclusion in the certification are the votes meeting the properly established legal requirements.

This case has shown that punch card balloting machines can produce an unfortunate number of ballots which are not punched in a clean, complete way by the voter. After the current counting, it is likely legislative bodies nationwide will examine ways to improve the mechanisms and machinery for voting.

B

The individual citizen has no federal constitutional right to vote for electors for the President of the United States unless and until the state legislature chooses a statewide election as the means to implement its power to appoint members of the Electoral College. U.S. Const., Art. II, §1. This is the source for the statement in *McPherson* v. *Blacker*, 146 U.S. 1, 35 (1892), that the State legislature's power to select the manner for appointing electors is plenary; it may, if it so chooses, select the electors itself, which indeed was the manner used by State legislatures in several States for many years after the Framing of our Constitution. *Id.*, at 28–33. History has now favored the voter, and in each of the several States the citizens themselves vote for Presidential electors. When the state legislature vests the right to vote for President in its people, the right to vote as the legislature has prescribed is fundamental; and one source of its fundamental nature lies in the equal weight accorded to each vote and the equal dignity owed to each voter. The State, of course, after granting the franchise in the special context of Article II, can take back the power to appoint electors. See *id.*, at 35 ("[T]here is no doubt of the right of the legislature to resume the power at any time, for it can neither be taken away nor abdicated") (quoting S. Rep. No. 395, 43d Cong., 1st Sess.).

The right to vote is protected in more than the initial allocation of the franchise. Equal protection applies as well to the manner of its exercise. Having once granted the right to vote on equal terms, the State may not, by later arbitrary and disparate treatment, value one person's vote over that of another. See, *e.g.*, *Harper* v. *Virginia Bd. of Elections*, 383 U.S. 663, 665 (1966) ("[O]nce the franchise is granted to the electorate, lines may not be drawn which are inconsistent with the Equal Protection Clause of the Fourteenth Amendment"). It must be remembered that "the right of suffrage can be denied by a debasement or dilution of the weight of a citizen's vote just as effectively as by wholly prohibiting the free exercise of the franchise." *Reynolds* v. *Sims*, 377 U.S. 533, 555 (1964).

There is no difference between the two sides of the present controversy on these basic propositions. Respondents say that the very purpose of vindicating the right to vote justifies the recount procedures now at issue. The question before us, however, is whether the recount procedures the Florida Supreme Court has adopted are consistent with its obligation to avoid arbitrary and disparate treatment of the members of its electorate.

Much of the controversy seems to revolve around ballot cards designed to be perforated by a stylus but which, either through error or deliberate omission, have not been perforated with sufficient precision for a machine to count them. In some cases a piece of the card—a chad—is hanging, say by two corners. In other cases there is no separation at all, just an indentation.

The Florida Supreme Court has ordered that the intent of the voter be discerned from such ballots. For purposes of resolving the equal protection challenge, it is not necessary to decide whether the Florida Supreme Court had the authority under the legislative scheme for resolving election disputes to define what a legal vote is and to mandate a manual recount implementing that definition. The recount mechanisms implemented in response to the decisions of the Florida Supreme Court do not satisfy the minimum requirement for non-arbitrary treatment of voters necessary to secure the fundamental right. Florida's basic command for the count of legally cast votes is to consider the "intent of the voter." *Gore* v. *Harris*, ___ So. 2d, at ___ (slip op., at 39). This is unobjectionable as an abstract proposition and a starting principle. The problem inheres in the absence of specific standards to ensure its equal application. The formulation of uniform rules to determine intent based on these recurring circumstances is practicable and, we conclude, necessary.

The law does not refrain from searching for the intent of the actor in a multitude of circumstances; and in some cases the general command to ascertain intent is not susceptible to much further refinement. In this instance, however, the question is not whether to believe a witness but how to interpret the marks or holes or scratches on an inanimate object, a piece of cardboard or paper which, it is said, might not have registered as a vote during the machine count. The factfinder confronts a thing, not a person. The search for intent can be confined by specific rules designed to ensure uniform treatment.

The want of those rules here has led to unequal evaluation of ballots in various respects. See *Gore* v. *Harris*, ___ So. 2d, at ___ (slip op., at 51) (Wells, J., dissenting) ("Should a county canvassing board count or not count a 'dimpled chad' where the voter is able to successfully dislodge the chad in every other contest on that ballot? Here, the county canvassing boards disagree"). As seems to have been acknowledged at oral argument, the standards for accepting or rejecting contested ballots might vary not only from county to county but indeed within a single county from one recount team to another.

The record provides some examples. A monitor in Miami-Dade County testified at trial that he observed that three members of the county canvassing board applied different standards in defining a legal vote. 3 Tr. 497, 499 (Dec. 3, 2000). And testimony at trial also revealed that at least one county changed its evaluative standards during the counting process. Palm Beach County, for example, began the process with a 1990 guideline which precluded counting completely attached chads, switched to a rule that considered a vote to be legal if any light could be seen through a chad, changed back to the 1990 rule, and then abandoned any pretense of a *per se* rule, only to have a court order that the county consider dimpled chads legal. This is not a process with sufficient guarantees of equal treatment.

An early case in our one person, one vote jurisprudence arose when a State accorded arbitrary and disparate treatment to voters in its different counties. *Gray* v. *Sanders*, 372 U.S. 368 (1963). The Court found a constitutional violation. We relied on these principles in the context of the Presidential selection process in *Moore* v. *Ogilvie*, 394 U.S. 814 (1969), where we invalidated a county-based procedure that diluted the influence of citizens in larger counties in the nominating process. There we observed that "[t]he idea that one group can be granted greater voting strength than another is hostile to the one man, one vote basis of our representative government." *Id.*, at 819.

The State Supreme Court ratified this uneven treatment. It mandated that the recount totals from two counties, Miami-Dade and Palm Beach, be included in the certified total. The court also appeared to hold *sub silentio* that the recount totals from Broward County, which were not completed until after the original November 14 certification by the Secretary of State, were to be considered part of the new certified vote totals even though the county certification was not contested by Vice President Gore. Yet each of the counties used varying standards to determine what was a legal vote. Broward County used a more forgiving standard than Palm Beach County, and uncovered almost three times as many new votes, a result markedly disproportionate to the difference in population between the counties.

In addition, the recounts in these three counties were not limited to so-called undervotes but extended to all of the ballots. The distinction has real consequences. A manual recount of all ballots identifies not only those ballots which show no vote but also those which contain more than one, the so-called overvotes. Neither category will be counted by the machine. This is not a trivial concern. At oral argument, respondents estimated there are as many as 110,000 overvotes statewide. As a result, the citizen whose ballot was not read by a machine because he failed to vote for a candidate in a way readable by a machine may still have his vote counted in a manual recount; on the other hand, the citizen who marks two candidates in a way discernable by the machine will not have the same opportunity to have his vote count, even if a manual examination of the ballot would reveal the requisite indicia of intent. Furthermore, the citizen who marks two candidates, only one of which is discernable by the machine, will have his vote counted even though it should have been read as an invalid ballot. The State Supreme Court's inclusion of vote counts based on these variant standards exemplifies concerns with the remedial processes that were under way.

That brings the analysis to yet a further equal protection problem. The votes certified by the court included a partial total from one county, Miami-Dade. The Florida Supreme Court's decision thus gives no assurance that the recounts included in a final certification must be complete. Indeed, it is respondent's submission that it would be consistent with the rules of the recount procedures to include whatever partial counts are done by the time of final certification, and we interpret the Florida Supreme Court's decision to permit this. See ____ So. 2d, at ____, n. 21 (slip op., at 37, n. 21) (noting "practical difficulties" may control outcome of election, but certifying partial Miami-Dade total nonetheless). This accommodation no doubt results from the truncated contest period established by the Florida Supreme Court in *Bush I*, at respondent's own urging. The press of time does not diminish the constitutional concern. A desire for speed is not a general excuse for ignoring equal protection guarantees.

In addition to these difficulties the actual process by which the votes were to be counted under the Florida Supreme Court's decision raises further concerns. That order did not specify who would recount the ballots. The county canvassing boards were forced to pull together ad hoc teams comprised of judges from various Circuits who had no previous training in handling and interpreting ballots. Furthermore, while others were permitted to observe, they were prohibited from objecting during the recount.

The recount process, in its features here described, is inconsistent with the minimum procedures necessary to protect the fundamental right of each voter in the special instance of a statewide recount under the authority of a single state judicial officer. Our consideration is limited to the present circumstances, for the problem of equal protection in election processes generally presents many complexities.

The question before the Court is not whether local entities, in the exercise of their expertise, may develop different systems for implementing elections. Instead, we are presented with a situation where a state court with the power to assure uniformity has ordered a statewide recount with minimal procedural safeguards. When a court orders a statewide remedy, there must be at least some assurance that the rudimentary requirements of equal treatment and fundamental fairness are satisfied.

Given the Court's assessment that the recount process underway was probably being conducted in an unconstitutional manner, the Court stayed the order directing the recount so it could hear this case and render an expedited decision. The contest provision, as it was mandated by the State Supreme Court, is not well calculated to sustain the confidence that all citizens must have in the outcome of elections. The State has not shown that its procedures include the necessary safeguards. The problem, for instance, of the estimated 110,000 overvotes has not been addressed, although Chief Justice Wells called attention to the concern in his dissenting opinion. See ____ So. 2d, at ____, n. 26 (slip op., at 45, n. 26).

Upon due consideration of the difficulties identified to this point, it is obvious that the recount cannot be conducted in compliance with the requirements of equal protection and due process without substantial additional work. It would require not only the adoption (after opportunity for argument) of adequate statewide standards for determining what is a legal vote, and practicable procedures to implement them, but also orderly judicial review of any disputed matters that might arise. In addition, the Secretary of State has advised that the recount of only a portion of the ballots requires that the vote tabulation equipment be used to screen out undervotes, a function for which the machines were not designed. If a recount of overvotes were also required, perhaps even a second screening would be necessary. Use of the equipment for this purpose, and any new software developed for it, would have to be evaluated for accuracy by the Secretary of State, as required by Fla. Stat. §101.015 (2000).

The Supreme Court of Florida has said that the legislature intended the State's electors to "participat[e] fully in the federal electoral process," as provided in 3 U.S.C. §5. ____ So. 2d, at ____ (slip op. at 27); see also *Palm Beach Canvassing Bd. v. Harris*, 2000 WL 1725434, *13 (Fla. 2000). That statute, in turn, requires that any controversy or contest that is designed to lead to a conclusive selection of electors be completed by December 12. That date is upon us, and there is no recount procedure in place under the State Supreme Court's order that comports with minimal constitutional standards. Because it is evident that any recount seeking to meet the December 12 date will be unconstitutional for the reasons we have discussed, we reverse the judgment of the Supreme Court of Florida ordering a recount to proceed.

Seven Justices of the Court agree that there are constitutional problems with the recount ordered by the Florida Supreme Court that demand a remedy. See post, at 6 (SOUTER, J., dissenting); post, at 2, 15 (BREYER, J., dissenting). The only disagreement is as to the remedy. Because the Florida Supreme Court has said that the Florida Legislature intended to obtain the safe-harbor benefits of 3 U.S.C. §5, JUSTICE BREYER's proposed remedy—remanding to the Florida Supreme Court for its ordering of a constitutionally proper contest until December 18—contemplates

action in violation of the Florida election code, and hence could not be part of an "appropriate" order authorized by Fla. Stat. §102.168(8) (2000).
* * *

None are more conscious of the vital limits on judicial authority than are the members of this Court, and none stand more in admiration of the Constitution's design to leave the selection of the President to the people, through their legislatures, and to the political sphere. When contending parties invoke the process of the courts, however, it becomes our unsought responsibility to resolve the federal and constitutional issues the judicial system has been forced to confront.

The judgment of the Supreme Court of Florida is reversed, and the case is remanded for further proceedings not inconsistent with this opinion.

Pursuant to this Court's Rule 45.2, the Clerk is directed to issue the mandate in this case forthwith. *It is so ordered.*

Cite as: 531 U.S. ____ (2000)

REHNQUIST, C. J., concurring

SUPREME COURT OF THE UNITED STATES

No. 00-949

GEORGE W. BUSH, ET AL., PETITIONERS

v. ALBERT GORE, JR., ET AL.

ON WRIT OF CERTIORARI

TO THE FLORIDA SUPREME COURT

[December 12, 2000]

CHIEF JUSTICE REHNQUIST, with whom JUSTICE SCALIA and JUSTICE THOMAS join, concurring.

We join the *per curiam* opinion. We write separately because we believe there are additional grounds that require us to reverse the Florida Supreme Court's decision.

I

We deal here not with an ordinary election, but with an election for the President of the United States. In *Burroughs* v. *United States*, 290 U.S. 534, 545 (1934), we said:

> "While presidential electors are not officers or agents of the federal government (*In re Green*, 134 U.S. 377, 379), they exercise federal functions under, and discharge duties in virtue of authority conferred by, the Constitution of the United States. The President is vested with the executive power of the nation. The importance of his elec-

tion and the vital character of its relationship to and effect upon the welfare and safety of the whole people cannot be too strongly stated."

Likewise, in *Anderson* v. *Celebrezze*, 460 U.S. 780, 794–795 (1983) (footnote omitted), we said: "[I]n the context of a Presidential election, state-imposed restrictions implicate a uniquely important national interest. For the President and the Vice President of the United States are the only elected officials who represent all the voters in the Nation."

In most cases, comity and respect for federalism compel us to defer to the decisions of state courts on issues of state law. That practice reflects our understanding that the decisions of state courts are definitive pronouncements of the will of the States as sovereigns. Cf. *Erie R. Co.* v. *Tompkins*, 304 U.S. 64 (1938). Of course, in ordinary cases, the distribution of powers among the branches of a State's government raises no questions of federal constitutional law, subject to the requirement that the government be republican in character. See U.S. Const., Art. IV, §4. But there are a few exceptional cases in which the Constitution imposes a duty or confers a power on a particular branch of a State's government. This is one of them. Article II, §1, cl. 2, provides that "[e]ach State shall appoint, in such Manner as the *Legislature* thereof may direct," electors for President and Vice President. (Emphasis added.) Thus, the text of the election law itself, and not just its interpretation by the courts of the States, takes on independent significance. In *McPherson* v. *Blacker*, 146 U.S. 1 (1892), we explained that Art. II, §1, cl. 2, "convey[s] the broadest power of determination" and "leaves it to the legislature exclusively to define the method" of appointment. *Id.*, at 27. A significant departure from the legislative scheme for appointing Presidential electors presents a federal constitutional question.

3 U.S.C. §5 informs our application of Art. II, §1, cl. 2, to the Florida statutory scheme, which, as the Florida Supreme Court acknowledged, took that statute into account. Section 5 provides that the State's selection of electors "shall be conclusive, and shall govern in the counting of the electoral votes" if the electors are chosen under laws enacted prior to election day, and if the selection process is completed six days prior to the meeting of the electoral college. As we noted in *Bush* v. *Palm Beach County Canvassing Bd.*, ante, at 6.

"Since §5 contains a principle of federal law that would assure finality of the State's determination if made pursuant to a state law in effect before the election, a legislative wish to take advantage of the 'safe harbor' would counsel against any construction of the Election Code that Congress might deem to be a change in the law."

If we are to respect the legislature's Article II powers, therefore, we must ensure that postelection state-court actions do not frustrate the legislative desire to attain the "safe harbor" provided by §5.

In Florida, the legislature has chosen to hold statewide elections to appoint the State's 25 electors. Importantly, the legislature has delegated the authority to run the elections and to oversee election disputes to the Secretary of State (Secretary), Fla. Stat. §97.012(1) (2000), and to state circuit courts, §§102.168(1), 102.168(8). Isolated sections of the code may well admit of more than one interpretation, but the general coherence of the legislative scheme may not be altered by judicial interpretation so as to wholly change the statutorily provided apportionment of responsibility among these various bodies. In any election but a Presidential election, the Florida Supreme Court can give as little or as much deference to Florida's executives as it chooses, so far as Article II is concerned, and this Court will have no cause to question the court's actions. But, with respect to a Presidential election, the court must be both mindful of the legislature's role under Article II in choosing the manner of appointing electors and deferential to those bodies expressly empowered by the legislature to carry out its constitutional mandate.

In order to determine whether a state court has infringed upon the legislature's authority, we necessarily must examine the law of the State as it existed prior to the action of the court. Though we generally defer to state courts on the interpretation of state law—see, *e.g.*, *Mullaney* v. *Wilbur*, 421 U.S. 684 (1975)—there are of course areas in which the Constitution requires this Court to undertake an independent, if still deferential, analysis of state law.

For example, in *NAACP* v. *Alabama ex rel. Patterson*, 357 U.S. 449 (1958), it was argued that we were without jurisdiction because the petitioner had not pursued the correct appellate remedy in Alabama's state courts. Petitioners had sought a state-law writ of certiorari in the Alabama Supreme Court when a writ of mandamus, according to that court, was proper. We found this state-law ground inadequate to defeat our jurisdiction because we were "unable to reconcile the procedural holding of the Alabama Supreme Court" with prior Alabama precedent. *Id.*, at 456. The purported state-law ground was so novel, in our independent estimation, that "petitioner could not fairly be deemed to have been apprised of its existence." *Id.*, at 457. Six years later we decided *Bouie* v. *City of Columbia*, 378 U.S. 347 (1964), in which the state court had held, contrary to precedent, that the state trespass law applied to black sit-in demonstrators who had consent to enter private property but were then asked to leave. Relying upon *NAACP*, we concluded that the South Carolina Supreme Court's interpretation of a state penal statute had impermissibly broadened the scope of that statute beyond what a fair reading provided, in violation of due process. See 378 U.S., at 361–362. What we would do in the present case is precisely parallel: Hold that the Florida Supreme Court's interpretation of the Florida election laws impermissibly distorted them beyond what a fair reading required, in violation of Article II.[1] This inquiry does not imply a disrespect for state *courts* but rather a respect for the constitutionally prescribed role of state *legislatures*. To attach definitive weight to the pronouncement of a state court, when the very question at issue is whether the court has actually departed from the statutory meaning, would be to abdicate our responsibility to enforce the explicit requirements of Article II.

II

Acting pursuant to its constitutional grant of authority, the Florida Legislature has created a detailed, if not perfectly crafted, statutory scheme that provides for appointment of Presidential electors by direct election. Fla. Stat. §103.011 (2000). Under the statute, "[v]otes cast for the actual candidates for President and Vice President shall be counted as votes cast for the presidential electors supporting such candidates." *Ibid.* The legislature has designated the Secretary of State as the "chief election officer," with the responsibility to "[o]btain and maintain uniformity in the application, operation, and interpretation of the election laws." §97.012. The state legislature has delegated to county canvassing boards the duties of administering elections. §102.141. Those boards are responsible for providing results to the state Elections Canvassing Commission, comprising the Governor, the Secretary of State, and the Director of the Division of Elections. §102.111. Cf. *Boardman* v. *Esteva*, 323 So. 2d 259, 268, n. 5 (1975) ("The election process . . . is committed to the executive branch of government through duly designated officials all charged with specific duties. . . . [The] judgments [of these officials] are entitled to be regarded by the courts as presumptively correct . . .").

After the election has taken place, the canvassing boards receive returns from precincts, count the votes, and, in the event that a candidate was defeated by .5% or less, conduct a mandatory recount. Fla. Stat. §102.141(4) (2000). The county canvassing boards must file certified election returns with the Department of State by 5:00 p.m. on the seventh day following the election. §102.112(1). The Elections Canvassing Commission must then certify the results of the election. §102.111(1).

The state legislature has also provided mechanisms both for protesting election returns and for contesting certified election results. Section 102.166 governs protests. Any protest must be filed prior to the certification of election results by the county canvassing board. §102.166(4)(b). Once a protest has been filed, "the county canvassing board may authorize a manual recount." §102.166(4)(c). If a sample recount conducted pursuant to §102.166(5) "indicates an error in the vote tabulation which could affect the outcome of the election," the county canvassing board is instructed to: "(a) Correct the error and recount the remaining precincts with the vote tabulation system; (b) Request the Department of State to verify the tabulation software; or (c) Manually recount all ballots," §102.166(5). In the event a canvassing board chooses to conduct a manual recount of all ballots §102.166(7) prescribes procedures for such a recount.

Contests to the certification of an election, on the other hand, are controlled by §102.168. The grounds for contesting an election include "[r]eceipt of a number of illegal votes or rejection of a number of legal votes sufficient to change or place in doubt the result of the election." §102.168(3)(c). Any contest must be filed in the appropriate Florida circuit court, Fla. Stat. §102.168(1), and the canvassing board or election board is the proper party defendant, §102.168(4). Section 102.168(8) provides that "[t]he circuit judge to whom the contest is presented may fashion such orders as he or she deems necessary to ensure that each allegation in the complaint is investigated, examined, or checked, to prevent or correct any alleged wrong, and to provide any relief appropriate under such circumstances." In Presidential elections, the contest period necessarily terminates on the date set by 3 U.S.C. §5 for concluding the State's "final determination" of election controversies."

In its first decision, *Palm Beach Canvassing Bd.* v. *Harris*, ___ So. 2d, ___ (Nov. 21, 2000) (*Harris I*), the Florida Supreme Court extended the seven-day statutory certification deadline established by the legislature.[2] This modification of the code, by lengthening the protest period, necessarily shortened the contest period for Presidential elections. Underlying the extension of the certification deadline and the shortchanging of the contest period was, presumably, the clear implication that certification was a matter of significance: The certified winner would enjoy presumptive validity, making a contest proceeding by the losing candidate an uphill battle. In its latest opinion, however, the court empties certification of virtually all legal consequence during the contest, and in doing so departs from the provisions enacted by the Florida Legislature.

The court determined that canvassing boards' decisions regarding whether to recount ballots past the certification deadline (even the certification deadline established by *Harris I*) are to be reviewed *de novo*, although the election code clearly vests discretion whether to recount in the boards, and sets strict deadlines subject to the Secretary's rejection of late tallies and monetary fines for tardiness. See Fla. Stat. §102.112 (2000). Moreover, the Florida court held that all late vote tallies arriving during the contest period should be automatically included in the certification regardless of the certification deadline (even the certification deadline established by *Harris I*), thus virtually eliminating both the deadline and the Secretary's discretion to disregard recounts that violate it.[3]

Moreover, the court's interpretation of "legal vote," and hence its decision to order a contest-period recount, plainly departed from the legislative scheme. Florida statutory law cannot reasonably be thought to *require* the counting of improperly marked ballots. Each Florida precinct before election day provides instructions on how properly to cast a vote, §101.46; each polling place on election day contains a working model of the voting machine it uses, §101.5611; and each voting booth contains a sample ballot, §101.46. In precincts using punch-card ballots, voters are instructed to punch out the ballot cleanly: AFTER VOTING, CHECK YOUR BALLOT CARD TO BE SURE YOUR VOTING SELECTIONS ARE CLEARLY AND CLEANLY PUNCHED AND THERE ARE NO CHIPS LEFT HANGING ON THE BACK OF THE CARD. Instructions to Voters, quoted in *Touchston* v. *McDermott*, 2000 WL 1781942, *6 & n. 19 (CA11) (Tjoflat, J., dissenting). No reasonable person would call it "an error in the vote tabulation," FLA. STAT. §102.166(5), or a "rejection of legal votes," FLA. STAT. §102.168(3)(c),[4] when electronic or electromechanical equipment performs precisely in the manner designed, and fails to count those ballots that are not marked in the manner that these voting instructions explicitly and prominently specify. The scheme that the Florida Supreme Court's opinion attributes to the legislature is one in which machines are *required* to be "capable of correctly counting votes,"

§101.5606(4), but which nonetheless regularly produces elections in which legal votes are predictably *not* tabulated, so that in close elections manual recounts are regularly required. This is of course absurd. The Secretary of State, who is authorized by law to issue binding interpretations of the election code, §§97.012, 106.23, rejected this peculiar reading of the statutes. See DE 00-13 (opinion of the Division of Elections). The Florida Supreme Court, although it must defer to the Secretary's interpretations, see *Krivanek* v. *Take Back Tampa Political Committee*, 625 So. 2d 840, 844 (Fla. 1993), rejected her reasonable interpretation and embraced the peculiar one. See *Palm Beach County Canvassing Board* v. *Harris*, No. SC00-2346 (Dec. 11, 2000) (*Harris III*).

But as we indicated in our remand of the earlier case, in a Presidential election the clearly expressed intent of the legislature must prevail. And there is no basis for reading the Florida statutes as requiring the counting of improperly marked ballots, as an examination of the Florida Supreme Court's textual analysis shows. We will not parse that analysis here, except to note that the principal provision of the election code on which it relied, §101.5614(5), was, as the Chief Justice pointed out in his dissent from *Harris II*, entirely irrelevant. See *Gore* v. *Harris*, No. SC00-2431, slip op., at 50 (Dec. 8, 2000). The State's Attorney General (who was supporting the Gore challenge) confirmed in oral argument here that never before the present election had a manual recount been conducted on the basis of the contention that "undervotes" should have been examined to determine voter intent. Tr. of Oral Arg. in *Bush* v. *Palm Beach County Canvassing Bd.*, 39–40 (Dec. 1, 2000); cf. *Broward County Canvassing Board* v. *Hogan*, 607 So. 2d 508, 509 (Fla. Ct. App. 1992) (denial of recount for failure to count ballots with "hanging paper chads"). For the court to step away from this established practice, prescribed by the Secretary of State, the state official charged by the legislature with "responsibility to . . . [o]btain and maintain uniformity in the application, operation, and interpretation of the election laws," §97.012(1), was to depart from the legislative scheme.

III

The scope and nature of the remedy ordered by the Florida Supreme Court jeopardizes the "legislative wish" to take advantage of the safe harbor provided by 3 U.S.C. §5. *Bush* v. *Palm Beach County Canvassing Bd.*, ante, at 6. December 12, 2000, is the last date for a final determination of the Florida electors that will satisfy §5. Yet in the late afternoon of December 8th—four days before this deadline—the Supreme Court of Florida ordered recounts of tens of thousands of so-called "undervotes" spread through 64 of the State's 67 counties. This was done in a search for elusive—perhaps delusive—certainty as to the exact count of 6 million votes. But no one claims that these ballots have not previously been tabulated; they were initially read by voting machines at the time of the election, and thereafter reread by virtue of Florida's automatic recount provision. No one claims there was any fraud in the election. The Supreme Court of Florida ordered this additional recount under the provision of the election code giving the circuit judge the authority to provide relief that is "appropriate under such circumstances." Fla. Stat. §102.168(8) (2000).

Surely when the Florida Legislature empowered the courts of the State to grant "appropriate" relief, it must have meant relief that would have become final by the cutoff date of 3 U.S.C. §5. In light of the inevitable legal challenges and ensuing appeals to the Supreme Court of Florida and petitions for certiorari to this Court, the entire recounting process could not possibly be completed by that date. Whereas the majority in the Supreme Court of Florida stated its confidence that "the remaining undervotes in these counties can be [counted] within the required time frame," ___ So. 2d. at ___, n. 22 (slip op., at 38, n. 22), it made no assertion that the seemingly inevitable appeals could be disposed of in that time. Although the Florida Supreme Court has on occasion taken over a year to resolve disputes over local elections, see, e.g., *Beckstrom* v. *Volusia County Canvassing Bd.*, 707 So. 2d 720 (1998) (resolving contest of sheriff's race 16 months after the election), it has heard and decided the appeals in the present case with great promptness. But the federal deadlines for the Presidential election simply do not permit even such a shortened process.

As the dissent noted:

> "In [the four days remaining], all questionable ballots must be reviewed by the judicial officer appointed to discern the intent of the voter in a process open to the public. Fairness dictates that a provision be made for either party to object to how a particular ballot is counted. Additionally, this short time period must allow for judicial review. I respectfully submit this cannot be completed without taking Florida's presidential electors outside the safe harbor provision, creating the very real possibility of disenfranchising those nearly 6 million voters who are able to correctly cast their ballots on election day." ___ So. 2d, at ___ (slip op., at 55) (Wells, C. J., dissenting).

The other dissenters echoed this concern: "[T]he majority is departing from the essential requirements of the law by providing a remedy which is impossible to achieve and which will ultimately lead to chaos." *Id.*, at ___ (slip op., at 67) (Harding, J., dissenting, Shaw, J., concurring).

Given all these factors, and in light of the legislative intent identified by the Florida Supreme Court to bring Florida within the "safe harbor" provision of 3 U.S.C. §5, the remedy prescribed by the Supreme Court of Florida cannot be deemed an "appropriate" one as of December 8. It significantly departed from the statutory framework in place on November 7, and authorized open-ended further proceedings which could not be completed by December 12, thereby preventing a final determination by that date.

For these reasons, in addition to those given in the *per curiam*, we would reverse.

Notes

1. Similarly, our jurisprudence requires us to analyze the "background principles" of state property law to determine whether there has been a taking of property in violation of the Takings Clause. That constitutional guarantee would, of course, afford no protection against state power if our inquiry could be concluded by a state supreme court holding that state property law accorded the plaintiff no rights. See *Lucas v. South Carolina Coastal Council*, 505 U.S. 1003 (1992). In one of our oldest cases, we similarly made an independent evaluation of state law in order to protect federal treaty guarantees. In *Fairfax's Devisee v. Hunter's Lessee*, 7 Cranch 603 (1813), we disagreed with the Supreme Court of Appeals of Virginia that a 1782 state law had extinguished the property interests of one Denny Fairfax, so that a 1789 ejectment order against Fairfax supported by a 1785 state law did not constitute a future confiscation under the 1783 peace treaty with Great Britain. See *id.*, at 623; *Hunter v. Fairfax's Devisee*, 1 Munf. 218 (Va. 1809).

2. We vacated that decision and remanded that case; the Florida Supreme Court reissued the same judgment with a new opinion on December 11, 2000, ___ So. 2d, ___.

3. Specifically, the Florida Supreme Court ordered the Circuit Court to include in the certified vote totals those votes identified for Vice President Gore in Palm Beach County and Miami-Dade County.

4. It is inconceivable that what constitutes a vote that must be counted under the "error in the vote tabulation" language of the protest phase is different from what constitutes a vote that must be counted under the "legal votes" language of the contest phase.

SUPREME COURT OF THE UNITED STATES
No. 00-949
GEORGE W. BUSH, ET AL., PETITIONERS v.
ALBERT GORE, JR., ET AL.
ON WRIT OF CERTIORARI TO THE FLORIDA
SUPREME COURT
[December 12, 2000]

JUSTICE STEVENS, with whom JUSTICE GINSBURG AND JUS-
TICE BREYER join, dissenting.

The Constitution assigns to the States the primary responsibility for
determining the manner of selecting the Presidential electors. See Art. II,
§1, cl. 2. When questions arise about the meaning of state laws, including
election laws, it is our settled practice to accept the opinions of the highest
courts of the States as providing the final answers. On rare occasions, however, either federal statutes or the Federal Constitution may require federal judicial intervention in state elections. This is not such an occasion.

The federal questions that ultimately emerged in this case are not substantial. Article II provides that "[e]ach *State* shall appoint, in such Manner
as the Legislature *thereof* may direct, a Number of Electors." *Ibid.* (emphasis added). It does not create state legislatures out of whole cloth, but rather
takes them as they come—as creatures born of, and constrained by, their
state constitutions. Lest there be any doubt, we stated over 100 years ago
in *McPherson* v. *Blacker*, 146 U.S. 1, 25 (1892), that "[w]hat is forbidden or
required to be done by a State" in the Article II context "is forbidden or
required of the legislative power under state constitutions as they exist." In
the same vein, we also observed that "[t]he [State's] legislative power is the
supreme authority except as limited by the constitution of the State." *Ibid.*;
cf. *Smiley* v. *Holm*, 285 U.S. 355, 367 (1932).[1] The legislative power in
Florida is subject to judicial review pursuant to Article V of the Florida
Constitution, and nothing in Article II of the Federal Constitution frees
the state legislature from the constraints in the state constitution that created it. Moreover, the Florida Legislature's own decision to employ a uni-
tary code for all elections indicates that it intended the Florida Supreme
Court to play the same role in Presidential elections that it has historically
played in resolving electoral disputes. The Florida Supreme Court's exercise of appellate jurisdiction therefore was wholly consistent with, and
indeed contemplated by, the grant of authority in Article II.

It hardly needs stating that Congress, pursuant to 3 U.S.C. §5, did not impose any affirmative duties upon the States that their governmental branches could "violate." Rather, §5 provides a safe harbor for States to select electors in contested elections "by judicial or other methods" established by laws prior to the election day. Section 5, like Article II, assumes the involvement of the state judiciary in interpreting state election laws and resolving election disputes under those laws. Neither §5 nor Article II grants federal judges any special authority to substitute their views for those of the state judiciary on matters of state law. Nor are petitioners correct in asserting that the failure of the Florida Supreme Court to specify in detail the precise manner in which the "intent of the voter," Fla. Stat. §101.5614(5) (Supp. 2001), is to be determined rises to the level of a constitutional violation.[2] We found such a violation when individual votes within the same State were weighted unequally, see, e.g., *Reynolds* v. *Sims*, 377 U.S. 533, 568 (1964), but we have never before called into question the substantive standard by which a State determines that a vote has been legally cast. And there is no reason to think that the guidance provided to the fact finders, specifically the various canvassing boards, by the "intent of the voter" standard is any less sufficient—or will lead to results any less uniform—than, for example, the "beyond a reasonable doubt" standard employed every day by ordinary citizens in courtrooms across this country.[3] Admittedly, the use of differing substandards for determining voter intent in different counties employing similar voting systems may raise serious concerns. Those concerns are alleviated—if not eliminated—by the fact that a single impartial magistrate will ultimately adjudicate all objections arising from the recount process. Of course, as a general matter, "[t]he interpretation of constitutional principles must not be too literal. We must remember that the machinery of government would not work if it were not allowed a little play in its joints." *Bain Peanut Co. of Tex.* v. *Pinson*, 282 U.S. 499, 501 (1931) (Holmes, J.). If it were otherwise, Florida's decision to leave to each county the determination of what balloting system to employ—despite enormous differences in accuracy[4]—might run afoul of equal protection. So, too, might the similar decisions of the vast majority of state legislatures to delegate to local authorities certain decisions with respect to voting systems and ballot design. Even assuming that aspects of the remedial scheme might ultimately be found to violate the Equal Protection Clause, I could not subscribe to the majority's disposition of the case. As the majority explicitly holds, once a state legislature determines to select electors through a popular vote, the right to have one's vote counted is of constitutional stature. As the majority further acknowledges, Florida law holds that all ballots that reveal the intent of the voter constitute valid votes. Recognizing these principles, the majority nonetheless orders the termination of the contest proceeding before all such votes have been tabulated. Under their own reasoning, the appropriate course of action would be to remand to allow more specific procedures for implementing the legislature's uniform general standard to be established.

In the interest of finality, however, the majority effectively orders the disenfranchisement of an unknown number of voters whose ballots reveal their intent—and are therefore legal votes under state law—but were for some reason rejected by ballot-counting machines. It does so on the basis of the deadlines set forth in Title 3 of the United States Code. *Ante*, at 11. But, as I have already noted, those provisions merely provide rules of decision for Congress to follow when selecting among conflicting slates of electors. *Supra*, at 2. They do not prohibit a State from counting what the majority concedes to be legal votes until a bona fide winner is determined. Indeed, in 1960, Hawaii appointed two slates of electors and Congress chose to count the one appointed on January 4, 1961, well after the Title 3 deadlines. See Josephson & Ross, Repairing the Electoral College, 22 J. Legis. 145, 166, n. 154 (1996).[5] Thus, nothing prevents the majority, even if it properly found an equal protection violation, from ordering relief appropriate to remedy that violation without depriving Florida voters of their right to have their votes counted. As the majority notes, "[a] desire for speed is not a general excuse for ignoring equal protection guarantees." *Ante*, at 10.

Finally, neither in this case, nor in its earlier opinion in *Palm Beach County Canvassing Bd.* v. *Harris*, 2000 WL 1725434 (Fla., Nov. 21, 2000), did the Florida Supreme Court make any substantive change in Florida electoral law.[6] Its decisions were rooted in long-established precedent and were consistent with the relevant statutory provisions, taken as a whole. It did what courts do[7]—it decided the case before it in light of the legislature's intent to leave no legally cast vote uncounted. In so doing, it relied on the sufficiency of the general "intent of the voter" standard articulated by the state legislature, coupled with a procedure for ultimate review by an impartial judge, to resolve the concern about disparate evaluations of contested ballots. If we assume—as I do—that the members of that court and the judges who would have carried out its mandate are impartial, its decision does not even raise a colorable federal question.

What must underlie petitioners' entire federal assault on the Florida election procedures is an unstated lack of confidence in the impartiality and capacity of the state judges who would make the critical decisions if the vote count were to proceed. Otherwise, their position is wholly without merit. The endorsement of that position by the majority of this Court can only lend credence to the most cynical appraisal of the work of judges throughout the land. It is confidence in the men and women who administer the judicial system that is the true backbone of the rule of law. Time will one day heal the wound to that confidence that will be inflicted by today's decision. One thing, however, is certain. Although we may never know with complete certainty the identity of the winner of this year's Presidential election, the identity of the loser is perfectly clear. It is the Nation's confidence in the judge as an impartial guardian of the rule of law.

I respectfully dissent.

Notes

1. "Wherever the term 'legislature' is used in the Constitution it is necessary to consider the nature of the particular action in view." 285 U.S., at 367. It is perfectly clear that the meaning of the words "Manner" and "Legislature" as used in Article II, §1, parallels the usage in Article I, §4, rather than the language in Article V. U.S. Term Limits, Inc. v. Thornton, 514 U.S. 779, 805 (1995). Article I, §4, and Article II, §1, both call upon legislatures to act in a lawmaking capacity whereas Article V simply calls on the legislative body to deliberate upon a binary decision. As a result, petitioners' reliance on Leser v. Garnett, 258 U.S. 130 (1922), and Hawke v. Smith (No. 1), 253 U.S. 221 (1920), is misplaced.

2. The Florida statutory standard is consistent with the practice of the majority of States, which apply either an "intent of the voter" standard or an "impossible to determine the elector's choice" standard in ballot recounts. The following States use an "intent of the voter" standard: Ariz. Rev. Stat. Ann. §16-645(A) (Supp. 2000) (standard for canvassing write-in votes); Conn. Gen. Stat. §9-150a(j) (1999) (standard for absentee ballots, including three conclusive presumptions); Ind. Code §3-12-1-1 (1992); Me. Rev. Stat. Ann., Tit. 21-A, §1(13) (1993); Md. Ann. Code, Art. 33, §11-302(d) (2000 Supp.) (standard for absentee ballots); Mass. Gen. Laws §70E (1991) (applying standard to Presidential primaries); Mich. Comp. Laws §168.799a(3) (Supp. 2000); Mo. Rev. Stat. §115.453(3) (Cum. Supp. 1998) (looking to voter's intent where there is substantial compliance with statutory requirements); Tex. Elec. Code Ann. §65.009(c) (1986); Utah Code Ann. §20A-4-104(5)(b) (Supp. 2000) (standard for write-in votes), §20A-4-105(6)(a) (standard for mechanical ballots); Vt. Stat. Ann., Tit. 17, §2587(a) (1982); Va. Code Ann.

§24.2-644(A) (2000); Wash. Rev. Code §29.62.180(1) (Supp. 2001) (standard for write-in votes); Wyo. Stat. Ann. §22-14-104 (1999). The following States employ a standard in which a vote is counted unless it is "impossible to determine the elector's [or voter's] choice": Ala. Code §11-46-44(c) (1992), Ala. Code §17-13-2 (1995); Ariz. Rev. Stat. Ann. §16-610 (1996) (standard for rejecting ballot); Cal. Elec. Code Ann. §15154(c) (West Supp. 2000); Colo. Rev. Stat. §1-7-309(1) (1999) (standard for paper ballots), §1-7-508(2) (standard for electronic ballots); Del. Code Ann., Tit. 15, §4972(4) (1999); Idaho Code §34-1203 (1981); Ill. Comp. Stat., ch. 10, §5/7-51 (1993) (standard for primaries), id., ch. 10, §5/17-16 (1993) (standard for general elections); Iowa Code §49.98 (1999); Me. Rev. Stat. Ann., Tit. 21-A §§696(2)(B), (4) (Supp. 2000); Minn. Stat. §204C.22(1) (1992); Mont. Code Ann. §13-15-202 (1997) (not counting votes if "elector's choice cannot be determined"); Nev. Rev. Stat. §293.367(d) (1995); N.Y. Elec. Law §9-112(6) (McKinney 1998); N.C. Gen. Stat. §§163-169(b), 163-170 (1999); N.D. Cent. Code §16.1-15-01(1) (Supp. 1999); Ohio Rev. Code Ann. §3505.28 (1994); 26 Okla. Stat., Tit. 26, §7-127(6) (1997); Ore. Rev. Stat. §254.505(1) (1991); S.C. Code Ann. §7-13-1120 (1977); S.D. Codified Laws §12-20-7 (1995); Tenn. Code Ann. §2-7-133(b) (1994); W. Va. Code §3-6-5(g) (1999).

3. Cf. Victor v. Nebraska, 511 U.S. 1, 5 (1994) ("The beyond a reasonable doubt standard is a requirement of due process, but the Constitution neither prohibits trial courts from defining reasonable doubt nor requires them to do so").

4. The percentage of nonvotes in this election in counties using a punch-card system was 3.92%; in contrast, the rate of error under the more modern optical-scan systems was only 1.43%. Siegel v. LePore, No. 00-15981, 2000 WL 1781946, *31, *32, *43 (charts C and F) (CA11, Dec. 6, 2000). Put in other terms, for every 10,000 votes cast, punch-card systems result in 250 more nonvotes than optical-scan systems. A total of 3,718,305 votes were cast under punch-card systems, and 2,353,811 votes were cast under optical-scan systems. *Ibid.*

5. Republican electors were certified by the Acting Governor on November 28, 1960. A recount was ordered to begin on December 13, 1960. Both Democratic and Republican electors met on the appointed day to cast their votes. On January 4, 1961, the newly elected Governor certified the Democratic electors. The certification was received by Congress on January 6, the day the electoral votes were counted. Josephson & Ross, 22 J. Legis., at 166, n. 154.

6. When, for example, it resolved the previously unanswered question whether the word "shall" in Fla. Stat. §102.111 or the word "may" in §102.112 governs the scope of the Secretary of State's authority to ignore untimely election returns, it did not "change the law." Like any other judicial interpretation of a statute, its opinion was an authoritative interpretation of what the statute's relevant provisions have meant since they were enacted. *Rivers v. Roadway Express, Inc.*, 511 U.S. 298, 312–313 (1994).

7. "It is emphatically the province and duty of the judicial department to say what the law is." *Marbury* v. *Madison.*, 1 Cranch 137, 177 (1803).

SUPREME COURT OF THE UNITED STATES
No. 00-949
GEORGE W. BUSH, ET AL., PETITIONERS *v.*
ALBERT GORE, JR., ET AL.
ON WRIT OF CERTIORARI
TO THE FLORIDA SUPREME COURT
[December 12, 2000]

JUSTICE SOUTER, with whom JUSTICE BREYER joins and with whom JUSTICE STEVENS and JUSTICE GINSBURG join with regard to all but Part C, dissenting.

The Court should not have reviewed either *Bush* v. *Palm Beach County Canvassing Bd.*, *ante*, p. ___ (*per curiam*), or this case, and should not have stopped Florida's attempt to recount all undervote ballots, see *ante* at ___, by issuing a stay of the Florida Supreme Court's orders during the period of this review, see *Bush* v. *Gore, post* at ____ (slip op., at 1). If this Court had allowed the State to follow the course indicated by the opinions of its own Supreme Court, it is entirely possible that there would ultimately have been no issue requiring our review, and political tension could have worked itself out in the Congress following the procedure provided in 3 U.S.C. §15. The case being before us, however, its resolution by the majority is another erroneous decision.

As will be clear, I am in substantial agreement with the dissenting opinions of JUSTICE STEVENS, JUSTICE GINSBURG and JUSTICE BREYER. I write separately only to say how straightforward the issues before us really are.

There are three issues: whether the State Supreme Court's interpretation of the statute providing for a contest of the state election results somehow violates 3 U.S.C. §5; whether that court's construction of the state statutory provisions governing contests impermissibly changes a state law from what the State's legislature has provided, in violation of Article II, §1, cl. 2, of the national Constitution; and whether the manner of interpreting markings on disputed ballots failing to cause machines to register votes for President (the undervote ballots) violates the equal protection or due process guaranteed by the Fourteenth Amendment. None of these issues is difficult to describe or to resolve.

A

The 3 U.S.C. §5 issue is not serious. That provision sets certain conditions for treating a State's certification of Presidential electors as conclusive in the event that a dispute over recognizing those electors must be resolved in the Congress under 3 U.S.C. §15. Conclusiveness requires selection under a legal scheme in place before the election, with results determined at least six days before the date set for casting electoral votes. But no State is required to conform to §5 if it cannot do that (for whatever reason); the sanction for failing to satisfy the conditions of §5 is simply loss of what has been called its "safe harbor." And even that determination is to be made, if made anywhere, in the Congress.

B

The second matter here goes to the State Supreme Court's interpretation of certain terms in the state statute governing election "contests," Fla. Stat. §102.168 (2000); there is no question here about the state court's interpretation of the related provisions dealing with the antecedent process of "protesting" particular vote counts, §102.166, which was involved in the previous case, *Bush* v. *Palm Beach County Canvassing Board*. The issue is whether the judgment of the state supreme court has displaced the state legislature's provisions for election contests: is the law as declared by the court different from the provisions made by the legislature, to which the national Constitution commits responsibility for determining how each State's Presidential electors are chosen? See U.S. Const., Art. II, §1, cl. 2. Bush does not, of course, claim that any judicial act interpreting a statute of uncertain meaning is enough to displace the legislative provision and violate Article II; statutes require interpretation, which does not without more affect the legislative character of a statute within the meaning of the Constitution. Brief for Petitioners 48, n. 22, in *Bush* v. *Palm Beach County Canvassing Bd., et al.*, 531 U.S. ___ (2000). What Bush does argue, as I understand the contention, is that the interpretation of §102.168 was so unreasonable as to transcend the accepted bounds of statutory interpretation, to the point of being a nonjudicial act and producing new law untethered to the legislative act in question.

The starting point for evaluating the claim that the Florida Supreme Court's interpretation effectively rewrote §102.168 must be the language of the provision on which Gore relies to show his right to raise this contest: that the previously certified result in Bush's favor was produced by "rejection of a number of legal votes sufficient to change or place in doubt the result of the election." Fla. Stat. §102.168(3)(c) (2000). None of the state court's interpretations is unreasonable to the point of displacing the legislative enactment quoted. As I will note below, other interpretations were of course possible, and some might have been better than those adopted by the Florida court's majority; the two dissents from the majority opinion of that court and various briefs submitted to us set out alternatives. But the majority view is in each instance within the bounds of reasonable interpretation, and the law as declared is consistent with Article II.

1. The statute does not define a "legal vote," the rejection of which may affect the election. The State Supreme Court was therefore required to define it, and in doing that the court looked to another election statute, §101.5614(5), dealing with damaged or defective ballots, which contains a provision that no vote shall be disregarded "if there is a clear indication of the intent of the voter as determined by a canvassing board." The court read that objective of looking to the voter's intent as indicating that the legislature probably meant "legal vote" to mean a vote recorded on a ballot indicating what the voter intended. *Gore* v. *Harris*, __ So. 2d __ (slip op., at 23–25) (Dec. 8, 2000). It is perfectly true that the majority might have chosen a different reading. See, *e.g.*, Brief for Respondent Harris et al. 10 (defining "legal votes" as "votes properly executed in accordance with the instructions provided to all registered voters in advance of the election and in the polling places"). But even so, there is no constitutional violation in following the majority view; Article II is unconcerned with mere disagreements about interpretive merits.

2. The Florida court next interpreted "rejection" to determine what act in the counting process may be attacked in a contest. Again, the statute does not define the term. The court majority read the word to mean simply a failure to count. ____ So. 2d, at___ (slip op., at 26–27). That reading is certainly within the bounds of common sense, given the objective to give effect to a voter's intent if that can be determined. A different reading, of course, is possible. The majority might have concluded that "rejection" should refer to machine malfunction, or that a ballot should not be treated as "reject[ed]" in the absence of wrongdoing by election officials, lest contests be so easy to claim that every election will end up in one. Cf. *id.*, at ____ (slip op., at 48) (Wells, C. J., dissenting). There is, however, nothing nonjudicial in the Florida majority's more hospitable reading.

3. The same is true about the court majority's understanding of the phrase

"votes sufficient to change or place in doubt" the result of the election in Florida. The court held that if the uncounted ballots were so numerous that it was reasonably possible that they contained enough "legal" votes to swing the election, this contest would be authorized by the statute.[1] While the majority might have thought (as the trial judge did) that a probability, not a possibility, should be necessary to justify a contest, that reading is not required by the statute's text, which says nothing about probability. Whatever people of good will and good sense may argue about the merits of the Florida court's reading, there is no warrant for saying that it transcends the limits of reasonable statutory interpretation to the point of supplanting the statute enacted by the "legislature" within the meaning of Article II.

In sum, the interpretations by the Florida court raise no substantial question under Article II. That court engaged in permissible construction in determining that Gore had instituted a contest authorized by the state statute, and it proceeded to direct the trial judge to deal with that contest in the exercise of the discretionary powers generously conferred by Fla. Stat. §102.168(8) (2000), to "fashion such orders as he or she deems necessary to ensure that each allegation in the complaint is investigated, examined, or checked, to prevent or correct any alleged wrong, and to provide any relief appropriate under such circumstances." As JUSTICE GINSBURG has persuasively explained in her own dissenting opinion, our customary respect for state interpretations of state law counsels against rejection of the Florida court's determinations in this case.

C

It is only on the third issue before us that there is a meritorious argument for relief, as this Court's *Per Curiam* opinion recognizes. It is an issue that might well have been dealt with adequately by the Florida courts if the state proceedings had not been interrupted, and if not disposed of at the state level it could have been considered by the Congress in any electoral vote dispute. But because the course of state proceedings has been interrupted, time is short, and the issue is before us, I think it sensible for the Court to address it.

Petitioners have raised an equal protection claim (or, alternatively, a due process claim, see generally *Logan v. Zimmerman Brush Co.*, 455 U.S. 422 [1982]), in the charge that unjustifiably disparate standards are applied in different electoral jurisdictions to otherwise identical facts. It is true that the Equal Protection Clause does not forbid the use of a variety of voting mechanisms within a jurisdiction, even though different mechanisms will have different levels of effectiveness in recording voters' intentions; local variety can be justified by concerns about cost, the potential value of innovation, and so on. But evidence in the record here suggests that a different order of disparity obtains under rules for determining a voter's intent that have been applied (and could continue to be applied) to identical types of ballots used in identical brands of machines and exhibiting identical physical characteristics (such as "hanging" or "dimpled" chads). See, *e.g.*, Tr., at 238–242 (Dec. 2–3, 2000) (testimony of Palm Beach County Canvassing Board Chairman Judge Charles Burton describing varying standards applied to imperfectly punched ballots in Palm Beach County during pre-certification manual recount); *id.*, at 497–500 (similarly describing varying standards applied in Miami-Dade County); Tr. of Hearing 8–10 (Dec. 8, 2000) (soliciting from county canvassing boards proposed protocols for determining voters' intent but declining to provide a precise, uniform standard). I can conceive of no legitimate state interest served by these differing treatments of the expressions of voters' fundamental rights. The differences appear wholly arbitrary.

In deciding what to do about this, we should take account of the fact that electoral votes are due to be cast in six days. I would therefore remand the case to the courts of Florida with instructions to establish uniform standards for evaluating the several types of ballots that have prompted differing treatments, to be applied within and among counties when passing on such identical ballots in any further recounting (or successive recounting) that the courts might order.

Unlike the majority, I see no warrant for this Court to assume that Florida could not possibly comply with this requirement before the date set for the meeting of electors, December 18. Although one of the dissenting justices of the State Supreme Court estimated that disparate standards potentially affected 170,000 votes, *Gore* v. *Harris, supra*, ___ So. 2d, at ___ (slip op., at 66), the number at issue is significantly smaller. The 170,000 figure apparently represents all uncounted votes, both undervotes (those for which no Presidential choice was recorded by a machine) and overvotes (those rejected because of votes for more than one candidate). Tr. of Oral Arg. 61–62. But as JUSTICE BREYER has pointed out, no showing has been made of legal overvotes uncounted, and counsel for Gore made an uncontradicted representation to the Court that the statewide total of undervotes is about 60,000. *Id.*, at 62. To recount these manually would be a tall order, but before this Court stayed the effort to do that the courts of

Florida were ready to do their best to get that job done. There is no justification for denying the State the opportunity to try to count all disputed ballots now.

I respectfully dissent.

Note

1. When the Florida court ruled, the totals for Bush and Gore were then less than 1,000 votes apart. One dissent pegged the number of uncounted votes in question at 170,000. *Gore v. Harris, supra,* __ So. 2d __ , (slip op., at 66) (opinion of Harding, J.). Gore's counsel represented to us that the relevant figure is approximately 60,000, Tr. of Oral Arg. 62, the number of ballots in which no vote for President was recorded by the machines.

SUPREME COURT OF THE UNITED STATES
No. 00-949
GEORGE W. BUSH, ET AL., PETITIONERS *v.*
ALBERT GORE, JR., ET AL.
ON WRIT OF CERTIORARI
TO THE FLORIDA SUPREME COURT
[December 12, 2000]

JUSTICE GINSBURG, with whom JUSTICE STEVENS joins, and with whom JUSTICE SOUTER and JUSTICE BREYER join as to Part I, dissenting.

I

THE CHIEF JUSTICE acknowledges that provisions of Florida's Election Code "may well admit of more than one interpretation." *Ante*, at 3 (concurring opinion). But instead of respecting the state high court's province to say what the State's Election Code means, THE CHIEF JUSTICE maintains that Florida's Supreme Court has veered so far from the ordinary practice of judicial review that what it did cannot properly be called judging. My colleagues have offered a reasonable construction of Florida's law. Their construction coincides with the view of one of Florida's seven Supreme Court justices. *Gore v. Harris,* __ So. 2d __, __ (Fla. 2000) (slip op., at 45–55) (Wells, C. J., dissenting); *Palm Beach County Canvassing Bd. v. Harris,* __ So. 2d __, __ (Fla. 2000) (slip op., at 34) (on remand) (confirming, 6-1, the construction of Florida law advanced in *Gore*). I might join THE CHIEF JUSTICE were it my commission to interpret Florida law. But disagreement with the Florida court's interpretation of its own State's law does not warrant the conclusion that the justices of that court have legislated. There is no cause here to believe that the members of Florida's high court have done less than "their mortal best to discharge their oath of office," *Sumner* v. *Mata*, 449 U.S. 539, 549 (1981), and no cause to upset their reasoned interpretation of Florida law.

This Court more than occasionally affirms statutory, and even constitutional, interpretations with which it disagrees. For example, when reviewing challenges to administrative agencies' interpretations of laws they implement, we defer to the agencies unless their interpretation violates "the unambiguously expressed intent of Congress." *Chevron U.S.A. Inc.* v. *Natural Resources Defense Council, Inc.*, 467 U.S. 837, 843 (1984). We do so in the face of the declaration in Article I of the United States Constitution that "All legislative Powers herein granted shall be vested in a Congress of the United States." Surely the Constitution does not call upon us to pay more respect to a federal administrative agency's construction of federal law than to a state high court's interpretation of its own State's law. And not uncommonly, we let stand state-court interpretations of *federal* law with which we might disagree. Notably, in the habeas context, the Court adheres to the view that "there is 'no intrinsic reason why the fact that a man is a federal judge should make him more competent, or conscientious, or learned with respect to [federal law] than his neighbor in the state courthouse.'" *Stone* v. *Powell*, 428 U.S. 465, 494, n. 35 (1976) (quoting Bator, Finality in Criminal Law and Federal Habeas Corpus for State Prisoners, 76 Harv. L. Rev. 441, 509 (1963)); see *O'Dell* v. *Netherland*, 521 U.S. 151, 156 (1997) ("[T]he *Teague* doctrine validates reasonable, good-faith interpretations of existing precedents made by state courts even though they are shown to be contrary to later decisions") (citing *Butler* v. *McKellar*, 494 U.S. 407, 414 (1990)); O'Connor, Trends in the Relationship Between the Federal and State Courts from the Perspective of a State Court Judge, 22 Wm. & Mary L. Rev. 801, 813 (1981) ("There is no reason to assume that state court judges cannot and will not provide a 'hospitable forum' in litigating federal constitutional questions").

No doubt there are cases in which the proper application of federal law may hinge on interpretations of state law. Unavoidably, this Court must sometimes examine state law in order to protect federal rights. But we have dealt with such cases ever mindful of the full measure of respect we owe to interpretations of state law by a State's highest court. In the Contract Clause case, *General Motors Corp.* v. *Romein*, 503 U.S. 181 (1992), for example, we said that although "ultimately we are bound to decide for ourselves whether a contract was made," the Court "accord[s] respectful consideration and great weight to the views of the State's highest court." *Id.*, at 187 (citation omitted). And in *Central Union Telephone Co. v. Edwardsville*, 269 U.S. 190 (1925), we upheld the Illinois Supreme Court's interpretation of a state waiver rule, even though that interpretation resulted in the forfeiture of federal constitutional rights. Refusing to supplant Illinois law with a federal definition of waiver, we explained that the state court's declaration "should bind us unless so unfair or unreasonable in its application to those asserting a federal right as to obstruct it." *Id.*, at 195.[1] In deferring to state courts on matters of state law, we appropriately recognize that this Court acts as an "'outside[r]' lacking the common exposure to local law which comes from sitting in the jurisdiction." *Lehman Brothers v. Schein*, 416 U.S. 386, 391 (1974). That recognition has sometimes prompted us to resolve doubts about the meaning of state law by certifying issues to a State's highest court, even when federal rights are at stake. Cf. *Arizonans for Official English v. Arizona*, 520 U.S. 43, 79 (1997) ("Warnings against premature adjudication of constitutional questions bear heightened attention when a federal court is asked to invalidate a State's law, for the federal tribunal risks friction-generating error when it endeavors to construe a novel state Act not yet reviewed by the State's highest court"). Notwithstanding our authority to decide issues of state law underlying federal claims, we have used the certification devise to afford state high courts an opportunity to inform us on matters of their own State's law because such restraint "helps build a cooperative judicial federalism." *Lehman Brothers*, 416 U.S., at 391. Just last Term, in *Fiore v. White*, 528 U.S. 23 (1999), we took advantage of Pennsylvania's certification procedure. In that case, a state prisoner brought a federal habeas action claiming that the State had failed to prove an essential element of his charged offense in violation of the Due Process Clause. *Id.*, at 25–26. Instead of resolving the state-law question on which the federal claim depended, we certified the question to the Pennsylvania Supreme Court for that court to "help determine the proper state-law predicate for our determination of the federal constitutional questions raised." *Id.*, at 29; *id.*, at 28 (asking the Pennsylvania Supreme Court whether its recent interpretation of the statute under which Fiore was convicted "was always the statute's meaning, even at the time of Fiore's trial"). THE CHIEF JUSTICE's willingness to *reverse* the Florida Supreme Court's interpretation of Florida law in this case is at least in tension with our reluctance in Fiore even to interpret Pennsylvania law before seeking instruction from the Pennsylvania Supreme Court. I would have thought the "cautious approach" we counsel when federal courts address matters of state law, *Arizonans*, 520 U.S., at 77, and our commitment to "build[ing] cooperative judicial federalism," *Lehman Brothers*, 416 U.S., at 391, demanded greater restraint.

Rarely has this Court rejected outright an interpretation of state law by a state high court. *Fairfax's Devisee* v. *Hunter's Lessee*, 7 Cranch 603 (1813), *NAACP* v. *Alabama ex rel. Patterson*, 357 U.S. 449 (1958), and *Bouie* v. *City of Columbia*, 378 U.S. 347 (1964), cited by THE CHIEF JUSTICE, are three such rare instances. See *ante*, at 4, 5, and n. 1. But those cases are embedded in historical contexts hardly comparable to the situation here. *Fairfax's Devisee*, which held that the Virginia Court of Appeals had misconstrued its own forfeiture laws to deprive a British subject of lands secured to him by federal treaties, occurred amidst vociferous States' rights attacks on the Marshall Court. G. Gunther & K. Sullivan, Constitutional Law 61–62 (13th ed. 1997). The Virginia court refused to obey this Court's *Fairfax's Devisee* mandate to enter judgment for the British subject's successor in interest. That refusal led to the Court's pathmarking decision in *Martin* v. *Hunter's Lessee*, 1 Wheat. 304 (1816). *Patterson*, a case decided three months after *Cooper* v. *Aaron*, 358 U.S. 1 (1958), in the face of Southern resistance to the civil rights movement, held that the Alabama Supreme Court had irregularly applied its own procedural rules to deny review of a contempt order against the NAACP arising from its refusal to disclose membership lists. We said that "our jurisdiction is not defeated if the nonfederal ground relied on by the state court is without any fair or substantial support." 357 U.S., at 455. *Bouie*, stemming from a lunch counter "sit-in" at the height of the civil rights movement, held that the South Carolina Supreme Court's construction of its trespass laws—criminalizing conduct not covered by the text of an otherwise clear statute— was "unforeseeable" and thus violated due process when applied retroactively to the petitioners. 378 U.S., at 350, 354.

THE CHIEF JUSTICE's casual citation of these cases might lead one to believe they are part of a larger collection of cases in which we said that the Constitution impelled us to train a skeptical eye on a state court's portrayal of state law. But one would be hard pressed, I think, to find additional cases that fit the mold. As JUSTICE BREYER convincingly explains, see *post*, at 6–9 (dissenting opinion), this case involves nothing close to the kind of recalcitrance by a state high court that warrants extraordinary action by this Court. The Florida Supreme Court concluded that counting every legal vote was the overriding concern of the Florida Legislature when it enacted the State's Election Code. The court surely should not be bracketed with state high courts of the Jim Crow South.

THE CHIEF JUSTICE says that Article II, by providing that state legislatures shall direct the manner of appointing electors, authorizes federal superintendence over the relationship between state courts and state legislatures, and licenses a departure from the usual deference we give to state court interpretations of state law. Ante, at 5 (concurring opinion) ("To attach definitive weight to the pronouncement of a state court, when the very question at issue is whether the court has actually departed from the statutory meaning, would be to abdicate our responsibility to enforce the explicit requirements of Article II"). The Framers of our Constitution, however, understood that in a republican government, the judiciary would construe the legislature's enactments. See U.S. Const., Art. III; The Federalist No. 78 (A. Hamilton). In light of the constitutional guarantee to States of a "Republican Form of Government," U.S. Const., Art. IV, §4, Article II can hardly be read to invite this Court to disrupt a State's republican regime. Yet THE CHIEF JUSTICE today would reach out to do just that. By holding that Article II requires our revision of a state court's construction of state laws in order to protect one organ of the State from another, THE CHIEF JUSTICE contradicts the basic principle that a State may organize itself as it sees fit. See, *e.g.*, *Gregory* v. *Ashcroft*, 501 U.S. 452, 460 (1991) ("Through the structure of its government, and the character of those who exercise government authority, a State defines itself as a sovereign"); *Highland Farms Dairy, Inc.* v. *Agnew*, 300 U.S. 608, 612 (1937) ("How power shall be distributed by a state among its governmental organs is commonly, if not always, a question for the state itself").[2] Article II does not call for the scrutiny undertaken by this Court.

The extraordinary setting of this case has obscured the ordinary principle that dictates its proper resolution: Federal courts defer to state high courts' interpretations of their State's own law. This principle reflects the core of federalism, on which all agree. "The Framers split the atom of sovereignty. It was the genius of their idea that our citizens would have two political capacities, one state and one federal, each protected from incursion by the other." *Saenz* v. *Roe*, 526 U.S. 489, 504, n. 17 (1999) (citing *U.S. Term Limits, Inc.* v. *Thornton*, 514 U.S. 779, 838 (1995) (KENNEDY, J., concurring)). THE CHIEF JUSTICE's solicitude for the Florida Legislature comes at the expense of the more fundamental solicitude we owe to the legislature's sovereign. U.S. Const., Art. II, §1, cl. 2 ("Each *State* shall appoint, in such Manner as the Legislature *thereof* may direct," the electors for President and Vice President) (emphasis added); *ante*, at 1–2 (STEVENS, J., dissenting).[3] Were the other members of this Court as mindful as they generally are of our system of dual sovereignty, they would affirm the judgment of the Florida Supreme Court.

II

I agree with JUSTICE STEVENS that petitioners have not presented a substantial equal protection claim. Ideally, perfection would be the appropriate standard for judging the recount. But we live in an imperfect world, one in which thousands of votes have not been counted. I cannot agree that the recount adopted by the Florida court, flawed as it may be, would yield a result any less fair or precise than the certification that preceded that recount. See, *e.g.*, *McDonald* v. *Board of Election Comm'rs of Chicago*, 394 U.S. 802, 807 (1969) (even in the context of the right to vote, the state is permitted to reform "'one step at a time'") (quoting *Williamson* v. *Lee Optical of Oklahoma, Inc.*, 348 U.S. 483, 489 (1955)).

Even if there were an equal protection violation, I would agree with JUSTICE STEVENS, JUSTICE SOUTER, and JUSTICE BREYER that the Court's concern about the December 12 date, *ante*, at 12, is misplaced. Time is short in part because of the Court's entry of a stay on December 9, several hours after an able circuit judge in Leon County had begun to superintend the recount process. More fundamentally, the Court's reluctance to let the recount go forward—despite its suggestion that "[t]he search for intent can be confined by specific rules designed to ensure uniform treatment," *ante*, at 7—ultimately turns on its own judgment about the practical realities of implementing a recount, not the judgment of those much closer to the process.

Equally important, as JUSTICE BREYER explains, *post*, at 12 (dissenting opinion), the December 12 date for bringing Florida's electoral votes into 3 U.S.C. §5's safe harbor lacks the significance the Court assigns it. Were that date to pass, Florida would still be entitled to deliver electoral votes Congress *must* count unless both Houses find that the votes "ha[d] not been . . . regularly given." 3 U.S.C. §15. The statute identifies other significant dates. See, *e.g.*, §7 (specifying December 18 as the date electors "shall meet and give their votes"); §12 (specifying "the fourth Wednesday in December"—this year, December 27—as the date on which Congress, if it has not received a State's electoral votes, shall request the state secretary of dissenting state to send a certified return immediately). But none of these dates has ultimate significance in light of Congress' detailed provisions for determining, on "the sixth day of January," the validity of electoral votes. §15.

The Court assumes that time will not permit "orderly judicial review of any disputed matters that might arise." *Ante*, at 1. But no one has doubted the good faith and diligence with which Florida election officials, attorneys for all sides of this controversy, and the courts of law have performed their duties. Notably, the Florida Supreme Court has produced two substantial opinions within 29 hours of oral argument. In sum, the Court's conclusion that a constitutionally adequate recount is impractical is a prophecy the Court's own judgment will not allow to be tested. Such an untested prophecy should not decide the Presidency of the United States.

I dissent.

Notes

1. See also *Lucas* v. *South Carolina Coastal Council*, 505 U.S. 1003, 1032, n. 18 (1992) (South Carolina could defend a regulatory taking "if an *objectively reasonable application* of relevant precedents [by its courts] would exclude . . . beneficial uses in the circumstances in which the land is presently found"); *Bishop* v. *Wood*, 426 U.S. 341, 344–345 (1976) (deciding whether North Carolina had created a property interest cognizable under the Due Process Clause by reference to state law as interpreted by the North Carolina Supreme Court). Similarly, in *Gurley* v. *Rhoden*, 421 U.S. 200 (1975), a gasoline retailer claimed that due process entitled him to deduct a state gasoline excise tax in computing the amount of his sales subject to a state sales tax, on the grounds that the legal incidence of the excise tax fell on his customers and that he acted merely as a collector of the tax. The Mississippi Supreme Court held that the legal incidence of the excise tax fell on petitioner. Observing that "a State's highest court is the final judicial arbiter of the meaning of state statutes," we said that "[w]hen a state court has made its own definitive determination as to the operating incidence, . . . [w]e give this finding great weight in determining the natural effect of a statute, and if it is consistent with the statute's reasonable interpretation it will be deemed conclusive." *Id.*, at 208.

2. Even in the rare case in which a State's "manner" of making and construing laws might implicate a structural constraint, Congress, not this Court, is likely the proper governmental entity to enforce that constraint. See U.S. CONST., amend. XII; 3 U.S.C. §§1–15; cf. *Ohio ex rel. Davis* v. *Hildebrant*, 241 U.S. 565, 569 (1916) (treating as a nonjusticiable political question whether use of a referendum to over-

ride a congressional districting plan enacted by the state legislature violates Art. I, §4); *Luther* v. *Borden*, 7 How. 1, 42 (1849).

3. "[B]ecause the Framers recognized that state power and identity were essential parts of the federal balance, see The Federalist No. 39, the Constitution is solicitous of the prerogatives of the States, even in an otherwise sovereign federal province. The Constitution . . . grants States certain powers over the times, places, and manner of federal elections (subject to congressional revision), Art. I, §4, cl. 1 . . ., and allows States to appoint electors for the President, Art. II, §1, cl. 2." *U.S. Term Limits, Inc.* v. *Thornton*, 514 U.S. 779, 841–842 (1995) (KENNEDY, J., concurring).

SUPREME COURT OF THE UNITED STATES
No. 00-949
GEORGE W. BUSH, ET AL., PETITIONERS *v.*
ALBERT GORE, JR., ET AL.
ON WRIT OF CERTIORARI
TO THE FLORIDA SUPREME COURT
[December 12, 2000]

JUSTICE BREYER, with whom JUSTICE STEVENS and JUSTICE GINSBURG join except as to Part I-A-1, and with whom JUSTICE SOUTER joins as to Part I, dissenting.

The Court was wrong to take this case. It was wrong to grant a stay. It should now vacate that stay and permit the Florida Supreme Court to decide whether the recount should resume.

I

The political implications of this case for the country are momentous. But the federal legal questions presented, with one exception, are insubstantial.

A

1

The majority raises three Equal Protection problems with the Florida Supreme Court's recount order: first, the failure to include overvotes in the manual recount; second, the fact that *all* ballots, rather than simply the undervotes, were recounted in some, but not all, counties; and, third, the absence of a uniform, specific standard to guide the recounts. As far as the first issue is concerned, petitioners presented no evidence, to this Court or to any Florida court, that a manual recount of overvotes would identify additional legal votes. The same is true of the second and, in addition, the majority's reasoning would seem to invalidate any state provision for a manual recount of individual counties in a statewide election.

The majority's third concern does implicate principles of fundamental fairness. The majority concludes that the Equal Protection Clause requires that a manual recount be governed not only by the uniform general standard of the "clear intent of the voter," but also by uniform subsidiary standards (for example, a uniform determination whether indented, but not perforated, "undervotes" should count). The opinion points out that the Florida Supreme Court ordered the inclusion of Broward County's undercounted "legal votes" even though those votes included ballots that were not perforated but simply "dimpled," while newly recounted ballots from other counties will likely include only votes determined to be "legal" on the basis of a stricter standard. In light of our previous remand, the Florida Supreme Court may have been reluctant to adopt a more specific standard than that provided for by the legislature for fear of exceeding its authority under Article II. However, since the use of different standards could favor one or the other of the candidates, since time was, and is, too short to permit the lower courts to iron out significant differences through ordinary judicial review, and since the relevant distinction was embodied in the order of the State's highest court, I agree that, in these very special circumstances, basic principles of fairness should have counseled the adoption of a uniform standard to address the problem. In light of the majority's disposition, I need not decide whether, or the extent to which, as a remedial matter, the Constitution would place limits upon the content of the uniform standard.

2

Nonetheless, there is no justification for the majority's remedy, which is simply to reverse the lower court and halt the recount entirely. An appropriate remedy would be, instead, to remand this case with instructions that, even at this late date, would permit the Florida Supreme Court to require recounting *all* undercounted votes in Florida, including those from Broward, Volusia, Palm Beach, and Miami-Dade counties, whether or not previously recounted prior to the end of the protest period, and to do so in accordance with a single, uniform substandard.

The majority justifies stopping the recount entirely on the ground that there is no more time. In particular, the majority relies on the lack of time for the Secretary to review and approve equipment needed to separate undervotes. But the majority reaches this conclusion in the absence of *any* record evidence that the recount could not have been completed in the time allowed by the Florida Supreme Court. The majority finds facts outside of the record on matters that state courts are in a far better position to address. Of course, it is too late for any such recount to take place by December 12, the date by which election disputes must be decided if a State is to take advantage of the safe harbor provisions of 3 U.S.C. §5. Whether there is time to conduct a recount prior to December 18, when the electors are scheduled to meet, is a matter for the state courts to determine. And whether, under Florida law, Florida could or could not take further action is obviously a matter for Florida courts, not this Court, to decide. See *ante*, at 13 (*per curiam*).

By halting the manual recount, and thus ensuring that the uncounted legal votes will not be counted under any standard, this Court crafts a remedy out of proportion to the asserted harm. And that remedy harms the very fairness interests the Court is attempting to protect. The manual recount would itself redress a problem of unequal treatment of ballots. As JUSTICE STEVENS points out, see *ante*, at 4 and n. 4 (STEVENS, J., dissenting opinion), the ballots of voters in counties that use punch-card systems are more likely to be disqualified than those in counties using optical-scanning systems. According to recent news reports, variations in the undervote rate are even more pronounced. See Fessenden, No-Vote Rates Higher in Punch Card Count, New York Times, Dec. 1, 2000, p. A29 (reporting that 0.3% of ballots cast in 30 Florida counties using optical-scanning systems registered no Presidential vote, in comparison with 1.53% in the 15 counties using Votomatic punch-card ballots). Thus, in a system that allows counties to use different types of voting systems, voters already arrive at the polls with an unequal chance that their votes will be counted. I do not see how the fact that this results from counties' selection of different voting machines rather than a court order makes the outcome any more fair. Nor do I understand why the Florida Supreme Court's recount order, which helps to redress this inequity, must be entirely prohibited based on a deficiency that could easily be remedied.

B

The remainder of petitioners' claims, which are the focus of the CHIEF JUSTICE's concurrence, raise no significant federal questions. I cannot agree that the CHIEF JUSTICE's unusual review of state law in this case, see *ante*, at 5–8 (GINSBURG, J., dissenting opinion), is justified by reference either to Art. II, §1, or to 3 U.S.C. §5. Moreover, even were such review proper, the conclusion that the Florida Supreme Court's decision contravenes federal law is untenable.

While conceding that, in most cases, "comity and respect for federalism compel us to defer to the decisions of state courts on issues of state law," the concurrence relies on some combination of Art. II, §1, and 3 U.S.C. §5 to justify the majority's conclusion that this case is one of the few in which we may lay that fundamental principle aside. *Ante*, at 2 (Opinion of REHN-QUIST, C. J.) The concurrence's primary foundation for this conclusion rests on an appeal to plain text: Art. II, §1's grant of the power to appoint Presidential electors to the State "Legislature." *Ibid*. But neither the text of Article II itself nor the only case the concurrence cites that interprets Article II, *McPherson* v. *Blacker*, 146 U.S. 1 (1892), leads to the conclusion that Article II grants unlimited power to the legislature, devoid of any state constitutional limitations, to select the manner of appointing electors. See *id.*, at 41 (specifically referring to state constitutional provision in upholding state law regarding selection of electors). Nor, as JUSTICE STEVENS points out, have we interpreted the Federal constitutional provision most analogous to Art. II, §1—Art. I, §4—in the strained manner put forth in the concurrence. *Ante*, at 1–2 and n. 1 (dissenting opinion).

The concurrence's treatment of §5 as "inform[ing]" its interpretation of Article II, §1, cl. 2, *ante*, at 3 (REHNQUIST, C. J., concurring), is no more convincing. The CHIEF JUSTICE contends that our opinion in *Bush* v. *Palm Beach County Canvassing Bd.*, *ante*, p. ____, *(per curiam) (Bush I)*, in which we stated that "a legislative wish to take advantage of [§5] would counsel against" a construction of Florida law that Congress might deem to be a change in law, *id.*, (slip op. at 6), now means that *this* Court "must ensure that post-election state court actions do not frustrate the legislative desire to attain the 'safe harbor' provided by §5." *Ante*, at 3. However, §5 is part of the rules that govern Congress' recognition of slates of electors. Nowhere in *Bush I* did we establish that this Court had the authority to enforce §5. Nor did we suggest that the permissive "counsel against" could be transformed into the mandatory "must ensure." And nowhere did we intimate, as the concurrence does here, that a state court decision that threatens the safe harbor provision of §5 does so in violation of Article II. The concurrence's logic turns the presumption that legislatures would wish to take advantage of § 5's "safe harbor" provision into a mandate that trumps other statutory provisions and overrides the intent that the legislature did express.

But, in any event, the concurrence, having conducted its review, now reaches the wrong conclusion. It says that "the Florida Supreme Court's interpretation of the Florida election laws impermissibly distorted them beyond what a fair reading required, in violation of Article II." *Ante*, at 4–5 (REHNQUIST, C. J, concurring). But what precisely is the distortion? Apparently, it has three elements. First, the Florida court, in its earlier opinion, changed the election certification date from November 14 to November 26. Second, the Florida court ordered a manual recount of "undercounted" ballots that could not have been fully completed by the December 12 "safe harbor" deadline. Third, the Florida court, in the opinion now under review, failed to give adequate deference to the determinations of canvassing boards and the Secretary.

To characterize the first element as a "distortion," however, requires the concurrence to second-guess the way in which the state court resolved a plain conflict in the language of different statutes. Compare Fla. Stat. §102.166 (2001) (foreseeing manual recounts during the protest period) with §102.111 (setting what is arguably too short a deadline for manual recounts to be conducted); compare §102.112(1) (stating that the Secretary "may" ignore late returns) with §102.111(1) (stating that the Secretary "shall" ignore late returns). In any event, that issue no longer has any practical importance and cannot justify the reversal of the different Florida court decision before us now.

To characterize the second element as a "distortion" requires the concurrence to overlook the fact that the inability of the Florida courts to conduct the recount on time is, in significant part, a problem of the Court's own making. The Florida Supreme Court thought that the recount could be completed on time, and, within hours, the Florida Circuit Court was moving in an orderly fashion to meet the deadline. This Court improvidently entered a stay. As a result, we will never know whether the recount could have been completed.

Nor can one characterize the third element as "impermissibl[e] distort[ing]" once one understands that there are two sides to the opinion's argument that the Florida Supreme Court "virtually eliminated the Secretary's discretion." *Ante*, at 9 (REHNQUIST, C. J, concurring). The Florida statute in question was amended in 1999 to provide that the "grounds for contesting an election" include the "rejection of a number of legal votes sufficient to . . . place in doubt the result of the election." Fla. Stat. §§102.168(3), (3)(c) (2000). And the parties have argued about the proper meaning of the statute's term "legal vote." The Secretary has claimed that a "legal vote" is a vote "properly executed in accordance with the instructions provided to all registered voters." Brief for Respondent Harris et al. 10. On that interpretation, punchcard ballots for which the machines cannot register a vote are not "legal" votes. *Id.*, at 14. The Florida Supreme Court did not accept her definition. But it had a reason. Its reason was that a different provision of Florida election laws (a provision that addresses damaged or defective ballots) says that no vote shall be disregarded "if there is a clear indication of the intent of the voter as determined by the canvassing board" (adding that ballots should not be counted "if it is impossible to determine the elector's choice"). Fla. Stat. §101.5614(5)(2000). Given this statutory language, certain roughly analogous judicial precedent, *e.g., Darby v. State ex rel. McCollough*, 75 So. 411 (Fla. 1917) (*per curiam*), and somewhat similar determinations by courts throughout the Nation, see cases cited *infra*, at 9, the Florida Supreme Court concluded that the term "legal vote" means a vote recorded on a ballot that clearly reflects what the voter intended. *Gore* v. *Harris*, ___ So. 2d ___, ___ (2000) (slip op., at 19). That conclusion differs from the conclusion of the Secretary. But nothing in Florida law requires the Florida Supreme Court to accept as determinative the Secretary's view on such a matter. Nor can one say that the Court's ultimate determination is so unreasonable as to amount to a constitutionally "impermissible distort[ion]" of Florida law.

The Florida Supreme Court, applying this definition, decided, on the basis of the record, that respondents had shown that the ballots undercounted by the voting machines contained enough "legal votes" to place "the results" of the election "in doubt." Since only a few hundred votes separated the candidates, and since the "undercounted" ballots numbered tens of thousands, it is difficult to see how anyone could find this conclusion unreasonable—however strict the standard used to measure the voter's "clear intent." Nor did this conclusion "strip" canvassing boards of their discretion. The boards retain their traditional discretionary authority during the protest period. And during the contest period, as the court stated, "the Canvassing Board's actions [during the protest period] may constitute evidence that a ballot does or does not qualify as a legal vote." *Id.*, at *13. Whether a local county canvassing board's discretionary judgment during the protest period not to conduct a manual recount will be set aside during a contest period depends upon whether a candidate provides additional evidence that the rejected votes contain enough "legal votes" to place the outcome of the race in doubt. To limit the local canvassing board's discretion in this way is not to eliminate that discretion. At the least, one could reasonably so believe.

The statute goes on to provide the Florida circuit judge with authority to "fashion such orders as he or she deems necessary to ensure that each allegation . . . is *investigated, examined,* or *checked,* . . . and to provide any relief appropriate." Fla. Stat. §102.168(8) (2000) (emphasis added). The Florida Supreme Court did just that. One might reasonably disagree with the Florida Supreme Court's interpretation of these, or other, words in the statute. But I do not see how one could call its plain language interpretation of a 1999 statutory change so misguided as no longer to qualify as judicial interpretation or as a usurpation of the authority of the State legislature. Indeed, other state courts have interpreted roughly similar state statutes in similar ways. See, *e.g., In re Election of U.S. Representative for Second Congressional Dist.,* 231 Conn. 602, 621, 653 A. 2d 79, 90–91 (1994) ("Whatever the process used to vote and to count votes, differences in technology should not furnish a basis for disregarding the bedrock principle that the purpose of the voting process is to ascertain the intent of the voters"); *Brown* v. *Carr,* 130 W. Va. 401, 460, 43 S. E.2d 401, 404–405 (1947) ("[W]hether a ballot shall be counted . . . depends on the intent of the voter. . . . Courts decry any resort to technical rules in reaching a conclusion as to the intent of the voter").

I repeat, where is the "impermissible" distortion?

II

Despite the reminder that this case involves "an election for the President of the United States," *ante,* at 1 (REHNQUIST, C. J., concurring), no preeminent legal concern, or practical concern related to legal questions, required this Court to hear this case, let alone to issue a stay that stopped Florida's recount process in its tracks. With one exception, petitioners' claims do not ask us to vindicate a constitutional provision designed to protect a basic human right. See, *e.g., Brown* v. *Board of Education,* 347 U.S. 483 (1954). Petitioners invoke fundamental fairness, namely, the need for procedural fairness, including finality. But with the one "equal protection" exception, they rely upon law that focuses, not upon that basic need, but upon the constitutional allocation of power. Respondents invoke a competing fundamental consideration—the need to determine the voter's true intent. But they look to state law, not to federal constitutional law, to protect that interest. Neither side claims electoral fraud, dishonesty, or the like. And the more fundamental equal protection claim might have been left to the state court to resolve if and when it was discovered to have mattered. It could still be resolved through a remand conditioned upon issuance of a uniform standard; it does not require reversing the Florida Supreme Court.

Of course, the selection of the President is of fundamental national importance. But that importance is political, not legal. And this Court should resist the temptation unnecessarily to resolve tangential legal disputes, where doing so threatens to determine the outcome of the election.

The Constitution and federal statutes themselves make clear that restraint is appropriate. They set forth a road map of how to resolve disputes about electors, even after an election as close as this one. That road map foresees resolution of electoral disputes by *state* courts. See 3 U.S.C. §5 (providing that, where a "State shall have provided, by laws enacted prior to [election day], for its final determination of any controversy or contest concerning the appointment of . . . electors . . . by *judicial* or other methods," the subsequently chosen electors enter a safe harbor free from congressional challenge). But it nowhere provides for involvement by the United States Supreme Court.

To the contrary, the Twelfth Amendment commits to Congress the authority and responsibility to count electoral votes. A federal statute, the Electoral Count Act, enacted after the close 1876 Hayes-Tilden Presidential election, specifies that, after States have tried to resolve disputes (through "judicial" or other means), Congress is the body primarily authorized to resolve remaining disputes. See Electoral Count Act of 1887, 24 Stat. 373, 3 U.S.C. §§5, 6, and 15.

The legislative history of the Act makes clear its intent to commit the power to resolve such disputes to Congress, rather than the courts:

> "The two Houses are, by the Constitution, authorized to make the count of electoral votes. They can only count legal votes, and in doing so must determine, from the best evidence to be had, what are legal votes. . . . The power to determine rests with the two Houses, and there is no other constitutional tribunal." H. Rep. No. 1638, 49th Cong., 1st Sess., 2 (1886) (report submitted by Rep. Caldwell, Select Committee on the Election of President and Vice-President).

The Member of Congress who introduced the Act added:

> "The power to judge of the legality of the votes is a necessary conse-

quence of the power to count. The existence of this power is of absolute necessity to the preservation of the Government. The interests of all the States in their relations to each other in the Federal Union demand that the ultimate tribunal to decide upon the election of President should be a constituent body, in which the States in their federal relationships and the people in their sovereign capacity should be represented." 18 Cong. Rec. 30 (1886).

"Under the Constitution who else could decide? Who is nearer to the State in determining a question of vital importance to the whole union of States than the constituent body upon whom the Constitution has devolved the duty to count the vote?" *Id.*, at 31.

The Act goes on to set out rules for the congressional determination of disputes about those votes. If, for example, a state submits a single slate of electors, Congress must count those votes unless both Houses agree that the votes "have not been . . . regularly given." 3 U.S.C. § 15. If, as occurred in 1876, one or more states submits two sets of electors, then Congress must determine whether a slate has entered the safe harbor of §5, in which case its votes will have "conclusive" effect. *Ibid.* If, as also occurred in 1876, there is controversy about "which of two or more of such State authorities . . . is the lawful tribunal" authorized to appoint electors, then each House shall determine separately which votes are "supported by the decision of such State so authorized by its law." *Ibid.* If the two Houses of Congress agree, the votes they have approved will be counted. If they disagree, then "the votes of the electors whose appointment shall have been certified by the executive of the State, under the seal thereof, shall be counted." *Ibid.* Given this detailed, comprehensive scheme for counting electoral votes, there is no reason to believe that federal law either foresees or requires resolution of such a political issue by this Court. Nor, for that matter, is there any reason to think that the Constitution's Framers would have reached a different conclusion. Madison, at least, believed that allowing the judiciary to choose the presidential electors "was out of the question." Madison, July 25, 1787 (reprinted in 5 Elliot's Debates on the Federal Constitution 363 (2d ed. 1876)).

The decision by both the Constitution's Framers and the 1886 Congress to minimize this Court's role in resolving close federal presidential elections is as wise as it is clear. However awkward or difficult it may be for Congress to resolve difficult electoral disputes, Congress, being a political body, expresses the people's will far more accurately than does an unelected Court. And the people's will is what elections are about.

Moreover, Congress was fully aware of the danger that would arise should it ask judges, unarmed with appropriate legal standards, to resolve a hotly contested Presidential election contest. Just after the 1876 Presidential election, Florida, South Carolina, and Louisiana each sent two slates of electors to Washington. Without these States, Tilden, the Democrat, had 184 electoral votes, one short of the number required to win the Presidency. With those States, Hayes, his Republican opponent, would have had 185. In order to choose between the two slates of electors, Congress decided to appoint an electoral commission composed of five Senators, five Representatives, and five Supreme Court Justices. Initially the Commission was to be evenly divided between Republicans and Democrats, with Justice David Davis, an Independent, to possess the decisive vote. However, when at the last minute the Illinois Legislature elected Justice Davis to the United States Senate, the final position on the Commission was filled by Supreme Court Justice Joseph P. Bradley. The Commission divided along partisan lines, and the responsibility to cast the deciding vote fell to Justice Bradley. He decided to accept the votes of the Republican electors, and thereby awarded the Presidency to Hayes.

Justice Bradley immediately became the subject of vociferous attacks. Bradley was accused of accepting bribes, of being captured by railroad interests, and of an eleventh-hour change in position after a night in which his house "was surrounded by the carriages" of Republican partisans and railroad officials. C. Woodward, Reunion and Reaction 159–160 (1966). Many years later, Professor Bickel concluded that Bradley was honest and impartial. He thought that "'the great question' for Bradley was, in fact, whether Congress was entitled to go behind election returns or had to accept them as certified by state authorities," an "issue of principle." The Least Dangerous Branch 185 (1962). Nonetheless, Bickel points out, the legal question upon which Justice Bradley's decision turned was not very important in the contemporaneous political context. He says that, "in the circumstances the issue of principle was trivial, it was overwhelmed by all that hung in the balance, and it should not have been decisive." *Ibid.*

For present purposes, the relevance of this history lies in the fact that the participation in the work of the electoral commission by five Justices, including Justice Bradley, did not lend that process legitimacy. Nor did it assure the public that the process had worked fairly, guided by the law.

Rather, it simply embroiled Members of the Court in partisan conflict, thereby undermining respect for the judicial process. And the Congress that later enacted the Electoral Count Act knew it.

This history may help to explain why I think it not only legally wrong, but also most unfortunate, for the Court simply to have terminated the Florida recount. Those who caution judicial restraint in resolving political disputes have described the quintessential case for that restraint as a case marked, among other things, by the "strangeness of the issue," its "intractability to principled resolution," its "sheer momentousness, . . . which tends to unbalance judicial judgment," and "the inner vulnerability, the self-doubt of an institution which is electorally irresponsible and has no earth to draw strength from." Bickel, *supra*, at 184. Those characteristics mark this case.

At the same time, as I have said, the Court is not acting to vindicate a fundamental constitutional principle, such as the need to protect a basic human liberty. No other strong reason to act is present. Congressional statutes tend to obviate the need. And, above all, in this highly politicized matter, the appearance of a split decision runs the risk of undermining the public's confidence in the Court itself. That confidence is a public treasure. It has been built slowly over many years, some of which were marked by a Civil War and the tragedy of segregation. It is a vitally necessary ingredient of any successful effort to protect basic liberty and, indeed, the rule of law itself. We run no risk of returning to the days when a President (responding to this Court's efforts to protect the Cherokee Indians) might have said, "John Marshall has made his decision; now let him enforce it!" Loth, Chief Justice John Marshall and the Growth of the American Republic 365 (1948). But we do risk a self-inflicted wound—a wound that may harm not just the Court, but the Nation.

I fear that in order to bring this agonizingly long election process to a definitive conclusion, we have not adequately attended to that necessary "check upon our own exercise of power," "our own sense of self-restraint." *United States* v. *Butler*, 297 U.S. 1, 79 (1936) (Stone, J., dissenting). Justice Brandeis once said of the Court, "The most important thing we do is not doing." Bickel, *supra*, at 71. What it does today, the Court should have left undone. I would repair the damage as best we now can, by permitting the Florida recount to continue under uniform standards.

I respectfully dissent.

Florida Attorney General Advisory Opinion of November 14

Advisory Legal Opinion
Number: AGO 2000-65
Date: November 14, 2000
Subject: Manual recount of ballots, error in voter tabulation
The Honorable Charles E. Burton
Chair, Palm Beach County Canvassing Board
County Courthouse
West Palm Beach, Florida 33401
Dear Judge Burton:

On behalf of the Palm Beach County Canvassing Board, you have asked this office's opinion as to the meaning of "error in voting tabulation which could affect the outcome of" an election as that phrase is used in section 102.166(5), Florida Statutes.

I am answering your request fully mindful that just yesterday the Division of Elections rendered Division of Elections Opinion 00-11 to the Chairman of the Republican Party, interpreting the duties of a county canvassing board pursuant to section 102.166(5), Florida Statutes.[1] Because the Division of Elections opinion is so clearly at variance with the existing Florida statutes and case law, and because of the immediate impact this erroneous opinion could have on the ongoing recount process, I am issuing this advisory opinion.

Section 102.166(4), Florida Statutes, permits a local canvassing board, upon request of a candidate or political party, to authorize a manual recount to include at least three precincts and at least 1 percent of the total votes cast for such candidate.[2] Section 102.166(5), Florida Statutes, provides "[i]f the manual recount indicates an error in vote tabulation which could affect the outcome of the election, the county canvassing board shall" among other options, manually recount all ballots.

Division of Election Opinion 00-11 concludes that the language "error in the vote tabulation" in section 102.166(5), Florida Statutes, refers only to a counting error in the vote tabulation system. The opinion concludes that the inability of a voting system to read an "improperly marked marksense or improperly punched punch-card ballot" is not an "error in the voter tabulation system" and would not, therefore, trigger a recount of all ballots. The division's opinion is wrong in several respects.

The opinion ignores the plain language of the statute which refers not to an error in the vote tabulation system but to an error in the vote tabulation. The Legislature has used the terms "vote tabulation system" and "automatic tabulating equipment" elsewhere in section 102.166, Florida Statutes, when it intended to refer to the system rather than the vote count. Yet the division, by reading "vote tabulation" and "vote tabulation system" as synonymous, blurs the distinctions that the Legislature clearly delineated in section 102.166.[3]

The error in vote tabulation might be caused by a mechanical malfunction in the operation of the vote-counting system, but the error might also result from the failure of a properly functioning mechanical system to discern the choices of the voters as revealed by the ballots. The fact that both possibilities are contemplated is evidenced by section 102.166(7) and (8), Florida Statutes. While subsection (8) addresses verification of tabulation software, subsection (7) provides procedures for an examination of the ballot by the canvassing board and counting teams to determine the voter's intent.

The division's opinion, without authority or support, effectively nullifies the language of section 102.166(7), Florida Statutes. Nothing in subsection (7) limits its application to the recount of all ballots. Rather, the procedures for a manual recount in subsection (7) equally apply to the initial sampling manual recount authorized in section 102.166(4)(d). Section 102.166(7)(b) states:

"If a counting team is unable to determine a voter's intent in casting a ballot, the ballot shall be presented to the county canvassing board for it to determine the voter's intent."

Yet under the division's interpretation, such language is rendered superfluous. It is fundamental principle of statutory construction that statutory language is not to be assumed to be surplusage; rather, a statute is to be construed to give meaning to all words and phrases contained within the statute.[4]

Section 102.166(7) clearly recognizes that an examination by a person of the ballot will occur to determine whether the voter complied with the statutory requirement, i.e., marked the marksense or punched the punch-card ballot. The statutes do not specify how a punch card must be punched. Clearly, there may be instances where a punch card or marksense ballot was not punched or marked in a manner in which the electronic or electromechanical equipment was able to read the ballot. Such a deficiency in the equipment in no way compromises the voter's intent or the canvassing board's ability to review the ballot and determine the voter's intent. In fact, section 101.5614(5) and (6), Florida Statutes, contemplate that such an examination will occur. Section 101.5614(6) provides that the ballot will not be counted if it is impossible to determine the elector's choice or if the elector marks more than one name than there are persons to be elected.

Clearly, the manual count of the sampling precincts which reveals a discrepancy between votes counted by the automatic tabulating equipment and valid ballots which were not properly read by the equipment but which constitute ballots in which the voter complied with the statutory requirements and in which the voter's intent may be ascertained constitutes an "error in vote tabulation." If the error is sufficient that it could affect the outcome of the election, then a manual recount of all ballots may be ordered by the county canvassing board.

The division's opinion fails to acknowledge the long- standing case law in Florida which has held that the intent of the voters as shown by their ballots should be given effect. Where a ballot is marked so as to plainly indicate the voter's choice and intent, it should be counted as marked unless some positive provision of law would be violated.[5]

As the state has moved toward electronic voting, nothing in this evolution has diminished the standards first articulated in such decisions as *State ex rel. Smith v. Anderson*[6] and *State ex rel. Nuccio v. Williams*[7] that the intent of the voter is of paramount concern and should be given effect if the voter has complied with the statutory requirement and that intent may be determined. For example, if a voter has clearly, physically penetrated a punch-card ballot, the canvassing board has the authority to determine that the voter's intention is clearly expressed even though such puncture is not sufficient to be read by automatic tabulating equipment.

In *State ex rel. Carpenter v. Barber*,[8] the Court stated:

"The intention of the voter should be ascertained from a study of the ballot and the vote counted, if the will and intention of the voter can be determined, even though the cross mark 'X' appears before or after the name of said candidate. See, *Wiggins, Co. Judge, v. State ex rel. Drane*, 106 Fla. 793, 144 So. 62; *Nuccio v. Williams*, 97 Fla. 159, 120 So. 310; *State ex rel. Knott v. Haskell*, 72 Fla. 176, 72 So. 651."

The Florida Statutes contemplate that where electronic or electromechanical voting systems are used, no vote is to be declared invalid or void if there is a clear indication of the intent of the voter as determined by the county canvassing board.[9]

In light of the plain language of section 102.166(5), Florida Statutes, authorizing a manual recount of all ballots when the sampling manual recount indicates an error in vote tabulation which could affect the outcome of the election and the general principles of election law, I must express my disagreement with the conclusions reached in Division of Election Opinion 00-11. Rather, I am of the opinion that the term "error in voter tabulation" encompasses a discrepancy between the number of votes determined by a voter tabulation system and the number of votes determined by a manual count of a sampling of precincts pursuant to section 102.166(4), Florida Statutes.

Sincerely,

Robert A. Butterworth

Attorney General

Notes

1. The validity of the opinion of the Division of Elections is questionable since it appears to exceed the authority granted to the division by Florida law. Section 106.23(2), Florida Statutes, provides the division with the authority to render advisory opinions interpreting the election code to, among others, a political party relating to actions such party has taken or proposes to take. Division of Elections Opinion 00-11, however, erroneously seeks to advise a political party about the responsibilities of the supervisor of elections and local canvassing board under section 102.166(5).

2. *See*, § 102.166(4)(d), Fla. Stat., stating that the person requesting the recount "shall choose three precincts to be recounted."

3. *See, e.g., Department of Professional Regulation, Board of Medical Examiners v. Durrani*, 455 So. 2d 515 (Fla. 1st DCA 1984) (legislative use of different terms in different portions of the same statute is strong evidence that different meanings were intended).

4. *See, Terrinoni v. Westward Ho!*, 418 So. 2d 1143 (Fla. 1st DCA 1982); *Pinellas County v. Woolley*, 189 So. 2d 217 (Fla. 2d DCA 1966); Ops. Att'y Gen. Fla. 95-27 (1995); 91-16 (1991) (operative language in a statute may not be regarded as surplusage); 91-11 (1991) (statute must be construed so as to give meaning to all words and phrases contained within that statute).

5. *See, State ex rel. Smith v. Anderson*, 8 So. 1 (Fla. 1890); *Darby v. State*, 75 So. 411 (Fla. 1917); *State ex rel. Nuccio v. Williams*, 120 So. 310 (Fla. 1929) (in performing their duty of counting, tabulating, and making due return of ballots cast in an election, the inspectors may, in some cases of ambiguity or apparent uncertainty in

the name voted for, determine, from the fact of the ballot as cast, the person for whom a vote was intended by the voter).

6. 8 So. 1 (Fla. 1890).

7. 120 So. 310 (Fla. 1929).

8. 198 So. 49, 51 (Fla. 1940).

9. *See, Wiggins v. State ex rel. Drane*, 144 So. 62, 63 (Fla. 1932) (separate tabulation and return of what may be deemed regular ballots does not mean that only regular ballots are to be counted; if the marking of the ballot should be irregular, but the voter casting such ballot has clearly indicated by an X-mark the candidate of his choice, the ballot should be counted as intended).

Remarks by Florida Senate President

Transcript of Remarks by Senate President John McKay
December 7, 2000
Good afternoon.

Earlier this afternoon, Speaker Feeney and I signed a proclamation calling for a special session to ensure that Florida's voters are not disenfranchised from the 2000 presidential election.

The action taken today is done so with considerable reluctance on my part due to the potential far-reaching effects of any actions. What we will do may impact the course of our country, and that is why I've approached the Legislature's role in this matter with—in a cautious and thoughtful manner.

My primary objective is simple, to ensure that the voters of Florida are not disenfranchised. I've been candid about who I've supported for the presidency. As a citizen of this state, I voted for George W. Bush.

But as Senate president I took an oath to represent all the people and not one single person or group. I embark on a special session not to advocate either position of the two protagonists but as a constitutional officer with a responsibility to represent the best interests of all Floridians.

On December 12 we may find ourselves in a position that calls for our involvement should there be no finality to the contests that are still pending. And it is possible that there may be more filed before this day is out. It would be irresponsible of us if we failed to put a safety net in place under the current court conditions.

Once again, if the election disputes are resolved by December 12 there may be a possibility that the Legislature will not have to act. We're convening on December 8 so that we will be in a position to act if necessary. We will not meet on either the Jewish or the Christian Sabbath. The current slate of electors that is in front of us, though, may be tainted because of the Supreme Court actions and other local county voting procedures.

Additionally, a reasonable person could conclude that the recent Supreme Court actions may cause Congress not to accept our electors that have already been sent to Washington. Our sole responsibility will be to put forth a slate of electors that is untainted and ensures that Florida's 25 electoral votes count in this election, regardless for whom they voted.

Transmittal Letter for Legislative Report on Special Session

December 4, 2000
The Honorable John McKay
President of the Senate
The Honorable Tom Feeney
Speaker of the House of Representatives
Dear President McKay and Speaker Feeney:
Your Select Joint Committee on the Manner of the Appointment of Presidential Electors having met, and after full and free conference, do recommend to their respective houses as follows:
1. The Florida Legislature convene in Special Session for the purpose of addressing the manner of appointment of presidential electors for the State of Florida; and, that
2. The Florida Legislature carefully consider the broad authority granted to it under Section I of Article III of the United States Constitution to establish the manner of appointment of the electors for the State of Florida; and, that
3. The Florida Legislature take appropriate action to ensure that Florida's 25 electoral votes for President and Vice President in the 2000 Presidential Election are counted.
Respectfully submitted,
Senator Lisa Carlton, Co-Chairman
Representative Johnnie Byrd, Co-Chairman

Excerpt from Ruling by Florida Supreme Court Mandating Statewide Manual Recount

Supreme Court of Florida
No. SC00-2431
ALBERT GORE, JR., and JOSEPH I. LIEBERMAN, Appellants,
vs.
KATHERINE HARRIS, as Secretary, etc., et al., Appellees.
[December 8, 2000]
PER CURIAM.
We have for review a final judgment of a Leon County trial court certified by the First District Court of Appeal as being of great public importance

and requiring immediate resolution by this Court. We have jurisdiction. See art. V, § 3(b)(5), Fla. Const. The final judgment under review denies all relief requested by appellants Albert Gore, Jr., and Joseph I. Lieberman, the Democratic candidates for President and Vice President of the United States, in their complaint contesting the certification of the state results in the November 7, 2000, presidential election. Although we find that the appellants are entitled to reversal in part of the trial court's order and are entitled to a manual count of the Miami-Dade County undervote, we agree with the appellees that the ultimate relief would require a counting of the legal votes contained within the undervotes in all counties where the undervote has not been subjected to a manual tabulation. Accordingly, we reverse and remand for proceedings consistent with this opinion.

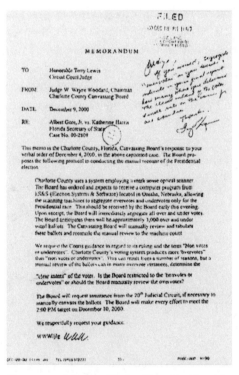

Figure 3.1. Memo to Judge Terry Lewis with handwritten notes

Chapter 4

The Electoral and Partisan Context

As we have seen, Republicans at the highest levels of Florida government took a number of steps to sabotage Florida's election system and block legally mandated recounts in the 2000 election. Their acts of malfeasance and misfeasance included Katherine Harris's flawed felon-disenfranchisement program, which differentially impacted Democrats and caused massive confusion on Election Day; the post-election threats by Jeb Bush's office to discourage Florida lawyers from working for Gore in the election litigation; the biased legal interpretations and administrative rulings by Harris and her staff that repeatedly caused confusion and delay; and the efforts by House Speaker Tom Feeney in coordination with the legal team of George Bush to create the appearance of a constitutional crisis. Whether any or all of these actions were illegal is unclear, but certainly they worked against the integrity of the election, undermined the rule of law, and used the powers of government to deflect the voters rather than to serve them.

Understanding the willingness of Republicans to resort to such behavior requires some familiarity with partisan trends in the Florida electorate and their effects on the political culture in Tallahassee. Republican actions to sabotage the election and block the recounts were not isolated incidents unique to a single, contested election; they were part of a larger pattern of political corruption that developed in the 1990s and continues to this day. The increasing ethnic and racial diversity of Florida's population has been eroding Republican electoral support, and Republican leaders have been trying to secure their power, while they still have it, by extending partisan control deep into the state's political institutions. In the process, Florida Republicans have developed a mind-set that is intolerant of dissent and insensitive to the rule of law.

This chapter examines the political context and partisan dynamics of the 2000 election. It begins by recounting the Republican Party's rise to power in Florida in the second half of the twentieth century. The chapter then discusses why Republican fortunes began to decline and what steps began to be taken to shore up the party's electoral position and strengthen its grip on the state government. The chapter concludes by explaining how Republican behavior in the 2000 election fit into this larger pattern of partisan entrenchment.

Why Voting Patterns Were Ignored

Voting patterns and other electoral dynamics received little attention either during or after the 2000 election controversy. In part this was because the election dispute centered on how the votes were to be counted and recounted, not on which groups had voted for which candidates and why. If demographic variations in voting were discussed by news reporters or expert commentators, it was almost always in terms of how they might affect the partisan distribution of ballot spoilage and the competitive situation of the candidates in light of the recounting trend of the moment. The implications of voting patterns for the long-term prospects of the Republican and Democratic parties were seldom if ever discussed.

Also reducing the attention given to electoral analysis was the absence of detailed information on voting patterns. In prior elections data on the voting tendencies of women, Hispanics, blacks, and other groups had been gathered in exit polls by Voter News Service (VNS), a company in New York City owned and operated by the five major television networks and the Associated Press, and this data had been used by the television networks to project winners and by the print media to assess turnout and analyze voting patterns. However, the exit polls on which VNS relied did not take voter error into account, which had apparently been much higher in Florida in 2000 than in previous elections, and the exit polls also ignored the effects of absentee ballots, which were up in 2000. After the election VNS concluded that its data from 2000 were not reliable. Consequently there was little information available during the election controversy for analyzing voting patterns even if they had been of interest.

Nonetheless electoral dynamics in Florida had a significant bearing on the election controversy. They influenced the election preparations of state officials, the candidates' assessment of their chances, the resources and attention devoted to Florida by the national parties, and the reactions of the citizenry as the election controversy unfolded.

An Unnoticed Surprise

Because voting patterns received little attention during the election controversy, most people failed to notice that the election outcome in Florida was a shocking blow to Republicans even though they prevailed in the Electoral College. When Republican George W. Bush first declared his candidacy, everyone thought that Florida would be his for the taking. After all, both the Florida legislature and Florida's congressional delegation were solidly Republican, and the state's popular Republican governor was George W.'s brother, Jeb. Hence Republicans looked to Florida to take them to the White House. Their strategy was to split the big states— win Texas and Florida to counterbalance expected Democratic victories in New York and California—and thereby push the election into the Midwest, where Gore was projected to do poorly because his staunch environmentalism would grate on industrial workers.

So much for expectations. Not only did Gore and Lieberman keep Florida in play through the entire campaign, thus forcing Bush and Cheney to spend time there instead of in Pennsylvania, Ohio, Michigan, and Illinois, the Democrats pulled in just as many Florida votes as their highly favored rivals.

Why did Bush and Cheney not win Florida by a substantial margin? Was it because of peculiar circumstances—fallout from Jeb's controversial policies on affirmative action, Gore's selection of a Jewish running mate, voter satisfaction with a booming economy—or were there deeper and more enduring reasons behind the Republicans' weak showing? A review of the evidence shows that Republican electoral support in Florida is waning. The widely shared view that Jeb could have delivered the state for George W. in 2000 underestimated Democratic strength in Florida and ignored the partisan impact of the rapidly changing demographic composition of the state's population.

Republican Fears in 2000

For Florida's leading Republicans, the 2000 election was an important opportunity to consolidate their power before the state's demographic trends overtake them. Not until 1998 had they been able to finally wrest control of both the state legislature and the governor's office from Florida Democrats, who had run the state for more than a century. Once Republicans had finally gained dominance, they became intent on solidifying their hold on the state's political institutions so that they would be able to maintain power in the face of rapid population growth among Democratic constituencies. Their strategy can be discerned from their actions. They sought to centralize power in the governor's office, change election laws to weaken Democratic voting power, facilitate absentee voting, stifle criticism from government analysts, and use privatization to replace state workers, who are inclined to favor the Democrats, with private service providers, whose dependence on government contracts would keep them loyal to the Republican power structure.

These tactics culminated in the 2000 election fiasco. The election, however, was not the Republicans' exclusive or even primary target. The actions they took that undermined the integrity of the 2000 election were part of a much larger assault on Florida's political institutions and civic culture. Their aim has never been merely to win a single election; they have been engaged in a long-term, multi-pronged effort to insert partisan Republican interests and people at key points throughout the state government, so that they can use the government resources and power to enforce party discipline, control public discourse, restrict access to information, and build support among doctors, state troopers, firefighters, and other groups amenable to Republican policies and seeking Republican favors. Winning the 2000 election was an important product of their tactics for subversion and entrenchment, but it was by no means the limit of their ambitions.

Despite their strength in the state, Republicans had reason to worry about Florida in the 2000 election and in future elections as well, because demographic trends had been (and still are) running against them. Since the 1950s Florida has been experiencing rapid population growth, and in the decades preceding the 2000 election the state had become steadily older and more diverse racially and ethnically. Although Republicans had been successful in attracting support from native Floridians, from in-migrating Midwesterners, and from Cuban Americans, the GOP had not done well with non-Cuban Hispanics, Caribbean blacks, African Americans, or senior citizens from the Northeast, and yet growth among all these Democratic constituencies, especially the minorities, was outpacing the much slower growth of the Republican base. In 2000 Florida's population was roughly 32 percent minority; by 2025 minorities are expected to make up 40 percent of state residents. Republicans anticipated problems in the 2000 election, and they saw even bigger problems later.

Similar electoral considerations were motivating Republicans nationally. In 2000 Florida was seen as a key state in Republican efforts to shatter the New Deal coalition once and for all, before it could be resuscitated and reinforced by rapid population growth among minorities. Beginning with Goldwater's nomination in 1964, the National Republican Party has been following a blueprint for pushing aside the Democrats by breaking their hold on the states of the Old Confederacy and creating an alliance of the West and the South against the Democrats' stronghold, the Northeast. This West-South coalition had been assembled temporarily by Presidents Nixon and Reagan but had broken apart under President Ford and the first President Bush. The South was the key to an electoral realignment, and one of the keys to the South was Florida.

But if a Republican-centered realignment is going to occur, it has to be soon. Population trends are running against Republicans not only in Florida but nationally, too. Florida is a picture of America's demographic future. If the Republicans could not take Florida in 2000, they would have trouble winning future presidential elections and would probably encounter increasing difficulty in states with large and growing minority populations.

The Modern Ascendance of Republican Power

The Republican Party's resurgence nationally after the success of the New Deal has depended considerably on Florida. The Republican road to the White House since the 1960s has been through the Old Confederacy, and

Florida has been the South's most Republican state. Florida has voted Republican in three out of every four presidential elections since 1952, and it was the first southern state since Reconstruction to have the governor's office and both houses of the legislature under Republican control.

Still, Republican power in Florida has always been tenuous. Although Republicans control the top tier of government, Florida is a competitive two-party state that favors centrist Democrats over Republicans in many national and statewide elections. In the 2000 election this was demonstrated quite clearly by the success of Democrat Bill Nelson over Republican Bill McCollum in the U.S. Senate race. It was also evident in voter registration. A table tracking voter registration by party between 1950 and 2000 is included in the appendix. Going into the 2000 election, Democrats outnumbered Republicans in Florida by more than 340,000 registered voters. To be sure, for several decades it had appeared that Florida was destined to become solidly Republican, but growth in Republican voter registration as a proportion of the statewide electorate peaked in 1996 at 43 percent and by 2000 had declined to 40 percent.

Florida's Three-Party System

The best way to understand the Republicans' success in Florida between 1964 and the mid-1990s is to think of Florida politics as a *regional* and *demographic* conflict involving *three* main voting blocks. One of these voting blocks is comprised of Republicans, who are concentrated in southwest and central Florida. Another is made up of liberal Democrats, who reside mainly in the retiree-rich counties on the southeast coast. In most statewide elections between 1960 and 1998, the votes from these two groups were roughly equal in number and therefore canceled each other out, leaving the third voting block, even though it is much smaller than the other two, to cast the deciding ballots.

The voters in this third group are referred to locally as Blue Dog Democrats. They are rural, white, traditional Southerners who register as Democrats but sometimes vote Republican, particularly in contests that are national or statewide in scope. The term "Blue Dog Democrats" comes from an earlier reference to "Yellow Dog Democrats," a phrase that originated in an old Florida saying among white southern Democrats prior to the 1950s. Supposedly these Democrats were so loyal to the Democratic Party and so hated the Republican Party—the Party of Lincoln—that they would vote for a Democrat, they claimed, "even if he were a yellow dog." When these Yellow Dog Democrats began to cross over to the Republican Party in presidential elections, they were initially called Dixiecrats after the name coined by Strom Thurmond in his third-party bid for the presidency in 1948. In the 1980s they came to be called Reagan Democrats, because, for a while prior to Reagan, they had returned to the National Democratic Party to support fellow Southerner Jimmy Carter, but Reagan pulled them back to the Republican side. In the 1990s many of these former Dixiecrats and Reagan Democrats came home once again to the Democratic Party, when the party put not one but two Southerners at the head of their ticket—Bill Clinton from Arkansas and Al Gore from Tennessee. Those Reagan Democrats who stayed with the Republicans through the Clinton-Gore administrations then began to be called Blue Dog Democrats, because blue was associated with the Republican Party and these were former Yellow Dogs.

Most of the Blue Dog counties are located in rural north Florida directly south of Tallahassee and in a thick band to the east and west about two counties out. Leon County itself, where Tallahassee is located, along with the counties immediately to Leon's east and west, do not qualify as Blue Dog territory because their voters have remained staunch Democrats. Conversely the counties approaching Pensacola to the west and Jacksonville to the east are not Blue Dog counties because they have become predominately Republican.

Another center of Blue Dog strength is a cluster of rural counties south of Orlando. This area is sometimes referred to collectively as "Forgotten Florida." Blue Dogs in Forgotten Florida are more likely than other Blue Dogs to identify with the Christian Right.

Blue Dogs were often the key to victory in Florida elections, because they did not vote consistently for the same political party. Since the mid-1960s Florida politics has been complicated and unstable in large part because Republicans and mainstream Democrats have remained loyal to their parties, whereas the Blue Dogs have shifted back and forth, depending on the nature of the office, the candidates, and the times.

The Republican Party rose to power in Florida by stressing conservative policies on civil rights and thereby attracting Blue Dog support in statewide elections. The split within the Democratic Party between, on the one hand, liberal and centrist Democrats and, on the other, Dixiecrats, Reagan Democrats, and Blue Dogs began in 1936 when President Roosevelt allowed black delegates to be seated at the National Democratic Convention, which caused a walkout by state delegations from the South. The Democrat-Dixiecrat breach widened in 1964 and 1965 when the Democrat-controlled Congress passed the civil rights and voting rights legislation that effectively dismantled racial segregation in the southern states. From that point forward, the Republican Party was suddenly a force in Florida politics. Indeed, by 1968 a Republican was in the governor's office.

Florida Democrats responded to this new electoral climate by distancing themselves from the National Democratic Party and running candidates who would appeal to Florida crackers. The gubernatorial election was moved to the off year between presidential elections so that the coattails of conservative presidential candidates, such as Goldwater in 1964 and Wallace and Nixon in 1968, would not hurt the chances of Democrats running for governor. Democratic elected officials began to refer to themselves as *southern* Democrats, as if the Democratic Party in the South was not the same party that had nominated Hubert Humphrey, George McGovern, and other northern liberals.

Florida Democrats also began to use the state's two-primary system to nominate centrists who could attract support from both the liberal and conservative wings of the party's base. In the two-primary system, if there are more than two candidates running to be the party's nominee for a particular office and if none of these candidates receives a majority in the first primary, a second primary is held to select between the top two vote getters in the first primary. The second primary is generally referred to as the "runoff."

The two-primary system has helped Democrats forge a coalition between conservative Democrats in north and central Florida and liberal Democrats in south Florida, because it gives moderates time to build support. The two-primary system was put in place in Florida's statewide races in 1932. Since then, for the Democratic Party nomination, there have been thirteen races involving runoffs. In almost half (six) of these, the runner-up in the first primary was the winner of the second primary. Among this six were three of Florida's greatest governors: Leroy Collins in 1954, Reubin Askew in 1970, and Bob Graham in 1978. All three ran well in both north and south Florida.

This was essential. After 1964 the only way Florida Democrats were able to prevent Republican mining of their base was by running moderate populists whose policies appealed to south Florida Democrats and whose character and background pulled Blue Dogs, at least temporarily, back into the Democratic fold.

Florida politics is a bellwether for the entire country, not only because of Florida's population trends but also because the voting pattern in Florida is a microcosm of the nation's. Nationally Republicans regained power after World War II by playing on the (white) South's hostility to racial desegregation. In response, the National Democratic Party began to nominate Southerners. Since 1964 Democrats have won the presidency only when they have regained the support of Blue Dog Democrats by placing a Southerner at the head of their ticket: Johnson in 1964, Carter in 1976, and Clinton in 1992 and 1996.

What Republicans Learned from the Old He Coon

Ironically it did not become apparent that Republican control of Florida was being built on a precarious and eroding foundation until 1998, just when the party gained control of the governor's office and both houses of the legislature for the first time since Reconstruction. In 1998 Jeb Bush won his second campaign for governor after having lost to incumbent governor Lawton Chiles in 1994. Chiles had taught Bush a tough lesson about the importance of the Blue Dogs. During his 1994 campaign Jeb paid little attention to rural Florida. He concentrated, instead, on the heavily populated region of southeast Florida, the midwestern retirement belt that runs down Florida's southwest coast, and the vast working-class neighborhoods in the expressway corridor connecting Tampa, Orlando, and Daytona Beach.

Chiles, on the other hand, recognized that Blue Dogs were the state's most important block of swing voters. In the first gubernatorial debate, which took place in Miami and was broadcast by radio, Bush received warm applause when he commented in Spanish to the local audience. Chiles, however, was focused on rural conservatives who were listening to the debate from afar. He announced proudly that he did not speak Spanish, he spoke "Cracker." Similarly, in the last debate of the campaign, he referred to himself as an "old he coon" and said that Bush was complaining about mudslinging because "a cut dog barks." These comments carried little weight and made little sense in the retirement communities of Broward County or in the black neighborhoods lining the I-95 corridor, but he knew he could count on the votes of these groups simply by virtue of his partisan affiliation. Blue Dog Democrats were another matter.

Chiles courted them because he knew that, as they say in rural Florida, crackers don't necessarily "go home from the dance with the one who brung 'em." Sometimes they sally off with liberal Democrats along the southeast coast. Reubin Askew put these strange bedfellows together in 1970, when he won his first election to statewide office. Askew was from Pensacola, which lies at the western edge of the Panhandle, but during his years in the state legislature he had forged alliances with southeastern liberals on such issues as reapportionment and civil rights. The same coalition elected Lawton Chiles to the U.S. Senate, brought Bob Graham (an urbane Miamian but also a dairy farmer) and Chiles to the Governor's Mansion, and took Graham from the governor's office to the U.S. Senate. This, too, was the coalition that allowed Jimmy Carter, a southern peanut farmer, to carry Florida in the presidential election of 1976.

At other times the Blue Dogs hook up with the Republicans. Prior to the 1994 governor's race between Chiles and Bush, they had done so in most presidential elections since 1968, in the gubernatorial elections of Republicans Claude Kirk (1966–1970) and Bob Martinez (1986–1990), and in the election of Connie Mack to the U.S. Senate (1988–2000).

Lessons from Jeb's Victory in 1998

Although four years later Jeb won a decisive victory in his second run at the governor's office, his win revealed not the growing popularity of Republicanism in Florida but rather the tenuous nature of the Republicans' grip on the state's government. Bush's opponent, Democrat Buddy MacKay, performed poorly not because Democrats who had supported Chiles in 1994 defected to the Republican ticket in 1998 but because many Democrats failed to go to the polls. In 1994 almost two-thirds of registered voters cast a ballot, whereas in November 1998 turnout was less than 50 percent. In Broward County, which in 1994 gave Chiles 123,000 more votes than it gave to Bush, turnout in November 1998 was a dismal 44 percent, down from 61 percent in the previous gubernatorial election. In Palm Beach County, which was the next largest source of votes for Chiles in 1994, turnout in 1998 was 50 percent, in contrast to 67 percent in 1994. Low turnout in these Democrat-rich counties doomed MacKay from the start.

Of particular concern for Bush and the Florida Republican Party was Bush's failure to become more popular between the 1994 and 1998 elections. Bush received a little over 2 million votes in 1994 and only about 2.1 million in 1998. This was true even though during this period the number of Republicans in Florida increased by more than 500,000 voters. Bush beat MacKay in 1998 not because the Republican vote surged in support of Jeb but because the Democrat vote ebbed. Chiles drew 2.1 million votes in 1994, but in 1998 MacKay received only 1.77 million votes, or 364,000 fewer votes, even though the number of registered Democrats had increased by 400,000.

Courting the Blue Dogs in 2000

During their campaigns for the presidency in 2000, both George W. Bush and Al Gore were active in seeking Blue Dog support. Gore came to Tallahassee very early in the campaign cycle—in March, after Jeb Bush had stirred up a huge controversy by issuing an Executive Order repealing the state's affirmative action policies in state hiring and contracting, and in admissions to state universities. Appearing at Leon High School, a north Florida emblem of "old Florida," Gore stood on stage with the widow of Lawton Chiles, and when he spoke he mentioned that earlier in the evening he had called the widow of Leroy Collins, a former governor, descendent of a nineteenth-century governor Keith Call, and a giant among Florida's historic statesmen. Clearly Gore was trying to link himself to the southern Democrats whom Blue Dogs continued to admire.

For his part, Bush waited to hit the Blue Dog counties in the Panhandle and north-central Florida until late in the campaign, when, despite spending much more time and money in the state than he had originally planned, Florida was still not firmly in the Bush-Cheney column. During the last week of the campaign, the entire Bush family showed up in rural north Florida. George H. W. Bush, the former president, toured the Panhandle and then linked up in Jacksonville with George W., Jeb, and the family matriarch, Barbara. Unless one knew the historic importance of Blue Dogs as the swing vote in Florida elections, it seemed crazy to invest this much time and energy, during the crucially important last days of the campaign, in some of the least populated counties of the state.

Voting Patterns in 2000

The results in 2000 provided further evidence of the Republicans' shaky hold on Florida. It revealed that the Blue Dogs—whose support had brought the Republican Party to power in the preceding three decades—are becoming less important as a deciding factor in Florida politics. If the Blue Dogs fade, the fortunes of Florida Republicans will fade with them.

As we have seen, since the late 1960s the Republican Party in Florida has achieved victory in statewide elections by forging a coalition between registered Republicans and Blue Dog Democrats. Democrats have countered this Republican gambit by running populists (like Lawton Chiles) who appeal to liberal Democrats in southeast Florida while also attracting Blue Dogs back to the Democratic fold. That Gore did not fit this populist mold but nevertheless did well in 2000 is demonstrable evidence that the Florida electorate is shifting out from under the Republican Party. Two demographic trends are particularly important. One is that the black population has begun to grow as a proportion of the total population for the first time since the 1940s. Second, there has been a rapid in-migration of Puerto Ricans, particularly in the Orlando area.

This means that Blue Dogs are becoming a smaller and smaller part of Florida's rapidly growing population, while the state's heavily Democratic Puerto Rican, Mexican, and black populations are becoming proportionally larger. Puerto Ricans and Mexicans demonstrated their presence dramatically in 2000: Orange County, in which Orlando is located, long a Republican stronghold, voted majority Democratic in a presidential election for the first time since 1948. As these population trends continue, Florida's partisan orientation will stop swinging on a Blue Dog hinge and will stabilize around a Democratic coalition of middle-class whites and urban minorities.

Republican Strategies for Expanding the Party's Electoral Base

Well aware that the demographic tide has turned against them, Republicans have been working aggressively on a number of fronts to improve their prospects while they still have control of the state government. One tactic has been perfectly legitimate. Republicans have been trying to improve their ability to attract supporters and get their supporters to the polls.

With respect to broadening their base in the electorate, at least since Jeb's election in 1998 they have been working to build support among non-Cuban Hispanics, especially Mexican Americans. Although Republican positions on most domestic issues alienate urban minorities, their positions on family values, religion, immigration, and international trade are consistent with the interests of Mexican Americans. Both Jeb and George W. Bush have made a point of stressing their Christian religiosity. Similarly one of the very first actions taken by Jeb after he became governor in 1998 was to go on a trade mission to Mexico. George W. did exactly the same shortly after his presidential inauguration. He also floated the idea of giving work permits and eventually citizenship to Mexicans who had immigrated to America illegally.

This strategy of using foreign policy to recruit traditionally Democratic constituencies has worked for Republicans previously. It was how they gained the enduring support of Cuban immigrants, who are now an important part of their Florida base.

Republicans are also using foreign policy to attract support among personnel in the armed services. For the first time in modern American history, the nation's soldiers have become aligned with one of the parties. A Duke University study of partisan orientations among military personnel is included in the appendix. It shows that 90 percent of the officer corps votes Republican in most elections.

Florida Republicans have been trying to recruit blacks but with less success. During his 1994 gubernatorial campaign, Jeb Bush made a notorious gaff that continues to haunt him. Asked by a reporter what he would do for blacks if he were elected, he quipped, "Probably nothing." In 1998 Jeb tried to overcome this mistake by describing himself as a compassionate conservative and also by seeking advice from prominent black clergy. Although he did better among blacks in the 1998 election, he lost all the ground he had gained with them and more when he issued the executive order for his One Florida initiative.

Republican Embattlements

Other tactics adopted by Florida Republicans to maintain their political dominance have not been limited to competing in the electoral arena. Some have been unlawful or at least have exceeded the bounds of acceptable political behavior, and have worked against the interests of the state and its citizens. Republicans at the highest levels of Florida government have been working in a variety of ways to entrench their power institutionally so that they can withstand the erosion of their electoral support which is already under way and is expected to accelerate. Even before the 2000 election fiasco occurred under the Republicans' watch, there were many signs that Republicans were intent on establishing a stranglehold on state government so that they will be difficult to dislodge as the state's population mix becomes increasingly inhospitable to Republican candidates.

One Republican tactic was to get tough with lobbyists. Beginning in the mid-1980s the pattern in Florida had been for special interests to donate equally to both parties and to candidates from both parties. However, after the election of 1998 Republicans spread the word that they expected donations of $2 for every $1 donated to Democrats. Lobbyists and others who did not comply were to be denied access to the governor and the legislative leadership, which would mean ruin for their businesses.

Another example of Republican efforts to consolidate their power occurred during the legislative session of 1999. Following the lead of state representative John Thrasher, who was the House Speaker that year and the year before, the Legislature eliminated the Florida Board of Regents, which had been responsible for overseeing the State University System. The board was replaced by separate boards of trustees at all ten of the state universities, and the governor was given the power to make all the trustee appointments. This created an enormous source of new patronage and also undermined the political neutrality of the state universities.

With the Board of Regents out of the way, Republicans quickly replaced many of the university presidents with political insiders. A former Speaker of the House was selected to head Florida State University. The Mayor of Jacksonville moved out of elected office and into the presidency of the University of North Florida. Jeb Bush's lieutenant governor resigned immediately after the 2002 gubernatorial election to become president of Florida Atlantic University.

In addition to politicizing university governance and administration, top Republicans used the powers of their offices to inject partisanship and instill fear down through the ranks of the state bureaucracy. In 1998 political operatives working for the Speaker of the House secretly examined voter registration records to learn the party affiliations of specific state employees and to identify agencies with high concentrations of Democrats. After it was determined that the most Democratic agency in the state government was the Florida Department of Education, the department was restructured and the positions of many of its employees were eliminated. Florida law forbids any consideration of partisan orientations in state hiring, firing, and contracting, but it fails to contemplate the more sinister possibility that highly partisan elected officials might purge the state bureaucracy indirectly by reorganization and privatization.

Some of the Republican assaults on state employees were more direct and personal. After a critic of the governor was invited by the state library director to speak at the 2002 annual conference of Florida librarians, the governor introduced legislation to privatize the state library and relocate its holdings to another part of the state. To its credit the state legislature balked at the measure but only after county libraries and their supporters across the state mobilized a grassroots campaign against the privatization proposal. Immediately after the legislative session, the state library director was forced out.

Misfeasance and Malfeasance Related to the 2000 Election

The partisan schemes of Florida's Republican elected officials during the 2000 election cycle took shape within this context of the party's declining electoral fortunes and rising partisan aggression. The acts of subterfuge and sabotage committed by Katherine Harris, Jeb Bush, Tom Feeney, and other Republicans were not peculiar to the special circumstances of a contested election; they were business as usual.

Consider the felon disenfranchisement program implemented by Katherine Harris in 1999 and 2000. Even if Harris had not corrupted its implementation, this program would inevitably weaken Democratic voting strength, because ex-felons are disproportionately black and poor. Republican legislators knew this when they passed it, but they claimed that the measure's partisan impacts were unintended and that the program was necessary to protect the integrity of Florida elections. However, this rationale was belied by a legislative requirement for the registered-voter list to be purged by a private company rather than by professionals in the Division of Elections. At no previous time in Florida history had the determination of voter eligibility been placed in private hands. Later, when Katherine Harris insisted that the firm use loose criteria that would cause many eligible voters to be improperly identified as ex-felons, she was simply using the tool that the legislature had established for this purpose.

By itself, the felon disenfranchisement program probably cost Gore the election. Not only did it cut into Democratic voting strength, it also resulted in massive confusion on election day when many voters were told by poll workers that they were no longer eligible to cast a ballot. Confusion and disorder was rampant at polling places serving black and low-income neighborhoods.

No doubt, neither Harris nor Republican legislators expected their felon disenfranchisement initiative to decide the election. It was just one of many Republican efforts to gain special advantages in Florida elections by rigging the system of voter registration and election administration. Despite the problems it caused, felon disenfranchisement would never have attracted much attention if the 2000 election had not ended in a virtual tie. Harris and her co-conspirators were like football players who normally play dirty and get away with it but who suddenly find their fouls in the spotlight when an opponent is seriously injured. The extraordinarily close outcome in 2000 was not the cause of isolated misdeeds that otherwise would have never been contemplated. Just the opposite: efforts to corrupt Florida's election system were under way well in advance of 2000 and involved top officials in both the legislative and executive branches; the close election simply brought this preexisting and widespread corruption to light.

Another pre-election example of top Republicans misusing the powers of public office for partisan gain involved Jeb Bush. In the months leading up to the election, he sent a letter to Florida Republicans calling on them to vote in 2000 and encouraging them to use an absentee ballot.

Not only was the letter itself illegal, it promoted illegal behavior. Although its production and mailing had been paid for by the Florida Republican Party, the letter violated Florida election law because it was printed on stationary bearing the state seal and appeared to be an official communication from the office of the governor.

The letter was encouraging illegal behavior, because Florida election law at the time allowed absentee voting only when circumstances prevented voters from going to the polls as usual. When they requested absentee ballots, voters had to certify that these circumstances applied. However, the governor's letter suggested that voters could use this option simply for the sake of convenience. The Florida Democratic Party went to court and succeeded in obtaining an injunction to prevent its continued use.

Another example of Republicans using their power to extend their power involved the judicial system. The appellate courts in Florida tend to be rather liberal by Republican standards. This is not so much because of their judicial philosophies as it is a result of the Florida Constitution, which is loaded with rights over and above those in the Constitution of the United States. For obvious reasons the state's Republican leaders have not wanted to try to remove popular provisions from the Florida Constitution, so they have chosen instead to use two tactics to try to alter the attitudes of the judges.

Their first effort along these lines was to attack the judicial branch with shrill language and threats. In 1998 Jeb Bush established the nation's first statewide voucher program. Eligibility for vouchers was limited to parents whose children were in the lowest performing schools as measured by student achievement scores. Vouchers enabled their recipients to receive state funds for all or part of the cost of sending their children to private schools. The Florida Supreme Court subsequently ruled that the program is unconstitutional, citing a requirement in the state constitution that calls for a system of free public education open to all residents. The justices argued that the voucher program would jeopardize the state's public education system. In response, the 1999 legislature threatened to try to amend the Florida Constitution to expand the size of the court so that the governor could pack it with Republicans. Legislation for this purpose was dropped only because of the ensuing outcry from scholars, editorial boards, and the Florida Bar.

Later, however, the governor and Republican legislators used a different tactic to again try to alter judicial decision making without changing the Florida Constitution. They targeted the process used to select judges. Florida has a four-tiered judicial system with two levels of trial courts (county courts and circuit courts) and two levels of appellate courts (district courts of appeals and the Florida Supreme Court). Trial court judges are elected, while appellant court judges are appointed by the governor. The governor also appoints trial court judges when a vacancy occurs between elections. In 1975 Florida established a system of merit selection for appellate judges, a system in which Judicial Nominating Commissions (JNCs) at the local level submit three nominees to the governor, who then must choose from among the three. There are separate JNCs for the Florida Supreme Court, each of the twenty judicial circuits, and each of the five courts of appeal districts. Prior to the 2001 legislative session, half the members of each Judicial Nominating Commission were appointed by the governor and half by the Florida Bar Association. The change made in 2001 was to give the governor the authority to appoint all the members of the committees rather than just half.

The End or the Beginning?

In summary, Republican misdeeds in relation to the 2000 election were nothing new or out of the ordinary. They were part of a general practice by Republican elected officials of subverting Florida's electoral system, politicizing state agencies, bullying the Florida Supreme Court, attacking judicial independence, and silencing critics.

These tactics and the political culture that approves of them emerged in the 1990s when it became clear that Florida was not going to become a one-party Republican state but would instead remain more or less evenly balanced and then gradually become more favorable to Democrats as the state's population became more and more ethnically and racially diverse. George W. Bush's surprisingly poor performance in Florida in 2000 went unnoticed in the post-election firestorm, but voting patterns in the election confirmed that Republican support in Florida is eroding. George W. Bush did better in Florida's Blue Dog counties than his father in 1992, Clinton in 1996, and Jeb in 1998, but he only managed to fight Gore to a draw, and only achieved that because of assistance from two outside factors: the system of election administration had been sabotaged, and the race included a third-party candidate (Ralph Nader) who pulled in 100,000 votes that would otherwise have gone to Gore.

In the years ahead, as growth among Florida's minorities continues to outpace the state's growth as a whole, Republicans will be under increasing electoral pressure, and their partisanship is likely to intensify. If so, their lawlessness in the 2000 presidential election may be eclipsed by far worse deeds in the future, especially if their actions continue to go unpunished, as they did in 2000. Certainly the moral of the 2000 election was not that cheaters never win. In 2002 Jeb Bush was reelected, and both Katherine Harris and Tom Feeney won seats in Congress.

Significantly Jeb's reelection in 2002 was aided, if not made possible, by continuing problems with election administration. In Broward County, which has more registered Democrats than any other county in the state, voter turnout in 2002 was the lowest ever experienced in a modern gubernatorial election. Turnout also fell to historic lows in Palm Beach and Miami-Dade counties, which, like Broward, are major sources of Democratic votes. The main cause of the low turnout in southeast Florida was a change made to Florida's election laws in 2001, when election administration was supposed to have been reformed to avoid a repeat of the fiasco in 2000. One of the changes made by the Republican-controlled legislature was to create a system of early voting, where ballots could be cast any time in the last two weeks leading up to a general election. Advocates of early voting claimed that it would reduce the number of voters going to the polls on election day and would therefore make the confusion and chaos witnessed at south Florida voting places in 2000 less likely. However, the turmoil in 2000 was caused in large part by the flawed felon-disenfranchisement program, which resulted in hundreds if not thousands of voters being told on election day that they were not on the registration list. Moreover, the provision for early voting was likely to be used most by Republicans, who tend to be wealthier than Democrats and hence to have travel and work schedules that are both more complicated and more flexible.

In any event, the provision for early voting ended up suppressing turnout in the Democrat-rich counties of southeast Florida. In the months leading up to the election, voters were encouraged to cast ballots early, and many did. However, because only a few polling places were opened for this purpose, the lines for early voting were long and sometimes took two hours or longer to get through. Consequently, for two weeks, south Florida television stations carried news reports of the crowds and delays, which discouraged voters from turning out on election day, even though, on that day, all of the voting places were opened and the crowds were not as large.

Appendix to Chapter 4

1999 Law on Felon Disenfranchisement

98.0975 Central voter file; periodic list maintenance.—
(1) By August 15, 1998, the division shall provide to each county supervisor of elections a list containing the name, address, date of birth, race, gender, and any other available information identifying the voter of each person included in the central voter file as a registered voter in the supervisor's county who:
(a) Is deceased;
(b) Has been convicted of a felony and has not had his or her civil rights restored; or
(c) Has been adjudicated mentally incompetent and whose mental capacity with respect to voting has not been restored.
(2) The division shall annually update the information required in subsection (1) and forward a like list to each supervisor by June 1 of each year.
(3)(a) In order to meet its obligations under this section, the division shall annually contract with a private entity to compare information in the central voter file with available information in other computer databases, in-

cluding, without limitation, databases containing reliable criminal records and records of deceased persons.

(b) The entity contracted by the division is designated as an agent of the division for purposes of administering the contract, and must be limited to seeking only that information which is necessary for the division to meet its obligations under this section. Information obtained under this section may not be used for any purpose other than determining voter eligibility.

(4) Upon receiving the list from the division, the supervisor must attempt to verify the information provided. If the supervisor does not determine that the information provided by the division is incorrect, the supervisor must remove from the registration books by the next subsequent election the name of any person who is deceased, convicted of a felony, or adjudicated mentally incapacitated with respect to voting.

History.—s. 8, ch. 98–129.

Transcript of Remarks by Florida Speaker of the House, Tom Feeney, November 22, 2000

Good afternoon. This is, uh, my second day on the job as speaker of the Florida House of Representatives. I can't wait to see what excitement waits us on the third day. Um, I will tell you that I have a brief statement to, uh, make, that we will be, uh, not taking any, uh, questions after that statement. I would encourage you to, um, uh, pay close attention to it.

In my view the court's ruling indicated the tremendous lack of respect that the Florida Supreme Court has for the laws of the State of Florida and the Legislature. The court continues to supplant its personal preferences over the statutory law of Florida, which was passed by the elected members of the legislature. Yesterday, if the Court had merely enforced firm and clear statutory deadlines, the Florida Supreme Court could have given us a resolution. Instead, I fear it has given us a potential constitutional crisis.

The people of Florida have elected 160 members of the Legislature and charged us with the creation and the protection of their laws. In my view the judicial branch has clearly overstepped their powers. Title 3, Section 2, of the United States Code, specifically delegates the power, authority, and responsibility to ensure an electoral college representation for Florida, and the Florida Legislature intends to uphold the Florida Constitution. This decision in my view was an expression of the court's view of appropriate deadlines or convenient deadlines rather than the deadlines strictly set out in law.

I'll tell you that every day the recount continues, with new decisions, new guidelines, boards and canvassing boards reversing their own procedures from a day or two earlier, reversing procedures that they have had in place for years, new courts issuing new guidelines for them to proceed by, continues to create a charade and undermine the public confidence in the entire system. There is increasingly compelling evidence of widespread mischief, human error, vote and ballot manipulation in the manual recount . . . process. One of the reasons the Florida Legislature was so clear in having a very definite deadline set out in statute, which the court has decided to ignore, is to make certain we never had to be in a position where you had the charade that is going on now.

I will share with you a bit of news. I'm told by our information technology department that the Florida website has had over one million hits today. Our offices have had over 200,000 e-mails, the large majority—we haven't done the tabulation—but the large majority asking us to do our constitutional duty to help resolve the crisis that the court in my view has created. The fax machines are jammed. We've received over 1,000 telephone calls from constituents and people from around the country and indeed the world. My press coordinator, her second week as a press communications, ah, coordinator, has received roughly 500 calls from the press alone. Obviously, if as my normal practice is, I just spent five or ten minutes with each of you, we wouldn't get much else done.

The last thing that I would like to say is that, um, I have spoken to a prominent, um, law professor today. I have invited him and have issued a, er um, issued an opportunity for him to decide to give the Florida House of Representatives advice about our constitutional responsibilities, our options, and prerogatives, and until I have that advice, I don't intend to take any further formal steps. Because the last thing I wish to say is that for those of you who are assigned to cover the Florida, ah, Legislature, or at least the Florida House and for those members that have been waiting, I think we can all stand down. This is Thanksgiving Eve. I think we can all relax, take a deep breath for at least 24 hours. Uh, and with that I appreciate your patience. We've tried to do the best we can. I want to thank Kim Stone and, um, we will be, ah, sharing more information with you as we have. Thank you.

Table 4.1. Voter Registrations and Deletions, 1995–2000

Date	New Valid	Deleted
1995	991,596	310,940
1996	1,180,050	298,052
1997	601,656	285,708
1998	618,681	350,738
2000	1,042,225	365,318
Jan. 2001	62,356	104,669
Totals	4,496,564	1,715,425

Table 4.2. Voter Turnout Percentages

Year	Presidential Preference Primary	First Primary	Second Primary	General Election
1954		53	58	47
1956		66		70
1958		54	30	37
1960		59	63	77
1962		43	29	46
1964		58	62	74
1966		51	58	60
1968		44	42	79
1970		41	42	62
1972	58	31		74
1974		33	26	50
1976	56	32		77
1978		36	33	60
1980	43	36	38	77
1982		30	15	55
1984	33			75
1986		30	24	61
1988	43	31	23	73
1990		34	25	60
1992	38	35	17	83
1994		29	12	66
1996	29	26		67
1998		17	7	49
2000	19	25	12	70
AVG	43	41	34	64

a. In several years both parties did not have statewide races on the ballot at the second primary.

b. There were no presidential preference primaries prior to 1972.

Table 4.3. Official Results, Federal Overseas Absentees November 17, 2000, Federal Overseas Absentees President of the United States

County	Bush/ Cheney (REP)	Gore/ Lieberman (DEM)	Browne/ Olivier (LIB)	Nader/ LaDuke (GRE)	Harris/ Trowe (SWP)	Hagelin/ Goldhaber (LAW)	Buchanan/ Foster (REF)	McReynolds/ Hollis (SPF)	Phillips/ Frazier (CPF)	Moorehead/ La Riva (WWP)	Chote/ Lancaster (WRI)	McCarthy/ Beifus (WRI)
Alachua	11	15	0	2	0	0	0	0	0	0	0	0
Baker	1	0	0	0	0	0	0	0	0	0	0	0
Bay	45	23	1	2	0	0	0	0	0	0	0	0
Bradford	2	0	0	0	0	0	0	0	0	0	0	0
Brevard	68	23	0	1	0	0	1	0	0	0	0	0
Broward	37	57	0	1	0	1	0	0	0	0	0	0
Calhoun	0	1	0	0	0	0	0	0	0	0	0	0
Charlotte	2	1	1	0	0	0	0	0	0	0	0	0
Citrus	34	6	0	4	0	0	0	0	0	0	0	0
Clay	167	36	0	3	0	0	0	0	0	0	0	0
Collier	17	18	0	5	0	0	0	0	0	0	0	0
Columbia	4	2	0	0	0	0	0	0	0	0	0	0
Desoto	0	1	0	0	0	0	1	0	0	0	0	0
Dixie	0	1	0	0	0	0	0	0	0	0	0	0
Duval	362	175	2	5	0	0	0	0	0	0	0	0
Escambia	154	47	1	6	0	0	0	0	0	0	0	0

County											
Flagler	5	0	0	0	0	0	0	0	0	0	0
Franklin	0	1	0	0	0	0	0	0	0	0	0
Gadsden	3	1	0	0	0	0	0	0	0	0	0
Gilchrist	0	0	0	0	0	0	0	0	0	0	0
Glades	0	0	0	0	0	0	0	0	0	0	0
Gulf	3	1	0	0	0	0	0	0	0	0	0
Hamilton	1	1	0	0	0	0	0	0	0	0	0
Hardee	0	3	0	0	0	0	0	0	0	0	0
Hendry	0	0	0	0	0	0	0	0	0	0	0
Hernando	12	4	0	0	0	0	0	0	0	0	0
Highlands	1	2	0	0	0	0	0	0	0	0	0
Hillsborough	34	19	0	6	0	1	0	0	0	0	0
Holmes	1	0	0	0	0	0	0	0	0	0	0
Indian River	4	1	0	0	0	0	0	0	0	0	0
Jackson	1	2	0	0	0	0	0	0	0	0	0
Jefferson	0	0	0	0	0	0	0	0	0	0	0
Lafayette	0	0	0	0	0	0	0	0	0	0	0
Lake	0	0	0	0	0	0	0	0	0	0	0
Lee	10	11	1	1	0	0	0	0	0	0	0
Leon	11	17	0	2	0	0	0	0	0	0	0
Levy	5	0	0	1	0	0	0	0	0	0	0
Liberty	0	0	0	0	0	0	0	0	0	0	0
Madison	0	1	0	0	0	0	0	0	0	0	0
Manatee	71	49	0	3	0	0	0	0	0	0	0

continued

Table 4.3.—continued

County	Bush/ Cheney (REP)	Gore/ Lieberman (DEM)	Browne/ Olivier (LIB)	Nader/ LaDuke (GRE)	Harris/ Trowe (SWP)	Hagelin/ Goldhaber (LAW)	Buchanan/ Foster (REF)	McReynolds/ Hollis (SPF)	Phillips/ Frazier (CPF)	Moorehead/ La Riva (WWP)	Chote/ Lancaster (WRI)	McCarthy/ Beifus (WRI)
Marion	5	9	0	1	0	0	0	0	0	0	0	0
Martin	2	1	0	0	0	0	0	0	0	0	0	0
Miami-Dade	41	59	0	3	0	0	0	0	0	0	0	0
Monroe	4	4	0	0	0	0	0	0	0	0	0	0
Nassau	4	3	0	0	0	0	0	0	—	0	0	0
Okaloosa	93	41	0	3	0	0	—	0	0	0	0	0
Okeechobee	0	1	0	0	0	0	0	0	0	0	0	0
Orange	14	16	0	0	0	0	0	0	0	0	0	0
Osceola	25	6	0	1	0	0	0	0	0	0	0	0
Palm Beach	13	22	0	1	0	0	0	0	0	0	0	0
Pasco	25	12	0	1	0	0	0	0	0	0	0	0
Pinellas	24	27	2	1	0	0	0	0	0	0	0	0
Polk	15	7	0	0	0	0	0	0	0	0	0	0
Putnam	10	5	0	2	0	0	0	0	0	0	0	0
Santa Rosa	65	16	0	2	0	0	0	0	0	0	0	0
Sarasota	17	16	0	2	0	0	—	0	0	0	0	0
Seminole	113	53	0	3	0	0	0	—	0	0	0	0
St. Johns	18	7	0	0	0	0	0	0	0	0	0	0

St. Lucie	0	1	0	0	0	0	0	0	0	0	0	0	0
Sumter	0	0	0	0	0	0	0	0	0	0	0	0	0
Suwannee	3	1	0	0	0	0	0	0	0	0	0	0	0
Taylor	2	0	0	0	0	0	0	0	0	0	0	0	0
Union	0	0	0	0	0	0	0	0	0	0	0	0	0
Volusia	11	9	0	0	0	0	0	0	0	0	0	0	0
Wakulla	0	0	0	0	0	0	0	0	0	0	0	0	0
Walton	4	1	0	0	0	0	0	0	0	0	0	0	0
Washington	1	0	0	0	0	0	1	5	1	1	1	0	0
Total	1,575	836	8	0	62	0	1	5	1	1	1	0	0
Percent	63.3	33.6	0.3	0.0	2.5	0.0	0.0	0.2	0.0	0.0	0.0	0.0	0.0

Table 4.4. 2000 Election, Official Results by County, with Absentees Separated Out

County	Bush/ Cheney (REP)	Gore/ Lieberman (DEM)	Browne/ Olivier (LIB)	Nader/ LaDuke (GRE)	Harris/ Trowe (SWP)	Hagelin/ Goldhaber (LAW)	Buchanan/ Foster (REF)	McReynolds/ Hollis (SPF)	Phillips/ Frazier (CPF)	Moorehead/ La Riva (WWP)	Chote/ Lancaster (WRI)	McCarthy/ Beifus (WRI)
Alachua	34,124	47,365	658	3,226	6	42	263	4	20	21	0	0
Baker	5,610	2,392	17	53	0	3	73	0	3	3	0	0
Bay	38,637	18,850	171	828	5	18	248	3	18	27	0	0
Bradford	5,414	3,075	28	84	0	2	65	0	2	3	0	0
Brevard	115,185	97,318	643	4,470	11	39	570	11	72	76	0	0
Broward	177,902	387,703	1,217	7,104	54	135	795	37	74	122	0	0
Calhoun	2,873	2,155	10	39	0	1	90	1	2	3	0	0
Charlotte	35,426	29,645	127	1,462	6	15	182	3	18	12	0	0
Citrus	29,767	25,525	194	1,379	5	16	270	0	18	28	2	0
Clay	41,736	14,632	204	562	1	14	186	3	6	9	0	0
Collier	60,450	29,921	185	1,400	7	34	122	4	10	29	0	0
Columbia	10,964	7,047	127	258	1	7	89	2	8	5	0	0
Desoto	4,256	3,320	23	157	0	0	36	3	8	2	3	3
Dixie	2,697	1,826	32	75	0	2	29	0	3	2	0	0
Duval	152,098	107,864	952	2,757	37	162	652	15	58	41	0	0
Escambia	73,017	40,943	296	1,727	6	24	502	3	110	20	0	0
Flagler	12,613	13,897	60	435	1	4	83	3	3	12	0	0

County												
Franklin	2,454	2,046	17	85	1	3	33	0	3	2	0	0
Gadsden	4,767	9,735	24	139	3	4	38	4	7	6	0	0
Gilchrist	3,300	1,910	52	97	0	1	29	0	2	4	0	0
Glades	1,841	1,442	12	56	0	3	9	1	0	1	0	0
Gulf	3,550	2,397	21	86	2	4	71	2	2	9	0	0
Hamilton	2,146	1,722	12	37	4	1	23	8	7	4	0	0
Hardee	3,765	2,339	17	75	0	2	30	0	2	3	0	0
Hendry	4,747	3,240	11	104	3	1	22	2	7	2	0	0
Hernando	30,646	32,644	116	1,501	8	26	242	4	10	22	0	0
Highlands	20,206	14,167	64	545	6	16	127	3	7	8	0	0
Hillsborough	180,760	169,557	1,138	7,490	35	217	847	29	68	154	0	
Holmes	5,011	2,177	18	94	1	7	76	3	6	2	0	0
Indian River	28,635	19,768	122	950	4	13	105	2	13	10	0	0
Jackson	9,138	6,868	40	138	0	2	102	1	4	7	0	0
Jefferson	2,478	3,041	14	76	2	1	29	1	0	0	0	1
Lafayette	1,670	789	6	26	2	0	10	1	1	0	0	0
Lake	50,010	36,571	204	1,460	4	36	289	1	21	15	0	0
Lee	106,141	73,560	538	3,587	30	81	305	5	34	96	0	0
Leon	39,062	61,427	330	1,932	9	28	282	7	16	31	0	0
Levy	6,858	5,398	92	284	1	1	67	1	10	12	0	0
Liberty	1,317	1,017	12	19	0	3	39	0	1	2	0	0
Madison	3,038	3,014	18	54	0	2	29	1	1	5	0	0

continued

Table 4.4.—continued

County	Bush/ Cheney (REP)	Gore/ Lieberman (DEM)	Browne/ Olivier (LIB)	Nader/ LaDuke (GRE)	Harris/ Trowe (SWP)	Hagelin/ Goldhaber (LAW)	Buchanan/ Foster (REF)	McReynolds/ Hollis (SPF)	Phillips/ Frazier (CPF)	Moorehead/ La Riva (WWP)	Chote/ Lancaster (WRI)	McCarthy/ Beifus (WRI)
Manatee	57,952	49,177	242	2,491	5	35	271	3	19	26	0	0
Marion	55,141	44,665	662	1,809	13	26	563	6	22	49	0	0
Martin	33,970	26,620	109	1,118	14	29	112	7	20	14	0	0
Miami-Dade	289,533	328,808	762	5,352	87	119	560	35	69	124	0	0
Monroe	16,059	16,483	162	1,090	1	26	47	0	3	7	9	0
Nassau	16,404	6,952	63	253	0	8	90	4	3	3	0	0
Okaloosa	52,093	16,948	313	985	4	15	267	2	33	20	0	0
Okeechobee	5,057	4,588	21	131	1	4	43	1	3	4	0	0
Orange	134,517	140,220	891	3,879	13	65	446	7	41	46	0	0
Osceola	26,212	28,181	309	732	10	20	145	5	10	33	1	0
Palm Beach	152,951	269,732	743	5,565	45	143	3,411	302	190	104	0	0
Pasco	68,582	69,564	413	3,393	19	83	570	14	16	77	0	0
Pinellas	184,825	200,630	1,230	10,022	41	442	1,013	27	72	170	0	0
Polk	90,295	75,200	366	2,059	8	59	533	5	46	36	0	0
Putnam	13,447	12,102	114	377	2	7	148	3	10	12	0	0
Santa Rosa	36,274	12,802	131	724	1	13	311	1	43	19	0	0
Sarasota	83,100	72,853	431	4,069	11	94	305	5	15	59	0	0
Seminole	75,677	59,174	550	1,946	6	38	194	5	18	26	0	0
St. Johns	39,546	19,502	210	1,217	4	11	229	2	12	13	0	0

St. Lucie	34,705	41,559	165	1,368	4	12	124	10	13	29	0	0
Sumter	12,127	9,637	53	306	2	2	114	0	3	17	0	0
Suwannee	8,006	4,075	52	180	2	4	108	0	9	5	16	0
Taylor	4,056	2,649	4	59	0	3	27	1	8	1	0	0
Union	2,332	1,407	15	33	1	0	37	0	1	0	0	0
Volusia	82,357	97,304	444	2,910	8	36	498	5	20	70	0	1
Wakulla	4,512	3,838	30	149	2	3	46	1	0	6	0	0
Walton	12,182	5,642	68	265	3	11	120	2	7	18	0	0
Washington	4,994	2,798	32	93	0	2	88	0	9	5	3	1
Subtotal	2,911,215	2,911,417	16,407	97,426	562	2,280	17,479	621	1,370	1,803	34	6
Federal												
Abssntee	1,575	836	8	62	0	1	5	1	1	1	0	0
Total	2,912,790	2,912,253	16,415	97,488	562	2,281	17,484	622	1,371	1,804	34	6
Percent	48.8	48.8	0.3	1.6	0.0	0.0	0.3	0.0	0.0	0.0	0.0	0.0

Table 4.5. Campaign Finance Information for George W. Bush and Al Gore, 2000 Presidential Election

Bush, George W.	Activity through 12/31/2000	
Total receipts	$193,866,253	
Contributions from individuals	$101,520,773	
Contributions from PACs	$2,229,056	
Contributions/loans from the candidate	$13,810	
Contributions from party	$28,728	
Coordinated expenditures	$13,255,560	
Independent expenditures	Against: $2,666,197	For: $7,473,993
Contributions from politicians' PACs	$108,642	
Contributions from other candidates/incumbents	$127,672	
Total disbursements	$186,638,415	
Contributions to others by this candidate	$4,789,031	
Outstanding debts	$671,145	
Cash available as of 12/31/2000	$7,262,776	

Gore, Al	Activity Through 12/31/2000	
Total receipts	$133,108,037	
Contributions from individuals	$45,612,601	
Contributions from PACs	$0	
Contributions/loans from the candidate	$0	
Contributions from party	$0	
Coordinated expenditures	$12,567,789	
Independent expenditures	Against: $378,758	For: $4,613,227
Contributions from politicians' PACs	$1,000	
Contributions from other candidates/incumbents	$8,634	
Total disbursements	$120,332,506	
Contributions to others by this candidate	($24,045)	
Outstanding debts	$1,748,949	
Cash available as of 12/31/2000	$12,775,524	

Table 4.6. Percentage of Voters Registered as Democrats, Republicans, and Independents, 1950–2002

Year	Percent Democrat	Percent Republican	Percent Independent
1950	94	6	
1960	83	17	
1970	72	25	3
1980	64	30	6
1990	52	41	7
1996	48	43	9
1999	45	40	15
2000	44	40	16
2002	43	39	16

Table 4.7. Breakdown of Ballots Received before and after November 7

	Bush	Gore
Ballots rec'd by Nov. 7	2,911,215	2,911,417
Late overseas ballots	1,575	836

Table 4.8. Breakdown of Flawed Ballots Accepted and Rejected, by County

	No. Accepted	No. Rejected	% Accepted
Counties won by Bush	530	523	50
Counties won by Gore	150	666	18
Total	680	1,189	36

Special Session Proclamation

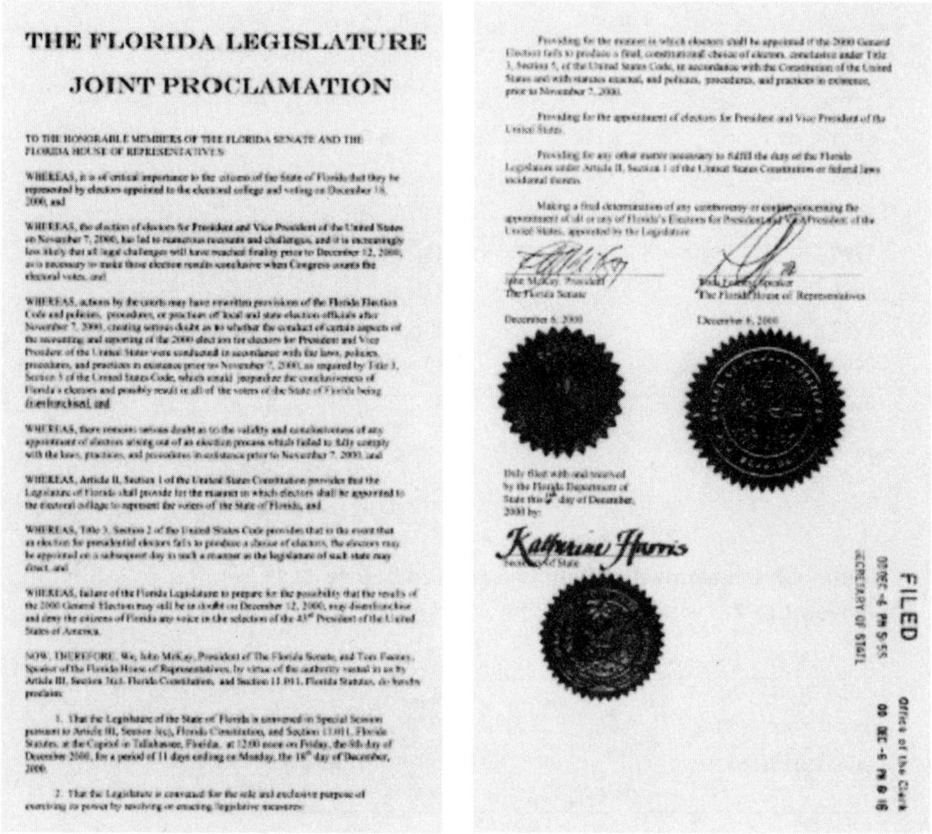
THE FLORIDA LEGISLATURE

JOINT PROCLAMATION

FILED

Figure 4.1. Proclamation for Special Session of the Florida Legislature

Duke University Study of Partisanship in the Military

Triangle Institute for Security Studies
Project on the Gap Between the Military and Civilian Society
Digest of Findings and Studies
Presented at the Conference on the Military and Civilian Society
Cantigny Conference Center, 1st Division Museum 28–29 October 1999
Peter D. Feaver
Associate Professor of Political Science
Duke University
919-660-4331
919-660-4330 fax
pfeaver@duke.edu
Richard H. Kohn
Professor of History
University of North Carolina at Chapel Hill
919-419-0323
919-962-2603 fax
rhkohn@juno.com

". . . one of the challenges for me is to somehow prevent a chasm from developing between the military and civilian worlds, where the civilian world doesn't fully grasp the mission of the military, and the military doesn't understand why the memories of our citizens and civilian policy makers are so short, or why the criticism is so quick and so unrelenting."

William S. Cohen, Secretary of Defense, in remarks at Yale University, 26 September 1997

This summary presents the results of a research project underwritten by the Smith Richardson Foundation and directed by Peter D. Feaver and Richard H. Kohn under the auspices of the Triangle Institute for Security Studies (TISS). With the issuing of this report and the papers appended, Phase I of the project is complete. Phase II will involve an extensive public discussion of the policy implications of these findings, with revisions and additional analysis as appropriate. In Phase III, the project's findings will be published in a scholarly edited volume and in relevant academic, policy, and general interest journals and magazines.

The project has examined the relationship between the military and society in the post–Cold War era, involving some two dozen scholars drawn from the academy, the military, and the national security policy community. The overall purpose is to strengthen the national defense by addressing an issue that has been identified as a priority concern by the Secretary of Defense, senior military officers, the media, and the national security community: whether there is a gap between civilian society and the military, and, if so, whether differing values, opinions, perspectives, and experience harm military effectiveness and civil-military cooperation.

Concerns about whether military forces shared the same background and values as the rest of society antedate the founding of the United States. Even before the American Revolution, Americans feared standing armies in peacetime, in large part because they were separate from society and had the means of coercing the population, installing a tyranny, or ruling by force. "Soldiers are apt to consider themselves as a Body distinct from the rest of the Citizens," wrote the revolutionary leader Sam Adams in 1776. "They have their Arms always in their hands. Their Rules and their Discipline is severe. They soon become attached to their officers and disposed to yield implicit obedience to their Commands. Such a Power should be watched with a jealous Eye." From then until the 1970s, Americans relied as much as possible on citizen soldiers, keeping up the smallest feasible body of regulars in peacetime for constabulary purposes, deterrence, and to prepare for war. Militia were the embodiment of freedom and liberty. "From a well-regulated militia we have nothing to fear; their interest is the same with that of the state," stated John Hancock in 1774.

Thus, while the nature and form of the American military has changed with Americas changing global position, a central and recurring problem for policy makers has been the need to reconcile the distinctive culture and mission of the armed forces with America's democratic ideals and practices. The issue has returned to center stage since the end of the Cold War and lies at the heart of much of the recent controversy attending military policy. This project contributes to the public discussion of these issues by addressing three questions:

Do post–Cold War military values, attitudes, opinions, and perspectives diverge from those in civilian society, and, if so, how?

Is this divergence, if it exists, growing and, if so, why?

How do any gaps affect policy in the areas of grand strategy, operations, and force structure? How does, or might in the future, a gap affect civil-military relationships?

The first phase of research has determined that the concerns expressed by the Secretary of Defense and others about a growing gap between the military and civilian worlds are justified but should not be exaggerated. Our research identified numerous schisms and trends that have undermined civil-military cooperation and, in certain circumstances, could degrade military effectiveness, but these problems cannot be called a crisis. Some of the concerns expressed in the policy community about the gap are not sustained by careful analysis.

There are numerous differences of opinion and attitude between elite military officers (defined in the study as officers selected for the courses in residence at staff and war colleges, their National Guard and Reserve counterparts, and new flag officers) and the civilian society they serve. Some differences are natural and even functional, deriving from the special mission of the military to prevail in armed combat. Other gaps are harder to link to the military's function but simply indicate that the values, perspectives, and opinions of people in uniform differ from those in the elite and general civilian public. (The elite public in this study consisted of a random sample of individuals from *Who's Who* and other samples drawn from similar reference works.) Not all attitude gaps are dangerous, nor are all convergences between the two cultures functional.

At the basic level of experience, which shapes values, attitudes, opinions, and perspectives, the gap between the U.S. military and civilian society is growing. As we leave the 20th century, the number of people have served in the military or have other personal connections with the military is declining. This "experience gap" is an artifact of the shrinking all-volunteer force and the passing of the World War II and Korea generations that, through personal experience, enjoyed such extensive ties to the U.S. armed forces. While the picture is complex, several findings emerge from our analysis: What is the nature of the gap?

Over the past quarter century, elite military officers have largely abandoned political neutrality and have become partisan Republicans (64%). The long tradition of an apolitical military has given way to a new reality in which the elite military is probably the most solidly Republican professional group in American society. The Republican identification has come at the expense of non-affiliation to the Democratic Party or identification as Independent. Elite military officers are Republican by a margin of 8 to 1 over Democrats while elite civilians and the mass public are split about evenly.

The partisan gap is matched by an ideological divide. The elite military are far more likely to identify themselves as conservative than are either mass or elite civilians (66% vs. 42%, or 38%), and many times less likely to identify themselves as liberal than either the mass or elite public.

The partisan ideological differences do not necessarily spill over into the full range of domestic and foreign policy issues, and, in any case, the gap appears to be wider and more pervasive in the realm of ideas and values than on more specific policy issues.

Americans in the national political elite are increasingly losing a personal connection to the military. For the first 75 years of the 20th century, there was a significant "veteran's advantage" in American politics: always a higher percentage of veterans in Congress than in the comparable age cohort in the general population. This veteran's advantage has eroded over the past twenty-five years in both chambers of Congress and across both parties. Beginning in the mid-1990s, there has been a lower percentage of veterans in the Senate and the House of Representatives than in the comparable cohort in the population at large. Thus, not only has the absolute number of people with military experience in the political elite declined, but the relative number has declined even further. Compared to historical trends, military veterans seem now to be under-represented in the national political elite.

The mass public, and the elite public only slightly less so, profess great confidence in the military and believe there is a fair degree of mutual respect between the military and society. The elite military likewise professes to respect civilian society and believes that relations with society generally are good. However, mutual professions of support and confidence between civilians and the military rest on an underlying alienation that may in time erode the surface support each claims for the other.

Elite military officers express great pessimism about the moral health of civilian society and strongly believe that the military could help society become more moral and that civilian society would be better off if it adopted more of the military's values and behaviors. Elite civilians share a pessimism about civilian society but strongly disagree that the military has a role in moral reform. Each harbors strong negative stereotypes about the other beneath a surface expression of respect and confidence.

The elite military is fairly critical about the quality of leadership in the political institutions that undergird American democracy. The elite military believe the political leadership is not well informed about military affairs (66% say "somewhat ignorant" or "very ignorant"). A significant portion (35%) believes the political leadership does not share the same values as the American people (only 41% say political leaders do share the same values while 23% say they are "not sure"). The elite military possess a pervasive hostility toward the media. At the same time, elite military (and the mass military) have more trust and confidence in government institutions than civilians, elite and mass.

On social values, elite military officers diverge from both elite and mass civilians, but in doing so fit somewhere on a continuum between the two civilian publics considerably more conservative than elite civilians but not quite as conservative as the general public. Given the larger gap between elite and mass civilians, the military cannot be said to be out of step with civilian society on this dimension.

Elite military officers are more supportive of gender equality in the services than is the general population, and no less supportive than elite civilians with the exception of women having a direct role in combat. Elite military officers strongly oppose (65%) women serving in all combat jobs. A comparable majority of civilian elites (58%) and only slightly fewer mass public (52%) support women serving in all combat jobs. Very few (14%) of civilian elites believe women should be required to serve in all combat jobs.

By a very large margin (76%), elite military officers oppose gays and lesbians openly serving in the military. But a majority of civilian elites (55%) and the mass public (57%) support gays and lesbians openly serving.

The elite military generally believes that the military has done what it should in dealing with the problem of sexual harassment, but civilian elites believe the military has not done enough.

The wide gap between the elite military and civilians on the issues of women in combat and homosexuals serving openly, on whether enough has been done to address sexual harassment, and on the necessity for traditional warrior (and male) culture for military effectiveness, suggests that these issues will continue to cause controversy and civil-military friction.

There is by and large a consensus between the elite military and both the elite and the mass public on many of the foreign policy issues that were contentious during the Cold War.

On some dimensions, a gap emerges between the mass public, on the one hand, and elite civilians and elite military officers, on the other. One of the very deepest chasms is on their attitude toward people, with elites far more willing (65% military, 60% civilian) to say that "most people can be trusted" and the mass far more likely (63%) to say that "you can't be too careful in dealing with people."

Elite military officers are not more "religious" than civilian elites, if measured by the frequency of attending religious services and the frequency of engaging in religious activity. But they are more religious, if measured by the degree of guidance respondents claim religion provides for their daily living and the specific content of those beliefs. In any case, contrary to some claims in the debate, any differences are not strikingly large. Except for a larger proportion of Roman Catholics and a smaller proportion of Jews, the elite military religious identification is congruent with that of the American population. Only 13% of elite military officers are evangelical Protestant, compared to 12% of elite civilians.

There appears to be a consensus across civilian and military elites on the relative efficacy of military and non-military tools in addressing various threats to national security.

Very few elites (7% of elite civilians, 1% of elite military) believe that the so-called "social engineering role" "redressing historical discrimination" is a very important role for the military, although somewhat more (23% of elite civilians, 14% of elite military) say it is at least "important."

Many of the gaps found at the more senior elite levels were not found at the level of the junior elite, that is, comparing officers in pre-commissioning courses at the service academies and ROTC with civilian students at Duke University. However, precommissioned officers were considerably more religious and conservative than a sample of Duke University students.

The partisan and ideological gaps found at the elite military level were considerably narrower at the level of accession to the mass military (defined as enlisted ranks and military personnel in the field). Those entering the enlisted ranks were more partisan Republican than civilians not going to college, but not by the margins seen at the elite level; the comparable cohort going into college was even more Republican than the cohort going into the military. A similar pattern emerges in ideological identification. The enlisted ranks are becoming more bourgeois, but not necessarily as Republican or conservative as the elite officer corps.

As was found at the elite level, people entering the enlisted ranks are more pro-military, more supportive of an activist but security-oriented foreign policy, and more supportive of defense spending than their peer cohort entering the labor force or college.

At the level of institutional presence, which refers to the significance of an institution in society, the military is not isolated, although there are trends that suggest this may happen in the future. The material presence of the military remains very high. It consumes a large, if shrinking, portion of the GDP; its reach is geographically distributed across the entire country in rough proportion to regional population share; and it is prominent on the public stage and especially in the media. However, the downsizing of the force is reducing social connections to the military and these will inevitably reduce its institutional presence.

The military also has a profound moral presence, having played such a crucial and public role in addressing a variety of societal problems including racism and drug abuse. The armed forces have been prominent in public debates over how best to expand opportunities to women. Over the last half century, the military has adapted to changes in American society. The U.S. armed forces has integrated racially and in gender, adjusted to the changing youth culture, and managed at the same time to retain both a moral and social legitimacy, and effectiveness in battle and in operations other than war. What factors shape the gap?

Many of the differences in opinion between the elite military and civilian society are due in part to the peculiar demographic makeup of the elite officer corps: disproportionately male, white, Catholic, and very highly educated. Nevertheless, most differences remain even when one controls for these demographic factors, suggesting both that the elite military may selectively attract a certain profile of officer and that certain "ideal types" rise to the elite ranks. Since virtually all opinion gaps are narrower at the accession level than at the more senior elite levels, the divergence of opinions is not merely a function of occupational selection (certain types of people entering the military). At least some of the gap is a result of other factors, possibly selective attrition and other socialization that occurs as an individual advances within the officer corps.

There are numerous factors that may have contributed to the "Republicanization" of the force, including the Vietnam experience, changes in support for defense by the two major political parties, and an increase in the proportion of young people who self-identified as Republican and expressed interest in joining the military during the Reagan administration military buildup. The "Republicanization" phenomenon, however, is not simply a function of the peculiar demographic makeup of the military.

Since the proportion of young people who self-identify as Republican and express interest in joining the military has recently declined, the skewed partisan distribution in the military may moderate over time. Seeking greater regional diversity, and much less so gender and racial diversity, may be an effective way to address some of the gaps between the elite military and civilian society.

Contrary to views widely held among elite military officers, the major daily newspapers do not emphasize negative stories about the military. The ratio of positive to negative stories is roughly 2:1. The Washington Post is considerably more positive in its depiction of the military than is the New York Times, but even the Times, on balance, treats the military positively. This may contribute to the military's favorable standing in the public eye.

Coverage of the military by military publications is overwhelmingly positive. This may explain why the elite military are more inclined than elite civilians to take a dubious view of the way the civilian press treats the military, since depictions of the military in military media are even more positive than the otherwise positive treatment in the civilian media. The military media may therefore be exacerbating the gap in civilian vs. military attitudes toward the military.

The belief that images of American casualties drives the American public's willingness to endure the human costs of war is based on an inaccurate understanding of how people respond to visual images. By setting the context for interpretation, leaders have far more leeway to shape the public's reaction even to the same kinds of images than is implied by the so-called "CNN effect" problem.

The popular media through fiction and film reinforces a diverse set of stereotypes about the military and civilian society. The action/thriller genre generally depicts the military as tough realists with higher moral standards and greater loyalty, responsibility, and technological expertise than their civilian counterparts. An important counterexample is the archetype of the senior officer who seizes unauthorized power, albeit often as a misguided effort to reform failings in civilian society.

High-brow fiction and film tend to present an especially critical view of the military.

The academic core curricula at the service academies and in ROTC are not adequate to give future officers a useful and coherent understanding of American society or its culture. Nor do the curricula present a coherent picture of the traditional principles of American civil-military relations.

Does the gap matter for public policy?

The culture gap extends back two centuries in American history but has traditionally been mitigated by a deeply ingrained acceptance of the principle of civilian control by the military, reinforced by the urgency of civil-military cooperation during the World Wars and the Cold War.

During the 1990s the principle of civilian control has been subjected to more ongoing strain than at any time in American history. The post–Cold War decade is the first period in American history that we are obliged to manage the culture gap whilst the military is large and powerful, yet without an external threat to focus civil-military cooperation. This suggests that future civil-military relations in the United States should be addressed by the national security community.

The presence of veterans in the national political elite has a profound effect on the use of force in American foreign policy. At least since 1816, there has been a very durable pattern in U.S. behavior: the more veterans in the national political elite, the less likely the United States is to initiate the use of force in the international arena. This effect is statistically stronger than many other factors known to influence the use of force, including the so-called democratic peace on which the Clinton National Security Strategy is based. The trend of a declining rate of veterans in the national political elite may suggest a continued high rate of military involvement in conflicts in the coming years.

Our results suggest that the trend of declining percentages of veterans in the national political elite cuts against efforts by the Clinton administration to strengthen the so-called "democratic peace" by championing the spread of democracy around the world. This strategy may indeed ultimately yield a peace dividend, but our results suggest that if the percentage of veterans serving in policy-making positions declines over time, other things being equal, the United States would be more likely to initiate the use of force overseas.

The gap in role, function, and responsibility at the top of government between military and civilian in wartime is traditional and functional. So, too, is the gap in background, experience, perspective, and professional behaviors and *mentalité*, in peacetime as well as war.

At the highest policy levels of the national command authority in recent years, the fusion of civilian and military leaders appears to dampen the influence of opinion gaps that might otherwise be prominent. While there is a high level of civil-military cooperation in policy and decision making, there is also conflict, and one result of the fusion is a blurring of roles by the most senior military, who become policy advocates and decision makers rather than solely advisers.

On average, the military elite and civilian elites without any military experience hold different views on the proper use of force: when and how to use force, and the appropriate role of the military in those decisions. The results suggest that the policy-making friction reported in recent uses of force is not as much the product of personality conflicts as a clash in the general approach to foreign policy and the use of force, a clash that could increase as the leavening effect of veterans in the political elite diminishes.

Contrary to a traditional understanding of civilian control, elite military officers believe that it is their role to insist and advocate rather than merely advise on key elements of decisions concerning the use of force, for instance: "setting rules of engagement" (83%), developing an "exit strategy" (80%), and "deciding what kinds of military units (air vs. naval, heavy vs. light) will be used to accomplish all tasks" (89%). Most likely a result of the Vietnam experience and the lessons the military elite drew therefrom, these views have already caused real friction in policy and decision making and will in the future, and could in some instances lead to unprofessional behavior.

The strong belief of civilian and military elites that the American public will not accept casualties is not supported by the survey data. The mass public says it will accept casualties. Indeed, in more traditional scenarios such as defending Taiwan against a Chinese invasion, the mass public gives estimates of acceptable casualties roughly equivalent to civilian and military elites. In nontraditional scenarios, such as restoring democracy in the Congo or preventing Iraq from obtaining weapons of mass destruction, the mass gives substantially higher estimates of acceptable casualties than do civilian or military elites.

On nontraditional missions, elite military officers are twice to four times as casualty averse as American civilians (mass or elite). This aversion is more pronounced among more senior than junior officers in rank. Furthermore, army officers are more casualty averse than marine officers or air force officers, but roughly comparable to navy officers. Casualty aversion in the military elite is unlikely to be a function of a desire for self-preservation. Casualty aversion does not correlate to service or specialty more prone to participation in combat. Younger officers who are more likely to be in combat are also more willing to accept higher casualties. Casualty aversion may be more a function of a zero-defect mentality among senior officers, in which casualties are viewed as indications that the mission will be perceived to be a failure; to the feelings of responsibility felt by more senior officers for the welfare of their troops; and to lack of confidence by more senior officers in the constancy and reliability of the senior civilian leadership.

The success of democracies at war has usually involved effective questioning, oversight, and, on occasion, intervention by civilian leaders into the technical aspects of military affairs. Contrary to remembered history, civilian meddling did not cause the United States to lose the Vietnam War nor did civilians abstain from overseeing the prosecution of the Persian Gulf War. Many of the problems and failures of recent American military interventions originated not in excessive or incompetent civilian meddling but in poor civilian oversight, particularly in failures to insist upon open and candid dialogue with the military, to plan, to ask difficult or unpleasant questions, and to scrutinize military activities so as to connect means with ends. Proper civil-military relations require civilian decision makers to immerse themselves in the conduct of war and exercise their authority and responsibility when needed, regardless of the theoretical or normative boundaries established in tradition or contemporary practice.

Although personal connections to the military are declining, this decline apparently has not greatly affected support for the armed forces through the defense budget, nor should recent accession and attrition woes be attributed to this gap. Personal connections do influence opinion about the defense budget, however, so efforts to "reconnect" the military to the general public will augment at the margins expressions of support for defense spending.

During the 1990s, being a veteran did not have a sizable impact on a U.S. senator's or representative's voting behavior, at least not compared to other factors that determine voting stance. Thus, if the decline in the congressional veterans is leading to significant changes in defense policy, its effects must be indirect, through changes in congressional agendas or in the quantity and kinds of information available to legislators.

At the margins, the "Republicanization" of the elite officer corps could affect the attractiveness of service in the military and hence recruiting. The declining propensity of African Americans to serve, whether in the enlisted ranks or officer corps, is probably primarily due to the strength of the American economy, but it may also be related to the "Republicanization" of the force.

The civilian population, both elite and especially mass, has very little understanding of civil-military relations and civilian control of the military. A surprisingly high percentage of the general population (30%) believes that the military most or all of the time seeks ways to avoid civilian orders with which it does not agree; a striking majority of the mass (68%) and a remarkably large percentage of elite civilians (46%) believe that the military does so at least some of the time. Nearly half of the mass (47%) and nearly one-third of civilian elites (30%) express doubt about the safety and security of civilian control in the United States.

Elite military officers showed better comprehension of the principle of civilian control. But pre-commissioned officers displayed serious misunderstandings about proper civil-military relations.

Chapter 5

The Failure of Post-Election Reform

With the U.S. Supreme Court's ruling on December 12 the election dispute ended. What did not end was the responsibility to investigate the problems of the election and take appropriate action to prevent similar problems in the future. At the very least, known crimes should have been prosecuted and suspected crimes investigated. Also warranting careful consideration were the election laws and supporting institutions of Florida and the nation. The end of the controversy should have marked the beginning of inquiry and the prelude to meaningful reform.

Instead, although election laws were indeed amended, investigations after the election were spotty, and reforms were mostly superficial. Ignoring the partisan intrigue that had preceded and accompanied the dispute, public officials treated the election fiasco as if it had simply been a consequence of outmoded vote-casting technology. No crimes from the election were prosecuted. No official studies were conducted of the role of the courts in electoral politics. None of the officials in charge of election administration in Florida was investigated, much less held accountable, for any contribution he or she may have made to the election's problems.

Similarly, when Florida's election laws were amended, the partisanship infecting Florida's system of election administration was left intact and in some ways exacerbated.

In part, this disappointing response in the aftermath of the controversy was a consequence of the same factors that had been responsible for much of the turmoil to begin with. Just as partisanship had corrupted Florida's system of election administration, it also posed a barrier to meaningful inquiry and corrective action. Republicans were in control of the state and national governments, and they had little to gain and much to lose from post-election investigations, prosecutions, and reforms.

But there was more to the limp response than just partisan manipulation. Not all citizens were tied to the Republican Party, and even those who were would not rank their ideological commitments above popular control of government and the rule of law. Most citizens must have found the post-election reforms adequate; otherwise more complaints would have been voiced.

This chapter describes the actions taken—and not taken—by public officials in the wake of the controversy and discusses cultural as well as political factors working against meaningful reform. To characterize the political situation and its cultural underpinnings, the chapter begins by reviewing and explicating the premises in speeches made by the candidates near the close of the dispute. The rest of the chapter is devoted to recapping post-election inquiries and reforms, and tracing some of their weaknesses, variously, to partisan intrigue, cultural blinders, and interactions between partisan politics and national ideology.

Parting Words

On December 13, when Al Gore made his concession speech for the presidential election which had begun thirty-six days earlier, he quoted Stephen Douglas's remark to Abraham Lincoln after the divisive election of 1860: "Partisan feeling must yield to patriotism." Whether or not Gore intended the quote to do so, it drew an analogy between George W. Bush and Abraham Lincoln, whose election had led to civil war. Only slightly more than a third of the voters had cast ballots for Lincoln, but he had won because the Democratic Party had split over the issue of slavery and had run two candidates for the presidency. The victory of a fervent abolitionist who stirred the emotions of his followers and the fears of opponents broke apart a nation that had been held together pragmatically for decades. In effect, Gore was implying that Bush faced a fractured nation because of his own demagoguery.

An hour later, when George W. Bush responded to Gore's concession speech with a speech of his own, he made absolutely no reference to history. He spoke from the assembly in Texas to accentuate his experience as a governor. He was introduced by a Democrat to symbolize his claim that he was a "uniter" not a divider. Almost as if he were making another campaign speech, he listed his goals for his term in office. From the very beginning of the dispute he had appeared bitter that Gore had contested the election, and even in his moment of victory it seemed that he was thinking only of himself, of his feelings and goals, and not of the divisions that had led to the close election and to the bitter conflict over its outcome.

The different rhetorical styles of Bush and Gore in the election dispute might have appeared to be opportunistic or idiosyncratic, but at a basic level they reflected the different philosophies of the nation's two dominant parties. This should not be surprising. Bush is a Republican and Gore a Democrat, and they are equally imbued with the ideals and premises of the political organizations they represent, organizations with long histories, written platforms, enduring goals, and distinct bases of support in the electorate. The parties' philosophies account for important aspects of the candidates' policy positions as well as for the ways in which Bush and Gore reacted to the election dispute and its controversial end.

Sore/Loserman

Spokespersons for Bush, and to some extent Bush himself, tended to personalize his differences with Gore during the election controversy. Gore was accused of being a poor sport, willing to do anything to achieve victory. He was said to have been "snippy" when he retracted his concession to Bush after learning, just before he was about to make his concession speech to the nation, that the outcome in Florida remained undecided. Gore's decision to contest the election was contrasted with Richard Nixon's when Nixon lost the 1960 presidential election to John Kennedy amid rumors that the vote in Chicago had been fudged to give Kennedy Illinois and ultimately the presidency. According to this criticism, even if Gore thought he might win with a recount, he should have conceded the election to spare the country political turmoil and perhaps social unrest.

An example of the rhetoric associated with Bush's personal attacks on Gore was a phrase that tagged Gore as a sore loser. The phrase was a play on the conjunction of Gore and Lieberman's names in the Democratic ticket, which was presented as "Gore/Lieberman." Twisting this to humorous effect, T-shirts and signs were printed that said "Sore/Loserman." The message was both memorable and powerful.

The claim that was being made, however, was rather unconvincing. This is why the play on words was necessary; an unadorned attack on Gore's personality because he was following the recount procedures specified in Florida law would have appeared petty—not to mention dismissive of millions of people who had cast votes for Gore in Florida and other states.

In addition to making a personal attack palatable to the watching citizenry, the Sore/Loserman rhetoric was also effective because it glossed over two very important but questionable premises in Bush's argument against recounting the Florida ballots. On its face, the idea that Gore should have conceded for the sake of the nation did not make much sense. It asserted that the outcomes of presidential elections should be accepted uncritically precisely because, or especially when, official election returns are thought to be unreliable. For this position to be at all logical, two conditions must be assumed: Social and political order in American is fragile, and stability depends on widespread acceptance of election outcomes regardless of their reliability. As we shall see momentarily, the first of these premises, if not also the second, pervaded the rhetoric of Bush and his advisers during and after the controversy.

Running Out the Clock

For his part, Gore claimed that he merely wanted all the votes to be counted. Rather than return Bush's personal attacks in kind, Gore suggested that Bush's opposition to reviewing the ballots in Florida was both rational and revealing. Bush did not want the machine-rejected ballots to be checked, Gore explained, because Bush knew that Gore had received more votes. Thus, by citing hidden motives to explain Bush's actions and demeanor, Gore sought to use Bush's own behavior against him. Bush's opposition to recounts became proof that the recounts were needed.

Like Bush's rhetoric, the rhetoric used by Gore and his advocates often drew on sports, but it did not exploit popular images of cheating and unsportsmanlike behavior. Instead, Bush was accused of being, as it were, *too* sporty. He was said to be trying to "run out the clock." This rhetorical analogy implied that Bush, while perhaps not cheating, was playing in the manner that prevented a valid contest. Gore supporters joked that "Bush did not want to get into a recount without first knowing what the outcome would be."

As with Bush's rhetoric, the rhetoric used by Gore was effective because it at once both concealed and conveyed important but problematic premises. Implicit in Gore's characterizations of Bush was the idea that social and political competition takes place on two levels, which correspond roughly to the distinctions between actions and words, motives and statements, truth and appearance, and so on. From this perspective, the potential for social disorder feared by Bush mistakes a single level for the whole; pointing to the constant competition, debate, and maneuvering apparent on the surface of American politics, Bush's imagery erroneously suggests that a war of all against all could break out at any moment, because it ignores the consensus beneath the superficial divisions. Gore's notion that Bush was running out the clock suggests that political infighting, even when it is very bitter, rests on a solid foundation of agreement and social solidarity. Players know what it means to run out the clock, because they know and agree on the purpose of the game, and this awareness implies that the game itself is not jeopardized by allowing competition to continue. Players may cheat but they know when they are cheating, and they tacitly endorse the rules whenever they cheat because cheating works only when it is concealed, and concealment implies guilt. From this perspective, there is no danger of a war of all against all. The real problem is dealing with people's natural inclination to skirt the rules and take advantage of the fair play of others.

Partisan Perspectives on American Politics, Society, and History

The premises embedded in the candidates' rhetoric flow from their partisan ideologies, which reflect the parties' bases of support in the electorate. Republicans and Democrats use different concepts and metaphors to describe the world, because, in effect, the parties look at the world from different social and economic locations.

The Miracle of Democracy: The View from Above

Republicans view the United States as a rare, almost miraculous creation. In the words of George W. Bush's Inaugural Address (in the appendix to this chapter), "Through much of the last century, America's faith in freedom and democracy was a rock in a raging sea. Now it is a seed upon the wind, taking root in many nations." This sense of democracy's fragility expresses the point of view of society's upper strata, whose members are vastly outnumbered and who therefore inevitably fear losing their assets and privileges to envious masses. Like "America's faith in freedom and democracy," they feel surrounded by a "raging sea." For this same reason Republicans often view American history as a descent from the nation's founding as a place with minimal government where people with ability and ambition could succeed to its current status as a political order in which, from the Republican perspective, free speech has been replaced by political correctness, Uncle Sam has given way to Big Brother, and individual initiative has been lost to group claims of victimization.

The view that liberty and popular control of government are rare and endangered was written into the U.S. Constitution of 1789, which replaced the Articles of Confederation. The American Founders thought that the greatest danger for a republican form of government was the potential for the less affluent majority to use its numbers in elections to take wealth and dignity from the more affluent upper classes. This is why the Founders constructed a political system with a democratic core surrounded by numerous checks and limitations. The core is the House of Representatives, which, when the Constitution was first implemented, was the only political unit whose members were selected through direct election by the people. All power flows from the House, because it alone can initiate the budget. The ability of this democratic element to act is constrained by the Senate, whose members were initially elected by the state legislatures; by the president and vice president, who are elected by the Electoral College; and by the Supreme Court, whose members are selected by the president but must be confirmed by the Senate.

One of the principal authors of the Constitution was John Adams. He formed the nation's first political party, the Federalists, which evolved through various incarnations into the Republican Party of today. The name of the Republican Party expresses support for representative government over direct democracy.

Over the past two centuries the Republican Party or its antecedents has stood against the tendency of American government to become increasingly democratic. In a few respects America's democratization has occurred formally through constitutional amendments, which included changes to limit presidents to two terms, allow senators to be elected by the people, and extend the franchise to women, to people of all races, and to young adults. These were significant amendments, but much of the nation's democratization has also happened through informal agreements, new practices at the state level, and changes in culture and technology. An example of the latter is the widespread use of public opinion polling and focus groups.

From the Republican perspective on the nation's history, the election dispute in 2000 reflected America's continuing downward slide from lawful government toward mob rule.

Unfulfilled Promise: The View from Below

For Democrats, American history has been an ascent—a long, difficult, and still incomplete climb that began with a social order based on slavery, gender oppression, and class privileges. Democrats see a path leading upward toward a truly democratic society in which all people will have equal rights, influence, and opportunity. This is the view of oppressed classes everywhere, although in the United States, as in other unique circumstances, its content is composed of historical examples from a singular past. People striving to rise within a hierarchy of social status and economic class notice the obstacles in their way and dream of a social order in which all such impediments have been wiped away. They reconstruct history as a struggle for liberation, a struggle by the human spirit to emerge clean and unblemished from the tar pit of oppression.

In American history the document most reflective of the utopian aspirations of the ascending classes is the Declaration of Independence, which was written by the American Founders to those powers which, at the time, held them in tutelage. The principal author of the Declaration was Thomas Jefferson, who was also the founder of the Democratic Party, the nation's oldest partisan organization. Most Americans are familiar only with the opening words of the Declaration, notably those stating that "all men are created equal" and that everyone has the right to "life, liberty, and the pursuit of happiness." But the bulk of the document is devoted to a lengthy description of the many grievances of the American colonies. Actually the Crown had its own complaints about the colonies—they were expensive to defend, they did not pay taxes commensurate to this expense, and they were unruly to boot—but the aspiring classes more quickly recognize their own suffering than the suffering of others and therefore invariably adopt the mantle of victims.

From the Democratic perspective, the 2000 election was simply another example of the imperfection of the existing political system. Gore analyzed it in these terms in his concession speech.

> While I strongly disagree with the [U.S. Supreme] Court's decision, I accept . . . the finality of this outcome . . . I also accept my responsibility . . . to honor the new president-elect and do everything possible to help him bring Americans together in fulfillment of the great vision that our Declaration of Independence defines and that our Constitution affirms and defends. . . . [The election's] closeness can serve to remind us that we are one people with a shared history and a shared destiny. Indeed, that history gives us many examples of contests as hotly debated, as fiercely fought, with their own challenges to the popular will. . . . And each time, both the victor and the vanquished have accepted the result peacefully and in the spirit of reconciliation. So let it be with us.

In this artful statement Gore suggests that the "shared history" and "shared destiny" of the American people is to fulfill "the great vision" of "our Declaration of Independence," a vision which, Gore implies, is not embodied in the Constitution but which the Constitution merely "affirms and defends." In other words, the Constitution is imperfect; "history gives us many examples" of elections that have involved "challenges to the popular will."

Gore tactfully says that such challenges have always been accepted "peacefully and in the spirit of reconciliation," but of course this is untrue; the unforgettable exception is the Civil War. We can be sure that Gore had not overlooked this counterexample, because, as we saw earlier, he referenced the Civil War indirectly by beginning his speech with a quote from Stephen Douglass about his loss to Abraham Lincoln in 1860. Thus Gore's concession speech alludes to a potentially explosive tension between America's political ideals and its institutions, between the will of the people and the decisions of its officials, and between the voters' decision in the 2000 presidential election and the Supreme Court's decision on December 12.

Ideology and Politics in the Post-Election Response

After the controversy had ended, the ideological premises and partisan interests that had divided Democrats and Republicans during the election dispute actually pushed them toward common ground as they evaluated the dispute and considered possible reforms. For obvious reasons, Republicans wanted to avoid any attempt to blame the problems of the election on those state officials who were responsible for maintaining and managing the system of voter registration and election administration. Conversely, Democrats were looking for reforms that would improve access to the polls and make voting easier and more accurate, for they believed, correctly, that the state's election system posed greater barriers to Democratic constituencies than to Republicans. These motivations, while different, caused both sides to gravitate toward technological accounts of the election breakdown and technological fixes.

The path of least resistance headed away from concerns about partisanship in election administration, even though such concerns had been central in the dispute. Three of the state's highest public officials—Secretary of State Katherine Harris, Governor Jeb Bush and Attorney General Bob Butterworth—had direct ties to one of the candidates in the dispute. Jeb Bush and Harris co-chaired George W.'s Florida campaign, and Butterworth chaired the Florida Campaign for Gore. Of course, Jeb Bush was also George W. Bush's brother. On its face, Florida's election process appeared vulnerable to partisan intrigues.

What was not known then but has since been documented is that partisan conniving was rampant during the election dispute among the very people who were supposed to be administering the election process to assure fairness. A series of articles published in the *Washington Post* a few weeks after the election controversy had been decided confirmed the electorate's worst suspicions. The articles revealed that at least some of the actions and decisions of Bush, Harris, and Butterworth were coordinated directly or indirectly with the strategies of the legal team for their party's candidate, and that Bush and Harris were indeed seeking to prevent the votes cast on Election Day from being fully and fairly counted, even though, or precisely because, they realized that careful review might show that Gore had won.

The *Post* series was followed in the summer of 2001 by a series in the *New York Times* suggesting the possibility of a conspiracy between Republican officials in Tallahassee, Republican members of Congress and their aids, and military personnel at home and abroad. The *Times* revealed that military personnel had been encouraged to vote after Election Day; that the delivery of overseas military ballots, at least some known to contain votes cast illegally, had been expedited to get the ballots to Florida in time to be counted; and that Republican operatives sent into Florida by the Bush campaign to pressure county canvassing boards had successfully pushed for improperly completed overseas ballots to be counted in Republican counties and rejected in Democratic counties.

In the center of these apparent conspiracies was Katherine Harris. As secretary of state, Harris was probably most to blame for election and post-election disorder even if she had not been party to criminal conspiracies, because she had had overall responsibility for administering Florida's election process. In the future, voters may be shocked to learn that, in order to receive advice as the election dispute unfolded, Harris brought into her inner circle one of the state's best-known Republican strategists, Mac Stipanovich, who has not denied being in regular contact with George W. Bush's legal team during the controversy. To be sure, during the dispute, accusations were hurled at Harris publicly—for example, that she was helping George W. in return for a promised ambassadorship. Rumors also circulated in Tallahassee that she and Jeb Bush had had an affair on one of their joint trips out of state during the primaries, rumors that became so pervasive by May 2001 that she had to deny them publicly. But, at the time, these accusations all seemed to have been contrived by her political enemies. However, once Stipanovich's role behind the scenes had come to light, Harris's repeated rulings that benefited Bush could no longer be easily dismissed as innocent expressions of her best judgment unfairly depicted as partisan sabotage.

For his part, Jeb Bush recused himself from the Election Commission but nevertheless played a very active role helping his brother behind the scenes. If his aid to George W. had been limited to offering advice and emotional support to his brother, Jeb's behavior would have been beyond public reproach. But, in fact, some of his actions appear to have been violations of Florida law. While employed by the state, he personally attended meetings with his brother's lawyers. Worse, he instructed or, at the very least, allowed his legal staff, while they, too, were working on state time, to contact the state's biggest law firms and discourage them from working for Gore. These calls involved more than a misappropriation of state resources for partisan political activities. Given that the law firms in question drew considerable income from state contracts and from lobbying contracts requiring access to the governor, the firms would have perceived these calls as veiled threats.

That Jeb Bush played such an active and legally risky role in the election controversy explains why, at the time, he overreacted to media inquiries about his actions. During the early days of the controversy Jeb was nowhere to be seen, and it was assumed that he was avoiding involvement to allay concerns that he might use his office to help his brother. However, about ten days into the controversy a television news crew caught up with him, and he was asked whether he would personally sign the letter certifying Florida's electors for his brother. Now an obvious and noncontroversial response would have been to say that he would do so if the law required it, which it did. But, instead, Jeb became indignant and said that he had "not stopped being a brother" just because of the election dispute and that he would help his brother if he could. The brief interview was widely aired on television news and reported in the print media, because it showed Jeb seemingly wanting to be involved and yet constrained by concerns about how his involvement would be interpreted. In retrospect, however, Jeb's visceral reaction to the TV reporter can be seen to have reflected his defensiveness about his behind-the-scenes maneuvers.

Although less extensive and more attenuated, partisanship was also evident among Democrats. Attorney General Bob Butterworth, a Democrat, had regular contact with the Gore team, went on television to defend the recounts, and had his staff suggest to the Palm Beach County Canvassing Board that it request an opinion from him about the recount deadline imposed by the secretary of state. On the other hand, Butterworth also took actions that worked against Gore. In particular, he stated in writing and on television that requirements in Florida election law requiring absentee ballots to have postmarks should be waived, because the mail of some members of the military stationed overseas and on ships would not have been stamped. Butterworth also demonstrated insight by arguing that equal treatment requirements in the U.S. Constitution needed to be addressed by conducting manual recounts statewide. Still, Butterworth's frequent contacts with the Gore legal and political team were inconsistent with the independence expected of his office.

In short, the officials who were supposed to keep Florida's election process fair and open did not appear at all neutral, and, in fact, they were not neutral. The series in the *Washington Post* summed up the role of partisanship as follows:

> What is clear is that Bush enjoyed an enormous advantage because of the presence of his brother in the governor's office and Katherine Harris as secretary of state. The role Jeb Bush and his team played in rounding up legal talent, providing political analysis and offering strategic advice is all the more clear from post-election interviews. With Jeb Bush as governor, the Republicans controlled the machinery of state government and with it the power to set deadlines, enforce election laws in ways that were beneficial to the then-Texas governor and put obstacles in Gore's path. Secretary of State Harris also relied on advice from one of the leading Republican strategists in the state—J. M. "Mac" Stipanovich, a well-connected Republican lobbyist who was an ally of Jeb Bush.

Troubling Questions about Possible Conspiracies

Even before the spring of 2001, when the leading newspapers of Florida and the nation began to uncover extensive evidence that Republicans had conspired to subvert Florida's election system, a number of statements and actions by Bush and his supporters were suspicious and should have generated demands for investigations. For example:

- How did Bush know early on election night that the television networks were in error when they called Florida for Gore? At the time there was no reason to doubt the exit polls. Up to Election Day the contest had been very close in Florida, and Gore appeared to be pulling ahead at the very end. However, when the networks announced Florida for Gore, Bush said that this simply could not be true.
- Why was Bush so sure that he had won Florida when Gore called him on election night to retract his concession? Bush is said to have told Gore that he was certain he had won because his brother had told him so. How would Jeb Bush have known this without talking to Katharine Harris, which would have been a violation of Florida's laws requiring public officials to meet publicly when discussing public business? Certainly Florida's government-in-the-sunshine laws would have covered any conversation about the election returns between Jeb Bush and Harris, for they were both members of the

Florida Elections Commission, which would be certifying the final vote.

- How did Jeb Bush and Katharine Harris separate their responsibilities as public officials in charge of Florida elections from their roles as co-chairs of the Bush presidential campaign in Florida? Harris and Jeb Bush had campaigned for George W. outside Florida during the presidential primaries and throughout Florida once Bush faced Gore in the general election. During all this time, when they must have discussed strategies for securing Bush's victory, had they never considered how they might use their resources and authority as governor and secretary of state to improve Bush's chances for victory? Had they never discussed felon disenfranchisement, Republican access to absentee ballots, or procedures for counting, reporting, and certifying the votes?

- Why were voting problems so much more widespread for African Americans than they had been in previous elections, and did Jeb Bush and Katherine Harris have any responsibility? African Americans complained about being rushed at the polling places, and they were disproportionately prevented from voting by the state's flawed program for removing felons from the registered-voter rolls in 1999 and 2000. High turnout among African American voters had been anticipated. Why were no steps taken to augment staff in the precincts with high percentages of black voters?

- In at least one county on Election Day officers of the Florida highway patrol, which reports to the governor, set up roadblocks to check drivers' licenses near polling places in predominantly black precincts. Was their intent to scare away black voters? By whose orders had the roadblocks been authorized, and how far up the chain of command had the existence of these orders been communicated?

- Why did the Republican leadership in the Florida legislature call the legislature into special session while the judicial branch of the state's government was still addressing the election issues? The legislature would not have been in a position to become involved in the election controversy until after December 12 and would have had until December 18 to take whatever action might have been necessary. The effect of the special session was to create fears that a constitutional crisis was imminent, thereby making Supreme Court intervention more likely. Although he initially denied it, the Florida Speaker of the House admitted that he had been in communication with the Bush team. Was the special session orchestrated directly or indirectly by George W. Bush or his agents?

- Why did Katherine Harris decide to keep her office open on Sunday, November 26, and thereby force the manual recounts in Florida to end at 5:00 p.m. on November 26 rather than at 9:00 a.m. on Monday the 27th? Dade County had decided to stop its recount in midstream because it thought it might be unable to meet the deadline. Palm Beach County missed the Sunday night deadline by a few hours. Why would the head of Florida's election process not want to do what she could to allow all the votes to be counted? When she had rigidly enforced an earlier deadline, she had explained her seemingly partisan behavior by saying that the election law gave her no other option, but deciding to end the recount on Sunday night of the 26th rather than Monday morning was entirely within her discretion.

- Had any or all members of the Florida Elections Commission discussed the meeting of November 26 ahead of time? Florida's public meeting laws would prohibit such communications, and yet the meeting on the 26th, when the election results were certified, seemed anything but spontaneous. Both Harris and Agricultural Commissioner Bob Crawford, who had replaced Jeb Bush on the Elections Commission after Bush had recused himself, delivered prepared speeches that dovetailed each other closely and seemed designed to put pressure on Gore to concede. How had both Harris and Crawford decided independently to assert that the election was over when, in fact, everyone knew that the results would be contested in the circuit court?

- Why did the U.S. Supreme Court stop the statewide recount that had been mandated by the Supreme Court of Florida? The statewide recount was under way and moving smoothly, and it would surely have been completed before December 12. The court's members had to be aware that by stopping the recount they would be giving the election to Bush regardless of what they might conclude in their subsequent deliberations. In this case the clock was being run out, not by the team that was in the lead but by the *referees*. How did they reach this decision prior to reviewing the evidence and hearing the arguments?

The Task Force of Governor Jeb Bush

On December 14, 2000, just one day after Gore's concession, Jeb Bush appointed the "Select Task Force on Election Procedures, Standards, and Technology." On the surface the task force appeared to be exactly what the situation called for: a balanced, independent body with the resources, authority, and credibility to conduct a through investigation of problems in the 2000 election and to recommend any statutory or constitutional reforms deemed necessary and practical for preventing similar problems in the future. In fact, however, the task force had minimal resources and a very limited scope. Its responsibilities, stated in Section D(4) of Executive Order 00–349, were to "study and make written policy recommendations and/or propose legislation *to improve the election procedures, standards and technology employed in each of Florida's 67 counties*" (emphasis added). (The full text of the order is contained in the appendix.)

The governor's motives in establishing the task force can only be inferred, but his haste, his failure to consult with top Democrats about the composition and charge of the task force, and the restrictions he placed on the scope of its inquiry and recommendations indicated that his purpose was, at least in part, to contain the post-election controversy and manage the pressures for reform. The formal name Bush gave to the commission—the Select Task Force on Election Procedures, Standards, and Technology—pointed the inquiry away from partisan corruption in election administration and toward the mechanics of voting and vote tabulation. Similarly the language quoted above from the executive order directed the task force away from Tallahassee and toward the election supervisors in the counties.

Further suggesting insincerity on the governor's part, Jeb advertised the task force as "nonpartisan," when, in fact, it was partisan to the extreme. Its members were not unconnected to political factions; they were appointed *specifically on the basis of* their party affiliations. Only one member was not attached to a party. The remaining twenty were divided equally between Democrats and Republicans. Either the governor was guilty of false advertising or he did not know the difference between *non*partisan and *bi*partisan.

In any event, the governor definitely understood how to use the partisan makeup of the task force to assure that it reflected partisan concerns. The task force was headed by partisan co-chairs, one Democrat and one Republican. Section 2 of the Executive Order further constrained the already limited scope of the task force by politicizing its decision making. It stipulated that,

> the two Co-Chairpersons shall limit the scope of the Select Task Force's study and written policy recommendations to those issues which can, *in the opinion of both Co-Chairpersons,* be manageably addressed by the entire Select Task Force within the time limits set herein. (emphasis added)

Requiring the co-chairs to agree on "the scope of . . . the study and . . . recommendations" meant that the Democrat, who might be inclined to press the inquiry into sensitive areas, could be vetoed by the Republican.

Bush further buttressed Republican strength on the task force by his appointments. For the Republican co-chair he selected Jim Smith, one of the shrewdest and most knowledgeable people in all Florida government. Smith had served two terms as attorney general and two terms as secretary of state. A protégé of Reubin Askew when Askew was governor in the first eight years of the 1970s, Jim Smith in 2001 had no peer in Florida politics except, perhaps, Jeb Bush. And even counting Bush, there is no elected official alive today with as much experience in Florida's executive branch as Smith.

In contrast to Smith, Bush's choice for the Democratic co-chair was Tad Foote, a former president of the University of Miami. Certainly Foote is an able university administrator and a popular figure in South Florida, but he has no real background in Florida politics and government. The comparison between Foote and Smith was more one-sided even than the matchup between Warren Christopher and Jim Baker during the election controversy. At least Christopher and Baker had both been secretaries of state; Foote, on the other hand, had never served as an official in Florida government.

Predestined to reach innocuous conclusions, the task force quickly became fixated on the technical aspects of elections. Out of the thirty-five recommendations made by the task force in its final report, sixteen dealt with voting equipment and related procedures, eight with voter education and poll worker qualifications, and eight with procedures for contesting elections and recounting ballots. In only three of its recommendations did the task force address the overall system of election administration. It called for the position of elections supervisor at the county level to be made nonpartisan, and for members of both the state elections commission and the county canvassing boards to be prohibited from working on other political campaigns.

However, when it came to removing partisanship from the system entirely, the task force punted. In the words of the final report,

> The Governor's Task Force tabled the idea of an independent, non-partisan elections board to replace the existing state Division of Elections. There are current efforts by the Florida Legislature for reorganizing the Florida Department of State, including the governance and duties of the Division of Elections, as part of ongoing statewide governmental reorganization following actions by the voters to change the Florida Constitution in 1998.

This rationale suggested that a major reorganization was in the works, that it was constitutionally mandated, and that recommendations for a nonpartisan election board might be disruptive. In fact, the Bush administration's proposal for reorganizing the Department of State, which was not completed until 2002, barely touched at all on election administration.

2001 Revisions to Florida's Election Laws

After the governor's task force issued its report in late February 2001, the Florida legislature acted on its recommendations in the legislative session that began in March, passing the Florida Election Reform Act of 2001. Announced with great fanfare, it received national attention and was in large measure favorably reviewed. Florida's governor Jeb Bush went to West Palm Beach, where much of the recounting had taken place, for a ceremonial signing. At the event he said that the legislation would create "one of the finest election systems anywhere." Among other changes, the legislation outlawed punch-card voting systems, provided for a standardized ballot, mandated an administrative process to develop detailed instructions for discerning voter intent in manual recounts, and stipulated that a statewide manual recount is required in any statewide contest decided by less than one-fourth of 1 percent of the votes cast.

Failure to Remove Partisanship

Some of these changes and additions to Florida's election laws had merit, but the legislation as a whole failed to correct the most serious problems revealed by the election. The central problem had been partisan corruption of the state's system of voter registration and election administration, corruption that had produced administrative actions that had subverted legally mandated recounts in a presidential election, had been intentionally prejudicial to the voting rights and electoral strength of historically oppressed minorities, and had allowed the nation's armed forces to engage in election fraud in a contest to decide who would become the next commander in chief. The legislation of 2001 left Florida's election system under the control of partisan officials, biased against African Americans and senior citizens, and even more likely than previously to produce election outcomes contradicting voters' intentions.

The 2001 legislation ignored the recommendation of the governor's task force to make county election supervisors nonpartisan. Similarly, although the act did include language to prohibit members of the state Elections Commission from leading political campaigns, the prohibition applied only to direct campaign involvement and did *not* mean that the officials themselves would be without partisan affiliations. The law assumed that Florida's election officials, who oversee voter registration, felon disenfranchisement, campaign finance limitations, and most other aspects of election administration in the state, would continue to be elected in partisan elections and would continue to be handicapped by an inherent conflict of interest between their stake in the success of their party, and their responsibility to assure open and fair elections.

Failure to Resolve Ballot Spoilage Issues

The election legislation of 2001 was similarly off target in its provisions for reducing ballot spoilage. The legislation addressed ballot spoilage in two ways: it outlawed punch-card systems, and it devoted monies to voter education. Moving away from punch cards may reduce voter error in general but not the tendency for African Americans and seniors to make more errors than are made by other voters. The high ballot-spoilage rates of these groups are not caused by faulty equipment or inadequate information. The high error rate of seniors probably stems from vision impairments, arthritis, and other physical characteristics that make many tasks more difficult. For them, newfangled voting equipment is likely to prove more difficult rather than less.

Africa Americans, on the other hand, experience high ballot-spoilage rates regardless of the type of equipment employed. As previously discussed, the highest rate of ballot spoilage in the state was in Gadsden County, which is the state's only majority African American county, and it uses an optical scan system. The inordinately high rate of ballot spoilage in predominantly black precincts probably stems from the sad experience blacks have had with American democracy. Historically as a people, African Americans were terrorized when they sought to exercise their voting rights, and, as a result, they are likely to feel uncomfortable in the polling place.

African Americans may also worry that the ballots they cast will not be counted. If so, their fears would not be groundless. The requirement in Florida law that votes, regardless of whether they have been properly filled out, must be counted whenever voter intent can be discerned was added to Florida election laws because, historically, many votes cast by blacks had been thrown out on technicalities. Fearing the same possibility today, blacks may be prone to mark their ballots in ways that, while inconsistent with instructions, make their choice thoroughly clear. This would explain why, in the 2000 election, valid write-in overvotes were concentrated in predominately black precincts. Many blacks marked Gore on the list of candidates and then, presumably to assure that their choice could not be misinterpreted, wrote Gore's name in the space for write-in candidates. It is doubtful that electronic and optical scan voting machines will remove these and similar sources of ballot spoilage in black voting.

More Potential for Confusion

The new voting equipment required by the 2001 legislation is also likely to result in more confusion and disorder at the polls. The legislation requires counties to use voting technologies that tabulate votes at the precinct level rather than sending all ballots to the county headquarters for counting there. Precinct tabulation allows ballot errors to be detected while voters are still on the scene to correct their mistakes. However, if the voting equipment is in fact programmed so that errors are identified immediately and voters are allowed to correct them, delays and traffic jams at the polls will be likely as voters are forced to work their way through the ballot properly. In past elections ballot spoilage has not created bottlenecks, because either the problems were not recognized at the time or those counties with precinct-level tabulation disengaged their error-detection systems to avoid delays when traffic became heavy. If, in future elections, many more ballot errors were to be detected because of the technology, the load at the polls would be much heavier than ever before in Florida history. Had the technology been in place in 2000, for example, the election system would have had to accommodate the ballot-salvaging activities of more than 175,000 voters.

Florida's 2001 election legislation did not expand the capacity of Florida's election system to handle this additional load. Hence, to the extent that new technology is successful in reducing ballot spoilage, it is likely to have the side effect of reducing turnout as voters see or hear about delays at the polls.

Delays May Reduce Democratic Turnout

Furthermore, bottlenecks at the polls will not be spread evenly throughout the system but instead will be concentrated in precincts with high concentrations of minorities and seniors. After all, these are the categories of voters with the highest incidence of ballot spoilage. Consequently any reductions in turnout caused by delays at the polls will be concentrated, once again, among traditionally Democratic constituencies.

In fact, as discussed in the previous chapter, this appears to have been exactly what happened in Broward County in the 2002 gubernatorial election between Jeb Bush and Bill McBride. After delays were reported during early voting, many voters stayed home, and Broward County experienced its lowest turnout ever in a modern gubernatorial election.

Inaccurate Election Returns More Likely

Yet another defect in Florida's 2001 election law was its see-no-evil approach to close elections. The 2000 election demonstrated that election returns based on mechanical tabulations are merely *estimates*, not precise and accurate indications of the *actual results*. This means that ballots should be manually inspected whenever the margin of victory in an election approaches the margin of error in mechanical vote tabulation. The election laws in effect in 2000 had set the trigger for manual recounts too low. They authorized manual recounts only when the margin of victory was less than one-half of 1 percent of the total votes cast, and yet mechanical tabulations typically err by 3 percent or more. Even the very best equipment available has an average error rate of 1 percent, which was double the manual-recount trigger in effect in Florida between 1990 and 2000.

However, the election law passed by the Florida legislature and signed by the governor in 2001 actually made the recount trigger *lower* rather than higher. Under the new provisions, a manual recount is not authorized unless the returns indicate that the election has been decided by one-quarter of 1 percent of the total votes cast. However, the normal error rate for optical scan and electronic voting systems—the types of election equipment counties will be adopting under the legislation—is between 1 and 3 percent. In the 2000 election the error rate for optical-scan systems with tabulation at the precincts varied in Florida from a low of .27 percent in Brevard County to 3.94 percent in Washington County. If the rate statewide is reduced to 1 percent—and this is a big "if"—then results from any Florida election in the foreseeable future decided by between .25 and 1 percent of the vote cast will be unreliable and yet will *not* be double-checked by recounting the votes manually. An example from recent Florida history where an election met these conditions was the 1988 contest between Mack and MacKay for the U.S. Senate, the very election targeted by the 1989 reforms that the 2001 reforms are supposed to have enhanced.

Surely not the result of coincidence, the weaknesses of the 2001 Florida Election Reform Act benefit the Republican Party, which controls the offices responsible for enacting and signing the law. On all voting systems, voter errors among Democrats appear to outrun Republican errors by about 2 to 1 until the votes with errors are read via manual recounts. This means that in statewide elections with a normal turnout, even with the new equipment and a low error rate of 1 percent, Republican candidates will start out with an advantage of 46,000 votes simply by virtue of the state's voting system. Given the closeness of many Florida elections and the importance of Florida in national elections, the bias in the system can lead to erroneous election returns that, like those in the 2000 presidential election, assign victory to candidates who have actually received fewer votes than their opponents have. Furthermore, because the trigger for manual recounts was lowered rather than raised by the 2001 legislation, the probability has increased that false election outcomes will go undetected and will therefore be allowed to stand.

Blatant Partisanship

On top of all this, under the guise of reform, the 2001 election law made changes to Florida's election system that were blatantly designed to harm the interests of Florida Democrats in the next election. Specifically for the 2002 election in which Jeb Bush was expected to be vulnerable, the legislation set aside the two-primary system that has historically enabled Democrats to nominate moderate candidates for statewide offices who can appeal to both their North Florida and South Florida constituencies. Because of this provision, Democrats nominated newcomer Bill McBride rather Janet Reno for governor. McBride lost to Bush when turnout in the general election, although high in the Panhandle and the I-4 corridor, was dismal in South Florida. Whether Reno could have defeated Bush in the general election is unclear, but certainly she would have attracted voters to the polls.

Official Evidence of Criminal Acts

The only government agency to investigate Florida's administration of the disputed 2000 presidential election was the U.S. Civil Rights Commission. It was also the only agency to use subpoena powers and require sworn testimony. For its efforts, the Commission received little attention and even less appreciation.

Contract for Identifying Felons

The Civil Rights Commission conducted hearings at several locations in Florida in January and February 2001. The hearings turned up evidence of a possible conspiracy by Florida's Republican secretary of state and other high-ranking Republican officials, perhaps including Florida governor Jeb Bush, to illegally remove predominantly Democratic voters from the registration rolls under the guise of removing felons, who, by Florida law, are ineligible to vote unless they have their civil rights restored by the governor and cabinet.

Most of the evidence of criminal acts came from the sworn statement of George Bruder, a vice president of Database Technologies (DBT), which was the private corporation that worked with the Florida secretary of state and the director of the Division of Elections in 1999 and 2000 to identify ex-felons on Florida's registered-voter rolls. Chapter 5 of the final report of the Civil Rights Commission covers the felon disenfranchisement program.

Among other things, it points out the suspicious character of the process used by the Division of Elections and the secretary of state's office to award DBT the contract for identifying voters who might be ex-felons. In the report's words:

The Division of Elections initially solicited private entities to bid for its list maintenance contract through requests for proposals. The first request resulted in an award to a private firm named Professional Analytical Systems & Services. Following its award of a contract to Professional Analytical Systems & Services, the Division of Elections, for reasons not evident in the record, submitted a second request for proposal. Next, the Division of Elections extended an invitation to negotiate to a Florida company then known as Database Technologies, Inc. and to Computer Business Services, a Georgia company. In response to the Division of Elections second Request for Proposal, Database Technologies, Inc. bid around $3.1 million, *an amount nearly 100 times higher than its first bid.* (emphasis added)

In his testimony to the Commission, Mr. Bruder was asked how he knew to make the price in his second bid so much higher than the price in his first bid. He answered that he had been advised to do so by "a little bird," and he refused to comment further.

Match Criteria Were Too Loose

In recounting his experiences with the project, Bruder explained that, as DBT began to match names and other information on lists of convicted felons with those on Florida's list of registered voters, he became concerned that the match criteria DBT had been instructed to use were too loose and resulted in "false positives." However, the Division of Elections insisted that DBT use the loosest criteria permissible within the scope of its contract, which called only for the use of first names, last names, and birthdates. The Division instructed DBT not to require that first and middle names be in any particular order to match. In other words, John Andrew Smith would be considered to match Andrew John Smith. The Elections Division also insisted that matches be allowed even when the last names of individuals on the list of ex-felons only approximated the last names of registered voters. The spelling needed to be just "90 percent" the same. This meant that John Andrew Smith would be counted as a match with John Andrew Smythe, Andrew John Smythe, John Adrew Smitt, Andrew John Smitt, and so on. Bruder summed up this part of his testimony by saying that "the state dictated to us that they wanted to go broader and we did it in the fashion that they requested."

The loose match criteria used by DBT under the direction of the Division of Elections resulted in a highly erroneous list of registered voters who were thought to be ex-felons. County elections supervisors were sent the names of the purported felons who were registered to vote their particular county. The supervisors were instructed to verify the information and remove voters from the rolls accordingly. How much care was taken by the supervisors is not known, but the investigation by the Civil Rights Commission found that procedures varied widely across the counties.

By June 2000 it became obvious to a number of the local supervisors of elections that the lists they had been given were full of errors. Numerous examples of problems are chronicled in the Civil Rights Commission's report. In addition to the loose match criteria, one source of many errors was the mistaken inclusion of misdemeanants on the list of felons from, of all states, Texas. This error alone caused more than 8,000 Florida voters to be improperly identified for removal from the registered voter rolls. Highlighting just how bad the lists distributed by the Division of Elections had been, in Madison County the name of the supervisor of elections (who was not a felon) was itself on the list.

Failure to Correct Known Problems

These and other problems were brought to the attention of the Division of Elections, which sent letters to all supervisors advising them of the mistakes. But many of the problems were never corrected at the county level, and thousands of voters were removed from the rolls improperly. Often, the first time voters learned that their voter registration had been revoked was when they arrived at the polls to cast their ballots in the 2000 presidential election. This accounts for much of the chaos that day.

The findings of the Civil Rights Commission were certainly sufficient to warrant a full investigation of actions of Florida secretary of state Katherine Harris, Florida governor Jeb Bush, and Elections Division director Clay Roberts. Either singly or in combination, all three may have used their offices to improperly influence the outcome of the 2000 election—a felony under the state's election laws. At the very least, one or more of them appear to have been guilty of either misfeasance or nonfeasance in issuing a contract that did not contain performance criteria regarding the accuracy of DBT's work, in failing to correct the problems with the felon disenfranchisement initiative once they became visible, and in not assuring that polling places were adequately staffed on election day in 2000 to handle the resulting confusion.

However, no follow-up investigation was ever conducted. Incredibly the hearings of the U.S. Civil Rights Commission received no live television coverage, and media stories about them always included Republican accusations that the Commission was biased because a majority of its members were Democrats or Democratic appointees. A few months later, when the Commission issued its draft report, the findings were written off as a hatchet job engineered by the chair, a black female who had come into conflict with Jeb Bush a year earlier over Bush's executive order eliminating affirmative action in state hiring, state contracting, and admissions to the state's public universities. The "One Florida Initiative," as the executive order was referred to, sparked a letter of inquiry from the Commission chair. None of these complaints about the Commission were fair, but they were apparently effective in neutralizing it politically. The Commission's substantial, detailed, and shocking findings about the disputed 2000 election had little impact on public opinion and were ignored by most policy makers.

Moreover, four years later Florida's top policy makers were responsible for producing yet another flawed list of potential felons in the months leading up to the presidential election of 2004, when George W. Bush would be seeking reelection in a contest expected to be very close. In 2001, state law governing felon disenfranchisement was amended to require the Florida Division of Elections to contract with the state's organization for court clerks to compile the "purge list." Nonetheless, the division subsequently complained that the clerks were asking for too much money to handle the project, and it used a technical loophole in the law to once again contract with a private company for this service. Using bidding procedures subsequently found by the state's inspector general to be improper, the division chose Accenture, an international technology consulting firm. The inspector general concluded that the bidding process was biased in Accenture's favor and the contract failed to include normal safeguards for contract compliance and quality control.

Once the purge list was finalized and transmitted to county elections supervisors, a number of organizations sought access to it under Florida's public-records laws, but Secretary of State Glenda Hood, who had been appointed by Governor Jeb Bush, fought to keep the list private. CNN took the issue to Florida circuit court, which ruled in CNN's favor and opened the purge list to outside scrutiny. The Brennan Law Center at New York University immediately found problems, as did journalists. The list of

48,000 registered voters included over 2,100 individuals who had been convicted of felonies but who, since then, had had their civil rights restored by Florida's governor and cabinet. Furthermore, excluded almost entirely from the purge list were Hispanics, many of whom in Florida would be expected to vote Republican.

Ultimately, Secretary of State Hood and Governor Bush announced that they would not require county supervisors to implement the purge, but supervisors were left free to apply the list if they so chose, and in any event many voters on the list had already been notified that they appeared to be ineligible to vote. The inevitable result was not only that the voting strength of Democratic constituencies was weakened for the 2004 presidential election, but also that the stage was set for confusion and chaos at the polls in African-American neighborhoods.

Appendix to Chapter 5

Al Gore's Concession Speech

Good evening. Just moments ago I spoke with George W. Bush and congratulated him on becoming the 43rd president of the United States. And I promised him that I wouldn't call him back this time. I offered to meet with him as soon as possible so that we can start to heal the divisions of the campaign and the contest through which we've just passed.

Almost a century and a half ago, Senator Stephen Douglas told Abraham Lincoln, who had just defeated him for the presidency, "Partisan feeling must yield to patriotism. I'm with you, Mr. President, and God bless you." Well, in that same spirit, I say to President-elect Bush that what remains of partisan rancor must now be put aside, and may God bless his stewardship of this country.

Neither he nor I anticipated this long and difficult road. Certainly neither of us wanted it to happen. Yet it came, and now it has ended, resolved, as it must be resolved, through the honored institutions of our democracy.

Over the library of one of our great law schools is inscribed the motto:

"Not under man, but under God and law." That's the ruling principle of American freedom, the source of our democratic liberties. I've tried to make it my guide throughout this contest, as it has guided America's deliberations of all the complex issues of the past five weeks. Now the U.S. Supreme Court has spoken. Let there be no doubt, while I strongly disagree with the court's decision, I accept it. I accept the finality of this outcome, which will be ratified next Monday in the Electoral College. And tonight, for the sake of our unity as a people and the strength of our democracy, I offer my concession.

I also accept my responsibility, which I will discharge unconditionally, to honor the new president-elect and do everything possible to help him bring Americans together in fulfillment of the great vision that our Declaration of Independence defines and that our Constitution affirms and defends.

Let me say how grateful I am to all those who've supported me and supported the cause for which we have fought. Tipper and I feel a deep gratitude to Joe and Hadassah Lieberman, who brought passion and high purpose to our partnership, and opened new doors, not just for our campaign, but for our country.

This has been an extraordinary election, but in one of God's unforeseen paths, this belatedly broken impasse can point us all to a new common ground, for its very closeness can serve to remind us that we are one people with a shared history and a shared destiny. Indeed, that history gives us many examples of contests as hotly debated, as fiercely fought, with their own challenges to the popular will. Other disputes have dragged on for weeks before reaching resolution, and each time, both the victor and the vanquished have accepted the result peacefully and in a spirit of reconciliation. So let it be with us.

I know that many of my supporters are disappointed. I am too. But our disappointment must be overcome by our love of country. And I say to our fellow members of the world community: Let no one see this contest as a sign of American weakness. The strength of American democracy is shown most clearly through the difficulties it can overcome. Some have expressed concern that the unusual nature of this election might hamper the next president in the conduct of his office. I do not believe it need be so.

President-elect Bush inherits a nation whose citizens will be ready to assist him in the conduct of his large responsibilities. I personally will be at his disposal and I call on all Americans—I particularly urge all who stood with us—to unite behind our next president. This is America. Just as we fight hard when the stakes are high, we close ranks and come together when the contest is done. And while there will be time enough to debate our continuing differences, now is the time to recognize that that which unites us is greater than that which divides us. While we yet hold and do not yield our opposing beliefs, there is a higher duty than the one we owe to political party. This is America and we put country before party. We will stand together behind our new president.

As for what I'll do next, I don't know the answer to that one yet. Like many of you, I'm looking forward to spending the holidays with family and old friends. I know I'll spend time in Tennessee and mend some fences, literally and figuratively. Some have asked whether I have any regrets. And I do have one regret—that I didn't get the chance to stay and fight for the American people over the next four years, especially for those who need burdens lifted and barriers removed, especially for those who feel their voices have not been heard. I heard you and I will not forget. I've seen America in this campaign and I like what I see. It's worth fighting for and that's a fight I'll never stop.

As for the battle that ends tonight, I do believe, as my father once said, that no matter how hard the loss, defeat may serve as well as victory to shake the soul and let the glory out. So for me this campaign ends as it began: with the love of Tipper and our family, with faith in God and in the country I have been so proud to serve, from Vietnam to the vice presidency, and with gratitude to our truly tireless campaign staff and volunteers including all those who worked so hard in Florida for the last 36 days.

Now the political struggle is over and we turn again to the unending struggle for the common good of all Americans and for those multitudes around the world who look to us for leadership in the cause of freedom. In the words of our great hymn, "America, America," let us crown thy good with brotherhood from sea to shining sea. And now, my friends, in a phrase I once addressed to others, it's time for me to go. Thank you and good night and God bless America.

George W. Bush's Victory Speech

Thank you very much. Good evening, my fellow Americans. I appreciate so very much the opportunity to speak with you tonight. Mr. Speaker, Lieutenant Governor, friends, distinguished guests, our country has been through a long and trying period, with the outcome of the presidential election not finalized for longer than any of us could ever imagine. Vice President Gore and I put our hearts and hopes into our campaigns; we both gave it our all. We shared similar emotions. So I understand how difficult this moment must be for Vice President Gore and his family. He has a distinguished record of service to our country as a congressman, a senator and a vice president. This evening I received a gracious call from the vice president. We agreed to meet early next week in Washington, and we agreed to do our best to heal our country after this hard-fought contest.

Tonight, I want to thank all the thousands of volunteers and campaign workers who worked so hard on my behalf. I also salute the vice president and his supporters for waging a spirited campaign, and I thank him for a call that I know was difficult to make. Laura and I wish the vice president and Senator Lieberman and their families the very best.

I have a lot to be thankful for tonight. I am thankful for America and thankful that we are able to resolve our electoral differences in a peaceful way. I'm thankful to the American people for the great privilege of being able to serve as your next president. I want to thank my wife and our daughters for their love. Laura's active involvement as First Lady has made Texas a better place, and she will be a wonderful First Lady of America. I am proud to have Dick Cheney by my side, and America will be proud to have him as our next vice president.

Tonight, I chose to speak from the chamber of the Texas House of Representatives because it has been a home to bipartisan cooperation. Here, in a place where Democrats have the majority, Republicans and Democrats have worked together to do what is right for the people we represent. We've had spirited disagreements, and in the end, we found constructive consensus. It is an experience I will always carry with me, an example I will always follow. I want to thank my friend, House Speaker Pete Laney, a Democrat, who introduced me today. I want to thank the legislators from both political parties with whom I've worked. Across the hall in our Texas Capitol is the State Senate, and I cannot help but think of our mutual friend, the former Democrat lieutenant governor, Bob Bullock. His love for Texas and his ability to work in a bipartisan way continue to be a model for all of us.

The spirit of cooperation I have seen in this hall is what is needed in Washington, D.C. It is the challenge of our moment. After a difficult election, we must put politics behind us and work together to make the promise of America available for every one of our citizens. I am optimistic that we can change the tone in Washington, D.C. I believe things happen for a reason, and I hope the long wait of the last five weeks will heighten a desire to move beyond the bitterness and partisanship of the recent past.

Our nation must rise above a house divided. Americans share hopes and goals and values far more important than any political disagreements. Republicans want the best for our nation. And so do Democrats. Our votes may differ, but not our hopes. I know America wants reconciliation and unity. I know Americans want progress. And we must seize this moment and deliver.

Together, guided by a spirit of common sense, common courtesy and common goals, we can unite and inspire the American citizens.

Together, we will work to make all our public schools excellent, teaching every student of every background and every accent, so that no child is left behind.

Together, we will save Social Security and renew its promise of a secure retirement for generations to come.

Together, we will strengthen Medicare and offer prescription drug coverage to all of our seniors.

Together, we will give Americans the broad, fair and fiscally responsible tax relief they deserve.

Together, we'll have a bipartisan foreign policy true to our values and true to our friends. And we will have a military equal to every challenge, and superior to every adversary.

Together, we will address some of society's deepest problems, one person at a time, by encouraging and empowering the good hearts and good works of the American people. This is the essence of compassionate conservatism, and it will be a foundation of my administration.

These priorities are not merely Republican concerns or Democratic concerns; they are American responsibilities. During the fall campaign, we differed about the details of these proposals, but there was remarkable consensus about the important issues before us: excellent schools, retirement and health security, tax relief, a strong military, a more civil society. We have discussed our differences. Now it is time to find common ground and build consensus to make America a beacon of opportunity in the 21st century. I'm optimistic this can happen. Our future demands it, and our history proves it. Two hundred years ago, in the election of 1800, America faced another close presidential election. A tie in the Electoral College put the outcome into the hands of Congress. After six days of voting, and 36 ballots, the House of Representatives elected Thomas Jefferson the third president of the United States. That election brought the first transfer of power from one party to another in our new democracy. Shortly after the election, Jefferson, in a letter titled "Reconciliation and Reform," wrote this: "The steady character of our countrymen is a rock to which we may safely moor. Unequivocal in principle, reasonable in manner, we shall be able to hope to do a great deal of good to the cause of freedom and harmony." Two hundred years have only strengthened the steady character of America. And so as we begin the work of healing our nation, tonight I call upon that character: respect for each other, respect for our differences, generosity of spirit and a willingness to work hard and work together to solve any problem.

I have something else to ask you, to ask every American. I ask for you to pray for this great nation. I ask for your prayers for leaders from both parties. I thank you for your prayers for me and my family, and I ask you to pray for Vice President Gore and his family. I have faith that with God's help we as a nation will move forward together, as one nation, indivisible. And together we will create an America that is open, so every citizen has access to the American dream; an America that is educated, so every child has the keys to realize that dream; and an America that is united in our diversity and our shared American values that are larger than race or party. I was not elected to serve one party, but to serve one nation. The president of the United States is the president of every single American, of every race and every background. Whether you voted for me or not, I will do my best to serve your interests, and I will work to earn your respect. I will be guided by President Jefferson's sense of purpose, to stand for principle, to be reasonable in manner, and, above all, to do great good for the cause of freedom and harmony.

The presidency is more than an honor. It is more than an office. It is a charge to keep, and I will give it my all.

Thank you very much, and God bless America.

George W. Bush's Inaugural Address

President Clinton, distinguished guests and my fellow citizens, the peaceful transfer of authority is rare in history, yet common in our country. With a simple oath, we affirm old traditions and make new beginnings.

As I begin, I thank President Clinton for his service to our nation.

And I thank Vice President Gore for a contest conducted with spirit and ended with grace.

I am honored and humbled to stand here, where so many of America's leaders have come before me, and so many will follow. We have a place, all of us, in a long story—a story we continue, but whose end we will not see. It is the story of a new world that became a friend and liberator of the old, a story of a slave-holding society that became a servant of freedom, the story of a power that went into the world to protect but not possess, to defend but not to conquer. It is the American story—a story of flawed and fallible people, united across the generations by grand and enduring ideals. The grandest of these ideals is an unfolding American promise that everyone belongs, that everyone deserves a chance, that no insignificant person was ever born.

Americans are called to enact this promise in our lives and in our laws. And though our nation has sometimes halted, and sometimes delayed, we must follow no other course. Through much of the last century, America's faith in freedom and democracy was a rock in a raging sea. Now it is a seed upon the wind, taking root in many nations. Our democratic faith is more than the creed of our country, it is the inborn hope of our humanity, an ideal we carry but do not own, a trust we bear and pass along. And even after nearly 225 years, we have a long way yet to travel.

While many of our citizens prosper, others doubt the promise, even the justice, of our own country. The ambitions of some Americans are limited by failing schools and hidden prejudice and the circumstances of their birth. And sometimes our differences run so deep, it seems we share a continent, but not a country. We do not accept this, and we will not allow it. Our unity, our union, is the serious work of leaders and citizens in every generation. And this is my solemn pledge: I will work to build a single nation of justice and opportunity.

I know this is in our reach because we are guided by a power larger than ourselves who creates us equal in His image. And we are confident in principles that unite and lead us onward. America has never been united by blood or birth or soil. We are bound by ideals that move us beyond our backgrounds, lift us above our interests and teach us what it means to be citizens. Every child must be taught these principles. Every citizen must uphold them. And every immigrant, by embracing these ideals, makes our country more, not less, American.

Today, we affirm a new commitment to live out our nation's promise through civility, courage, compassion and character. America, at its best, matches a commitment to principle with a concern for civility. A civil society demands from each of us good will and respect, fair dealing and forgiveness. Some seem to believe that our politics can afford to be petty because, in a time of peace, the stakes of our debates appear small. But the stakes for America are never small. If our country does not lead the cause of freedom, it will not be led. If we do not turn the hearts of children toward knowledge and character, we will lose their gifts and undermine their idealism. If we permit our economy to drift and decline, the vulnerable will suffer most. We must live up to the calling we share. Civility is not a tactic or a sentiment. It is the determined choice of trust over cynicism, of community over chaos. And this commitment, if we keep it, is a way to shared accomplishment.

America, at its best, is also courageous. Our national courage has been clear in times of depression and war, when defending common dangers defined our common good. Now we must choose if the example of our fathers and mothers will inspire us or condemn us. We must show courage in a time of blessing by confronting problems instead of passing them on to future generations.

Together, we will reclaim America's schools, before ignorance and apathy claim more young lives. We will reform Social Security and Medicare, sparing our children from struggles we have the power to prevent. And we will reduce taxes, to recover the momentum of our economy and reward the effort and enterprise of working Americans.

We will build our defenses beyond challenge, lest weakness invite challenge.

We will confront weapons of mass destruction, so that a new century is spared new horrors. The enemies of liberty and our country should make no mistake: America remains engaged in the world by history and by choice, shaping a balance of power that favors freedom. We will defend our allies and our interests. We will show purpose without arrogance. We will meet aggression and bad faith with resolve and strength. And to all nations, we will speak for the values that gave our nation birth.

America, at its best, is compassionate. In the quiet of American conscience, we know that deep, persistent poverty is unworthy of our nation's promise. And whatever our views of its cause, we can agree that children at risk are not at fault. Abandonment and abuse are not acts of God, they are failures of love.

And the proliferation of prisons, however necessary, is no substitute for hope and order in our souls. Where there is suffering, there is duty. Americans in need are not strangers, they are citizens, not problems, but priorities. And all of us are diminished when any are hopeless.

Government has great responsibilities for public safety and public health, for civil rights and common schools. Yet compassion is the work of a nation, not just a government. And some needs and hurts are so deep they will only respond to a mentor's touch or a pastor's prayer. Church and charity, synagogue and mosque lend our communities their humanity, and they will have an honored place in our plans and in our laws.

Many in our country do not know the pain of poverty, but we can listen to those who do. And I can pledge our nation to a goal: When we see that wounded traveler on the road to Jericho, we will not pass to the other side.

America, at its best, is a place where personal responsibility is valued and expected. Encouraging responsibility is not a search for scapegoats, it is a call to conscience. And though it requires sacrifice, it brings a deeper fulfillment. We find the fullness of life not only in options, but in commitments. And we find that children and community are the commitments that set us free. Our public interest depends on private character, on civic duty and family bonds and basic fairness, on uncounted, unhonored acts of decency which give direction to our freedom. Sometimes in life we are called to do great things. But as a saint of our times has said, every day we are called to do small things with great love. The most important tasks of a democracy are done by everyone.

I will live and lead by these principles: to advance my convictions with civility, to pursue the public interest with courage, to speak for greater justice and compassion, to call for responsibility and try to live it as well. In all these ways, I will bring the values of our history to the care of our times. What you do is as important as anything government does. I ask you to seek a common good beyond your comfort; to defend needed reforms against easy attacks; to serve your nation, beginning with your neighbor. I ask you to be citizens: citizens, not spectators; citizens, not subjects; responsible citizens, building communities of service and a nation of character.

Americans are generous and strong and decent, not because we believe in ourselves, but because we hold beliefs beyond ourselves. When this spirit of citizenship is missing, no government program can replace it. When this spirit is present, no wrong can stand against it.

After the Declaration of Independence was signed, Virginia statesman John Page wrote to Thomas Jefferson: "We know the race is not to the swift nor the battle to the strong. Do you not think an angel rides in the whirlwind and directs this storm?" Much time has passed since Jefferson arrived for his inauguration. The years and changes accumulate. But the themes of this day he would know: our nation's grand story of courage and its simple dream of dignity. We are not this story's author, who fills time and eternity with his purpose. Yet his purpose is achieved in our duty, and our duty is fulfilled in service to one another. Never tiring, never yielding, never finishing, we renew that purpose today, to make our country more just and generous, to affirm the dignity of our lives and every life. This work continues. This story goes on. And an angel still rides in the whirlwind and directs this storm.

God bless you all, and God bless America.

Jeb Bush's Executive Order Establishing a Task Force

Executive Order Number 00-349

WHEREAS, the Year 2000 Presidential Election was extremely close and concerns were raised regarding the election procedures, standards and technology employed in each of the 67 counties of the State of Florida, and

WHEREAS, regardless of the outcome of the election, all Floridians would benefit from an immediate review of the State's election procedures, standards and technology, and

WHEREAS, any review of the State's election procedures, standards and technology should be conducted on a non-partisan basis in an effort to ensure the highest level of public confidence in Florida's system for conducting elections;

NOW, THEREFORE, I, JEB BUSH, Governor of the State of Florida, by the powers vested in me by the Constitution and laws of the State of Florida, do hereby promulgate the following executive order, effective immediately:

Section 1.

A. There is hereby created the Select Task Force on Election Procedures, Standards and Technology.

B. The Select Task Force shall be comprised of no more than 21 members, ten of whom shall be Republicans, ten of whom shall be Democrats and one of whom shall be affiliated with neither party. At least two of the members shall be representatives from a county Supervisor of Elections Office, and four members shall be legislators, a Republican and Democrat from the Florida House of Representatives and a Republican and Democrat from the Florida Senate. The Governor shall designate two members, of different parties, to serve as Co-Chairpersons. Select Task Force members shall receive no compensation, but shall be entitled to per diem and travel expenses while attending meetings of the Select Task Force, to the extent allowed by Section 112.061, Florida Statutes. Per diem and travel expenses shall be paid by the Secretary of State's Office in accordance with Chapter 112, Florida Statutes. The Select Task Force may include an executive director who shall serve at the pleasure of the Co-Chairpersons and the Secretary of State's Division of Elections will provide technical assistance. The Select Task Force may also call upon experts to testify, and such experts shall be reimbursed for reasonable and necessary expenses of attending Select Task Force meetings.

C. The Select Task Force shall act by a vote of the majority of its members. A quorum of at least eleven members shall be required for an act of the Select Task Force to have effect. No member may grant a proxy for his or her vote to any other member except with the prior approval of the Co-Chairpersons.

D. The first meeting of the Select Task Force shall be held no later than January 3, 2001.

Section 2.

The Select Task Force shall study and make written policy recommendations and/or propose legislation to improve the election procedures, standards and technology employed in each of Florida's 67 counties. Such recommendations and/or proposed legislation shall be submitted by March 1, 2001, to the Governor, the President of the Florida Senate, the Speaker of the House of Representatives, and the Secretary of State. In the interest of facilitating immediate action during the 2001 Legislative Session, the two Co-Chairpersons shall limit the scope of the Select Task Force's study and written policy recommendations to those issues which can, in the opinion of both Co-Chairpersons, be manageably addressed by the entire Select Task Force within the time limits set herein. The Co-Chairpersons shall, in addition, identify any issues raised by Select Task Force members which cannot be manageably addressed, but which may merit further study or examination in an alternative forum at a later time.

Section 3.

All agencies under the control of the Governor are directed, and all other agencies are requested, to render full assistance and cooperation to the Select Task Force.

Section 4.

The Select Task Force shall continue in existence only until its objectives are achieved, but not later than March 1, 2001.

IN TESTIMONY WHEREOF, I have hereunto set my hand and have caused the Great Seal of the State of Florida to be affixed at Tallahassee, the Capitol, this 14th day of December, 2000.

Oath of Office from the Florida Constitution

Article II, Section 5(b) of the Florida Constitution.

(b) Each state and county officer, before entering upon the duties of the office, shall give bond as required by law, and shall swear or affirm:

"I do solemnly swear (or affirm) that I will support, protect, and defend the Constitution and Government of the United States and of the State of Florida; that I am duly qualified to hold office under the Constitution of the state; and that I will well and faithfully perform the duties of (title of office) on which I am now about to enter. So help me God.," and thereafter shall devote personal attention to the duties of the office, and continue in office until a successor qualifies.

Epilogue

The disputed 2000 presidential election offers important lessons about the nation's political institutions and civic culture. The dispute could and should have been decided by a manual recount carried out pursuant to the procedures specified in Florida law. Very early in the dispute, Attorney General Bob Butterworth had called on the secretary of state and others to initiate a statewide recount. Public officials operating in good faith could have quickly devised uniform procedures for interpreting voter intent to fulfill the equal protection requirements of the U.S. Constitution, and all uncounted ballots could have been visually inspected and tabulated in a couple of weeks.

That the system of election administration was derailed by partisan intrigue is an obvious sign of problems, but we need to know whether these problems originate from weaknesses in the nation's election procedures, judicial institutions, political parties, elected officials, candidates, citizens, or what. The three general questions raised in chapter 1 of this compendium were offered as specific lines of inquiry for investigating the source of the breakdown:

- What individuals or institutional disabilities were responsible for producing the flawed election outcome?
- What characteristics of the nation's political culture prevented the electorate at large from reasoning effectively during and after the election breakdown?
- What reforms are needed to correct or mitigate these problems so that the polity can be returned to health or at least prevented from degenerating further?

In closing, let us consider these questions in light of the evidence from 2000.

Critical Categories in Western Political Thought

To evaluate the performance of our political institutions, leaders, and citizens in the disputed 2000 presidential election, we must consider ideas in traditional political philosophy that underpin America's system of representative democracy. For it was from the classics of political philosophy that the Founder's drew their reasoning for separating governmental powers into distinct branches, pitting the branches against one another in a system of checks and balances, designating certain rights as fundamental and inalienable, and so on. The premises underlying these and other institutional features of the American republic offer a framework of expectations for assessing the performance of the political system and for differentiating institutional disabilities from failures of leadership and citizenship.

America's political institutions are based on a simple but profoundly important theoretical framework that was formulated within Western Civilization during two millennia of experiment and experience with monarchical, aristocratic, democratic, theocratic, and totalitarian political formations. Among scholars of Western political thought, a distinction is typically drawn between classical political philosophy and modern political science, because political philosophy and political science have different aims, draw on different evidence, and address different audiences. But these differences flow primarily from the distinct challenges facing political inquiry in the ancient and modern eras, not from substantive disagreements between ancient and modern scholarship over the nature of politics and society.

Classical political philosophy and modern political science are in agreement that politics and government are best understood as a dynamic relationship between two distinct categories of citizens. Classical political philosophy differentiates these political groupings in terms of capabilities and resources. The most capable and affluent group is referred to as the *aristoi* or *oligoi*, and the less capable and affluent as the *mazza* or *demos*. Modern political scientists draw the same distinction and use almost identical terms; they say that the members of all political systems are divided into "elites" and "masses." The term "masses" actually originates from the ancient Greek word "mazza," which means "bread dough." Modern political scientists are also in agreement with classical political philosophy in recognizing that many factors—some universal and others idiosyncratic—determine in which of the two groupings particular individuals end up.

The great insight of Socrates, and another overarching theme uniting political philosophy and political science, is the conclusion that differences in the nature, character, and capabilities of human communities originate in politics and government, not religion, geography, economic organization, kinship patterns, or other dimensions of variation in human life unrelated to power. Political philosophy and political science teach us that political systems differ in terms of the procedures, criteria, and rules that are used to limit access to the elite level, to select office holders from among the elite class, and to maintain limits on the actions of office holders while they are in power. Office holders can be selected on the basis of family origins, expressions of mass preferences (such as mass elections), expressions of elite preferences (elite elections, as when U.S. senators were elected by state legislatures), random assignment (as is done today in selecting juries), and so on. Political systems function well, and the societies they govern are capable of maintaining their economic and political independence, when mass and elite are in agreement on the elites' qualifications to rule, on the procedures for office-holder selection and removal, and on the limits of elite authority. Conversely, political systems will fall into disorder if the consensus on these matters breaks down or if either elites or masses, or a subset of elites or masses, begin to subvert the established consensus to gain personal advantages.

Both political philosophy and political science are concerned about system change, but in different ways. A primary interest of classical political philosophy has been to prevent stable, law-abiding political systems from degenerating into disorder, civil war, and tyranny. Modern political science has not been indifferent to this issue, but it has been much more interested in understanding how to prompt positive change, that is, how to transform primitive, autocratic, or bureaucratic systems into law-abiding, stable republics.

Classical political philosophy identifies a number of factors that affect political order. Stability is more likely when, for example, there is a large middle class, when political speech is protected but also limited, when opportunities are made available for masses to express their preferences on select issues and to remove public officials under certain conditions, and when elites are pitted against one another in a competition for authority and popular support. Political philosophy warns that political systems most often degenerate into unbridled disagreement and then tyranny because of actions by elites, but it also notes that masses quickly become complicit. Elites usually initiate the downward slide in two ways. One is that, as a group, they begin to use their power to enhance their own wealth at the expense of the masses, which are then ground into debt, poverty, and servitude.

Political degeneration is also initiated when the competition between elites for mass support gets out of hand, that is, when elites start trying to achieve power and status through trickery, bribery, intimidation, demagoguery, or violence. The historical record of antiquity suggests that, in such circumstance, elites who advocate the interests of the wealthiest classes may be more likely to use lawless tactics as those who speak for the poor and the powerless. In classical Rome, Julius Caesar and the two Gracchus brothers were assassinated by conservative members of the Roman Senate because they had gained popularity advocating a redistribution of land from large landowners to itinerate citizens.

When a society becomes characterized by mass debt and unmitigated elite ambition, the masses may join the march to tyranny by foolishly supporting elites who call for a temporary suspension to the rule of law. The masses are never well informed, and poverty and injustice can make them especially vulnerable to politicians who promise quick and radical changes to intractable conditions. The road to political oblivion is, in this sense, paved with legitimate grievances and understandable hopes. However, it ends in a cul-de-sac of death and despair, because, once the rule of law is abandoned, order can be maintained only by force and indoctrination, which are themselves applied lawlessly. Moreover, lawlessness will tend to grow increasingly extreme because the abuses of each side will provoke worse abuses in response.

For its part, modern political science teaches that democracy's development is best initiated and sustained by vesting certain specific responsibilities and powers in a single official empowered to speak and decide for the whole nation while at the same time being accountable to the masses or their representatives. The responsibilities that political scientists say should be assigned to the executive have to do with trade and international affairs. The executive must be empowered to enforce contracts, provide facilities and services for communication and commerce, take advantage of opportunities for expanding the nation's territories and resources, and engage in diplomacy and warfare. The masses or their representatives must retain control over access to the public purse and must be able to remove the executive under specified conditions.

These concepts and insights by no means exhaust the content of political philosophy and political science, and their simplified presentation here glosses over many important issues. But they are sufficient to bring to our attention aspects of the 2000 election beyond those issues that happened to animate the candidates, their supporters, and the citizenry. Among other things, consideration is directed to the resources and values of elites and masses, patterns of elite recruitment, conditions of citizenship and electoral participation, socialization of elites and masses, institutional constraints on competition between elites, channels of communication between elites and masses, and so on. The election controversy tested the character of the elites and masses, and offered a rare look into the guts of American politics and government. Political philosophy and political science tell us where to search for symptoms of political degeneration and how to trace those symptoms to their origins in the body politic.

Institutional Failures

The failure of American democracy in the 2000 presidential election occurred in part because at least four components of the political system are malfunctioning. One is the framework of checks and balances that is supposed to prevent top leaders in government from using their power lawlessly or for tyrannical aims. Most of the checks and balances envisioned by the Founders are no longer effective because the development of political parties has made them largely inoperative. The procedures for electing officials to legislative and executive positions, enacting legislation, appointing the judiciary, approving treaties, and, yes, resolving election disputes were intended to maintain a healthy tension between the branches of government. However, when a single political party has effective control over two or more branches the system of checks and balances is likely to fail, because the branches will collude rather than clash.

Political parties formed early in the nation's history, and the danger they posed to the nation's politics and government were immediately recognized. The parties originated in the competition between John Adams and Thomas Jefferson to be George Washington's successor. Toward the end of Washington's second term, when it became known that Washington would not be seeking a third term, Adams formed the Federalist Party, which was the precursor to the Republican Party of today. In the Electoral College of 1796, Adams outpolled Jefferson and was elected president, while Jefferson, as the second-highest vote getter, became vice president. Jefferson and his running mate, Aaron Burr, came in first four years later after Jefferson formed the political organization that today is called the Democratic Party. In his farewell address in 1796, Washington foresaw the rise of partisanship that Adams was initiating, and he warned against it.

At many points in the disputed 2000 presidential election, it was evident that partisan allegiances crippled the system of checks and balances.

- A number of the justices of the U.S. Supreme Court became animated by partisan loyalties and ultimately misused the Court's authority to secure the presidency for George W. Bush. This misuse of authority involved (1) preempting the role assigned to Congress by the U.S. Constitution as the ultimate arbiter of election disputes; and (2) interfering in matters of state government reserved to the states by the Constitution. Justices also violated their oath of office to uphold the Constitution.
- The Speaker of the Florida House colluded with the Bush campaign to create false fears of an impending constitutional crisis.
- Through intermediaries, the Florida secretary of state colluded with Florida's governor and legislative leaders, as well as with the Bush campaign, to create confusion, cause repeated delays, and ultimately prevent a legally mandated tabulation of uncounted ballots.
- Military personnel, presumably at very high levels of authority, collaborated with Republican members of Congress or their staff, the Florida secretary of state or her staff, and the Bush campaign to deliver illegally cast ballots to Florida and have them counted in the official tabulation.

A second area of institutional breakdown is the system of federalism, in which state authority is supposed to be protected from unwarranted national intrusion. Like the failure of checks and balances, the malfunctioning of federalism was evident early in the Republic's history. Less than a decade after the U.S. Constitution had been adopted, ambiguity concerning the relative authority of the two levels of government surfaced in a conflict, again between John Adams and Thomas Jefferson, over the Alien and Sedition Acts. These acts authorized the president and other agents of the national government to deport aliens and to arrest citizens simply for speaking out against the actions of the government or its officials. The Acts had been pushed through by President Adams and the newly formed Federalist Party in Congress. In response to the Alien and Sedition Acts, which he vociferously opposed, Jefferson, although vice president, left Washington and returned to Virginia, where he authored the doctrine of nullification. The latter asserted that states were not bound by federal laws that were not in compliance with the "plain meaning" of the Constitution. The doctrine of nullification eventually became the intellectual justification for the South's secession from the Union.

Confusion and ambiguity in the U.S. Constitution over the boundary between state and federal authority was responsible for the judicial meltdown in the 2000 election controversy. Judicial decision making became bogged down over the question of which court system, state or federal, had jurisdiction over the issues. Although the partisan bias of the U.S. Supreme Court was obvious, the Court's partisan majority could rationalize its actions and therefore was emboldened to act, because the Constitution leaves the state and national roles in federalism open to interpretation.

A third area where the nation's political institutions are no longer functioning as intended involves the system of congressional representation. The Founders chose to have large congressional districts because they believed that large districts would make it unlikely for ideological extremists to be elected. This expectation was dashed after political parties formed in the new Republic and partisan officials took control of legislative and congressional districting. Gerrymandering became an accepted practice, and legislative and congressional districts began to be drawn to protect incumbents and to strengthen the dominant party's hold on the legislative branch.

This meant that representatives became increasingly partisan and ideological. Congressional districts that are safe for the nominee of one party or another are safe precisely because they do not reflect the actual partisan mix of the larger communities from which they have been carved out. In redistricting, a large region with a more or less even division of support across the two major parties is typically split along borders that leave most Republicans in one district and most Democrats in another. Consequently the representatives subsequently elected will be, in one case, far more conservative and, in the other, far more liberal than the community at large.

The partisanship of state and national legislators was evident throughout the dispute over the outcome of the 2000 presidential election. The Speaker of Florida's House of Representatives became actively involved in a conspiracy with the Bush campaign to foment popular anger and create the impression that political disorder was imminent. The Speaker was motivated by a partisan ideology that was not only more conservative than the public philosophy of the average Floridian but was also more conservative than the outlook of Florida Republicans and even of Republicans in the Florida House of Representatives.

Similarly, extremism was also apparent in the partisan shenanigans of Republicans in Congress. Only extremists would collude with military leaders to deliver ballots to Florida that had been illegally cast. Extremism, too, may have been what clouded the thinking of those Republicans in Congress who sent staff members to Palm Beach, Broward, and Miami-Dade counties to disrupt the legally mandated recount that was then under way, and to pressure local election officials to count ballots from overseas military personnel even when the ballots had not been properly dated and stamped.

Last on the list of institutional problems is the method of appointing justices to the U.S. Supreme Court. The Founders divided this power between the president and the Senate. The president nominates members to the Court, and the Senate can veto the nomination by refusing to consent to the appointment. This system has been broken not only by the destructive impact of partisanship on checks and balances but also by the efforts of the Supreme Court itself to control the appointment of its members and thereby become an authority unto itself.

Today members of the U.S. Supreme Court have become actively involved in selecting their own selector, that is, in determining who will be president and thus who will choose their replacements. This was obvious in 2000 when the U.S. Supreme Court intervened to stop the recount in Florida. However, this was not the first time in recent years that the Court had sought to influence presidential politics in a blatantly partisan manner. Just two years earlier the Court had issued its remarkable ruling that a private individual could sue a sitting president in civil court and require his deposition. Paula Jones was given the go-ahead for her litigation against President Clinton, who was subsequently deposed. To be sure, President Clinton brought calamity on himself when he prevaricated in some of his answers, but his failings were personal, not institutional. The Supreme Court justices who authorized Jones's civil suit to proceed could not have been unaware that this would entangle the president in an inquiry that would be, at the very least, damaging to his popularity and therefore harmful to the prospects of Democrats in 2000. As it turned out, the Court's ruling led indirectly to Clinton's impeachment. When in 2000 the Court intervened to aid George W. Bush, it was finishing the job it had started earlier in trying to assure that Clinton would be followed in office by a Republican.

Each of these institutional breakdowns individually poses serious dangers to freedom and popular control of government in the United States, but together they amplify one another and multiply the possibilities for partisan intrigue to triumph over democracy. Untoward actions by one branch of government or political party provoke corresponding reactions elsewhere in the political system. The potential for a downward spiral of partisan lawlessness is real and appears to be growing stronger rapidly.

Failures of Leadership

Viewed from the perspective of political philosophy and political science, the 2000 election exposed more than malfunctions in the nation's political institutions. The character of public discourse during the controversy revealed major disabilities in the thinking of elites and masses alike.

Among elites, Republicans were less reasonable and more emotional than Democrats. An example of the kind of statesmanship that the controversy called for was the proposal by Attorney General Bob Butterworth, a Democrat, for the secretary of state to lead a statewide recount. Another example was the tone set by Warren Christopher, who, in stark contrast to James Baker, remained calm, called for an orderly determination of the election's winner, and avoided shrill attacks on the decisions of the courts. A third example was Lieberman's and also Butterworth's willingness to support Republican calls for including in the vote tabulation the many undated, unstamped, and otherwise invalidly marked ballots received after Election Day from military personnel serving overseas.

Of course, when Lieberman and Butterworth advocated that special exceptions be made for overseas military ballots, they, like most other people outside the circle of top Republicans, were unaware that at that very moment Republicans were working with the U.S. military to collect illegally cast ballots and expedite their delivery to Florida. Given that the concessions of Butterworth and Lieberman were repaid with Republican deceit, Democrats may be less reasonable in any election disputes that may arise in the future. In politics, bad faith destroys the trust that makes good faith possible.

Why were Republicans so intent on winning that they were willing to undermine the democracy? They appear to have been enraged by Bill Clinton's continued popularity in the face of numerous accusations about his personal improprieties. Presumably this frustration, which had accumulated for eight years, motivated Republican support for Kenneth Starr's misuse of the Whitewater investigation to probe into President Clinton's statements in the Paula Jones case, statements wholly unrelated to Whitewater. Republican elites throughout the country had become incensed by Clinton's political skills, when earlier the public had proven to be indifferent to revelations that he had had an affair with Gennifer Flowers, that Mrs. Clinton had caused White House staff to be fired so that she could replace them with her own loyalists, and that a longtime aid to the Clintons, Vince Foster, had supposedly committed suicide just when he had reached the pinnacle of his career. Although it is no excuse for their actions, the frustration of Republicans might be considered understandable.

Still, if we step back and consider the course of national politics since 1960, we can see that Republican elites, if not others, have been becoming increasingly willing to use lawless tactics in presidential politics. In 1973 and 1974 the public learned that Republican president Richard Nixon, who was in his second term, had succeeded in rigging the 1972 presidential election by causing the Democrats to nominate a weak candidate. When Nixon subsequently resigned from office, his vice president, Republican Gerald Ford, became president and promptly pardoned Nixon for any crimes he may have committed. Ford also appointed the first and only politician to head the CIA, George H. W. Bush, who had been in the White House as a close adviser to Nixon when the Watergate crimes had been committed. During the 1980s Bush, who had become vice president, and Republican president Ronald Reagan were involved in illegally selling arms to Iran and channeling money to anticommunist revolutionaries in Nicaragua. Their unlawful relations with Iran began during their campaign for the White House in 1980, when they promised the Iranians that their administration would channel arms to Iran if Iran would damage Jimmy Carter's chances of reelection by not releasing the hostages before the election. Kenneth Starr's Whitewater investigation and the decision by House Republicans to impeach President Clinton were simply part of this larger pattern of Republican indifference to the requirements of federal law, constitutional principles, and democratic civility.

Also needing to be placed in historical perspective is the comparatively lackadaisical attitudes of Democrats during the dispute in the 2000 election. Viewed in isolation, the Democrats' low-key response to Republican tactics might seem to reflect nothing more than an assessment of the candidates. After all, there were good reasons for Democrats to have mixed feelings about Bill Clinton and Al Gore. Democrats had had to acknowledge the serious failures of judgment by President Clinton in his private life, as well as Clinton's willingness to lie about this to the American people. By the same token, it would have been normal for Democrats to have harbored doubts about Vice President Gore, because Gore had stood by Clinton during the impeachment, and he had been accused of violating campaign finance laws by soliciting campaign contributions from his government office.

But recent American history suggests that the Democrats' posture in 2000 reflects an enduring trait, not a momentary response to the circumstances. Typically, when top Democrats behave lawlessly, it is in their personal lives, not in their pursuit and use of political power. Democrats may simply be more committed than Republicans are to democratic principles of fair play. Political scientists have found that schools attended by working-class students tend to stress civic duty in their courses on American history and government, whereas the schools of upper-class students present politics as a struggle for power between organized movements. Perhaps when it comes to political conflicts, Democratic elites are better sports because the party is imbued with the conventional perspective of its base in the middle and working classes.

In any event, the failure of political elites to work in good faith to resolve the election dispute in 2000 is symptomatic of a leadership class that is becoming increasingly lawless and corrupt. This is not to say that in the

United States all political elites or even most political elites are untrust-
worthy and Machiavellian in their conduct of public affairs. No doubt a
large majority of America's political leaders are people of principal and
moderation. But elite behavior in the disputed 2000 presidential election
suggests that America's elite strata contains more than a few rotten apples,
which may be beginning to spoil the whole barrel.

Failures of Citizenship

Unfortunately mass political opinion and behavior during the election dispute offers little support for those elites who may be hoping that the citizenry will eventually recognize and reject the manipulative tactics of partisan leaders. Although citizens in modern representative democracies are
expected to be self-directing participants in public discourse, citizen reactions to the disputed 2000 presidential election raises questions about the
citizenry's ability to think for itself. Most citizens mindlessly parroted the
statements of Democratic and Republican elites. There was no search for
common ground and no real effort to get at the truth through discussion
and evidence. This was partly because the issues were somewhat technical
and outside the expertise of most people, but it also stemmed from the
widespread tendency of U.S. citizens to substitute partisanship for reason.
In short, the masses were as combative, emotional, and unreasonable as the
worst of the elites.

In this respect, the mass public's behavior was entirely consistent with
the findings of modern political science. After five decades of public opinion research, political scientists are in general agreement that mass publics
cannot reason independently. Mass opinion mirrors elite opinion, albeit in
a much less sophisticated form, because the masses take their cues from the
particular elites with whom they happen to identify. Democratic masses
listen to Democratic elites, and Republican masses listen to Republican
elites. Hence the more divided the elites are, the more divided are the
masses.

These problems of public discourse were well recognized in classical
political philosophy. In the works of Plato, Aristotle, Thucydides, and others, a distinction is drawn between *logos* and *ergon*, that is, between speech
and actuality, or words and facts. Classical political philosophers reported
that the mass public of ancient Athens failed to adequately appreciate this
distinction. The citizenry thought that the better a plan sounded, the bet-

ter it would prove in action. In turn, the philosophers explained, this unwarranted confidence in catchy phrases and enticing descriptions repeatedly caused the Assembly to make foolish decisions and to accept leadership from those who proposed daring actions and unrealistic goals rather
than from those who reasoned carefully from facts and experience. As a
result, Athens became overextended in pursuit of empire, engaged in unnecessary wars with Sparta and other Greek cities, and eventually lost its
independence.

Modern social science has added an emotional dimension to this account of irrationality in public discourse. Freud explained that human
motivation at both the individual and group or societal levels is rooted in
certain fantasies, fears, and misunderstandings from infancy and childhood. The masses gravitate toward leaders who are dogmatic, insensitive,
and unreflective, because they subconsciously seek the political equivalent
of an all-powerful father. Similarly mass publics are inclined to racism,
anti-Semitism, and other forms of xenophobia, because scapegoating re-
lieves feelings of inadequacy that are developed during maturation.

The cognitive limitations and emotional needs of mass publics helps to
explain the failure of American voters in 2000 to insist on an end to
partisan intrigue and to demand that the election's outcome be accurately
and transparently determined. For the mass public, intense partisanship
works on many levels. It allows for strong opinions while leaving all the
thinking to others. It divides the world into two groups, one good and the
other bad. It replaces any sense of doubt left over from childhood with
feelings of power and self-righteousness.

Implications for Speech and Action

Of the problems revealed by the disputed 2000 presidential election, the
institutional malfunctions are easiest to understand, but they may be
impossible to address until the civic culture, which is more elusive to
comprehension, is subjected to reflection and improved by criticism. The
political system needs to be reformed to make it less partisan and more
accountable. At this point in history, it does not appear that political
parties and other organized factions can be eliminated, but certainly their
influence can be reduced. This end could be served by any or all of the
following changes:

- Remove election administration from partisan influences. Elections should be administered by a professional civil service. Also, the penalties for election fraud and other illegal efforts to influence election outcomes should be made much more severe.

- Extend the duration of the election process to allow revoting in cases where outcomes are ambiguous. Elections should be scheduled far enough in advance of a new term of office that an election can be held again if the outcome is tainted or too close to call.
- Place legislative redistricting at all levels of government in the hands of nonpartisan boards and civil-service professionals. Require redistricting to aim for accuracy in representation. The aggregate partisan composition of a legislative body should be expected to reflect roughly the partisan composition of the overall citizenry that the legislative body is supposed to represent.
- Move away from winner-take-all systems or representation. This could be done by eliminating the Electoral College. Alternatively it could be accomplished without a constitutional amendment if states were to choose to apportion electoral votes on the basis of each party's proportion of the popular vote rather than giving all electoral votes to the top vote getter.
- Establish an ethical framework to prohibit and condemn partisanship in judicial decision making. Amend the oath of office for appellant judges to include a provision requiring nonpartisan objectivity. Adopt a code of ethics for judges that requires their recusal on cases in which they have, or could reasonably be considered to have, a conflict of interest.

Obviously this list of recommended reforms is by no means exhaustive. For example, no attempt is made to strengthen the system of checks and balances nor is consideration given to campaign finance. The list of reforms is intended to be suggestive. The important point is for Americans to recognize that our political institutions are flawed, that popular control of government is at risk, and that the trajectory of unbridled partisanship is tyranny.

Of course, before most Americans are likely to admit any of this even as a possibility, the nation's civic culture must be healed. As it stands, public discourse is taking place in an echo chamber of ignorance, suspicion, and cynicism. All proposals for reform are evaluated by partisans in terms of their partisan implications and are favored or opposed accordingly. In this situation even the most laudable initiatives for political improvement end up reinforcing partisanship rather than reducing it.

No doubt mindless partisanship among elites would vanish if it were suddenly condemned by the mass public, but this is highly unlikely without sound leadership. Everything we know about mass opinion tells us that civic culture depends on elite discourse. The mass public will not become tolerant, reasonable, and curious until political elites begin to shed their ideological armor, become mutually respectful, and commit fully to the rule of law and reason.

On the other hand, political elites cannot lead this cultural transformation, because the current environment of media commentary and mass hysteria selects against public officials who acknowledge ignorance or express uncertainty. In contemporary American politics it is more important for leaders to be certain than right. We are thus caught in a catch-22: politicians cannot change until citizens change, but citizens will not change until politicians change first.

The responsibility for initiating a return to civility therefore falls to elites who are not directly involved in partisan politics. A number of groups fall into this category. Professors, lawyers, physicians, clergy, journalists, and students are all committed by their roles and socialized by their training to seek truth and eschew prejudice. Admittedly all these elite groups are today infected to various degrees by the nation's partisan fever. Doctors and lawyers have squared off politically over medical malpractice litigation. Many Christian ministers seem to have decided that God is a Republican. Media outlets often have obvious partisan loyalties even if the journalists who work for them do not. However, none of these groups has succumbed to the fever entirely, and all are predisposed to support an open and honest society.

The citizenry, too, contains people who love truth more than advantage. Thinking people everywhere were appalled by the disputed 2000 presidential election. They could see that the democratic aspirations of a large and powerful republic, a republic conceived in liberty and dedicated to universal political equality, were being trampled under the feet of clashing partisans, who had forgotten that elections are a fragile but essential mechanism of self-government, not a personal contest and certainly not a sport or a game. During the election dispute in 2000, thinking people watched, slack-jawed, as ruthless partisans chopped and fitted every fact to the Procrustean bed of the party line. They could see the hypocrisy, and they sensed the danger even though they did not understand its origins.

The challenge for reformers among elite and mass alike is to learn how to reason with unreasonable people. In this, modern political science is not a good teacher, for it has only recently begun to notice the problem. Indeed, science in general shares the naïve confidence of our times that unadorned truth will win out in any competition of ideas that is unconstrained by censorship.

However, opening closed minds was one of the defining objectives of classical political philosophy, because political philosophy originated in democratic Athens as it began to degenerate and undergo the convulsions of a polarized society. The founder of political philosophy, Socrates, was noted for his use of irony, his preference for dialogues over speeches and lectures, and for his claim that wisdom comes from recognizing one's own ignorance. Socrates did not go around chastising demagogues for their sophistry or urging citizens in the Assembly to be logical and realistic. Instead, he tried to remedy dogmatism as he encountered it in his everyday life. He did so by posing questions to the many people he met who were self-righteous about their virtues and unreflective about their convictions. When Socrates met someone who was indignant at some perceived injustice, he asked the person, "What is the meaning of justice?" and then he would pose further questions about the answer he was given. When he was with people who said they were his friends, he would ask, "What is friendship and what is love?"

Socrates used irony, or what today we would call sarcasm or dry wit, as a way to expose overconfidence and plant seeds of doubt. Standing outside the court prior to the trial that would end in his conviction and execution, Socrates ran into an acquaintance, Euthyphro, a boastful young man who claimed to be able to see the future and who was prosecuting his own father for manslaughter. It seems that a slave in the household had committed a murder, and the father had tied the slave up and left him in a ditch while he went for the authorities. Suddenly a storm came up, a flash flood ensued, and the slave drowned. Euthyphro explained that he felt obligated by his strong sense of duty and piety to prosecute his father for the slave's death.

Upon hearing this story, Socrates asked Euthyphro to let him, Socrates, become Euthyphro's student, since Euthyphro was wise enough to know with certainty what was right and wrong in this complex tragedy. Although Socrates was being ironic, Euthyphro thought that he was serious and went on to offer Socrates his guidance. Socrates, playing along with his own gag, took on the role of pupil and began asking Euthyphro questions about duty and goodness. Soon it became clear that Euthyphro could not give a reasonable account of even the most basic moral concepts. Whether Euthyphro learned anything from the exchange was unclear, but he was definitely shaken, for he left hastily, telling Socrates that he had an "urgent engagement somewhere."

Perhaps it is time to ask partisan extremists to instruct the rest of us on the meaning and nature of democracy.

Bibliography

Florida History

Akin, Edward N. *Flagler: Rockefeller Partner and Florida Baron.* Kent, Ohio: Kent State University Press, 1988.

Arsenault, Raymond, "The End of the Long Hot Summer: The Air Conditioner and Southern Culture." *Journal of Southern History* 6, no. 4 (November 1984): 597–628.

———. *St. Petersburg and the Florida Dream, 1888–1950.* Norfolk, Va.: Donning, 1988.

Billinger, Robert D., Jr. "With the Wehrmacht in Florida: The German POW Facility at Camp Blanding, 1942–1946." *Florida Historical Quarterly* 58, no. 2 (October 1979): 160–73.

Carr, Patrick. *Sunshine States: Wild Times and Extraordinary Lives in the Land of Gators, Guns, and Grapefruits.* Garden City, N.Y.: Doubleday, 1990.

Cash, William T. *A History of the Democratic Party in Florida.* Tallahassee: Florida Democratic Historical Foundation, 1936.

Chalmers, David. "The Ku Klux Klan in the Sunshine State: The 1920s." *Florida Historical Quarterly* 42, no. 3 (January 1964): 209–15.

Chandler, David Leon. *Henry Flagler: The Astonishing Life and Time of the Visionary Robber Baron Who Founded Florida*. New York: Macmillan, 1986.

Cox, Merlin G. "David Sholtz: New Deal Governor of Florida." *Florida Historical Quarterly* 43, no. 2 (October 1964): 142–52.

Dovell, Junius E. *History of Banking in Florida, 1828–1954*. Orlando, 1955.

———. "A History of the Everglades of Florida." Ph.D. dissertation, University of North Carolina, 1947.

Dunn, James William. "The New Deal and Florida Politics." Ph.D. dissertation, Florida State University, 1971.

Flynt, Wayne. *Cracker Messiah: Governor Sidney J. Catts of Florida*. Baton Rouge: Louisiana State University Press, 1977.

———. *Duncan Upshaw Fletcher: Dixie's Reluctant Progressive*. Tallahassee: Florida State University Press, 1971.

Gannon, Michael V. *Florida: A Short History*. Gainesville: University Press of Florida, 1993.

———. *Operation Drumbeat: The Dramatic True Story of Germany's First U-Boat Attacks along the American Coast in World War II*. New York: Harper and Row, 1990.

———. ed. *The New History of Florida*. Gainesville: University Press of Florida, 1996.

George, Paul S. "Passage to the New Eden: Tourism in Miami from Flagler through Everest G. Sewell." *Florida Historical Quarterly* 59, no. 4 (April 1981): 440–63.

———. "Submarines and Soldiers: Fort Lauderdale and World War II." *Broward Legacy* 14 (winter–spring 1991): 2–14.

Ginzl, David J. "The Politics of Patronage: Florida Republicans during the Hoover Administration." *Florida Historical Quarterly* 61, no. 1 (July 1982): 1–19.

Hughes, Melvin Edward, Jr. "William J. Howey and His Florida Dreams." *Florida Historical Quarterly* 66, no. 3 (January 1988): 243–64.

Ingalls, Robert P. *Urban Vigilantes in the New South: Tampa, 1881–1936*. Knoxville: University of Tennessee Press, 1988. Reprint, Gainesville: University Press of Florida, 1993.

Long, Durward. "Key West and the New Deal, 1934–1936." *Florida Historical Quarterly* 46, no. 3 (January 1968): 209–18.

McDonnell, Victoria H. "The Businessman's Politician: A Study of the Administration of John Wellborn Martin, 1925–1929." Master's thesis, University of Florida, 1968.

Morris, Allen. *The Florida Handbook*. Tallahassee: Peninsular Publishing. Bi-annual publication.

Proctor, Samuel. *Napoleon Bonaparte Broward: Florida's Fighting Democrat*. Gainesville: University Press of Florida, 1993 [1950].

———. "The National Farmers' Alliance Convention of 1890 and Its 'Ocala Demands,'" *Florida Historical Quarterly* 28, no. 3 (January 1950): 161–81.

Rogers, Ben F. "Florida in World War II: Tourists and Citrus." *Florida Historical Quarterly* 39, no. 1 (July 1960): 34–41.

Rogers, William Warren. *Outposts on the Gulf: Saint George Island and Apalachicola from Early Exploration to World War II.* Gainesville: University Press of Florida, 1986.

Shofner, Jerrell H. "Roosevelt's 'Tree Army': The Civilian Conservation Corps in Florida." *Florida Historical Quarterly* 65, no. 4 (April 1987): 433–56.

Tebeau, Charlton W. *A History of Florida.* Rev. ed. Coral Gables: University of Miami Press, 1980 [1971].

Tindall, George B. *The Emergence of the New South, 1913–1945.* Baton Rouge: Louisiana State University Press, 1967.

Vance, Linda D. *May Mann Jennings, Florida's Genteel Activist.* Gainesville: University Press of Florida, 1980.

Vickers, Raymond B. *Panic in Paradise: Florida's Banking Crash of 1926.* Tuscaloosa: University of Alabama Press, 1994.

Wynne, Lewis N., ed. *Florida at War.* Saint Leo, Fla.: Saint Leo College Press, 1993.

Waters, Roderick D. "Gwendolyn Cherry: Educator, Attorney, and the First African-American Female Legislator in the History of Florida." Master's thesis, Florida State University, 1990.

Florida Policy and Politics

Askew, Reubin O'D., and Lance deHaven-Smith. *"E Pluribus Unum* in a Multi-Racial, Multi-Cultural State," Introduction to *Review of Legislation.* Tallahassee: Florida State University Law Review, winter 2000.

Blake, Nelson M. *Land into Water — Water into Land: A History of Water Management in Florida.* Tallahassee: Florida State University Press, 1980.

Colburn, David R., and Lance deHaven-Smith. *Government in the Sunshine State: Florida since Statehood.* Gainesville: University Press of Florida, 1999.

Colburn, David R., and Richard K. Scher. *Florida's Gubernatorial Politics in the Twentieth Century.* Gainesville: University Press of Florida, 1980.

Dauer, Manning, ed. *Florida's Politics and Government.* Gainesville: University Press of Florida, 1980.

deHaven-Smith, Lance. *The Atlas of Florida Voting and Public Opinion.* Tallahassee: Florida Institute of Government, 1998.

———. "Constitution Revision in Florida." In *The Florida Public Policy Management System,* ed. Richard Chackerian, 116–39. Dubuque, Iowa: Kendall/Hunt, 1998.

———. "Environmental Belief Systems: Public Opinion Toward Land Use Regulation in Florida." *Environment and Behavior* (March 1988).

———. *Environmental Concern in Florida and the Nation*. Gainesville: University Press of Florida, 1989.

———. *Environmental Publics: Public Opinion on Environmental Protection and Growth Management*. Monograph #87–2. Boston: Lincoln Institute of Land Policy, 1987.

———. "Florida's Economy Is E-volving." *Florida Trend: 2001 Annual TopRank Florida*, December 2000, 8–11.

———. "Florida's Issue Cycles." *Tampa Tribune*, May 6, 1999.

———. "Florida's Unfinished Agenda in Growth Management and Environmental Protection." In *Florida Politics and Government*, ed. Robert J. Huckshorn, 2nd ed., 147–61. Gainesville: University Press of Florida, 1998 [1991].

———. *The Florida Voter*. Tallahassee: Florida Institute of Government, 1995.

———. "Graham Amendment Is about Academic Freedom." *Tallahassee Democrat* (September 2003).

———. "Ideology and the Tax Revolt: Florida's Amendment 1." *Public Opinion Quarterly* 49 (fall 1985): 300–309.

———. "News from the Economic Frontline." Cover story for Florida CEO Trends. *Florida Trend*, December 2001, 8–14.

———. "Profiles in Cowardice." *Florida Trend*, August 1995.

———. "Questions and Answers about 2000 Election." *Tallahassee Democrat* (September 2003).

———. "Regulatory Theory and State Land-Use Regulation: Implications from Florida's Experience with Growth Management," *Public Administration Review* 44, no. 5 (September/October 1984): 413–20.

———. "Republican Era Hinges on 2002 Florida Election." *Tallahassee Democrat* (August 2003).

———. "Term Limits May Increase Home Rule." *Florida Counties: The Magazine of the Florida Association of Counties*, March/April 1999.

———. "Tough Times Ahead." Cover story for *Florida CEO Trends. Florida Trend*, December 2002, 6–10.

———. "Toward a Communicative Theory of Environmental Opinion: A Rejoinder to Audirac and Shoemyen." *Environment and Behavior* 21 (September 1989): 630–35.

———. "What's Wrong with Florida's Cabinet System, The Debate." Published by the Lincoln Center for Public Service, vol. 1, no. 2.

deHaven-Smith, Lance, and Allen Imershein. "Florida." In *Reagan and the States: Federalism Under Stress*, ed. Richard C. Nathan, Fred Doolittle, and Associates. Princeton, N.J.: Princeton University Press, 1987.

Douglas, Marjory Stoneman. *The Everglades: River of Grass*. New York: Rinehart, 1947.

Dye, Thomas R. *Public Policy in Florida: A Fifty-State Perspective*. Tallahassee: Policy Sciences Program, Florida State University, 1992.

Fiedeler, Tom, and Lance deHaven-Smith. *The 2000 Almanac of Florida Politics*. Dubuque, Iowa: Kendall-Hunt, 2000.

Fjellman, Stephen M. *Vinyl Leaves: Walt Disney World and America*. Boulder, Colo.: Westview, 1992.

Huckshorn, Robert J., ed. *Government and Politics in Florida*. 2nd ed. Gainesville: University Press of Florida, 1998 [1991].

Kallina, Edward. *Claude Kirk and the Politics of Confrontation*. Gainesville: University Press of Florida, 1993.

Key, V. O., Jr. *Southern Politics in the State and Nation*. New York: Vintage, 1949.

Lamis, Alexander P. *The Two Party South*. 2nd exp. ed. New York: Oxford University Press, 1990.

MacManus, Susan S. *Young v. Old: Generational Combat in the 21st Century*. Boulder, Colo.: Westview, 1996.

Wagy, Thomas R. *Governor LeRoy Collins: Spokesman of the New South*. Tuscaloosa: University of Alabama Press, 1985.

Florida Demographics

Bernard, Richard M., and Bradley R. Rice, eds. *Sunbelt Cities: Politics and Growth since World War II*. Austin: University of Texas Press, 1983.

Boswell, Thomas D., and James R. Curtis. *The Cuban-American Experience: Culture, Images, and Perspectives*. Totowa, N.J.: Rowman and Allanheld, 1983.

Bouvier, Leon F., and Bob Weller. *Florida in the 21st Century: The Challenge of Population Growth*. Washington, D.C.: Center for Immigration Studies, 1992.

Colburn, David, and Lance deHaven-Smith. *Florida's Megatrends*. Gainesville: University Press of Florida, 2002.

Frey, William H. "Minority Magnet Metros in the 1990s." In *Research Report*. The article is available from the University of Michigan, Ann Arbor, Mich. 48104.

Grenier, Guillermo J., and Alex Stepick. *Miami Now: Immigration, Ethnicity, and Social Change*. Gainesville: University Press of Florida, 1992.

McGovern, James R. *The Emergence of a City in the Modern South: Pensacola, 1900–1945*. DeLeon Springs, Fla.: E. O. Painter, 1976.

Miller, Randall M., and George E. Pozzetta, eds. *Shades of the Sunbelt: Essays on Ethnicity, Race, and the Urban South*. Westport, Conn.: Greenwood, 1988. Reprint, Gainesville: University Press of Florida, 1989.

Mohl, Raymond A. "Florida's Changing Demography: Population Growth, Urbanization, and Latinization." *Environmental and Urban Issues* 17 (winter 1990): 22–30.

————. "Miami: The Ethnic Cauldron." In *Sunbelt Cities: Politics and Growth Since World War II*, ed. Richard M. Bernard and Bradley R. Rice. Austin: University of Texas Press, 1983.

————. "Miami: New Immigrant City." In *Searching for the Sunbelt: Historical Perspectives on a Region*, ed. Raymond A. Mohl, 149–75. Knoxville: University of Tennessee Press, 1990.

————. "Race and Space in the Modern City: Interstate 95 and the Black Community in Miami." In *Urban Policy in Twentieth-Century America*, ed. Arnold R. Hirsch and Raymond A. Mohl. New Brunswick, N.J.: Rutgers University Press, 1993.

————, ed. Searching for the Sunbelt: Historical Perspectives on a Region. Knoxville: University of Tennessee Press, 1990.

Mohl, Raymond A., and Gary Mormino. "The Big Change in the Sunshine State: A Social History of Modern Florida." In *The New History of Florida*, ed. Michael V. Gannon, 418–47. Gainesville: University Press of Florida, 1996.

Moore, Deborah Dash. *To the Golden Cities: Pursuing the American Jewish Dream in Miami and L.A.* New York: Free Press, 1994.

Mormino, Gary R., and George E. Pozzetta. *The Immigrant World of Ybor City: Italians and Their Latin Neighbors in Tampa, 1885–1985.* Urbana: University of Illinois Press, 1987.

Nolan, David. *Fifty Feet in Paradise: The Booming of Florida.* New York: Harcourt Brace Jovanovich, 1984.

Portes, Alejandro, and Alex Stepick. *City on the Edge: The Transformation of Miami.* Berkeley: University of California Press, 1993.

Smith, Stanley K., and June Marie Nogle. "Population Projections by Age, Sex, and Race for Florida and Its Counties, 2002–2025." *Florida Population Studies* 36, no. 3 (July 2003).

Civil Rights in Florida

Button, James. *Blacks and Social Change: Impact of the Civil Rights Movement in Southern Communities.* Princeton, N.J.: Princeton University Press, 1989.

Colburn, David R. "Florida Governors Confront the Brown Decision: A Case Study of the Constitutional Politics of School Desegregation, 1954–1970. In *An Uncertain Tradition: Constitutionalism and the History of the South*, ed. Kermit L. Hall and James W. Ely Jr., 326–55. Athens: University of Georgia Press, 1989.

————. *Racial Change and Community Crisis: St. Augustine Florida, 1877–1980.* New York: Columbia University Press, 1985. Reprint, Gainesville: University Press of Florida, 1991.

Colburn, David R., and Jane L. Landers, eds. *The African American Heritage of Florida*. Gainesville: University Press of Florida, 1995.

Dalfiume, Richard M. *Desegregation of the U.S. Armed Forces: Fighting on Two Fronts, 1939–1953*. Columbia: University of Missouri Press, 1969.

Daniel, Pete. "County Considerations in Commission Redistricting." In *Mapping Florida's Political Landscape: The Changing Art and Politics of Reapportionment and Redistricting*, Susan MacManus. Tallahassee: Florida Institute of Government, 2001.

———. "Going among Strangers: Southern Reactions to World War II." *Journal of American History* 77, no. 3 (December 1990): 886–911.

Hall, Kermit L., and James W. Ely Jr., eds. *An Uncertain Tradition: Constitutionalism and the History of the South*. Athens: University of Georgia Press, 1989.

Havard, William C., and Loren P. Beth. *The Politics of Mis-representation: Rural-Urban Conflict in the Florida Legislature*. Baton Rouge: Louisiana State University Press, 1962.

Kersey, Harry A., Jr. *The Florida Seminoles and the New Deal, 1933–1942*. Gainesville: University Presses of Florida, 1989.

Kousser, J. Morgan. *The Shaping of Southern Politics: Suffrage Restriction and the Establishment of the One-Party South, 1880–1910*. New Haven: Yale University Press, 1974.

Lawson, Steven. *Black Ballots: Voting Rights in the South, 1944–1969*. New York: Columbia University Press, 1976.

Lawson, Steven F. "The Florida Legislative Investigation Committee and the Constitutional Readjustment of Race Relations, 1956–1963." In *An Uncertain Tradition: Constitutionalism and the History of the South*, ed. Kermit L. Hall and James W. Ely Jr., 296–325. Athens: University of Georgia Press, 1989.

McGovern, James R. *Anatomy of a Lynching: The Killing of Claude Neal*. Baton Rouge: Louisiana State University Press, 1982.

Mormino, Gary R. "G.I. Joe Meets Jim Crow: Racial Violence and Reform in World War II Florida." *Florida Historical Quarterly* 73, no.1 (July 1994): 23–42.

———. "World War II." In *The New History of Florida*, ed. Michael V. Gannon, chap. 18. Gainesville: University Press of Florida, 1996.

Price, Hugh. *The Negro and Southern Politics: A Chapter of Florida History*. New York: New York University Press, 1957.

Rabby, Glenda A. "Out of the Past: The Civil Rights Movement in Tallahassee, Florida." Ph.D. dissertation, Florida State University, 1984.

Richardson, Joe M. *The Negro in the Reconstruction of Florida, 1865–1877*. Tallahassee: Florida State University Press, 1965.

Shofner, Jerrell H. "Custom, Law, and History: The Enduring Influence of Florida's 'Black Code.'" *Florida Historical Quarterly* 57, no. 3 (January 1977): 277–98.

———. "Florida and Black Migration," *Florida Historical Quarterly* 57, no. 3 (January 1979): 267–88.

———. *Nor Is It Over Yet: Florida in the Era of Reconstruction, 1865–1877.* Gainesville: University Press of Florida, 1974.

Sitkoff, Harvard. "Racial Militancy and Interracial Violence in the Second World War." *Journal of American History* 58, no. 3 (December 1971): 661–81.

Smith, Charles U., ed. *The Civil Rights Movement in Florida and the United States.* Tallahassee: Father and Son, 1993.

Sosna, Morton. "More Important Than the Civil War? The Impact of World War II on the South." In *Perspectives on the American South*, ed. James Cobb, 4:145–63. New York: Gordon and Breach, 1987.

Political Philosophy

Adorno, Theodore W., Else Frenkel-Brunswick, Daniel J. Levinson, and R. Nevitt. *The Authoritarian Personality.* New York: Harper, 1950.

Dahl, Robert A., and Charles E. Lindblom. *Politics, Economics, and Welfare.* Chicago: University of Chicago Press, 1953.

deHaven-Smith, Lance. "Collective Will-Formation: The Missing Dimension in Public Administration." *Administrative Theory and Praxis* 20, no. 2 (1998): 126–40.

———. *Foundations of Representative Democracy.* New York: Peter Lang, 1999.

———. *Philosophical Critiques of Policy Analysis: Lindblom, Habermas, and the Great Society.* Gainesville: University Press of Florida, 1988. Winner of the Manning J. Dauer Prize.

deHaven-Smith, Lance, and Randall B. Ripley. "The Political-Theoretical Foundations of Public Policy." In *Handbook of Political Theory and Policy Science*, ed. Edward B. Portis and Michael B. Levy. Westport, Conn.: Greenwood, 1988.

Drury, Shadia B. *The Political Ideas of Leo Strauss.* New York: St. Martin's, 1988.

Erskine, Andrew. *The Hellenistic Stoa: Political Thought and Action.* Ithaca, N.Y.: Cornell University Press, 1990.

Finley, M. I. *The Ancient Greeks.* New York: Penguin, 1963.

Gibbon, Edward. *The Decline and Fall of the Roman Empire.* New York: Dell, 1963.

Habermas, Jurgen. *Knowledge and Human Interests.* Translated by Jeremy J. Shapiro. Boston: Beacon, 1971 [1968].

———. *Legitimation Crisis.* Translated by Thomas McCarthy. Boston: Beacon, 1975 [1973].

———. *The Philosophical Discourse of Modernity.* Boston: MIT Press, 1990.

———. *The Theory of Communicative Action.* Vol. 1: *Reason and the Rationalization of Society.* Translated by Thomas McCarthy. Boston: Beacon, 1981.

Keat, Russell. *The Politics of Social Theory: Habermas, Freud, and the Critique of Positivism.* Chicago: University of Chicago Press, 1981.

Kuhn, Thomas S. *The Structure of Scientific Revolutions.* Chicago: University of Chicago Press, 1962.

Lindblom, Charles. *Politics and Markets.* New York: Basic Books, 1977.

Mannheim, Karl. *Ideology and Utopia.* London: Routledge and Kegan Paul, 1936.

Pelikan, Jaroslav. *The Excellent Empire: The Fall of Rome and the Triumph of the Church.* San Francisco: Harper and Row, 1987.

Popper, Karl R. *The Open Society and Its Enemies.* Princeton, N.J.: Princeton University Press, 1962 [1944].

Spinoza, Benedict de. *A Theologico-Political Treatise.* Translated by R.H.M. Elwes. New York: Dover, 1951.

Strauss, Leo. *Liberalism Ancient and Modern.* Chicago: University of Chicago Press, 1989 [1968].

———. "The Mutual Influence of Theology and Philosophy." *Independent Journal of Philosophy* 3.

———. *Persecution and the Art of Writing.* Chicago: University of Chicago Press, 1988 [1952].

———. *The Rebirth of Classical Political Rationalism: An Introduction to the Thought of Leo Strauss.* Selected and Introduced by Thomas L. Pangle. Chicago: University of Chicago Press, 1989.

Weber, Max. *The Protestant Ethic and the Spirit of Capitalism.* New York: Scribner, 1958.

The 2000 Presidential Election

Abramson, Paul R., John H. Aldrich, and David, W. Rohde. *Change and Continuity in the 2000 and 2002 Elections.* Washington, D.C.: CQ Press, 2003.

Achenbach, Joel. *It Looks Like a President Only Smaller: Trailing Campaign 2000.* New York: Simon and Schuster, 2001.

Barry, Dave. *Dave Barry Hits below the Beltway.* London: Random House Large Print, 2001.

Caesar, James W., and Andrew Busch. *The Perfect Tie.* Lanham, Md.: Rowman and Littlefield, 2001.

Cook, Rhodes. *Race for the Presidency Winning the 2000 Nomination.* Washington, D.C.: CQ Press, 1999.

Crotty, William J. *America's Choice 2000 Entering a New Millennium.* Bolder, Colo.: Westview, 2001.

Denton, Robert E. *The 2000 Presidential Campaign: A Communication Perspective.* Westport, Conn.: Praeger, 2002.

Dionne, E. J., Jr., Gerald M. Pomper, William G. Mayer, Majorie Randon Hershey, and Kathleen A. Frankovix. *The Election of 2000: Reports and Interpretations.* London: Chatham House, 2001.

Dover, E. D. *The Disputed Presidential Election of 2000: A History and Reference Guide,* Westport, Conn.: Greenwood, 2003.

———. *Missed Opportunity: Gore, Incumbency, and Television in Election 2000.* Westport, Conn.: Praeger, 2002.

Fife, Brian L., and Geralyn M. Miller. *Political Culture and Voting Systems in the United States: An Examination of the 2000 Presidential Election.* Westport, Conn.: Praeger, 2002.

Greenfield, Jeff. *Oh, Waiter! One Order of Crow! Inside the Strangest Presidential Election Finish in American History.* New York: Putnam, 2001.

Harris, Katherine. *Center of the Storm.* Nashville: WND Books, 2002.

Institute of Politics at Harvard University. *Campaign for President: The Managers Look at 2000.* Middlesex, U.K.: Hollis, 2003.

Jacobson, Arthur J., and Michel Rosenfeld. *The Longest Night: Polemics and Perspectives on Election 2000.* Berkeley: University of California Press, 2002.

Jacobson, Gary C., and Samuel Kernell. *The 2000 Elections and Beyond.* Washington, D.C.: CQ Press, 2001.

Jamieson, Kathleen, and Paul Waldman. *Electing the President, 2000: The Insiders' View.* Philadelphia: University of Pennsylvania Press, 2001.

Johnston, Richard, Michael G. Hagen, and Kathleen Hall Jamieson. *The 2000 Presidential Election and the Foundations of Party Politics.* Cambridge: Cambridge University Press, 2004.

Kaplan, David A. *The Accidental President: How 413 Lawyers, 9 Supreme Court Justices, and 5,963,110 Floridians (Give or Take a Few) Landed George W. Bush in the White House.* New York: William Morrow, 2001.

Kellner, Douglas. *Grand Theft 2000: Media Spectacle and a Stolen Election.* Lanham, Md.: Rowman and Littlefield, 2001.

Lewis, Charles. Center for Public Integrity. *The Buying of the President 2000.* New York: Avon, 2000.

Lieberman, Joseph I., and Hadassah Lieberman. *An Amazing Adventure: Joe and Hadassah's Personal Notes on the 2000 Campaign.* New York: Simon and Schuster, 2003.

Magleby, David B., Raymond J. La Raja, and Nelson W. Polsby. *Financing the 2000 Election.* Washington, D.C.: Brookings Institution, 2002.

McHale, John P., Glenn J. Hansen, P. M. Pier, John P. McGuire, and William L. McHale Benoit. *Campaign 2000: A Functional Analysis of Presidential Campaign Discourse.* Lanham, Md.: Rowman and LittleField, 2003.

Merzer, Martin. *The Miami Herald Report: Democracy Held Hostage.* New York: St. Martin's, 2001.

Moore, James. *Bush's Brain: How Karl Rove Made George W. Bush Presidential.* Wiley, 2003.

Nader, Ralph. *Crashing the Party: How to Tell the Truth and Still Run for President.* New York: St. Martin's, 2002.

New York Times. 36 Days: The Complete Chronicle of the 2000 Presidential Election Crisis. New York: Times Books, 2001.

Nichols, John, and David DesChamps. *Jews for Buchanan: Did You Hear the One about the Theft of the American Presidency?* New York: New Press, 2001.

Novak, Robert D. *Completing the Revolution: A Vision for Victory in 2000.* New York: Free Press, 2000.

Rakove, Jack N., Alex Keyssar, and Henry Brady. *The Unfinished Election of 2000.* New York: Basic Books, 2001.

Sammon, Bill. *At Any Cost: How Al Gore Tried to Steal the Election,* Regnery, 2001.

Simon, Roger. *Divided We Stand: How Al Gore Beat George Bush and Lost the Presidency.* New York: Crown, 2001.

Steed, Robert P., and Laurence W. Moreland. *The 2000 Presidential Election in the South: Partisanship and Southern Party Systems in the 21st Century.* Westport, Conn.: Praeger, 2002.

Toobin, Jeffrey. *Too Close to Call: The Thirty-Six-Day Battle to Decide the 2000 Election.* New York: Random House, 2001.

Wayne, Stephen J., and Clyde Wilcox. *The Election of the Century and What It Tells Us about the Future of American Politics.* Armonk, N.Y.: M.E. Sharpe, 2002.

Weisberg, Herbert F., and Clyde Wilcox. *Models of Voting in Presidential Elections: The 2000 U.S. Election.* Stanford, Calif.: Stanford University Press, 2003.

Public Opinion

Adorno, Theodore W., Else Frenkel-Brunswick, Daniel J. Levinson, and R. Nevitt. *The Authoritarian Personality.* New York: Harper, 1950.

Berger, Peter L., and Thomas Luckman. *The Social Construction of Reality.* Garden City, N.Y.: Doubleday, 1966.

Campbell, A., P. E. Converse, W. E. Miller, and D. E. Stokes. *The American Voter.* Chicago: Rand-McNally, 1960.

Converse, P.E. "The Nature of Belief Systems in Mass Publics." In *Ideology and Discontent,* ed. D. E. Apter. New York: Free Press, 1964.

———. "Public Opinion and Voting Behavior." *Nongovernmental Politics* 4 (1973): 124–25.

deHaven-Smith, Lance. "Environmental Belief Systems: Public Opinion Toward Land Use Regulation in Florida." *Environment and Behavior* 20 (1988): 176–99.

————. *Environmental Concern in Florida and the Nation.* Gainesville, Fla.: University Press of Florida, 1991.

————. *Environmental Publics: Public Opinion on Environmental Protection and Growth Management.* Boston: Lincoln Institute of Land Policy, 1987.

————. "Ideology and the Tax Revolt: Florida's Amendment 1." *Public Opinion Quarterly* 49 (1985): 300–309.

————. "Toward a Communicative Theory of Environmental Opinion: A Rejoinder to Audirac and Shoemyen." *Environment and Behavior* 21 (September 1989): 630–35.

Field, J. O., and R. E. Anderson. "Ideology in the Public's Conceptualization of the 1964 Election." *Public Opinion Quarterly* 33 (1973): 380–98.

Fiorina, M. P. *Retrospective Voting in American National Elections.* New Haven, Conn.: Yale University Press, 1981.

Lane, R. E. *Political Ideology.* New York: Free Press, 1962.

Lippman, Walter. *Public Opinion.* New York: Free Press, 1922.

Luttbeg, N. "The Structure of Beliefs among Leaders and the Public." *Public Opinion Quarterly* 32 (1968): 398–409.

McKlosky, H. "Consensus and Ideology in American Politics." *American Political Science Review* 58 (1964): 361–82.

Miller, Warren E., and J. Merril Shanks. *The New American Voter.* Cambridge, Mass.: Harvard University Press, 1996.

Natchez, P.B. *Images of Voting / Visions of Democracy.* New York: Basic Books, 1985.

Nie, N., with C. Anderson. "Mass Belief Systems Revisited: Political Change and Attitude Structure." *Journal of Politics* 36 (1974): 540–91.

Niemi, R. G., R. D. Ross, and J. Alexander. "The Similarity of Political Values of Parents and College-age Youths." *Public Opinion Quarterly* 43 (1978): 503–20.

Pappi, Franz Urban. "Political Behavior: Reasoning Voters and Multi-Party Systems." In *A New Handbook of Political Science*, ed. Robert E. Goodin and Hans-Dieter Klingemann, 255–75. Oxford: Oxford University Press, 1996.

Pierce, J. C. "Party Identification and the Changing Role of Ideology in American Politics." *Midwest Journal of Political Science* 16 (1970): 25–42.

Pomper, G. M. "From Confusion to Clarity: Issues and American Voters, 1956–1968." *American Political Science Review* 66 (1972): 415–28.

Popkin, S. L. *The Reasoning Vote.* Chicago: University of Chicago Press, 1991.

Prothro, J. W., and C. M. Grigg. "Fundamental Principles of Democracy: Bases of Agreement and Disagreement." *Journal of Politics* 22 (1960): 276–94.

RePass, D. E. "Issues Salience and Party Choice." *American Political Science Review* 65 (1971): 389–400.

Smith, Eric R.A.N. "Changes in the Public's Political Sophistication." In *Controversies in Voting Behavior*, ed. Richard G. Niemi and Herbert F. Weisberg. Washington, D.C.: CQ Press, 1993.

———. *The Unchanging American Voter*. Berkeley: University of California Press, 1989.

Stallings, R. A. "Patterns of Belief in Social Movements: Clarifications from an Analysis of Environmental Groups." *Sociological Quarterly* 14 (1973): 465–80.

Index

Note: Page numbers in *italics* indicate figures and tables.

Absentee ballots: J. Bush and, 210–11; federal overseas, 80, *220–23*; reforms of 1999 and, 29; trials regarding, 23, 24

Accenture, 267

Adams, John, 248, 288, 289

Adams, Sam, 232

African Americans: ballot spoilage and, 260–61; errors made by, 31; population of, 206; voting problems for, 255; write-in overvotes and, 13

Alien and Sedition Acts, 289

Analysis of Florida election, 8–9

Ansted, Justice, 102

Appointment of justices to U.S. Supreme Court, 290–91

Arguments, judgment of validity of, xvi

Aristoi, 285

Aristotle, 294

Askew, Reubin, 202, 204, 258

Athens, political system in, xiv–xv, 295

Attorney General. *See* Butterworth, Robert

Baker, James, 21, 104, 258, 291

Baker County, 67–68

Ballots: ambiguously marked, 8–9; design of, 27, 31, 32–34; dimpled, 95, 99; flawed, accepted and rejected, *229*; military, 19, 20, 260; overseas, 18, 80, *220–23*; received before and after November 7, *229*; segregation of, 65–67, 74–76; spoilage issues and Election Reform Act, 260–61. *See also* Absentee ballots

Beckstrom v. Volusia County Canvassing Board, 37

Blue Dog Democrats, 200–204, 205–6, 212

Boardman v. Esteva, 37

Boise, David, 98–99, 100, 101, 102

Brennan Law Center, 267

Brevard County, 263

Breyer, Justice, 104

Broder, John, 84

Broward County, 65–66, 213, 262

Broward County Canvassing Board, 18, 20

Bruder, George, 264, 265

Buchanan, Patrick (Reform Party candidate), 33

Burton, Charles, 17

Bush, Barbara, 205

Bush, George H. W., 205, 292–93

Bush, George W.: Blue Dog Democrats and, 205; campaign finance information, *228*; Florida Supreme Court and, 104; Gore accusations about, 246–47; Inaugural Address by, 276–79; legal team of, 252; Motion to Expedite Consideration, 133–34; as personalizing differences with Gore, 245–46; Petition for Writ of Certiorari, 134–37; U.S. Supreme Court and, 291; victory speech of, 245, 272–75

Bush, Jeb: absentee ballots and, 210–11; G. W. Bush campaign and, 251, 254; certification of election returns by, 22, 98; Chiles and, 26, 203; conspiracies and, 254–55; felon disenfranchisement program and, 264; Florida Election Reform Act and, 259; intervention by legislature and, 21; legal staff of, 252–53; media and, 253; phone calls to law firms from office of, 16, 252–53; popularity of, 205; purge list and, 267, 268; recusal from Florida Elections Commission, 16, 252; reelection of, 212–13, 262; return to Florida by, 15; Select Task Force on Election Procedures, Standards, and Technology, 257–59, 280–81

Butterfly ballot, 27, 32–34

Butterworth, Robert: actions of, 283, 291–92; advisory opinion written by, *187–91*; Gore campaign and, 16, 251, 253; military ballots and, 20; Palm Beach County and, 92

Caesar, xv

Caldwell, Alicia, 77

Calhoun County, 79

Caplan, Jane, 60

Cardenas, Al, 17, 21

Carnac the Magnificent, 99

Carter, Jimmy, 201, 203, 204, 293

Carvin, Michael, 20

Casualty aversion, 240–41

Certification of election, 22, 88, 96, 98

Certitude, as widespread, 6–7

Chads, 27–28

Chappell v. Martinez, State ex rel., 37

Checks and balances, framework of, 287–88

Chiles, Lawton, 26, 203, 204

Chote, May, 83

Christopher, Warren, 258, 291

Cicero, xv

Citizenship: categories of, 284–85; failures of, 294–95

Civic culture, 296–97

Civil-military relations, 241, 242

Civil War, 250, 289

Classes: communication pathology between, xv; Democratic Party and, 249–50; education in politics and, 293; Republican Party and, 247–49

Classical political philosophy: modern political science and, 284–85; opening closed minds and, 298–99; political order and, 286; primary interest of, 285; public discourse and, 294–95

Clinton, Bill: Blue Dog Democrats and, 201, 203; impeachment of, 291, 293; Republicans and, 292

CNN, 267

Collier County, 79, 82

Collins, Leroy, 202

Communication pathology: certitude, foolish, 6–7; disinformation, 25–27; facts compared to words, 294–95; polarization, cynicism, and, xv–xvii; taboo about 2000 election, xii–xiv; words, dysfunctional use of, xvi–xvii

Confusion: fomented by Republicans, 25–26; potential for, with Election Reform Act, 261–62

Congress: counting electoral votes in, 44–46; Democratic Party, and U.S. Civil Rights Commission report, xiii; staff members of, 290; veteran's advantage and, 234

Congressional representation, system of, 289–90

Conspiracies, issues regarding, 251–52, 254–56, 264–68

Constitutional crisis, creation of sense of, 23, 95–96, 255–56

Contract for identifying felons, 264–65, 266

Controversy, end to, 7

Crawford, Bob, 256

Crenson, Sharon, 60, 76

Crime, evidence of, 11, 264–68

Culling of election rolls, 29

Cynicism: danger of, xvii; events influencing, 3; in history of republican governments, xv

Damron, David, 77

Database Technologies (DBT), 264, 265

December 12, 4–6. *See also* U.S. Supreme Court Decision of December 12

Declaration of Independence, 249

Democracy: Democratic Party view of, 249–50; as fragile, 297–98; lawless tactics and, 291–94; meaning of, 299; Republican Party view of, 247–49. *See also* Classical political philosophy; Modern political science

Democratic Party: Blue Dog Democrats, 200–204, 205–6, 212; in Congress, and U.S. Civil Rights Commission report, xiii; in Florida, 197, 202–3, 204; of Jefferson, 288; lawlessness and, 293; low turnout of, 213; silence of, after election, xiii; view of democracy by, 249–50

Democratization of America, 248–49

Demographic trends, 206, 212

Demos, 285

Design of ballot, 27, 31, 32–34

Dimpled ballots, 95, 99

Disinformation, dissemination and power of, 25–27

Dixiecrats, 201–2

Douthat, Bill, 77

Drama, election as, 4–5

Drogin, Bob, 60

Duke University Study of Partisanship in the Military: attitude gaps and, 233–34; gaps, causes of, 237–38; gaps, types of, 234–37; overview of, 231–32; public policy implications, 238–42; Republican Party and, 207

Duration of election process, 296

Duval County, 75

Early voting system, 213

Election administration, reforms to, 295–96

Election administration system in state: corruption of, 6; as derailed, 283; partisanship and, 251–54; task force and, 258–59

Election laws: legally valid vote, standard for, 37; misconceptions about, 26–27; statewide recounts and, 91; subversion of, 14. *See also* Reforms

Election Reform Act (2001), 259–64

Elections: disputed, in history, xi, 26, 96, 107–8; as drama, 4–5; emotional character of, 3–4

Election timeline, 15–24

Electoral College, 296

Electors, 43–44, 108, *193*

Elites, 285, 286, 287, 293–94, 297

Emotional character of elections, 3–4

Equal Protection Clause of 14th Amendment to Constitution, 90, 105

Ergon, 294

Escambia County, 38, 75, 79

Euthyphro, 298–99

Experience gap, 233

Extremism, 290, 299

Facts compared to words, 294–95

Feaver, Peter D., 231

Federalism, 289

Federalist party, 248, 288

Feeney, Tom: J. Bush and, 95; G. W. Bush campaign and, 256; collusion by, 288; election of, 212; intervention by legislature and, 16, 21; partisanship of, 290; remarks by, 216–17

Felon disenfranchisement law, 214–15

Felon disenfranchisement program, 209–10, 264–68

Felons, convicted, 29, 209

Fessenden, Ford, 60, 76

Florida Board of Regents, 208

Florida Circuit Court: Gore lawsuit in, 19, 93–94, 98–100; ruling on deadline by, 18

Florida Constitution: Article III, Legislature, 46; Article V, Judiciary, 46–47; Article XI, Amendments, 47–48; need for amendment to, 14–15; Oath of Office, 282; rights in, 211

Florida Division of Elections: contract for identifying felons and, 264, 265; Palm Beach County and, 17–18, 92; purge list and, 267

Florida Election Reform Act, 14

Florida Elections Commission, 254–55, 256

Florida Redistricting Economic and Demographic System, 35

Florida statutes: Canvass of returns, 48–50; Contest of election, 52–54; Protest of Election Returns; Procedure, 50–52

Florida Supreme Court: G. W. Bush appeal of ruling by, 21, 23; circuit court and, 24; criticisms of, 104; decision changing recount deadline, 112–32; focus of, 90–91; Gore appeal and, 23; legislative special session and, 23; oral arguments to, 20; Palm Beach County and, 93; pass through jurisdiction and, 19; ruling by,

20–21, *193*; ruling mandating statewide recount, 102–3, *193*; U.S. Supreme Court and, 97–98, 104–5

Flowers, Gennifer, 292

Foldessy, Ed, 60

Foote, Tad, 258

Ford, Gerald, 292

"Forgotten Florida," 201

Foster, Vince, 292

Franklin County, 80–81

Freud, Sigmund, 295

Gadsden County, 27, 31, 87, 261

Gerrymandering, 289–90

Ginsburg, Justice, 104

Glades County, 79

Gore, Al, Jr.: accusations about G. W. Bush by, 246–47; Blue Dog Democrats and, 205; G. W. Bush attacks on, 245–46; campaign finance information, *228*; concession speech of, 244–45, 250, 269–71; Democrats and, 293; performance of in Florida, 206; Reagan Democrats and, 201; as winner of election in Florida, 8, 9, 12, 38–39

Gore legal team: Boise and, 98–99, 100, 101, 102; fatal flaw in case by, 100–102; statistician on, 101–2; undervotes and, 99–100

Governor. *See* Bush, Jeb

Gracchus brothers, 286

Graham, Bob, 202, 204

Guardian (newspaper), 40

Hamilton, Bill, 84

Hancock, John, 232

Hannon, Tom, 84

Harris, Katherine: G. W. Bush campaign and, 251, 254; cell phone call of, 15; certification of election returns by, 19, 22, 98; collusion by, 288; conspiracies and, 252, 254–55; election of, 212; felon disenfranchisement program of, 209–10, 264–68; manual recounts and, 92–93; office hours issue, 256; overseas ballots and, 18; Palm Beach County Canvassing Board and, 22; ridicule of, 7; Stipanovich and, 16

Hayes, Rutherford B., 108
Herron, Mark, 19
Highway patrol, 255
Hispanics, 206, 268
Holland, Keating, 60
Holmes County, 79
Holton, Sean, 60
Hood, Glenda, 267, 268
Humburg, Connie, 60

Institutional failures: appointment of justices to U.S. Supreme Court, 290–91; checks and balances, framework of, 287–88; congressional representation, 289–90; federalism, 289; implications of, 295
Investigation: failure to implement, 243–44; by U.S. Civil Rights Commission, xiii, 264–68
Iran-Contra deal, 292–93
Irony, 298

Jaspin, Elliot, 60, 76
Jefferson, Thomas, 248, 288, 289
Jefferson County, 79
Jergovic, Diana, 60
Jimenez, Frank, 15, 16, 17
Johnson, Lyndon, 203
Jokes, 7, 99
Jones, Paula, 291, 292
Judicial decision making: breakdown in, 106; federalism and, 289; Gore campaign and, 98–100; Gore loss in contest phase, 100–103; jurisdiction issue, 90–91; legislature and, 95–96; November 23 filings and, 91–93; partisanship and, 106–7, 296; principal decisions, *110–11*; side issues, 94–95; state courts, 93–94; U.S. Supreme Court, 96–98, 103–5
Judicial Nominating Commissions, 211–12
Judicial system in state, 211–12
Julius Caesar, 286

Jurisdiction: candidates' positions on, 91; U.S. Constitution and, 106

Kast, Ed, 15
Keating, Dan, 60, 76
Kennedy, Justice, 104
Kirk, Claude, 204
Klock, Joseph, 20
Kohn, Richard H., 231
Kuntz, Phil, 84

Lafayette County, 79, 81
Law firms, phone calls to, 16, 252–53
Lawless tactics, 286, 291–94
Leadership class, 291–94
Legislature (state): intervention by, 16, 21, 23, 95–96, 255–56; maneuvers by, 107; Senate President, remarks by, *192*; Speaker of House, remarks by, 216–17; special session, proclamation regarding, *193*, 230. *See also* Feeney, Tom; McKay, John
Lehr, Myriam, 20
Lewis, Terry, 77, 103
Lieberman, Joseph, 20, 246, 291–92
Lincoln, Abraham, 244–45
Logos, 294

Machine counts, accuracy of, 26–28
Mack, Connie, 28, 204, 263
MacKay, Buddy, 28, 204, 263
Madison County, 265
Manual recounts: accuracy of, 26–27, 34; administrative blocking of, 92–93; belittling of, 99; bias of, 13; Broward County, 18, 20; G. W. Bush campaign and, 17, 25–26, 92; deadline for, 92; Florida Supreme Court and, 20–21, 102–3; Gore campaign and, 16; governor's office and, 16; legal requirement for, 14; Miami-Dade County, 18, 19–20, 21, 40–41; Palm Beach County, 16–18, 21; time constraints and, 41–42; trigger for, 262–63; U.S. Supreme Court and, 105; Volusia County, 18, 19

Marion County, 81

Martin County, 23, 24, 79

Martinez, Bob, 204

Masses: definition of, 285; elites and, 286; modern political science and, 287; partisanship and, 295; truth and, 297–98; as uninformed and unreasonable, 294

Match criteria for felon disenfranchisement program, 265–66

Mazza, 285

McBride, Bill, 262, 264

McCarthy, Ken, 83

McCollum, Bill, 200

McKay, John, 21, *192*

McManus, Doyle, 84

Media: J. Bush and, 253; information presented by, 2; military and, 238; non-events and, 7; post-election studies by, 40–41; postmortem on election by, xii–xiii, 14, 251–52

Meyer, Meghan, 77

Meyers, Andrew, 20

Miami-Dade Canvassing Board: decision of, 94; halt of recount by, 98; manual recount of, 19–20, 21; meeting of, 18

Miami-Dade County: governor election in, 213; NORC data and, 81, 82; undervotes in, 40–41

Miami Herald (newspaper), 40, 41

Military: collusion by personnel in, 252, 288; media and, 238. *See also* Duke University Study of Partisanship in the Military

Military ballots: extremism and, 290; fraud and, 260; Lieberman, Butterworth, and, 20, 291–92; partisanship and, 19. *See also* Overseas ballots

Militia, 232

Modern political science: change and, 285–86; classical political philosophy and, 284–85; role of executive in, 286–87; masses and, 294

Murphy, Chuck, 84

Nader, Ralph, 212

Nassau County, 79–80, 81

National Opinion Research Center (NORC): accuracy of data and, 57; data sets, 57–58; description of, 55; findings of, 39–40; goal of, 55; news organizations involved with, 55; study by, 8; tabulations by, *39*; uncertified ballots examined by, *36*, 55–57; undervotes and, 38–39. *See also* NORC Media "Read_me" File

Nelson, Bill, 200

New Yorker magazine, 40

New York Times (newspaper): military and, 238; postmortem on election by, xii–xiii, 14, 251–52

Nixon, Richard, 292

NORC. *See* National Opinion Research Center (NORC)

NORC Media "Read_me" File: adjusted certified totals, 71–72; Analytical Assumptions and Terminology, 60–65; Appendices, 85–86; ballot segregation, 74–76; ballots with multiple markings, 64; Broward County, 65–66; Coder-comment Override Table, 67; Coder Issues, 67–68; Consortium Steering Committee Representatives, 84; County Data, 76–77; Data Analysis Working Group, 59–60; Exceptional Counties, 65–67; missing data assumptions, 64; negation marks, 64; Orange County, 66–67; pencil marks, 65; Precinct Data, 77–84; Relating NORC-coded Ballot Data to State-certified Totals, 71–76; Scenarios, 68–71; Table of Contents, 58–59; Tabulator, 76; Volusia County, 65; voter intent, assessment of, 61, 62–63; write-ins, rules on, 63

Nullification, doctrine of, 289

O'Connor, Justice, 104

Oligoi, 285

One Florida Initiative, 267

Opinion, erroneous, held by citizens, 8
Optical scan system, 31, 261, 263
Orange County, 66–67, 78–79, 206
O'Reilly, Richard, 60, 76
Osceola County, 80, 81
Outcome of election: by county, with absentees separated out, *224–27*; as flawed, 9, 42; Gore as winner, 8, 9, 12, 38–39
Overseas ballots, 18, 80, *220–23*. *See also* Military ballots
Overvotes: description of, 30; NORC coding of, 60; as predominately for Gore, 41; as valid, 35–37, *36*; write-in, 13, 38, 261

Palm Beach County, 27, 32–34, 213
Palm Beach County Canvassing Board: deadline and, 22; dimpled ballots and, 95; Florida Division of Elections and, 17–18; manual recount initiated by, 92; sunshine rule and, 16–17; voter intent and, 21
Partisanship: ambiguities of U.S. Constitution and, 106–7; among elite military officers, 233–34; as barrier to inquiry and corrective action, 244; checks and balances, framework of, 288; congressional representation and, 289–90; differences in error rates and, 31–32; in election administration system in Florida, 6, 251–54; Florida Election Reform Act and, 259–60, 263–64; of justices to U.S. Supreme Court, 290–91; masses and, 295; reason compared to, 294; reforms addressing, 295–96; Select Task Force on Election Procedures, Standards, and Technology and, 257–58, 259; time constraints and, 41–42; voting machines and, 10
Penelas, Alex, 21
Periente, Justice, 94
Pinellas County, 81
Plato, dialogues of, xvii, 294–95
Polarization of leaders and citizens, xv, 6

Political corruption, pattern of, 196
Political culture, 9–10, 212–13
Political parties: percentage of voters registered by, *229. See also* Democratic Party; Republican Party
Political system: in Athens, xiv–xv, 295; citizens, categories of, 284–85; congressional representation in, 289–90; degeneration of, 286; differences in, 285; recommendations for, 295–96; in Rome, xiv–xv
Polk County, 82
Population growth in state, 199
Post-election studies, 12–13, 40–41
Privatization, 198, 209
Public discourse, 291–92, 294–99. *See also* Communication pathology
Puerto Rican population, 206
Punch card system: butterfly ballot, 32–34; error rate and, 31–32; false undervote and, 35; Florida Election Reform Act and, 260; machine reading and, 27–28; undervotes and, 99–100
Purge list, 267–68

Reagan, Ronald, 292–93
Reagan Democrats, 201–2
Reasoning with unreasonable people, 298–99
Recount, automatic, provision for, 29
Redistricting, legislative, 289–90, 296
Reform Party, 33, *33*
Reforms: criticism of, 10; disputed elections and, xi–xii; to election administration system, 295–96; in Florida in 1989, 28–29; in Florida in 1999, 29–30; in Florida in 2001, 259–64; motivations for, 251; needed, in Florida, 14–15; Select Task Force on Election Procedures, Standards, and Technology, 257–59, 280–81; as step backward, 14
Rehnquist, Chief Justice, 104
Reno, Janet, 264
Republican governments, history of, xiv–xv

Republican Party: absentee ballots and, 210–11; base-broadening by, 206–7; demographic trends and, 198–99; early voting system and, 213; Florida and, 199–200; Florida Election Reform Act and, 263–64; foreign policy and, 207; judicial system and, 211–12; lawless tactics of, 292–94; lobbyists and, 208; malfeasance and misfeasance by, 195–96; mindset of, 196; state bureaucracy and, 208–9; strategy of, 197, 199; view of democracy by, 247–49; voter registration, 200; voting patterns and, 196–98

Resource materials, 2

Returns, inaccurate, as more likely with reform, 262–63

Roberts, Clay, 15, 17, 92, 266

Rome, political system in, xiv–xv

Rose, Bill, 84

Rubottom, Don, 16

Rule of law: commitment to, 297; suspension of, 286

Running out the clock rhetoric, 246–47

Sauls, N. Sander, 98, 100, 102, 103

Scalia, Justice, 97, 104

Schulte, Fred, 77

Secretary of State. *See* Harris, Katherine

Segregation of ballots, 65–67, 74–76

Select Task Force on Election Procedures, Standards, and Technology, 257–59, 280–81

Seminole County, 23, 24

Senior citizens, voting errors made by, 13, 31, 260

Smith, Jim, 258

Smith Richardson Foundation, 231

Socrates, xv, xvii, 285, 298–99

Sore/Loserman rhetoric, 245–46

Souter, Justice, 104

St. Johns County, 80

Starr, Kenneth, 292, 293

Statesmanship, 291–92

Stevens, Justice, 104

Stipanovich, Mac, 16, 252, 254

Stonehill, Dave, 76

Suwannee County, 82–83

Taboo, conversational, about 2000 election, xii–xiv

Technology for voting, 10

Terrorist attacks, 40

Texas Election Code, 54–55

Thomas, Justice, 104

Thrasher, John, 208

Thucydides, 294

Thurmond, Strom, 201

Time constraints, 41–42

Title III of U.S. Code. *See* U.S. Code, Title III

Tobin, Tom, 77

Triangle Institute for Security Studies, 231

Tribe, Laurence, 91

Tse, Archie, 60

Turnout: delays as reducing Democratic, 262; high, as expected in 2000, 30, 255

Two-primary system, 202, 263–64

Tyranny: classical political philosophy and, 285, 286; history of, xiv–xv, xvii; partisanship and, 296

Undervotes: definition of, 30; Gore legal team and, 99–100; NORC coding of, 60; valid, as discarded by machines, 34–35

U.S. Civil Rights Commission, investigation by, xiii, 264–68

U.S. Code, Title III: counting electoral votes in Congress, 44–46; Determination of Controversy as to Appointment of Electors, 44; election dispute of 1876 and, xi; Failure to Make Choice on Prescribed Day, 44; safe harbor and, 96; time constraints and, 41–42; Time of Appointing Electors, 43; U.S. Supreme Court and, 22

U.S. Constitution: Article II, 43; contradictions in, 89; Equal Protection Clause of 14th Amendment to, 90, 105; jurisdiction issues and, 106; Republican Party and, 248; 12th Amendment to, xi

U.S. Court of Appeals for 11th Circuit, 19, 23

U.S. Supreme Court: appointment of justices to, 290–91; G. W. Bush appeal to, 21, 24, 103; conclusion of, as anticlimactic, 5; creation of sense of constitutional crisis and, 23, 95–96, 255–56; Florida Supreme Court decision and, 23; focus of, 90; issue considered by, 21; misuse of authority by, 288; Motion to Expedite Consideration, 133–34; oral arguments heard by, 23; Petition for Writ of Certiorari, 134–37; public perception and, 103–4; rulings by, 24, 96–98, 103–5, 256; Writ Stopping All Recounting, 138–40

U.S. Supreme Court Decision of December 12: justices concurring with, 150–58; justices dissenting with, 159–86; text of, 141–50

Veteran's advantage, 234
Veterans effect, 239
Volusia County: co-mingling of ballots in, 65; lawsuit by, 18, 19; NORC study in, 81, 82
Vote: definitions of, xvi; legally valid, standard for, 25, 37; valid, as discarded by machines, 34–35
Voter error: partisan differences in, 31–32; senior citizens and, 13, 260; types of, 30–31

Voter registrations and deletions, *218*
Voters News Service, 15, 196–97
Voter turnout percentages, *219*
Voting equipment: cleaning of, 99; confusion and, 261–62; error rate in, 262–63; machine counts, accuracy of, 26–28; reforms and, 10; sources of error in casting and tabulating votes and, 27–28; valid votes discarded by, 34–35. *See also* punch card system
Voting patterns, 196–98, 206
Voucher program, 211

Walsh, Kevin, 84
Washington, George, 288
Washington County, 263
Washington Post (newspaper): military and, 238; postmortem on election by, xii–xiii, 14, 251; on role of partisanship, 254
Wells, Justice, 24, 102
West-South coalition, 199
Whitewater investigation, 292, 293
Winner-take-all system, 296
Words: dysfunctional use of, xvi–xvii; facts compared to, 294–95
Write-in overvotes, 13, 38, 261

Xenophon, xvii

Yellow Dog Democrats, 201

Zeleny, Jeff, 77

Lance deHaven-Smith is professor of public policy at the Reubin O'D. Askew School of Public Administration and Policy at Florida State University. His publications include *The Florida Voter* (1996), *Environmental Concern in Florida and the Nation* (UPF, 1991), *Philosophical Critiques of Policy Analysis* (UPF, 1989), and *Foundations of Representative Democracy* (1999). He is also coauthor with David Colburn of *Government in the Sunshine State* (UPF, 1999) and *Florida's Megatrends* (UPF, 2002).